Successful elite sport policies

For mutual inspiration!

Thank you,

hopefully we can collaborate

in some way in the future.

Cheers

Veerle De Bosscher

This book was anonymously peer-reviewed by authors of *International Journal of Physical Education.*

The authors thank the reviewers for their contribution!

Veerle De Bosscher, Simon Shibli,
Hans Westerbeek & Maarten van Bottenburg

SUCCESSFUL ELITE SPORT POLICIES

An international comparison of the Sports Policy factors Leading to International Sporting Success (SPLISS 2.0) in 15 nations

Meyer & Meyer Sports

Co-authors involved in writing different sections:

David Barrett (Pillar 8), Camilla Brockett (Pillar 4 and 6), Bake Dijk (Pillar 3), Jari Lämsä (Pillar 9), Popi Sotiriadou (Pillar 7), Anna Vilanova (Pillar 5).

British Library Cataloguing in Publication Data
A catalogue record for this book is available from the British Library

Successful elite sport policies
Maidenhead: Meyer & Meyer Sport (UK) Ltd., 2015
ISBN: 978-1-78255-076-1

Aachen, Auckland, Beirut, Cairo, Cape Town, Dubai, Hägendorf, Hong Kong, Indianapolis, Manila, New Delhi, Singapore, Sydney, Tehran, Wien

 Member of the World Sport Publishers' Association (WSPA)

Total production by: Print Consult GmbH, Munich, Germany
ISBN: 978-1-78255-076-1
E-Mail: info@m-m-sports.com
www.m-m-sports.com

Table of Contents

Preface

THANK YOU!

Twelve years ago we were at the European Association for Sport Management conference in Stockholm and discovered that we had common research interests in elite sport policy. We agreed to collaborate and from this modest beginning the SPLISS project was formed. Since then, SPLISS-related papers have been published in Europe, America and Australasia and in 2008 we celebrated the publication of our first book *The Global Sporting Arms Race*.

It is hard to believe that a research project that started off as a small-scale pilot study at the heart of a PhD thesis would somehow develop into having its own international conference and be a key research strand at sport management conferences. Today we have 15 nations (regions) from four continents taking part in SPLISS 2.0. We get regular requests for new countries to join the project, there is a demand for a Paralympic version of SPLISS, and there is probably a lifetime's work for somebody to roll out the SPLISS methodology on a sport-by-sport basis.

In this book we present the key findings from the SPLISS 2.0 project and have the opportunity to discuss the 'state of the art' that is international elite sport policy. This book presents the results of an international comparative study on elite sport policies of 15 nations worldwide: Australia, Belgium (separated into Flanders and Wallonia), Brazil, Canada, Denmark, Estonia, France, Finland, Japan, South Korea, the Netherlands, Northern Ireland (as part of the United Kingdom), Portugal, Spain and Switzerland. The focus is on the relationship between policies and international sporting success and, accordingly, insights into the factors that shape elite sport policies and the pathways to success in different nations. 3,142 elite athletes, 1,376 elite coaches and 241 high performance directors have provided their views about elite sport policies in their nation.

None of this would have been possible without the hard work and commitment of the contributing partner researchers from the different nations. Many have worked tirelessly and with limited resources to undertake the vast amount of work involved in compiling the various inventories and surveys that make up the raw data. In Brussels we have also worked diligently to pull the data together to make a coherent whole. The level of dedication shown by those involved in the project mirrors that of elite athletes in their pursuit of sporting excellence.

Thanks to all these people!

Furthermore we would like to thank numerous people and organisations:

- The elite athletes, coaches and performance directors who completed lengthy questionnaires and the different policy organisations and NOCs, who freely gave their time and provided valuable insights into their policies and programmes
- The sport organisations and governments in different nations that provided funding to carry out this project
- The researchers from the different partner nations that have freely offered their help to contribute in the data analysis (see list further in this book)
- External experts who have been willing to comment and make suggestions on the research instruments; their critical thoughts have been really useful (see list further in this book)
- Infostrada Sports who provided access to their awesome Podium Performance database which was so helpful in deriving our success measures
- The city of Antwerp, which—as a European Sports capital 2013—indirectly supported this project by funding the conference 'elite sport success: society boost or not?' as an outcome of this project
- Our sponsors, who provided us with some helpful co-ordination funding: the Flemish (Belgium) government (Topsport Vlaanderen/Ministry of Culture, Youth, Sport, Media); the Dutch Sport agency NOC*NSF and the ministry of Health, Welfare and Sport; and, Ernst & Young (Belgium)
- The Vrije Universiteit Brussel (VUB) for its ongoing support financially and in the co-ordination of the SPLISS project since inception

SPLISS has been a great project in which to be involved. In addition to the papers and the book there has been the opportunity to present the findings at conferences all over the globe. Researchers involved in the project have gone on to achieve doctorates and professorships whereas others have been elected to prestigious national level sports committees in their countries. In addition we have all formed productive research collaborations and made many new friends along the way. These outcomes are the essence of successful international research projects—long may they continue.

The SPLISS consortium group

Veerle De Bosscher, Simon Shibli, Hans Westerbeek and Maarten van Bottenburg

1 Chapter 1: Introduction

1.1 Rationale

The research presented in this book is built on the premise that nation states and their leadership deem elite sport (increasingly) important, and success in elite sport, in particular, is an important objective to achieve on behalf of the nation. It will be shown in this book that most nations in our sample continue to increase their national spending on elite sport, which can be taken as a direct sign that elite sport success is considered a worthy cause in which to invest taxpayers' funds. Ironically, with more nations investing in elite sport—a phenomenon we called the 'global sporting arms race' in SPLISS 1.0—comes the need to invest more, simply to stay in the game, because other nations are investing more and raising the stakes.

In recognition of this scenario the first SPLISS project has been well timed, as it served as the launching pad for the current project (SPLISS 2.0) of which the results are presented and discussed in this book. Obviously, and logically, we build on the conceptual model that was developed in the first project and enhance it on the basis of our subsequent learning. Where we naively started the SPLISS 1.0 project thinking that we could identify a uniform best practice pathway towards building a perfect elite sport development system, we now know that it is not so much the whole of a system structure, but much more the unique combination of system pieces that result in a variety of different approaches that deliver elite sport success.

In this project, we have started the process of further and deeper investigation of the different components that make up an elite sport policy development and implementation system (called *Pillars* in this book). We acknowledge that our model is still complex and that our research instruments are demanding and not yet sufficiently lean to deal with a bigger sample of countries. However, by collecting data from more countries, with further developed research instruments and with a bigger team of highly skilled and passionate researchers, we feel that we have significantly advanced our knowledge about the composition of what are the critical success factors that drive success in elite sport. We have also advanced our knowledge about the interplay between different success factors and between the nine different Pillars of the SPLISS model. Some are indeed sequential and depend on each other; others can be developed in isolation, or in parallel to other Pillars. Some Pillars are highly developed in some nations, and not at all in others. That, in essence, leads to the purpose of SPLISS 2.0, to identify what policy works, when and in which national context.

During the past 10 years, the first SPLISS project has also sparked a wide range of related research that has fed into the development of our own model, and we have gratefully sourced the research as input into our own theoretical advancement. When the SPLISS project began in 2003 elite sport policy research was largely uncharted territory and very much a niche area for a small group of researchers. In 12 years the SPLISS project:

- has grown into a global collaboration between 15 nations, 58 researches and 33 policymakers;
- has at least in part inspired other researchers to do similar research in other nations;
- has become a key strand in most sport management related conferences; and
- has staged its own international conferences in Antwerp 2013 and Melbourne 2015.

These achievements and the continued interest of policymakers, sports administrators and academics is clear evidence of the importance of the systematic study of elite sport policy in the third millennium.

1.2 Background to SPLISS

SPLISS (Sports Policy factors Leading to International Sporting Success) is an international network of research co-operation that aims to co-ordinate, develop and share expertise in innovative high performance sport policy research in co-operation with policymakers, National Olympic Committees (NOCs), international (sport) organisations, and researchers worldwide.

The first SPLISS project (SPLISS 1.0), delivered in 2008 by an international consortium of researchers, was a study comparing elite sport policies in six nations (Belgium [Flanders & Wallonia], Canada, Italy, the Netherlands, Norway and the United Kingdom). Based on the development of a theoretical model a pilot study in six nations to test the model resulted in a published PhD study and a book:

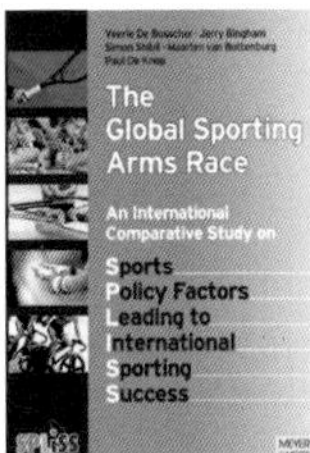

De Bosscher, V., Bingham, J., Shibli, S., van Bottenburg, M., De Knop, P. (2008). The global Sporting Arms Race. An international comparative study on sports policy factors leading to international sporting success. Aachen: Meyer & Meyer. ISBN: 978-1-84126-228-4. (173p)

De Bosscher, V. (2007). Sports Policy Factors Leading to International Sporting Success. Published doctoral thesis, supervised by De Knop, P., van Bottenburg, M. Brussel: VUBPRESS. ISBN-978-905487-421-8 (347p)

This project was the first joint initiative of the 'SPLISS' group, led by the Vrije Universiteit Brussel in collaboration with Utrecht University, Sheffield Hallam University and UKSport. A summary of the SPLISS 1.0 study is freely available from the website: www.SPLISS.net/publications and several scientific papers have been published over the past years (see website for an overview).

The SPLISS 1.0 study was characterised by three elements:

1. The development of a theoretical model of sport policy factors leading to international sporting success, consisting of nine Pillars, with the identification of more than 100 critical success factors (CSF).
2. The use of mixed methods research, including development of a scoring system to measure the competitive position of nations in elite sport. This was presented as a 'traffic light' to indicate the relative performance of each nation for each Pillar measured.
3. The involvement of the main stakeholders in elite sport as part of the research methodology: 1,090 athletes, 273 coaches and 71 performance directors in the six nations were asked to express and rate their views about the elite sport system in their nation. The SPLISS research takes existing inputs (e.g., money) and outputs (e.g., medals) calculations and takes the 'black box' of throughput or processes of elite sport policies into consideration as the critical link between resources put into the system and results that are delivered.

The SPLISS project, in that regard, moves beyond other studies on elite sport policies, for example by Andersen and Ronglan (2012); Bergsgard, Houlihan, Mangset, Nordland and Rommetveldt (2007); Digel, Burk and Fahrner (2006); Green and Houlihan (2005) and Houlihan and Green (2008). These studies, all with their own approaches and foci, compare and describe elite sport policy of nations with the purpose of analysing the policy formulation process and the context in which elite sport operates. The SPLISS research seeks to complement to this and considers the continuum of resources, process, and sporting results more holistically.

1.3 From SPLISS 1.0 to 2.0

Despite advancing our knowledge about theory, methodology and policies, the SPLISS 1.0 study also delivered numerous new research challenges. Irrespective of anecdotal evidence about the relationship between policy actions and elite sport success, SPLISS 1.0 did not fully provide conclusive evidence. In policy research it is hard to conduct an experiment where the impact of a single or series of policy factor(s) on output measures is determined in a controlled environment. It also became clear that various research paradigms deliver multiple (causal) models that may explain the production of elite sporting success. Country specific context based on, for example, history or culture may provide nations with various options to design and implement successful elite sport systems. In this respect, Houlihan and Green (2008) state that 'one crucial indicator of convergence of sport systems is the extent to which a broad range of countries with different political, socio-economic and cultural profiles adopt similar policy goals' (p. 20). This is confirmed by Svein Andersen and Lars Tore Ronglan (2012) in their book *Nordic Elite Sport: Same Ambitions, Different Tracks*. The SPLISS methodology has largely focused on countries where policy systems were increasingly institutionalised by government. This has led to a research focus on government-funded, mainly Olympic, sports and to a lesser extent to commercialised sports. The SPLISS model and its CSFs may be less applicable to countries where elite sport policy is (also) the remit of Non-governmental organisations or private organisations. SPLISS has therefore been typified as a functionalistic approach to elite sport (Bogerd, 2010).

To address these issues the SPLISS methodology has developed further to take in more nations and delve deeper into the different CSFs and their relationship with success reflected in the name SPLISS 2.0. This large-scale project, of which this book is the outcome, includes 15 nations, as shown in Figure 1: ten European nations, two countries in Asia, and two in America and Australia (Oceania). For specific reasons, explained later in the book, these nations actually represent 16 systems for elite sport development because Flanders and Wallonia have politically independent sport policy structures, and Great Britain did not participate in the project, but Northern Ireland as one of the home nations did. In the remainder of this study we consider Flanders, Wallonia and Northern Ireland as independent national sporting systems.

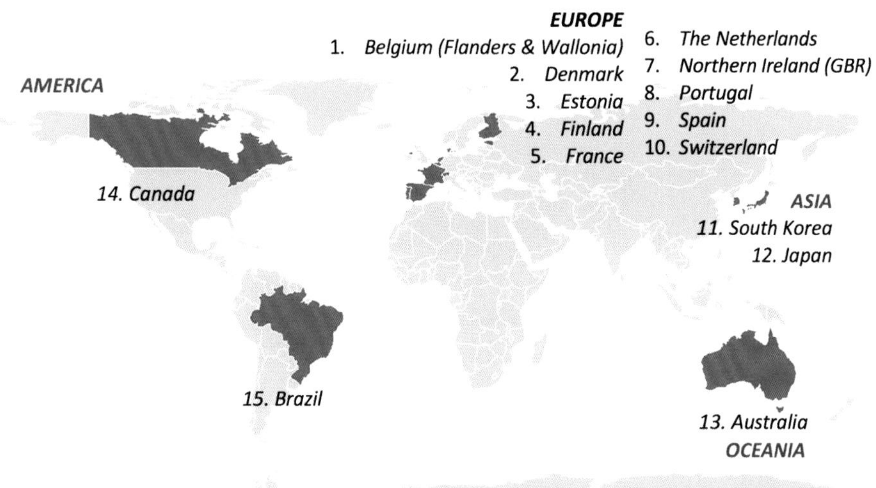

Figure 1: Countries involved in SPLISS 2.0[1]

SPLISS 1.0 also delivered further evidence that policy factors leading to elite sport success may differ by sport. As it was stated by Porter (1990), commenting on the competitive advantage of nations,

'No nation can be competitive in everything. ...A high level of competitiveness in all areas is very unlikely in the economy and therefore nations may specialise in one domain' (p. 8).

Sport-by-sport comparisons may reveal that certain Pillars are more conditional to success than others. Clusters of policy success models may be found, for example, for early versus late (talent) specialisation sports, or for team sports versus individual sports. Accordingly, to address these issues, several SPLISS-related studies look into sport specific comparisons and from different viewpoints, for example:

- Athletics: a resource-based perspective on countries' competitive advantage in elite athletics (Jasper Truyens, PhD, Vrije Universiteit Brussel, Belgium).
- Tennis: the examination of the tennis policy factors that influence the tennis performance of a country (Jessie Brouwers, PhD, Griffith University (AUS) in collaboration with Vrije Universiteit Brussel).
- Judo, high performance judo: organisational determinants for international sporting success (Leandro Mazzei, PhD, University of Sao Paulo (BRA) in collaboration with Vrije Universiteit Brussel).

---

1 13 full nations and three regions: Flanders and Wallonia (Belgium) and Northern Ireland

- Snow sports: a market-based view of nations on the medal market of the Winter Olympic Games (Andreas Christophe Weber, PhD, Swiss Federal Institute of Sport Magglingen SFISM/ Vrije Universiteit Brussel, SUI).

Smaller (Masters) studies are also conducted, such as horse riding: key success determinants in sports policies (Clara Van Laer, Masters thesis at Vrije Universiteit Brussel, 2012); commercial speed skating teams: key figures in skating about the consequences of the development of branding teams for the elite sport climate and talent development, in particular, a case study in the Netherlands (Renneke Bogerd, Masters thesis at Utrecht University, 2011); swimming: comparing elite sport policy factors leading to international sporting success in Flanders and the Netherlands (Sepp Meyers, Masters thesis at Vrije Universiteit Brussel, 2009); and canoe: elite sport culture and policy interrelationships: the case of sprint canoe in Australia (Sotiriadou, Gowthorp & De Bosscher, 2013).

Other sport policy-specific projects are being developed as well such as:

- Pillar 2, a network approach to elite sport policies (Susana Rodrigues, PhD, Lisbon University (POR) in collaboration with Vrije Universiteit Brussel);
- analysis of the policies and the climate/environment for elite sport on the different organisational levels of Brazil: governmental and non-governmental–with emphasis on the relations of school sport and participative sport with sports talents identification and development programmes (led by Maria Thereza Ter Böhme, Universidade de Sao Paulo); and
- elite sport and cities, a comparison between five Dutch cities and three Belgian cities (Fenke van Rossum, Masters thesis at Vrije Universiteit Brussel).
- PARA-SPLISS: Sport policy factors influencing success in paralympic sports (Aurélie Pankowiak, Victoria University (AUS) in collaboration with Vrije Universiteit Brussel (BE) and Jacqueline Patatas, Vrije Universiteit Brussel (BE)).

Projects regarding elite sport policies in developing countries and in regard to military sport are also under consideration. These projects contribute to further developing, adapting and validating the SPLISS model and methods in different settings and contexts.

1.4 SPLISS 2.0 objective

The objective of the SPLISS 2.0 project is to better understand which (and how) sport policies lead to international sporting success and to obtain a better insight into the effectiveness and efficiency of elite sport policies of nations at an overall sports level. To triangulate our findings we use the insights of athletes, coaches and performance directors in the 15 'participating nations.

The sub-objectives of this research project are threefold:

1. From a practitioner's view, we aim to use our newfound theoretical and methodological knowledge to inform policymakers about the keys to effective elite sport policies and international policy developments in an increasingly competitive environment. This should also allow (participating) nations to identify critical success factors that apply most to their specific context and stage of development, allowing for accelerated development of sport system components.
2. From a scientific view, we want to improve and refine the theoretical model–following from SPLISS 1.0–that helps explain how sport policy factors lead to international sporting success, and to further enhance and validate the methodological approach allowing for better and valid international comparisons.
3. Ultimately we aim to develop an instrument that can be used by policymakers and academics alike to evaluate the effectiveness of elite sport policies.

The SPLISS 2.0 study builds on the model and methodologies developed in SPLISS 1.0. We take this project beyond SPLISS 1.0 by collecting more information about certain Pillars, sampling more nations and questioning more respondents. The project involved 15 nations and responses from more than 3,000 elite athletes, over 1,300 coaches and 241 performance directors that provide deeper insights into the effectiveness of elite sport policies. This allowed us to develop a more comprehensive scoring methodology and to obtain deeper insights into the relationship between elite sport policies and sporting success of nations. In this study we maintain a focus at the national sport policy level. We do not go into sport-by-sport comparisons, nor do we consider the policy systems that drive the development of commercial sport success.

1.5 Organisation of SPLISS 2.0: Research team and partners

In every nation individual researchers and teams in research institutes were the drivers of the SPLISS 2.0 project. They collected the data and co-ordinated the research project in their own country; they sourced local research funding; and they ensured that the objectives of their funders, policymakers, NOCs, and national governing bodies were achieved. Table 1 provides a detailed overview of the SPLISS 2.0 team and policymakers. The project resulted in collaboration between 58 researchers and 33 policymakers from the 15 nations.

Research team

The SPLISS project was set up by Veerle De Bosscher and her team and is based at and managed by the Vrije Universiteit Brussel (Belgium). They took the lead in reviewing the relevant literature, the research design, theory development and methodological design, and the development and distribution of research instruments, guiding and mentoring participating researchers; and overseeing the comparative analysis and reporting of data. The project is a collaboration of a consortium of researchers at Sheffield Hallam University (England) (Simon Shibli), Utrecht University (Netherlands) (Maarten van Bottenburg) and Victoria University (Australia) (Hans Westerbeek). Furthermore a team of researchers from the consortium partners and other countries has made substantial contributions to the data inputs and analysis. These colleagues are:

- Anna Vilanova (National Institute of Physical Education of Catalonia (INEFC), ESP, Pillar 5, athletic career and post-career support)
- Bake Dijk (Utrecht University, NED, Pillar 3, sports participation and SPLISS website)
- Ben Corbett (Griffith University, AUS, Pillar 7, coach provisions and development)
- Camilla Brockett (Victoria University, AUS, Pillar 4, talent identification and development and Pillar 6, training facilities)
- David Barrett (Sheffield Hallam University, UK, Pillar 8, (inter)national competition)
- Geert De Wael (Vrije Universiteit Brussel, BEL, elite sport climate survey)
- Jari Lämsä (KIHU/Research institute for Olympic Sports, FIN, Pillar 9, scientific research and innovation)
- Jasper Truyens (Vrije Universiteit Brussel, BEL, Pillar 2, governance, structure and organisation of elite sport policies and general methodology)
- Mikko Kärmeniemi (Research institute for Olympic Sports, FIN, Pillar 3, sports participation)
- Popi Sotiriadou (Griffith University, AUS, Pillar 7, coach provisions and development)
- Stephanie De Croock (Vrije Universiteit Brussel, BEL, Pillar 1, financial support)
- Sophie Noyens (Vrije Universiteit Brussel, BEL, elite sport climate survey)

Expert team

We also are thankful to the expert team that was involved in providing feedback during the development of the research instruments:

- Adrian Bürgi (Federal Office of Sport FOSPO, SUI)
- Ariane Caplin (Vrije Universiteit Brussel, BE)
- Anke Reints (Vrije Universiteit Brussel, BE)
- Barrie Houlihan (Loughborough University, UK)
- Jonas Schafer (University of Fribourg, SUI)
- Kristel Taelman ((Vrije Universiteit Brussel/Bloso, BE)
- Michael Dooms (Vrije Universiteit Brussel, BE)
- Rasmus K. Storm (Danish Institute for Sports Studies, DEN)
- Rüdisüli Ralph (Federal Office of Sport FOSPO, SUI)

Table 1: SPLISS partners

Country and lead researcher	Research team
AUSTRALIA 	Hans Westerbeek, Camilla Brockett CONTACT: Hans.Westerbeek@vu.edu.au
BELGIUM–FLANDERS 	Veerle De Bosscher, Stephanie De Croock, Jasper Truyens, Geert De Wael, Sophie Noyens CONTACT: veerle.de.bosscher@vub.ac.be
BELGIUM–WALLONIA 	Mathieu Winand,[1] Thierry Zintz,[2] Emilie Malcourant,[2] CONTACT: mathieu.winand@stir.ac.uk Thierry.zintz@uclouvain.be
BRAZIL 	Maria Tereza Silveira Bohme, in collaboration with: Carla Nascimento Luguetti, Catalina Naomi Kaneta, Flávia da Cunha Bastos, Flório Joaquim Silva Filho, Leandro Mazzei, Luciana Perez Bojikian, Luiz Fernando Medeiros Nóbrega, Luiz Ricardo de Lima, Marcelo Alves Kanasiro, Maressa D'Paula Gonçalves Rosa Nogueira, Tatiana de Barros Meira, Valniria Maria Lopes de Souza, Victor Pignotti Maielo CONTACT: terbohme@usp.br
CANADA 	David Legg, Geoff Schoenberg, Suzanne Hamilton, Winston Wing Hong To CONTACT: dlegg@mtroyal.ca

Research institutes	Local funding partners	Policymakers
Victoria University, Institute of Sport, Exercise and Active Living (ISEAL) VICTORIA UNIVERSITY INSTITUTE OF SPORT, EXERCISE AND ACTIVE LIVING	ISEAL, Victoria University Australian Sports Commission	Australian Institute of Sport Australian Sports Commission
Vrije Universiteit Brussel, Department Sport Policy and Management (SBMA) Vrije Universiteit Brussel	Vrije Universiteit Brussel, Department of Government Culture, Youth, Sport and Media (CJSM)–Topsport Vlaanderen	Bloso BOIC (Olympic Committee)
[2]Université catholique de Louvain [1]Stirling University UCL Université catholique de Louvain	–	Olympic Chair in Management of Sport Organisations (Université Catholique de Louvain)
School of Physical Education and Sports of University of São Paulo, Maria Tereza Silveira Bohme USP	University of São Paulo	Federal Department of Sport, Elite Sport department; Brazilian Army Major
Mount Royal University, Department of Physical Educion and Recreation St MOUNT ROYAL UNIVERSITY 1910 CALGARY, CANADA	Sport Canada	–

Country and lead researcher	Research team
DENMARK 	Rasmus K. Storm, Henrik Brandt, Lau Tofft, Nynne Mortensen CONTACT: Rasmus.Storm@idan.dk
ESTONIA 	Eerik Hanni CONTACT: Eerik.Hanni@riigikontroll.ee
FRANCE 	Patrick Mignon, Emanuel Lelore CONTACT: patrick.mignon@gmail.com
FINLAND 	Jari Lämsä, Jarmo Mäkinen, Mikko Kärmeniemi CONTACT: jari.lamsa@kihu.fi
JAPAN 	Yoshiyuki Mano, Hiroaki Funahashi in collaboration with: Takahiro Waku, Shirai Katsuyoshi, Shuhei Yamashita, Hiromi Nakamura, Etsuko Yamada, Kazumi Kitagawa CONTACT: y-mano@waseda.jp hiro0721funa@gmail.com
THE NETHERLANDS 	Maarten van Bottenburg, Bake Dijk CONTACT: M.vanBottenburg@uu.nl

Research institutes	Local funding partners	Policymakers
Danish Institute for Sports Studies & University of Southern Denmark Idrættens Analyseinstitut	The National Olympic Committee and the Sports Confederation of Denmark	Team Denmark
National Audit Office of Estonia riigikontroll National Audit Office of Estonia	–	Estonian Olympic Committee, Estonian Ministry of Culture
Institut National du Sport et de l'Éducation Physique (INSEP) INSEP Institut National du Sport	INSEP	–
KIHU-Research institute for Olympic Sports KIHU	Ministry of Culture and Education, Finland	Finnish Olympic Committee
Waseda University	Japan Society for the Promotion of Science	Department of Information & International Relations at Japan Sport Council (ex-Department of Sports Information at Japan Institute of Sports Sciences)
Utrecht University School of Governance Universiteit Utrecht	Ministry van VWS, NOC*NSF	Mulier Institute

Country and lead researcher	Research team
NORTHERN IRELAND  	Simon Shibli CONTACT: S.Shibli@shu.ac.uk Paul Donnelly, Jamie Uprichard CONTACT: pauldonnelly@sportni.net
PORTUGAL 	Pedro Guedes De Carvalho, Rui Canelas CONTACT: pedro.guedes.carvalho@gmail.com rncanelas@gmail.com
SPAIN 	Anna Vilanova, Adrià Martin, Eduard Inglés, Laura Bou, Maria Romero, Sílvia Gonzalez CONTACT: anna.vilanova@gencat.cat
SWITZERLAND 	Hippolyt Kempf, Marco Stopper, Andreas Christoph Weber, Anne Renaud CONTACT: Hippolyt.Kempf@baspo.admin.ch
SOUTH KOREA	Eunha Koh CONTACT: eunha.koh@gmail.com

Research institutes	Local funding partners	Policymakers
Sheffield Hallam University in collaboration with Sport Northern Ireland Sheffield Hallam University | Sport Industry Research Centre Sport Northern Ireland	Sport Northern Ireland	Sport Industry Research Centre at Sheffield Hallam University
Faculty of Social and Human Sciences, Beira Interior University UNIVERSIDADE DA BEIRA INTERIOR	–	CIDESD–I&D Research Unity; Secretário de Estado do Desporto e Juventude and Comité Olimpico de Portugal
National Institute of Physical Education of Catalonia, INEFC INEFC Generalitat de Catalunya	Consejo Superior de Deportes	Centre d'Alt Rendiment CAR, AsociaciónEspañola de Investigación Social Aplicada al Deporte, AEISAD
Swiss Federal Institute of Sport Magglingen SFISM–Sport and Society Division Schweizerische Eidgenossenschaft Confédération suisse Confederazione Svizzera Confederaziun svizra Federal Office of Sport FOSPO Swiss Federal Institute of Sport Magglingen SFISM	Federal Office of Sport FOSPO; Swiss Olympic Lamprecht und Stamm Sozialforschung und Beratung AG	Federal Office of Sport FOSPO Swiss Olympic
Korea Institute of Sport Science KISS 한국스포츠개발원 Korea Institute of Sport Science	–	–

1.6 Local publication reports

Different SPLISS partners have produced their own policy reports and numerous publications. A summary, of those that are known to us, are shown here. For additional publications by the researchers, we refer to the website: www.spliss.net.

- Brazil: Ter Böhme, M.T. et al.–GEPAE, EEFE, LATECA (2014). International comparison of elite sport policies (SPLISS)–descriptive analysis of Brazilian results. Universiade De Sao Paulo.
- ENGLISH VERSION: www.eefe.usp.br/lateca/web/index.php/en/gepetij/research-reports/218-international-comparison-of-elite-sport-policies-spliss-descriptive-analysis-of-brazilian-results
- PORTUGUESE VERSION: www.eefe.usp.br/lateca/web/index.php/pt/2-sem-categoria/143-analise-descritiva-dos-resultados-brasileiros-spliss
- Canada: Legg, D. (2014). Sport Policies Leading to International Sporting Success–Blog for Canadian Sport for Life, canadiansportforlife.ca/blog/sport-policies-leading-international-sporting-success-spliss-dr-david-legg
- Denmark: Storm, R.K., & Jørgensen, L.T. (2012), Elitesportsmiljøet i Danmark (2012): Analyse af det danske eliteidrætsmiljø baseret på undersøgelsen. 'Sport Policy Factors Leading to International Sporting Success' (SPLISS). Copenhagen: Danish Institute for Sports Studies. www.idan.dk/vidensbank/downloads/elitesportsmiljoeet-i-danmark-2012/e6428881-cad5-49ce-bca7-a1b3008dc3bb
- Denmark: Storm, R.K., & Jørgensen, L.T. (2014), Sport Policy Factors Leading to International Sporting Success (SPLISS): Dansk eliteidræt i international sammenligning–foreløbige resultater. Copenhagen: Danish Institute for Sports Studies. www.idan.dk/vidensbank/downloads/sport-policy-factors-leading-to-international-sporting-success-(spliss)/2b831502-c6aa-408e-a7bd-a30800a59764
- Estonia: Report in Estonian: www.riigikontroll.ee/DesktopModules/DigiDetail/FileDownloader.aspx?FileId=11334&AuditId=2209
- Estonia: Summary in English: www.riigikontroll.ee/DesktopModules/DigiDetail/FileDownloader.aspx?FileId=11572&AuditId=2209
- Finland: Kärmeniemi, M., Mäkinen, J. & Lämsä, J. (2012).SPLISS –urheilujärjestelmät. Suomen kansallinen väliraportti (SPLISS–sport systems. The I national report of Finland). KIHUn julkaisusarja nro 39. www.kihu.fi/tuotostiedostot/julkinen/2012_kar_spliss_ii__sel21_11949.pdf
- Flanders: De Bosscher, V., De Croock, S. (2012). Trends in het Vlaams topsportklimaat. Evaluatie volgens topsporters, trainers en topsportcoördinatoren: 2-meting (2003-2007-2011)[Trends

in the elite sport climate in Flanders. Evaluation according to elite athletes, coaches and high performance directors]. Brussel: VUB. ISBN: 9789090272788. www.vub.ac.be/SBMA/sites/default/files/Trends%20in%20het%20Vlaams%20topsportklimaat-2012.pdf

- Japan: Funahashi, H., Nagamatsu, J., Shirai, K., Yamashita, S., Nakamura, H., Yamada, E., Waku, T., De Bosscher, V., Mano, Y. (2013). International Journal of Sport and Health Science Success Drivers in the Japanese Elite Sport System: An Examination Based on Evaluations of the Elite Sport Climate by Elite Athletes. *Asian Sports Management Review, 7*, 1999
- Japan: Japan Sport Council & Waseda University (2012). Elite sport kankyo chousa: chousa houkokusho [Elite sport climate survey: Analysis report] Retrived from: www.manosemi.net/direct/topics/topics_pdf_download/topics_id=240&no=1
- The Netherlands: van Bottenburg et al. (2012). Bloed, zweet en tranen en een moment van glorie [blood, sweat, tears and a moment of glory]. Niewegein. Arko Sports Media.
- Northern Ireland: Donelly, P., Shibli , S. (2014). Sport Policy Factors Leading To International Sporting Success: An audit of the elite sport development system in Northern Ireland–www.sportni.net/research/recent-research/2013-2/?pg=2
- Portugal: Carvalho, Pedro e Canelas, Rui (2013) RELATÓRIO NACIONAL DO SPLISS–versão em língua portuguesa. Ed. impressa única
- Spain: Vilanova, A; Inglés, E.; Martin, A & Gonzàlez, S. (2011). Memoria Científico-Tècnica: Factores de la política deportiva española que conducen al éxito deportivo a nivel internacional (Report: Sports Policy Factors Leading to International Spanish Sporting Success'). Consejo Superior de Deportes. Expedient 095/UPB10/11. Registro: 11329. www.inefcgiseafe.files.wordpress.com/2014/11/splissspain4.pdf
- Switzerland: Kempf, H., Weber, A. Ch., Renaud, A., & Stopper, M. (2014). Elitesport in Switzerland. Snapshot SPLISS-CH 2011. Magglingen: Federal Office of Sport. Document available at: www.baspo.admin.ch/internet/baspo/de/home/dokumentation.parsys.000104.downloadList.92617.DownloadFile.tmp/brospliss2011escreen.pdf

1.7 Funding the research

A key feature of the SPLISS collaboration was that the individual researchers from each of the participating nations organised funding for domestic data collection. Available funding per nation varied significantly in that regard, and it also needs to be noted that several SPLISS partners indirectly funded the project by the engagement of their own personnel.

SPLISS has largely depended on institutional investments to ensure the national co-ordination of this large-scale project. The SPLISS consortium partners did not seek any financial contribution from the participating nations as a return for the massive co-ordinating work. All such costs were met by the Vrije Universiteit Brussels and supported by the consortium members, and engaged researchers from the partner countries. Additional co-ordination funding was provided by the government in Flanders (topsport Vlaanderen and the Department of Culture, Youth, Sports and Media), the National Sport Association in the Netherlands (NOC*NSF), and Ernst & Young in Belgium. Despite limited funding, the SPLISS 2.0 project is a showcase of collaboration, as the consortium group estimated the value of work to date to be approximately 1.3 million Euros and 5 full-time researchers.

1.8 Structure of this book

As this book aims to advance both academic knowledge and contribute to effective elite sport policies for practitioners, a mix of theoretical and practical insights are provided. Following this chapter we present the nine Pillar model that is used in this book as the framework to explain international sporting success in chapter 2. This is followed by a detailed discussion of our research methodology and its limitations in chapter 3. Following the introduction of the nine Pillar SPLISS model, the subsequent chapters introduce and analyse the different Pillars that make up the SPLISS model and as such create a broader understanding of what the building blocks of elite sport systems are. Figure 2 illustrates this multidimensional approach towards determining the effectiveness of elite sport policy (Chelladurai, 2001). Starting with outputs (results of elite sport competition), the purpose of chapter 4 is to provide a structured overview of how various measures of performance can be rationalised and measured and as such, how we can approach success in the 15 nations. The Pillars—or policy areas—are then discussed in chapter 5, starting with the inputs or financial resources (Pillar 1), which provides insights into how elite sport in the various countries is resourced. Throughputs refer to the efficiency of sports policies, that is, the optimum way the inputs can be managed to produce the required outputs in elite sport (De Bosscher et al., 2006). Pillars 2-9 are throughput factors and are evaluated and discussed in the subsequent parts of chapter 5. In addition to the data collected by the researchers in the nine Pillars, the elite sport climate is measured through interviews with elite athletes, elite coaches and performance directors in the various nations. What is meant by the term 'elite sports climate' is defined by van Bottenburg (2000) as 'the social and organisational environment that provides the circumstances in which athletes can develop into elite sport athletes and can continue to achieve at the highest levels in their branch of sport' (2000, p. 24). The results are discussed throughout the different Pillars. Finally, beyond the medals there are the impacts (outcomes) of elite sport success on society at large, the apparent reasons that governments invest in any elite sport system. Due to the complexity of defining and measuring such outcomes, they are not the subject of analysis in this study. In the last chapter we will discuss the country-by-country benchmarks and how these relate to the relationships between inputs, throughputs and outputs.

Figure 2: The SPLISS process diagram

1.9 Key terminology

- **National Governing Body (NGB):** In general, we use the term 'National Governing Body' to describe the governing body for a specific sport (similar to Federations and National Sport Organisations [NSOs]). The NGBs manage competitions, rules, regulations and championships for their sport. Each NGB sanctions competitions in its country and those competitions follow NGB rules. Typical examples of NGBs include Athletics Canada, the Flemish Gymnastics Federation, and the Lawn Tennis Association (also known as British Tennis).
- **Performance director:** The head of the elite sport department of a National Governing Body (or National Sport Organisation/Federation), who manages elite sport development for a particular sport. Sometimes, when no such person is available (especially in smaller nations or smaller NGBs), it means the person responsible for sport development and elite sport development (e.g., development of the nine Pillars) in general within that sport, or a sport technical director.
- **National Olympic Committee (NOC):** The NOC for any given nation is the body recognised by the International Olympic Committee (IOC) to promote Olympism and to ensure that athletes from their nation attend the Olympic Games. Examples could be the Belgium Olympic and Interfederal Committee (BOIC) and the British Olympic Association (BOA).
- **National sport agencies (NSA):** The national sport agencies act as a leading organisation working in partnership with others to promote sport generally or elite sport in particular. They can be governmental, quasi-governmental or non-governmental. For example, in the UK, UK Sport is the lead body for the development of elite sport. In some nations, for example the Netherlands, the National Olympic Committee and the umbrella organisation for sport have merged to form a single body: NOC*NSF (National Olympic Committee*National Sport Federation).
- **Critical success factor (CSF):** A factor or activity within a strategic elite sport policy planning process that drives the strategy forward and that can contribute to the international sporting success of countries.
- **Purchasing power parity (PPP)** is an economic concept and a technique used to determine the relative value of currencies to be equivalent to (or on par with) each currency's purchasing power. It asks how much money would be needed to purchase the same goods and services in two countries, and uses that to calculate an implicit foreign exchange rate.

Chapter 1 references

Andersen, S., and Tore Ronglan, L. (2012). *Nordic Elite Sport. Same ambitions, different tracks.* Norway: AIT Otta AS.

Bergsgard, N. A., Houlihan, B., Mangset, P., Nordland, S. I. and Rommetveldt, H. (2007). *Sport policy. A comparative analysis of stability and change.* London: Elsevier.

Bogerd, J. (2010). *Twee kanten van de medaille. Sleutelfiguren uit de schaatssport over de gevolgen van de ontwikkeling van de merkenteams voor het topsportklimaat van het langebaanschaatsen en talentontwikkeling in het bijzonder [Two sides of the medal. Key points from skating about the consequences of the development of commercial teams for the elite sport climate in long distance skating and talent development in particular].* Master thesis in sportbeleid en management, Utrecht University, Utrecht.

Chelladurai, P. (2001). *Managing organisations for sport and physical activity: A systems perspective.* Scottsdale, AZ: Holcomb Hathaway Publishers.

De Bosscher, V., De Knop, P., van Bottenburg, M. and Shibli, S. (2006). A Conceptual Framework for Analysing Sports Policy Factors Leading to International Sporting Success. *European Sport Management Quarterly, 6* (2), 185-215.

De Bosscher, V. (2007). Sports Policy Factors Leading to International Sporting Success. Published doctoral thesis, supervised by De Knop, P., van Bottenburg, M. Brussels: VUBPRESS.

De Bosscher, V., Bingham, J., Shibli, S., Van Bottenburg, M. and De Knop, P. (2008). *The global Sporting Arms Race.* An international comparative study on sports policy factors leading to international sporting success. Aachen: Meyer & Meyer.

Digel, H., Burk, V. and Fahrner, M. (2006). High-performance sport. An international comparison. *Edition Sports international, 9.* Weilheim/Teck, Tubingen, DE: Bräuer.

Green, M. and Houlihan, B. (2005). *Elite sport development. Policy learning and political priorities.* London and New York: Routledge.

Houlihan, B. and Green, M. (2011). *Handbook of Sports Development.* London and New York: Routledge.

Porter, M. E. (1990). *The competitive advantage of nations.* London: the Macmillan Press LTD.

Sotiriadou, P., Gowthorp, L. and De Bosscher, V (2013). Elite sport culture and policy interrelationships: The case of Sprint Canoe in Australia. Leisure studies, 32, 6, pp. 598-617, http://dx.doi.org/10.1080/02614367.2013.833973. ISSN 0261-4367.

van Bottenburg, M. (2000). *Het topsportklimaat in Nederland [The elite sports climate in the Netherlands].* Hertogenbosch, Netherlands: Diopter-Janssens and van Bottenburg bv.

2 Chapter 2: Theoretical underpinnings of the SPLISS model

2.1 Introduction: Elite sport success is developable

Without talent, athletes like Ian Thorpe, Sidney Crosby, Inge De Bruin or Neymar would never have enjoyed the level of success that they achieved in their impressive sporting careers, nor would countless other elite athletes around the globe. But it has not been talent alone that enabled them to win medals and championships. They grew up in sport clubs where training and competition opportunities honed their skills; where the guidance from coaches, physiotherapists, doctors, dieticians and sports scientists improved their performance and enhanced their physical and mental readiness; and where the support services from national governing bodies, governments, Olympic Committees and private partners made working towards a sporting career more attractive. Talent, whether it is in sport, arts, sciences, or other life endeavours, is an individual quality that can only be fully expressed in a specific social environment and with the support of others (van Bottenburg 2009). In other words, people are not born as athletes; they need to invest great time, energy, resources and passion to their sport, surrounded by people who provide a range of support services. Over the years, this has raised questions among researchers and policymakers about the extent to which success at international competitions is 'developable'. *Macro-level* factors such as population, welfare, climatic variation and political systems highly influence national success and have been considered in various studies. Research showed that over 50% of international success of countries can be explained by three variables: population, wealth (expressed as Gross Domestic Product per capita) and (former) communism (referring to a particular political system) (e.g., De Bosscher, 2007). These factors are relatively stable and cannot be influenced significantly by direct human influence such as policymakers. However, these factors are important to consider when determining elite sport development strategy (Bergsgard, Houlihan, Mangset, Nordland and Rommetveldt, 2007; Houlihan and Green, 2008).

International success is determined by factors at three levels: macro (environment), meso (policy) and micro (talent). Only at the meso-level, can success be cultivated

As nations have become strategic in the way that they produce elite athletes, *'they rely less on these uncontrollable variables and more on variables which are widely regarded as being components of an elite sports development system'* (De Bosscher et. al., 2008, p 18). As such elite sport has attracted mainstream policy attention from governments around the world, and also policy researchers who increasingly believe that 'elite sport success is developable': That is it can be achieved more effectively as the result of proactive resourcing and creation of an elite sports development system, rather than simply relying on passive macroeconomic variables. This influence is exercised at the *meso-level* and is related to factors that operate at the level of politics and policy formulation (De Bosscher, De Knop, van Bottenburg and Shibli, 2006). As such, an increasing number of studies have been conducted into identifying which policies lead to elite sport success. Table 2 provides an overview of recent comparative elite sport policy research, each with a different approach and methodology.

Such studies can be divided into two categories. On the one hand there are studies that aim to determine and analyse the key success determinants of elite sport policies at the national policy level (e.g., De Bosscher et al, 2006; De Bosscher et al., 2008; Digel, Burk and Fahrner, 2006; Oakley and Green, 2001). On the other hand, there are studies aiming to understand elite sport from a broader political or historical perspective (e.g., Andersen and Ronglan, 2012; Bergsgard et al., 2007; Green and Houlihan, 2005; Houlihan and Green, 2008). In addition a plethora of meso-level studies is starting to develop at a sport-specific level (e.g., Andersen and Ronglan, 2012; Böhlke, 2007; Böhlke and Robinson, 2009; Brouwers, Sotiriadou and De Bosscher, in press; Robinson and Minikin, 2011; Sotiriadou, Gowthorp and De Bosscher, 2013; Truyens, De Bosscher, Heyndels and Westerbeek, 2013), as 'success of countries tends to be concentrated in sports or specific events, in other words, countries typically specialize' (Truyens et al., 2013, p.1). What can be concluded from these studies is that broad common categories of elite sport systems exist across multiple countries. These are based on a similar model of elite sports development with only slight variations between countries (Bergsgard et al., 2007; Green and Houlihan, 2005; Oakley and Green 2001). As stated by Houlihan (2009):

One important and possibly crucial indicator of convergence in elite sports systems is the extent to which a broad range of countries with different political, socio-economic and cultural profiles adopt similar policy goals and instruments. [...] if it is accepted that there is convergence in policy goals, then the next area for investigation is in relation to the policy instruments that have been selected to achieve that goal and, crucially, whether the choice of policy instruments is constrained by the nature of the policy objective (p. 64).

This convergence of elite sport policies can be explained by internationalisation and globalisation processes during which elite sport systems have been copied, especially from former communist countries during the 1970s (e.g., Broom, 1991; Douyin, 1988; Krüger, 1984; Riordan, 1989; Semotiouk, 1990) and later from countries such as Australia and France.

Table 2: An overview of key success factors described in international comparative elite sport policy studies (books) compared to SPLISS (ranked chronologically)

Authors **Methods and study characteristics**	**Focus Countries and sports**	**Factors analysed**	**Comparison with SPLISS**
Green and Houlihan, (2005) • *descriptive and comparative;* qualitative data collection: interviews and document analysis • *advocacy coalition framework (ACF) to analyze policy changes* • *aims to identify the degree of similarity in elite sport development models*	3 countries: Australia, UK and Canada overall + 3 sports: swimming, athletics, sailing/ yachting.	• Support for full-time athletes	Pillar 5
		• A hierarchy of competition opportunities centred on preparation for international events	Pillar 8
		• Elite facility development	Pillar 6
		• Provision of coaching, sports science and sports medicine support services	Pillar 7 and 9
Digel et al. (2006) • descriptive and comparative; qualitative data collection: interviews and document analysis; questionnaires (3 sport associations), • Ministries responsible for HP sport, National Olympic committees, country specific organisations	8 countries: Australia, China, France, Germany, Italy, Russia, UK, USA Overall + 3 sports: athletics, swimming, volleyball	Resources	Pillar 1
		Politics	– (macro)
		Education	Pillar 3 + macro
		Competition	Pillar 8
		Talent search	Pillar 4
		Science	Pillar 9
		Mass media and sponsorship	Environment
Bergsgard et al. (2007) • *contextual and historical* • *descriptive; contributors from each country*	4 countries: Germany, England, Canada, Norway Overall (national) level	Context , cultural background, and historical development	– (macro)
Houlihan and Green (2008) • *contextual and historical* • *descriptive;* author(s) from each country describe elite sport policies, generally based on literature and document analysis • *Builds on Green and Houlihan's (2005) ACF*	9 countries: China Japan, Singapore, Germany, France, Poland, Norway, New Zealand, USA Overall (national) sports level	Historical	–
		Political	– (macro)
		Organisational	Pillar 2 + all Pillars
		Context	–
		Talent ID and development	Pillar 4

Authors Methods and study characteristics	Focus Countries and sports	Factors analysed	Comparison with SPLISS
De Bosscher et al. (2008)–SPLISS • *focus on meso-level factors, using SPLISS model and comparing 103 critical success factors* • *mixed methods research: qualitative phase 1 (model); qualitative + quantitative phase 2* • *stakeholder involvement (athletes, coaches, performance directors)* • *scoring system: to move beyond the descriptive level of comparison*	6 countries: Belgium (Flanders + Wallonia), Canada, Italy, the Netherlands, Norway, UK Overall (national) sports level	Pillar 1: Financial support	
		Pillar 2: Governance, organisation and structure of elite sport	
		Pillar 3: Sport participation	
		Pillar 4: Talent identification and development	
		Pillar 5: Athletic and post-athletic support	
		Pillar 6: Facilities	
		Pillar 7: Coach provision and development	
		Pillar 8: (Inter)national competition	
		Pillar 9: Scientific research and innovation	
Andersen and Tore Ronglan (2012) • *contextual and historical; aims to look beyond the designated sport organisations and to capture the more detailed structures as well as intentions and processes behind national elite sports systems* • *descriptive; contributors from each country* • *aims to identify how national elite sport systems came about, how they relate to success in individual sports, how they differ in terms of centralisation, responsibilities and roles, and how this influences the capacity for successful elite sport development*	4 Nordic countries (with similar systems) + success stories of sports: Norway (women's handball), Finland (men's ice hockey), Denmark (track cycling), Sweden (tennis and golf);	1) Historical sport developments in Nordic countries, in relation to elite versus mass sport; critical decisions; resources; controversies 2) Success stories–different roads to excellence 3) Differences and similarities; policy issues; systematic comparisons	– (different approach)
		Key dimensions in elite sport development:	
		Mass sport foundation	Pillar 3
		Facilities	Pillar 6
		Strategies and key factors	Pillar 2
		Team building focus	–
		International influence	–
		Interaction with national elite sport system	–

Despite the fact that in the SPLISS 1.0 study (2008) we agreed with the opinions of other authors that homogeneity and convergence has increased, the study itself revealed substantial differences in the way elite sport policies were implemented in the different nations. This was also one of the key findings by Anderson and Ronglan (2012), comparing Nordic countries in an analysis of their paths to excellence over the last 30 years:

the systems often contain elements of dynamics and change, where interdependencies, intensity of interaction, mechanisms of decision-making and integration of individual actions vary considerably. Even within a highly competitive domain of elite sport, subject to strong pressures toward convergence, there is considerable space for local ingenuity in identifying and making most out of their local resources (p. 284).

The lack of a coherent theoretical model about sports policy factors that influence international sporting success lies at the root of the formulation of the SPLISS model. The SPLISS model differs from these studies in its scope, methodology and integration, as will be explained in the next sections.

2.2 The SPLISS model

2.2.1 Nine Pillars as policy components of elite sport success

The various building blocks that lead to elite sport success are complex, multi-faceted and multi-layered. As noted earlier it can be argued that factors influencing success can be classified at three levels: macro-, meso-, and micro-level (De Bosscher et al., 2006). The SPLISS model is based on this classification. *Macro-level* factors influence the (dynamic) social and cultural environments in which people live, including economy, demography, geography and climate, urbanisation, politics, and national culture. *Meso-level* factors influence the policy environment of nations (e.g., policies on coach development, policies on talent identification and selection). At the *micro-level* are factors that influence the success of individual athletes, ranging from the influence of inherited genes to social influence of parents, friends and coaches. Many researchers have tried to explain the success of individual athletes instead of comparing nations (e.g., Conzelmann and Nagel, 2003; Duffy, Lyons, Moran Warrington and McManus, 2006; Gibbons, McConnel, Forster, Riewald and Peterson, 2003; Greenleaf, Gould and Diefen, 2001; van Bottenburg, 2000; Wylleman and Lavallee, 2004). However, the interaction of factors at the micro-, meso- and macro-levels is what best explains achieving elite success, but it is also the most complex analysis to undertake.

SPLISS aims to model the relationship between elite sport policy systems and policies and international success

The purpose of the SPLISS framework is to model the relationship between elite sport policy policies and international success—the focus of research therefore is directed at meso-level factors. The SPLISS model (Figure 3) is based on a comprehensive literature review regarding the organisational context of elite sport development in countries (meso-level), supplemented by two studies at the micro-level, where the focus was on better understanding of the determinants of success for individual athletes. The first study examined the views of international tennis experts on the factors determining tennis success. The second study examined the views of Flemish athletes, coaches and performance directors as the main stakeholders. Based on these studies the SPLISS model was developed and tested in six countries including Belgium (separated in Flanders and Wallonia), Canada, Italy, the

Netherlands, the UK and Norway, now better known as the SPLISS 1.0 study. We refer to previous publications for more in-depth information on the SPLISS model and the methodology (De Bosscher et al., 2006; De Bosscher De Knop, van Bottenburg, Shibli and Bingham, 2009).

SPLISS measures nine Pillars or policy components, at the level of inputs (Pillar 1) and throughputs (Pillars 2-9), that can lead to increased outputs or success

It was concluded that most critical success factors that can be influenced by policies can be distilled down to nine key areas or 'Pillars', including inputs (Pillar 1) and throughputs (Pillars 2-9) (Figure 3).

- Inputs are reflected in Pillar 1, as the financial support for sport and elite sport. Countries that invest more in (elite) sport can create more opportunities for athletes to develop their talent.
- Throughputs are the policy actions that script and deliver the processes ('what' is invested and 'how' it is used) that may lead to increasing success in international sport competitions. They refer to the efficiency of sport policies, that is, the optimum way the inputs can be managed to produce the required outputs. All of Pillars 2-9 are indicators of the throughput stage.

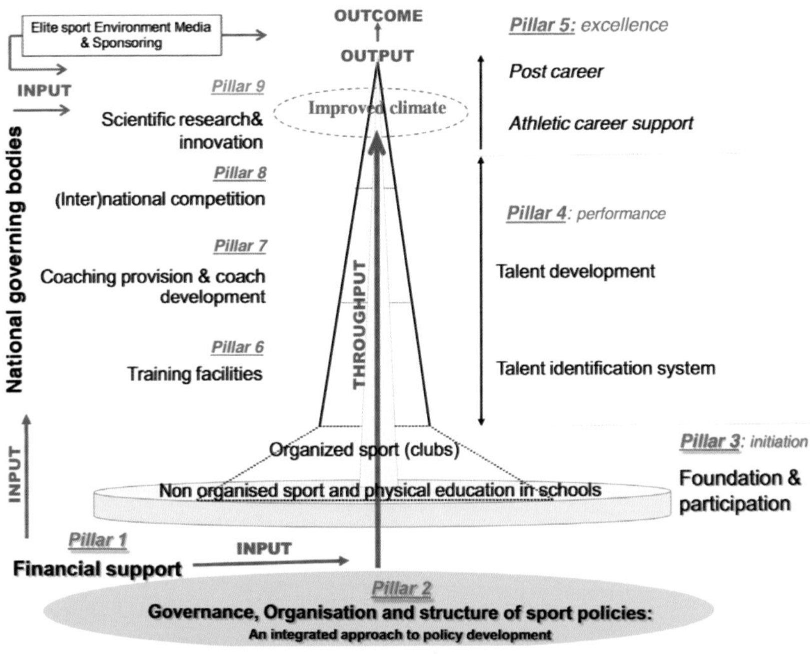

Figure 3: The SPLISS model: Theoretical model of 9 Pillars of sports policy factors influencing international success (adapted from De Bosscher et al., 2006) (reprinted with permission from Taylor & Francis Ltd, www.informaworld.com, and slightly adapted from De Bosscher et al., 2006)

The SPLISS model uses the actual performance of nations in elite sport competitions as the output measure of the system. There are various indicators by which the outputs of an elite athlete production system can be measured. For example, by counting the number of medals won during the Olympic Games or other events; by counting the number of finals achieved (top eight places); by determining the relative success (e.g., medals per head of population or number of medals corrected for country GDP) or even the number of participants qualifying to take part in major events. All of these methods appear to correlate significantly ($r_s > 0.8$) (De Bosscher et al., 2007). Chapter 4 will delve deeper into these measures.

The nine Pillars are underpinned by Critical Success Factors (CSFs) as will be explained in this chapter. The shape of the SPLISS model (a pyramid) accounts for the fact that of many talented athletes entering elite sport systems only a few will reach the international top and achieve medal-winning success. Our contention is that for a national sporting system to merely have the nine Pillars in place is only the start to achieving elite sporting success; what then becomes important is how the Pillars connect, interact and are invested in by policymakers (and others) (De Bosscher, 2007). It is the unique combination and variation of inputs and throughputs that will determine success levels.

Input

Pillar 1: Financial support

Financial resources are measures of **input**. Previous research clearly indicates that countries that invest more in (elite) sport create more opportunities for athletes to achieve success. Hogan and Norton (2000) found a linear relationship between money spent and total medals won by Australia since the 1980s. An important outcome of the SPLISS 1.0 study was that:

'In terms of input-output analysis, the best predictor of output appears to be the absolute amount of funding allocated to elite sport (p. 134).'

However, the SPLISS 1.0 findings also suggested that over the past decade, this relationship has become less pronounced. With more countries investing in elite sport there are diminishing returns on (base) investments and it seems that successful countries need to continue investing in elite sport simply to maintain existing performance levels (De Bosscher et al., 2008).

Throughput

Pillar 2: Governance, organisation and structure of (elite) sport policies, an integrated approach to policy development

The amount of resources devoted to elite sport is important, but it is the organisation and structure of sport and its relationship to (a national) society that enables efficient use of these resources to further the chances of elite sporting success (SIRC, 2002). There is, in that regard, no consensus or preference regarding the necessity for centralisation or high level of government intervention in elite sports policies (Houlihan, 2009). Furthermore, it has been argued that it is equally important to have a good national communication system, clear distribution and description of roles in the system, and simple (efficient) administration (Clumpner, 1994; Oakley and Green, 2001). The importance of involving stakeholders in elite sport policy development has also been noted (Thibault, Kihl and Babiak, 2010). Besides these elements, important variables of this Pillar also relate to organisational, historical and cultural contexts that differ per country. It is therefore important to observe how policymakers and policy systems respond and adapt to change, such as the increasing commercialisation and professionalisation of elite sport (Houlihan and Green, 2008).

Pillar 3: Participation in sport

Although the (lacking) relationship between sport for all and elite sport is often debated, most top athletes originate from grassroots participation. Van Bottenburg (2002) found a significant correlation between mass participation and medals won during the Olympic Games (Barcelona and Sydney) especially when grassroots sport was 'intensive and competitive.' Similarly, at a sport-specific level, a high correlation was found between the number of tennis players and international success in 40 nations (De Bosscher and De Knop, 2002). On the other hand, there are examples of low participation sports that deliver high levels of success, such as diving and cycling in Australia (Elphinson, 2004; Green, 2005). It can be argued that a broad base of sport participation is not always a condition for success, but it may deliver a foundation for potential success because it provides a supply of young talent and various training and competition opportunities for this talent to hone their skills.

Pillar 4: Talent identification and development system

Pillar 4 concerns the discovery and development of talented athletes. A well-developed talent identification and development system is particularly important in countries with small populations (talent pools) (Harre, 1982; Régnier, Salmela and Russel, 1993). Policymakers therefore need to focus their attention on creating monitoring systems to identify talent characteristics, robust talent detection systems that minimise drop-out, and well-organised scouting systems (Rowe, 1994). In most nations talented athletes are recruited in single sports, by the national governing bodies. Therefore, much data related to this Pillar needs to be studied on a sport-specific basis. The second part of this Pillar concerns talent development, where young talents follow a period of intensive training during which they develop a mastery of their sport. Many countries have developed nationally co-ordinated initiatives to support governing bodies in setting up high-level training and competition programmes and to support athletes to combine their academic career with a sport career.

Pillar 5: Athletic and post-career support

The logical extension of the talent identification and development phase is the production of elite athletes capable of competing at the highest level. Many athletes who have the potential to reach the top, drop out of the system before they achieve true success. National sport governing bodies play an important role in supporting athletes during and after their career which is why factors important in this Pillar also need to be analysed at a sport-specific level. In only a few sports can athletes make a living from their sporting earnings and pay for all the costs they incur. We look at the different ways in which governments provide financial support for athletes to meet their living costs and have support programmes to provide access to the services required to realise their potential. Finally, athletes also need to be assisted in preparing for life after sport.

Pillar 6: Training facilities

Training facilities (Pillar 6) are an important success factor in the process of enabling athletes to train in a relevant and high-quality sporting environment. The extent of facility provision also provides a link between participation and excellence. De Bosscher and De Knop (2002) showed that the number of tennis courts was highly correlated with international success of nations in tennis ($r = 0.858$). At the top level, this Pillar is concerned with a network of high-quality national and regional facilities, specifically for elite sport purposes, including administrative headquarters, overnight accommodation, a close link with sports medics, a close link with sports scientists/ co-operation with universities, and a close link with the education institutes of younger athletes.

Pillar 7: Coaching and coach development

With regard to Pillar 7, the quality and quantity of coaches is important at each level of the sport development continuum. At the high-performance level, two criteria provide points of comparison. The first considers the quality and organisation of training certification systems where, for example, in some countries like France and Australia, certification of coaches is required in sport clubs (D'amico, 2000). The second is concerned with the level of time and resource commitment that (elite) coaches can give to achieving excellence with their athletes. In some nations professional coaches are the standard; in other nations coaching largely remains an undervalued and underpaid or even voluntary activity.

Pillar 8: (Inter)national competition

A co-ordinated approach to staging international events is the eighth identified indicator for successful elite sports policies. It has been shown in many studies on the Olympic Games (Clarke, 2002; Johnson and Ali, 2002; Kuper and Sterken, 2003) that the organisation of international events in the home country has a positive effect on international success. Athletes performing in their home country have the benefit of low travel costs and familiar weather conditions and facilities. In addition, a well-developed and high-level national competition structure is a significant criterion as frequent exposure to sporting competition is a necessary factor in athlete development (Crespo, Miley and Couraud, 2001). National competition structures mainly need to be analysed at a sport-specific level.

Pillar 9: Scientific research and innovation in elite sport

Pillar 9 seeks to examine the extent to which nations take a co-ordinated approach to the development, organisation and dissemination of scientific research and knowledge. It also is concerned with the extent that (technological) innovation plays a role in elite sport success. At the core of the Pillar are the ways in which nations systematically gather and disseminate scientific information in areas such as talent identification and development, medicine, nutrition, psychology, physiology, biomechanics and sport coaching.

As shown in Table 2, the SPLISS model has combined information that other authors also consider to be the elements of an elite sport system. The main difference is that the nine Pillars in the SPLISS study have been further extended by detailed critical success factors (De Bosscher et al., 2009) that will be explained further. The focus of SPLISS in that regard is on meso-level factors (sport policy) unlike many studies that focus their attention on explaining elite sport policies in a broader political or historical context. The SPLISS study can therefore be seen as complementary to these other studies.

We feel it is important to stress that the nine Pillars of the SPLISS model are general elite sport policy dimensions, for which it can be argued that all the factors that can be influenced by sport policies, can be classified under one of these Pillars. However, as indicated in earlier work: *'Its (SPLISS) function is not deterministic: rather it aims to identify pivotal issues and to generate crucial questions in a benchmark study of elite sport systems'* (De Bosscher et al, 2006, p. 209). The SPLISS model is therefore dynamic, and will continuously be adapted over time and to different sport settings, different sport contexts and situations. Nations might not necessarily increase their chances of success by investing in some or all Pillars but rather they need to find the most suitable blend of Pillars and CSFs that best fit the unique situation of that nation.

2.2.2 INPUT-THROUGHPUT-OUTPUT: A multidimensional model to measure effectiveness of elite sport policies

The SPLISS model provides a multidimensional approach to effectiveness evaluation of elite sport policies a the levels of input, throughput, output and feedback

Input-throughput-output models, such as the SPLISS model, are also well known in strategic management literature. With the advent of total quality management (TQM), statistical process control (Deming, 1982) and the balanced scorecard (Kaplan & Norton, 1996), the emphasis in strategic management has shifted away from output measures (such as success) and input measures (such as financial resources) to measures of processes and strategy (Neely, Gregory and Platts, 2005). The SPLISS model integrates the elite sport policy literature that focuses on sport policy factors that are important for international sporting success (see earlier) and the literature that deals with effectiveness (quality of output) (De Bosscher, Shilbury et al., 2011). We have used a multidimensional approach to evaluate effectiveness of organisations by Chelladurai (2001) and applied this to a national sport policy context. This is illustrated in Figure 4.

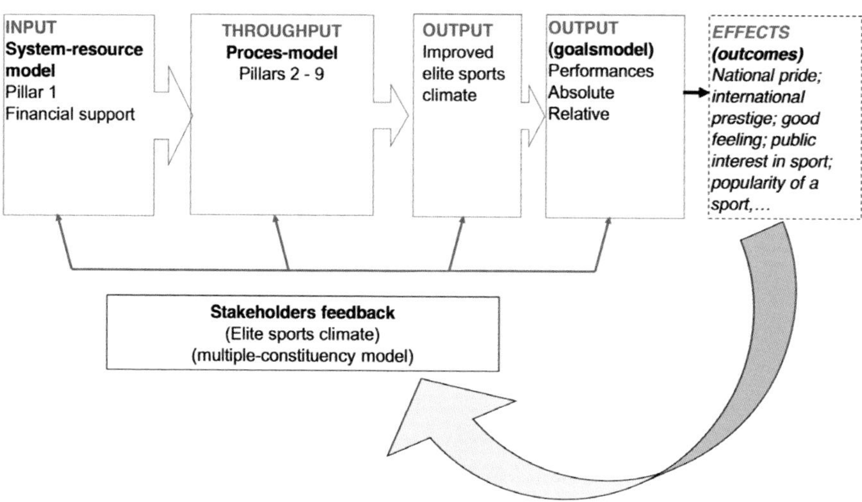

Figure 4: SPLISS as a multidimensional model to measure effectiveness of elite sport policies (De Bosscher et al., 2011)

The model's multidimensional structure stems from the integration of (a) the measuring system-resource model (e.g., Frisby, 1986; Yuchtman and Seashore, 1967) that suggests measure inputs, (b) the internal process approach that evaluates throughputs (Pfeffer, 1977; Steers, 1977),

(c) the 'goals' model (Etzioni, 1964; Price, 1972) where effectiveness is defined as the degree to which an organisation has achieved its goals, and (d) the multiple constituency model (feedback) or the participant satisfaction model (e.g., Connolly, Conlon and Deutsch, 1980; Papadimitriou and Taylor, 2000) which defines organisational effectiveness according to an organisation's 'ability to satisfy key strategic constituencies in their environment' (Sowa et al., 2004, p. 713). All of these elements are integrated in the SPLISS model and considered in our study. To that end it is assumed that elite athletes, coaches, performance directors and others should be formally involved in the policy evaluation process.

The outcomes concern: why do nations invest in elite sport? These are not measured in SPLISS

In addition to the input-throughput-output relationship, the 'outcomes' in Figure 4 refer to the multitude of reasons why nations may want to invest in elite sport and how governments justify why it is important to win more medals. Politicians and policymakers often argue that elite sport affects national identity, pride, international prestige, diplomatic recognition, international prestige, feel good factors, public interest in sport and an increasing popularity of a sport (De Bosscher, Sotiriadou and van Bottenburg, 2013). Governments tend to justify large investments of public money using the argument that elite athlete success and hosting international events generate many of these positive outcomes. Policy documents often refer to the positive impact of elite sport on society, including economic impact, social impact, individual development of talented people and the capacity to inspire increased mass participation in sport (van Bottenburg, Elling, Hover, Brinkhof and Romijn, 2011). Because millions of people are emotionally connected to (elite) sport, there is a widespread trust in the 'good of (elite) sport' (Coalter, 2007). Interestingly, little research evidence has been generated to support these widely acclaimed broader societal benefits of elite sport. Apart from a few studies on the (mainly economic) impact of events,[2] the evidence of impact that elite sport has in society remains scant (De Bosscher et al., 2013). Given the complexity of collecting such evidence, the impact (outcomes) of elite sport success are not considered in the SPLISS study and as such present an opportunity for future SPLISS related research.

2 See a literature overview in De Bosscher, Sotiriadou and van Bottenburg, 2013. Due to differences in methodology, perspective and definitions, the estimation of economic value of elite sport events differs quite strongly between studies.

2.2.3 Critical success factors (CSF): The processes that drive the Pillars

One of the key characteristics of the SPLISS model is that Pillars are operationalised into measurable items, named critical success factors (CSFs):

'The SPLISS study does not just identify 'what' characterises successful elite sport policies, but also 'how' these different dimensions can be developed. The unique feature of this research is that in addition to measuring easily quantifiable variables, such as inputs (e.g., money) and outputs (e.g., medals), it also delves into understanding the 'black box' of throughput (De Bosscher et al., 2008, p. 35).'

In strategic management literature a 'critical success factor' is the term describing a process or activity that is required for ensuring the success of a company or an organisation. CSFs are vital components of a company strategy and critical to an organisation's operating activities. A CSF drives the strategy forward; it makes or breaks the success of the strategy (hence 'critical') (Friesen and Johnson, 1995). CSFs should not be confused with key performance indicators (KPIs) which are measures that quantify management objectives and enable the measurement of strategic progress and performance. Accordingly, the CSFs identified in the SPLISS model are vital for the evaluation of each Pillar, but are not essentially performance indicators (such as the number of medals). The term 'Leading' in the SPLISS acronym can in this respect be mistaken for pointing at a (not implied) cause–effect relationship. In the SPLISS model the CSFs drive and measure each Pillar rather than being indicators of performance (De Bosscher, Shibli, van Bottenburg, De Knop and Truyens, 2010). They may increase chances of international success but do not guarantee success, due to the many other confounding variables that can also influence success.

The nine Pillars and 750 CSFs are underpinned by a total of 96 CSFs in PLISS 2.0. These CSFs are the elements that can drive the Pillar forward

The Pillars and the critical success factors that make up each Pillar can be seen as the ingredients of an elite sport system. As stated by Marcel Sturkenboom, former director of the Dutch National Olympic Committee and National Sport Federation (NOC*NSF) (2007): *'having the ingredients does not automatically lead to success. How you bring the ingredients together is what counts'*. As outlined in Table 3, a total of 96 CSFs and 750 sub-factors have been measured in the SPLISS 2.0 project.

Table 3: Overview of the number of CSFs in the 9 Pillars measured in the SPLISS model

	CSF	Sub-factors
Pillar 1: Financial support	8	9
Pillar 2: Governance, organisation and structure	18	119
Pillar 3: Sports participation	10	31
Pillar 4: Talent identification and development	12	169
Pillar 5: (Post-)career support	7	122
Pillar 6: Training facilities	9	84
Pillar 7: Coach provision and development	16	100
Pillar 8: (Inter)national competition	7	51
Pillar 9: Scientific research and innovation	9	65
TOTAL	96	750

2.3 Final remarks

2.3.1 The environment of elite sport: Culture, politics, sponsorship and media... Pillar 10?

The environment of elite sport, such as culture, politics, sponsorship and media are not measured in SPLISS 2.0

The underpinning logic of the SPLISS model is that elite sporting success can be influenced by elite sport policies. We have already introduced the interdependency of factors at the meso- and macro-levels. There are a range of other factors that are increasingly important in elite sport development but not included in SPLISS because they cannot be controlled, influenced and as such cannot contribute to developing or managing elite sporting success. This was identified by Digel (2000) as 'the environment of elite sport' as a source of world-class performance in sport. This environment includes, for example, the role that a national education system can play, the influence of the private sector as a partner of sport, the role of the mass media as a promoter (or detractor) of sport's interests and the attitudes of the wider population as a sounding board for world-class sport performances. We could identify these factors as 'Pillar 10' of the SPLISS model. However, while the importance of these variables is recognised, they are hard to measure and difficult to compare between nations. It can be argued that some components are included as part of Pillar 2, in regard to the national co-ordination and collaboration with the private sector. However, we would like to acknowledge that 'Pillar 10' factors are largely absent in our analysis, for good methodological reasons, and that future research should be conducted separately into such issues, probably at a sport-specific level (e.g., Truyens et al., 2013).

2.3.2 Evaluation of national-level public policies

SPLISS measures the national level of publicly funded policies and does not include commercialised funding that is not nationally co-ordinated

The focus of SPLISS is on sports funded primarily through public sector bodies and therefore excludes the more commercial or 'market models' of elite athlete development. Elite sport development in commercial sport is quite different from publicly funded elite sport systems, although hybrid models continue to develop around the world (e.g., speed skating in the Netherlands is still nationally co-ordinated by the NGB but largely commercially funded). Westerbeek and Hahn (2013) in that regard argue that explosive growth of commercial sport driven through global mass media exposure will lead to dramatic changes in the composition of national elite sport systems. The private sector increasingly acts as a co-financier of the system of high-performance sport. These private investments have increased the prospects of athletes making a living from their sport. However, private sector investment (and ownership) of sport is not only hard to measure, but also hard if not impossible to regulate and govern by national governments. One only has to consider the takeover of world football by super wealthy businessmen. Elite sport system development in corporate sport for that matter justifies separate and sport-specific approaches. This is also the reason that the SPLISS model would demand a different approach when used to analyse sport policy in the United States, one of the most developed sport business nations in the world, where elite sport development is delegated to (often privately owned) sport organisations and where nationally driven elite sport policies are virtually nonexistent (Sparvero, Chalip and Green, 2007).

2.3.3 Many roads lead to Rome!

What works for whom in what circumstances, in what respects, and how?

Although the SPLISS model and its constituting CSFs is comprehensive, it is not an all-embracing model that can be applied to any situation, any country or any context. It is impossible to create one single model for explaining international success and as previously noted different systems may lead to similar levels of success (De Bosscher, 2007). As stated by other authors, high performance sport development is characterised by the prevailing local culture in sport that has been developed over a long time (Digel et al., 2006) and which is influenced by the local politics and political system. As such similar policy actions may have different outcomes across nations. This also means that initial policy decisions can determine future policy choices, which is referred to as 'path dependency' by Houlihan and Green (2008). This concept, originally introduced by Kay (2005, cited in Houlihan and Green) states that the trajectory of change up to a certain point constrains the trajectory after that point (p. 553). The process of policy transfer and benchmarking and as an outcome of that the improvement of the (elite sporting) system, is constrained by the historical, cultural and political context of nations. The relatively high level of success of a nation such as Italy, in the SPLISS 1.0 study, combined with its low Pillar scores, can be explained by the context in which these results emerged. With its great sporting culture, large talent pool, and lower level of international competition at the time, Italy was at the tail end of an era. The last bit of success was squeezed out of a system that required an overhaul. There are many roads that lead to Rome in that regard, and each nation has to find its own path that best fits its history, context, culture and here and now (Pawson and Tilley, 1997).

Chapter 2 references

Andersen, S. S. and Ronglan, L. T. (2012). *Nordic Elite Sport: Same Ambitions, Different Tracks.* Copenhagen Business School Press.

Bergsgard, N. A., Houlihan, B., Mangset, P., Nrdland, S. I. and Rommetveldt, H. (2007). *Sport policy. A comparative analysis of stability and change.* London: Elsevier. Bernard, and Busse. (2000). Bernard and Busse Spreadsheet.

Böhlke, N. (2007). New insights in the nature of best practive in elite sport system management–examplified with the organisation of coaches education. *New Studies in Athletics, 45* (3), 49-59.

Böhlke, N. and Robinson, L. (2009). Benchmarking of élite sport systems. *Management Decision, 47* (1), 67-84.

Broom, E. F. (1991). Lifestyles of aspiring high performance athletes: A comparison of national models. *Journal of Comparative Physical Education and Sport, 8* (2), 24-54.

Brouwers, Sotiriadou and De Bosscher (in press). Sport specific policies and factors that influence international success: The case of tennis. *Sport Management Review.*

Chelladurai, P. (2001). *Managing organisations for sport and physical activity: A systems perspective.* Scottsdale, AZ: Holcomb Hathaway Publishers.

Clarke, S. R. (2002). Home advantage in the Olympic Games. Retrieved November 27, 2003, from University of Technology website http://www.swo,/edu.au/sport/olympics/HAOlympicgames.pdf. Swinnburn.

Clumpner, R. A. (1994). 21ste century success in international competition. In *Sport in the global village* (pp.298-303). R. Wilcox (Ed.). Morgantown, WV: Fitness Information Technology.

Coalter, F. (2007). *A wider social role for sport. Who's keeping the score?* New York: Routledge.

Connolly, T., Conlon, E. J. and Deutsch, S. J. (1980). Organizational effectiveness: A multiple-constituency approach. *Academy of Management Review, 5* (211-217).

Conzelmann, A. and Nagel, S. (2003). Professional Careers of the German Olympic Athletes. *International Review for the Sociology of Sport, 38* (3), 259-280. doi: 10.1177/10126902030383001

Crespo, M., Miley, D. and Couraud, F. (2001). An overall vision of player development. In *Tennis Player Development* (pp. 13-18). M. Crespo, M. Reid and D. Miley (Eds). London: ITF LTd.

De Bosscher, V. (2007). *Sports policy factors leading to international sporting success.* Published doctoral thesis. Brussels: VUBPRESS.

De Bosscher, V. and De Knop, P. (2002). *The influence of sports policies on international success: An international comparative study.* Paper presented at the 9th World Sport for All Congress, 'Sport for All and Elite Sport: Rivals or partners?' Ahrnem, the Netherlands.

De Bosscher, V., Bingham, J., Shibli, S., van Bottenburg, M. and De Knop, P. (2008). *The global sporting arms race. An international comparative study on sports policy factors leading to international sporting success.* Aachen: Meyer & Meyer.

De Bosscher, V., De Knop, P., van Bottenburg, M. and Shibli, S. (2006). A conceptual framework for analysing sports policy factors leading to international sporting success. *European Sport Management Quarterly, 6* (2), 185-215.

De Bosscher, V., De Knop, P., van Bottenburg, M., Shibli, S. and Bingham, J. (2009). Explaining international sporting success: An international comparison of elite sport systems and policies in six countries. *Sport Management Review, 12* (3), 113-136.

De Bosscher, V., Shibli, S., van Bottenburg, M., De Knop, P. and Truyens, J. (2010). Developing a methodology for comparing the elite sport systems and policies of nations: A mixed research methods approach. *Journal of Sport Management, 24*, 467-600.

De Bosscher, V., Shilbury, D., Theeboom, M., Hoecke, J. V. and Knop, P. D. (2011). Effectiveness of national elite sport policies: A multidimensional approach applied to the case of Flanders. *European Sport Management Quarterly, 11* (2), 115-141.

De Bosscher, V., Sotiriadou, P. and van Bottenburg, M. (2013). Scrutinizing the sport pyramid metaphor: an examination of the relationship between elite success and mass participation in Flanders. *International Journal of Sport Policy and Politics, 5* (3), 319-339. doi: 10.1080/19406940.2013.806340

D'amico, R. L. (2000). *Organisation and Regulations in National Sport Bodies: A comparative study in artistic gymnastics.* (Doctor of Philosophy), University of Sydney.

Deming, W. E. (1986). *Out of the crisis.* Cambridge, MA: MIT Press.

Digel, H. (2000). *Resources for world class performances in sport – a comparison of competitive sport systems.* Institut National du Sport Expertise in Elite Sport 2nd International Days of Sport Sciences, 46–49.

Digel, H., Burk, V. and Fahrner, M. (2006). *High-performance sport. An international comparison* (Vol. 9). Weilheim/Teck, Tubingen: Bräuer.

Douyin, X. (1988). A comparative study on the competitive sports training systems in different countries. *Journal of Comparative Physical Education and Sport, 2* (3), 3-12.

Duffy, P., Lyons, D., Moran, A., Warrington, G. and McManus, C. (2006). How we got here: Perceived influences on the development and success of international athletes. *Irish Journal of Psychology, 27* (3-4), 150-167

Elphinston, B. (2004). *Win to win models in sport. The Australian experience 1896-2004.* Paper presented at the IOC-technical seminar, http://w3.uniroma1.it/compass, Warschau, PL.

Etzioni, A. (1964). *Modern organisations.* Englewood Cliffs, NJ: Prentice-Hall.

Friesen, M. E. and Johnson, J. A. (1995). *The Success Paradigm: Creating Organizational Effectiveness Through Quality and Strategy.* US: Greenwood publishing group.

Frisby, W. (1986). Measuring the organizational effectiveness of national sport governing bodies. *Canadian Journal of Applied Sport Sciences, 11* (2), 94-99.

Gibbons, T., McConnel, A., Forster, T., Riewald, S. T. and Peterson, K. (2003). *Reflections on success: US Olympians describe the success factors and obstacles that most influenced their Olympic development.* Report phase II, United States Olympic Committee (USOC).

Green, B. C. (2005). Building Sport programs to optimize athlete recruitment, retention and transition: toward a normative theory of sport development. *Journal of Sport Management, 19*, 233-253.

Green, M. and Houlihan, B. (2005). *Elite sport development. Policy learning and political priorities.* New York: Routledge.

Greenleaf, C., Gould, D. and Diefen, K. (2001). Factors influencing Olympic performance with Atlanta and Nagano US Olympians. *Journal of Applied Sport Psychology, 13*, 154-184.

Harre, D. (1982). *Trainingslehre [training methods].* Berlin: Sportverlag.

Hogan, K. and Norton, K. (2000). The 'price' of Olympic gold. *Journal of Science & Medicine in Sport, 3* (2), 203-218.

Houlihan, B. (2009). Mechanisms of international influence on domestic elite sport policy. *International Journal of Sport Policy and Politics, 1* (1), 51-69. doi: 10.1080/19406940902739090

Houlihan, B., and M. Green. 2008. *Comparative Elite Sport Development. Systems, structures and public policy.* London, UK: Elsevier.

Johnson, K. N. and Ali, A. (2002). A tale of two seasons: Participation and medal counts at the summer and winter Olympic Games. Retrieved February 15, 2003, from Wellesley college, Massachusetts www.wellesley.edu/economics/wkpapers/wellwp_0010.pdf

Kaplan, R. S. and Norton, D. P. (1996). Using the Balanced Scorecard as a strategic management system. *Harvard Business Review, 74* (1), 75-85.

Kay, A. (2005). A critique of the use of path dependency in policy studies. *Public Administration, 83*, 553-571.

Krüger, A. (1984). *To Moscow and back: International status of comparative research in regard to physical activity outside of schools. Proceedings of the 4th International Seminar on Comparative Physical Education and Sport.* Malente-Kiel, West Germany, 213-227.

Kuper, G. and Sterken, E. (2003). Olympic participation and performance since 1896. University of Groningen, Research Institute SOM (Systems, Organisations and Management).

Neely, A., Gregory, M. and Platts, K. (2005). Performance measurement system design: A literature review and research agenda. *International Journal of Operations & Production Management, 25* (12), 1228-1263.

Oakley, B. and Green, M. (2001). The production of Olympic champions: International perspectives on elite sport development system. *European Journal for Sport Management, 8*, 83-105.

Papadimitriou and Taylor (2000). 'Organisational effectiveness of Hellenic national sports organisations: A multiple constituency approach.' *Sport Management Review 3* (1), 23-46. doi: http://dx.doi.org/10.1016/S1441-3523(00)70078-7.

Pawson, R. and Tilley, N. (1997). *Realistic Evaluation.* London: Sage.

Pfeffer, J. (1977). Usefulness of the concept. In *New perspectives on organizational effectiveness* (pp. 132-143). P. S. Goodman and J. M. Pennings (Eds.). San Francisco, CA: Jossey-Bass.

Price, J. L. (1972). The study of organizational effectiveness. *The Sociological Quarterly, 13* (1), 3-15. doi: 10.2307/4105817

Régnier, G., Salmela, J. and Russell, S. J. (1993). Talent detection and development in sport. In *Handbook of research on sport psychology* (pp. 290-313). R. N. Singer, M. Murphy and K. L. Tennant (Eds.). New York: Macmillan Publishers.

Riordan, J. (1989). Soviet sport and perestroika. *Journal of Comparative Physical Education and Sport, 6*, 7-18.

Robinson, L. and Minikin, B. (2011). Developing strategic capacity in Olympic sport organisations. *Sport, Business and Management, 1* (3), 219-233.

Rowe (1994). *Talentdetectie in basketbal [Talent detection in basketball].* Unpublished doctoral dissertation, Catholic University of Leuven, BE.

Semotiuk, D. M. (1990). East Bloc athletics in the Glasnost era. *Journal of Comparative Physical Education and Sport, 9* (1), 26-29.

SIRC. (2002). European sporting success. A study of the development of medal winning elites in five European countries. Final Report, Sheffield, Sport Industry Research Centre.

Sotiriadou, P., Gowthorp, L. and De Bosscher, V. (2013). Elite sport culture and policy interrelationships: The case of Sprint Canoe in Australia. *Leisure Studies, 1-20.* doi: 10.1080/02614367.2013.833973

Sowa, Jessica E., Sally Coleman Selden and Jodi R. Sandfort. (2004). 'No longer unmeasurable? A multidimensional integrated model of nonprofit organizational effectiveness.' *Nonprofit and Voluntary Sector Quarterly, 33* (4): 711-728. doi: 10.1177/0899764004269146.

Sparvero, E., Chalip, L. and Green, B. C. (2008). Chapter 10–United States. In *Comparative Elite Sport Development* (pp. 242-271). H. Barrie and G. Mick (Eds.). Oxford: Butterworth-Heinemann.

Steers, R. M. (1977). *Organizational effectiveness: A behavioral view.* Santa Monica, CA: Goodyear.

Thibault, L., Kihl, L. and Babiak, K. (2010). Democratization and governance in international sport: addressing issues with athlete involvement in organizational policy. *International Journal of Sport Policy and Politics, 2* (3), 275-302. doi: 10.1080/19406940.2010.507211

Truyens, J., De Bosscher, V., Heyndels, B. and Westerbeek, H. (2014). A resource-based perspective on countries' competitive advantage in elite athletics. *International Journal of Sport Policy and Politics, 1-31.* doi: 10.1080/19406940.2013.839954

van Bottenburg, M. (2000). *Het topsportklimaat in Nederland [The elite sports climate in the Netherlands].* Hertogenbosch, Netherlands: Diopter-Janssens and van Bottenburg bv.

van Bottenburg, M. 2002. *'Sport for all and elite sport: Do they benefit one another?' 9th World Sport for All Congress, 'Sport for all and elite sport: Rivals or partners?,* Ahrnem, NL.

van Bottenburg, M. (2009). *Op jacht naar goud. Het topsportklimaat in Nederland, 1998-2008. [the hunt for gold. The elite sport climate in the Netherlands, 1998-2008].* Niewegein, Netherlands: Arko Sports Media.

van Bottenburg, M., Elling, A., Hover, P., Brinkhof, S. and Romijn, D. (2011). De maatschappelijke betekenis van topsport. [The social meaning of elite sport]: Departement voor Bestuurs- en Organisatiewetenschap (USBO) Universiteit Utrecht, Mulier Instituut.

Westerbeek, H. M. and Hahn, A. (2013). The influence of commercialisation and globalisation on high performance sport. *In Managing High Performance Sport.* P. Sotiriadou, and V. De Bosscher (Eds.). London: Routledge.

Wylleman, P. and Lavallee, D. (2004). A developmental perspective on transitions faced by athletes. In *Developmental sport and exercise psychology: A lifespan perspective* (pp. 507-527). M. Weiss (Ed.). Morgantown, WV: Fitness Information Technology.

Yuchtman, E. and Seashore, S. E. (1967). A system resource approach to organizational effectiveness. *American Sociological Review, 32* (6), 891-903.

Swiss athlete Dario Cologna completing the survey

3 Chapter 3: Methodologies and samples

3.1 Introduction: International comparisons are complicated

International comparative studies are some of the most complicated areas of research (Henry, Amara and Al-Tauqi, 2005; Porter, 1990). In sport the issue is even more convoluted because sport systems are closely interwoven with the culture of a nation, and therefore each system is unique. Different extraneous and uncontrollable factors make comparability problematic. Accordingly most comparative sport studies either use quantitative macro-data in a large number of nations (called large n-studies), or they are descriptive studies and when comparing nations examine general trends or similarities/differences between them. Most studies in (elite) sport policy and sport management are in the latter category. This is largely due to a lack of standardisation in comparative research methods, as well as limited publicly available and quantifiable data on sport policies within and across nations (Henry et al., 2005). These constraints are indicative of the complexity of cross-national comparisons. Furthermore, policy instruments are often dependent on politics and policy regimes, which implies that similar policy actions may have different outcomes in different nations.

It will therefore never be possible in comparative elite sport policy studies to reduce all success factors to one all-embracing theory. The key point of note, as stated by Hofstede (1998) is to identify how one can pare down typical problems to an extent that a common language can be found for those factors that càn be compared. Hofstede (1998) provided the metaphor that every comparison of values and norms between nations is like a comparison between apples and oranges, and it is important to find a common language:

Popular wisdom deems that one cannot compare apples with oranges. But what do we mean by 'compare'? Scientifically speaking, apples and oranges come under the general category of 'fruits' and can be compared on many criteria, such as availability, price, colour, vitamin content or keeping quality. Comparing apples with oranges, cross-cultural psychologist Harry Triandis once said, is okay as long as we possess a fruitology, a theory of fruits. (p. 16)

The SPLISS 'fruitology' is developed in the theoretical model (chapter 2), consisting of nine Pillars and 96 CSFs (750 sub-factors) that can be managed by national sports policies or national sport organisations and that may influence the potential for athletes to perform at the international level. The methodologies are further characterised by two elements, as will be further explored in the next sections:

- A mixed methods research design
- The development of a scoring system in the data analysis to 'measure' elite sport policy effectiveness

3.2 Study design: Mixed methods research

The key purpose driving the SPLISS project is to develop insights into the relationship between elite sport policies (inputs and throughputs) and international sporting success (outputs). In other words, we seek to identify how policy (actions) derived from the nine Pillars can contribute to performance. Performance management involves the use of tools or operational principles aimed at helping decision-makers and managers in their practices regarding strategy, control, performance evaluation or organisational operations (Chappelet and Bayle, 2005). The link between strategy and performance is also the cornerstone of the Kaplan and Norton (1996) balanced scorecard and has been acknowledged in strategic management literature as a way to complement financial performance measures of industry efficiency. The complexity of input-throughput-output evaluation lies in the variety of factors that influence success, and this becomes even more complicated in an international comparative context. For these reasons, we have used a mixed methods research protocol, to collect and analyse a comprehensive amount of data on the nine Pillars and its CSFs.

1. SPLISS model	2a. SPLISS 2.0 Data collection	2b. SPLISS 2.0 Data analysis
96 CSFs (750 sub-factors) across nine Pillars at the level of inputs-throughputs-outputs (chapter 2). **Procedures:** 1. Content analysis of literature and documents; interviews to reflect expert opinion and consumer perspective (face and content validity) 2. Pilot testing in an empirical study with six sample nations, or rather SPLISS 1.0 (in addition, criterion and construct validity; external validity)	Qualitative and quantitative data in 15 countries to operationalise CSFs and outputs. **Procedures:** 1. Output analysis, using infostrada (chapter 4) Data collected and validated by local SPLISS partners using: 2. Overall sport policy inventory (212 questions and 184 pages), collected from policy documents and interviews 3. Elite sport climate survey with elite athletes, coaches and performance directors	• Measurement of the competitive position of the sample nations in Nine Pillars • Descriptive comparison **Procedures:** 1. Content analysis of qualitative information 2. Scoring system (composite indicators) based on quantitative and qualitative indicators from the inventory and the surveys: transform quantitative + qualitative data into 0-1 scores; aggregated scores for CSFs and each Pillar

Figure 5: (simplified) SPLISS 2.0 mixed methods research design

The advantage of mixed methods research is that it provides strengths that offset the weaknesses of both quantitative and qualitative research (e.g., Creswell and Plano Clark, 2007; Rudd and Johnson, 2010). Building on the theories and methods developed in SPLISS 1.0, the SPLISS study employed mixed research methods with a two-phase sequential design that has both an exploratory and an explanatory character. In the second phase qualitative and quantitative data are concurrently collected and analysed as is illustrated in Figure 5: (simplified) SPLISS 2.0 mixed methods research design.

3.2.1 Data collection and protocol

The national SPLISS research partner collected the data locally in each country, using pre-defined research instruments. Comparability of data as well as the reliability of the comparison was a major concern of the research consortium. Researchers received a research protocol that provided guidance on the process of data of collection aiming to standardise data gathering procedures and as such to increase reliability of the data. All documents were provided through a joint web platform. To improve international comparability, the partners were allowed to add locally relevant questions, but not to delete or change any. Several international meetings were organised to fine-tune the data collection and identify possible gaps in the research methodology. The involvement of local (nation-based) researchers led to:

- The translation of research instruments to a local context (12 languages in total);
- Validation of research data during the stage of data collection, data analysis and results;
- Collaboration with and involvement of local policymakers and sport organisations; and
- Expanding international networks and collaboration opportunities for the local researchers.

The 9 Pillars and 96 'Critical Success Factors (CSF)' were operationalised through two types of research instruments: an overall sport policy inventory for each of the nine Pillars and an elite sport climate survey targeting elite athletes, elite coaches and performance directors (federations). The inventory was aimed at collecting objective data on the nine Pillars from elite sport policy organisations, the survey was aimed at evaluating the elite sports climate (in the nine Pillars) from the perspective of important stakeholders in elite sport.

a. Overall sport policy inventory

This instrument is an extensive semi-structured inventory of all the indicators in the nine Pillars (and their evolution over the past 10 years). The inventory originally consisted of 126 CSFs (later reduced/merged to 96), 212 questions and 184 pages covering all the nine Pillars.

The inventory was completed by the researchers in each country through interviews with policy agencies and analysis of secondary sources such as policy documents. Open-ended questions initially sought to gain insight into each country's policy system, closed questions were added to ensure a degree of comparability across nations for the various sub-criteria. Space was left for additional comments that were helpful in creating a deeper understanding.

b. Elite sport climate survey

This structured questionnaire was completed by (a) athletes, (b) coaches and (c) performance directors in each country. The survey served two purposes: (1) to gather information on indicators or 'facts' that cannot easily be measured (using dichotomous questions) (De Pelsmacker and Van Kenhove, 1999) and (2) to measure success indicators as they are perceived by their primary users (using a five point Likert scale). The surveys were of substantial size (around 60 questions and 18 pages) in order to cover all the Pillars and the relevant CSFs.

By involving athletes, coaches and performance directors as the main stakeholders, this research focuses on a multidimensional effectiveness evaluation of elite sport policies (Chelladurai, 2001; Papadimitriou and Taylor, 2000; Shilbury, 2006). This method is similar to, for example, the World Competitiveness Yearbook in economies (Garelli, 2008; Rosselet, 2008) and to methods in performance management literature (Kloot and Martin, 2000).

3.2.2 Definitions

For reasons of comparability, the SPLISS project focussed only on able-bodied Olympic summer and winter sports and as such excluded disabled athletes. To guarantee the international homogeneity and comparability of the benchmarking process, there were strict definitions of the different stakeholders included in this project. The elite coach, elite athlete and performance directors in each country had to be selected based on these definitions. Each country was free to add additional groups of stakeholders, although they were asked to (try to) ensure at least a minimum response rate of 20% for the different key stakeholder groups.

a. Elite athlete was defined as:

1. *'An elite athlete should be regarded as an (able-bodied) athlete who, whether as an individual, or as part of a team, is ranked in the world top 16 for his or her discipline, or in the top 12 of any equivalent continental ranking system.' OR*
2. *'An athlete who receives direct or indirect funding and/or other services via a support programme funded and/or organised on a national (or regional) basis for the purpose of achieving success at least one of the following levels: the Olympic Games; the senior World Championships; and the senior Continental Championships in his or her sport (European, Asian, Pan American etc).' Countries that had such programmes had to survey these athletes, and advise the SPLISS group about the standard of the athletes concerned in their study. As a minimum, all athletes identified via definition (1) above had to be included in the survey.*

b. Elite coach was defined as:

'A coach who trains elite athletes (as defined here) or talented youths in a national/regional trainings centre. Sub-elite coaches training talented youths will be included in the study as a separate category.'

c. Performance director was defined as:

'The head of the elite sport department of a National Governing Body (or National Sport Organisation/ Federation), who manages elite sport development for a particular sport. Sometimes, when no such person is available (especially in smaller nations or smaller NGBs), the performance director will be the person responsible for sport development and elite sport development (e.g., development of the nine Pillars) in general within that sport, or a sport technical director.'

3.2.3 Data analysis: Scoring system methodology

We are aware of the shortcomings of a rational-technocratic perspective on performance management. Management practices can often better be characterised as emergent, recursive and ambiguous rather than planned, linear and clear (Mintzberg, Lampel and Ahlstrand, 2005). Nonetheless, we start from the premise that the performance management process is based on rational goals of informed decision making (De Lancer Julnes, 2008). At the heart of the performance management process is the performance measurement system, which is of critical importance to the effective and efficient functioning of the management system (Van Hoecke, Schoukens and De Knop, 2013). It is seen as the process of quantifying the efficiency and effectiveness of action (Neely, Gregory and Platts, 2005).

By combining quantitative measurement techniques to the qualitative data, we provided some rigor to underpinning the (opinion driven) insights regarding the relationship between policies and success. Useful methodological insights can be gained from considering research beyond the sport sector, for example in the economic sector where the concept of national competitiveness is more developed, notably in the fields of international trade, industrial organisation and business economics (Siggel, 2009). According to Garelli (2008), *'The measurement of world competitiveness is routinely used in economic studies to provide a framework to assess how nations manage their economic future'* (p. 1). Although this does not imply that nations can be 'in control' of their economic future, in SPLISS, we replicated such an approach in an elite sport setting and in this respect explore a method to assess how nations try to manage their future success in international sport competitions (De Bosscher et al., 2010).

The basic principles of economic competitiveness studies are quite similar in design. Linssen (1998) used the four steps, to measure 110 indicators clustered in 10 determinants and compared across six nations: (1) generating the determinants of competitiveness; (2) expressing relevant factors in indicators and sub indicators; (3) scoring each indicator and in some cases applying weightings; and (4) comparing the scores and, if possible, explaining differences between nations. Similar methods can be found in the IMD World Competitiveness Yearbook or the Global Competitiveness Report (World Economic Forum, 2008). For example in the World Competitiveness Yearbook, 55 economies are analysed and ranked on 331 criteria that are grouped into 20 factors and then regrouped into four competitiveness determinants (Rosselet, 2008).

Consistent with these studies, this section details how we transformed the critical success factors of the nine Pillar model into measurable units that were individually scored and aggregated into a final score for each Pillar, called composite indicators (OECD, 2008). Composite indicators are also increasingly recognised as a useful tool in policy analysis and public communication (OECD, 2008). The scoring system helped to test the hypotheses addressing relationships between the Pillars and success (outputs); it provided simple comparisons of countries that can be used to illustrate complex and sometimes elusive issues (OECD, 2008). It also facilitated the recognition of patterns and to extract meaning from qualitative data, account for all data, document analytic moves, and verify interpretations (Sandelowski, Voils and Knafl, 2009). The scoring system development consisted of two stages:

1. Within the 96 CSFs in the nine Pillars, a total of 750 sub-factors were measured. All 750 sub-factors over nine Pillars were allocated a score between 0 and 1. Depending on the source (elite sport climate survey or sport policy inventory) and type of question (open-ended, dichotomous, or assessment), the standards for this scale differed (De Bosscher et al., 2010).
    - The most complex ratings derived from the overall sport policy inventory, because qualitative information on the elite sport systems for each Pillar had to be transformed into a score. These (mostly) open-ended questions were grouped and assessed in terms of 'availability of the criterion in a stronger or weaker form', to indicate the level of development. For each CSF, the standards and ratings were discussed within the consortium group until consensus was reached.
    - For quantitative data from the overall sport policy inventory (e.g., elite sport expenditures), data were standardised. 'z-scores' were created for all quantitative data sets. This standardised the different data types on a common scale and allows fair comparisons between different types of data. Each data point was given a score based on its distance from the mean average of the entire data set, where the scale is the standard deviation of the data set. Subsequently the Z-score was turned into a 'cumulative probability score' to arrive at the final totals (between 0-1) for each CSF.

- In the elite sport climate survey quantitative data were available based on two types of questions: dichotomous questions (yes/no) and ratings on a five-point Likert scale (ordinal). For the dichotomous questions absolute standards were used to calculate the scores (the percentage 'yes' answers divided by 100). For the five-point Likert scale questions 'ratings' were calculated, by multiplying the response values respectively by 1 (highly developed), 0.75 (sufficiently developed), 0.5 (reasonably developed), 0.25 (insufficiently developed), and 0 (not developed). This resulted in a score that lies between 0 and 1.
- When the CSFs contained several sub-indicators the scores were aggregated taking into account the non-available answers.

2. The scores for each CSF were aggregated into a sub-dimensional score and finally into a total percentage score. The total score was allocated a conditional formatting color ranging from a low level of development (red) to a high level of development (dark green). This is illustrated in Figure 6: example of scoring 3 CSFs within one sub-dimension of Pillar 2. Figure 7 shows how three CSFs within Pillar 2 (governance, organisation and structure of elite sport) are scored separately for the sport policy inventory (black) and elite sport climate survey (blue), and aggregated into a final percentage score for each nation on a sub dimension 'athletes, coaches and other important stakeholders are involved in the elite sport policy development' and subsequently for the whole Pillar (Figure 7), taking into account the non-available answers.

COUNTRIES		N	AUS	BRA	CAN	DEN	ESP	FIN	FLA	JPN	S. KOR	NED	N. IRL	POR	SUI	WAL	FRA	EST
III. Athletes, coaches and other important key stakeholders are involved in the elite sport policy development																		
	subtotal III		0,58	0,32	0,78	0,42	0,47	0,56	0,52	0,54	0,44	0,63	0,22	0,60	0,66	0,26	NA	NA
CSF 2.7	Policy of the NSA is regularly evaluated with athletes, coaches, performance directors who are formally invited to be involved in the evaluation process PRIOR and AFTER policy takes place	4	1,00	0,00	0,88	0,38	1,00	0,94	0,69	0,88	0,56	0,94	0,00	0,63	1,00	0,25	0,19	NA
CSF 2.7 (b)	Policy of the NSA is regularly evaluated with athletes, coaches, performance directors who are formally invited to be involved in the evaluation process PRIOR and AFTER policy takes place	16	0,45	0,33	0,47	0,40	0,38	0,40	0,48	0,48	0,33	0,47	0,31	0,37	0,38	0,31	NA	0,34
CSF 2.8	Athletes and coaches are represented within national governing bodies	2	0,00	0,00	1,00	0,00	0,00	0,00	0,00	0,00	0,00	0,00	0,00	1,00	0,00	0,00	0,00	NA
CSF 2.8 (b)	Athletes and coaches are represented within national governing bodies	4	0,71	0,38	0,57	0,42	0,54	0,53	0,73	0,53	0,43	0,58	0,75	0,62	0,44	0,26	NA	0,65
CSF 2.9	Athletes and coaches are represented in the decision making process of the NSA	4	0,40	0,40	0,50	0,50	0,00	0,60	0,00	0,40	0,33	0,67	0,00	0,00	0,00	0,00	0,00	NA
CSF 2.9(b)	Athletes and coaches are regularly consulted (by NSA) about their specific needs	2	0,35	0,49	0,50	0,39	0,43	0,32	0,71	0,39	0,54	0,48	0,06	0,37	0,49	0,48	NA	0,43

Figure 6: Example of scoring 3 CSFs within one sub-dimension of Pillar 2

COUNTRIES	AUS	BRA	CAN	DEN	ESP	FIN	FLA	JPN	S. KOR	NED	N. IRL	POR	SUI	WAL	FRA	EST
Percentage Score for Pillar 2-INVENTORY	0,67	0,37	0,60	0,56	0,48	0,48	0,43	0,60	0,45	0,76	0,44	0,27	0,60	0,32	0,37	NA
Percentage Score for Pillar 2-ELITE SPORT CLIMATE	0,55	0,43	0,53	0,45	0,54	0,43	0,59	0,55	0,50	0,49	0,34	0,55	0,50	0,47	NA	0,34
Percentage Score for Pillar 2	0,64	0,38	0,58	0,53	0,50	0,47	0,47	0,58	0,47	0,69	0,42	0,34	0,58	0,36	NA	

Figure 7: Illustration of total score and traffic lights for Pillar 2 for 18 CSFs and 119 sub-factors

Some CSFs were weighted to reflect their relative importance. These weightings were largely based on the number of sub-factors by which a CSF was measured and on the (expert) validation process conducted in the SPLISS 1.0 study. Weights were required because each CSF was not measured by the same number of questions, and to 'lock in' the impact of each CSF on the overall score (i.e., 'not weighting is also weighting').

The scoring method in SPLISS 2.0 differed from SPLISS 1.0 in regard to the scales; the original 1-5 scale has been replaced by scores between 0-1 to accommodate for a higher number of sub-variables that were aggregated into a score for each CSF. There is no general consensus on the use of scales (Ochel and Röhen, 2006). For example the World Competitiveness Yearbook converts data from a 1-6 scale to a 0-10 scale and then calculates standard deviation values to determine rankings (Rosselet, 2008). The World Economic Forum converts the data to a scale of 1-7 (Önsel et al., 2008) and Sledge (2005) used a Likert scale of −1 to +2 to assess firms' strategies.

3.3 Sample countries: Key points and characteristics

When the SPLISS 2.0 project was announced, any nation interested was invited to participate, under the condition that they were able to collect the comprehensive data set and follow the research protocol.

The SPLISS sample for this study can be described as 13 nations and 3 regions: Flanders, Wallonia and Northern Ireland. These represent 16 national sport systems from 15 nations in total. For readability reasons, we will further use 15 nations throughout this book. Northern Ireland is the smallest of the four countries of the United Kingdom in terms of both area and population, containing 2.9% of the UK population and 5.7% of the total area of the United Kingdom. In 2008 the United Kingdom was part of the SPLISS 1.0 project, when they were upgrading their elite sport policies since their worst-ever Olympic performance in 1996 in Atlanta. After 2008, many nations were looking at the UK as a best practice benchmark and as such the UK felt less eager to take part in SPLISS 2.0. Northern Ireland did take part and was therefore seen as a 'nation in its own right' within the project. UK Sport is the co-ordinating authority for elite sport, where DCAL (government department for culture, media and sport) in Northern Ireland sets the policy direction and Sport NI puts this into practice. Some sports are supported at UK level, others are supported at the home nation level of Northern Ireland.

Sport policy directions in Belgium are formulated in a unique way and cannot be understood without taking the regional differences into account. As the responsibility for sport is delegated to the independent regions (Dutch-speaking Flanders, French-speaking Wallonia and German-speaking community), there is no national sport policy ministry or administration. Consequently, Flanders and Wallonia (Dutch- and French-speaking part together) can be seen as two distinct nations. There are three ministries of sport, for which the law (i.e., decree) determines that they cannot fund another region or a federal (Belgian) sport structure; accordingly there are three national sports administrations and also the national governing bodies are separated (although for Wallonia and the German-speaking community, many NGBs are merged). At the federal (Belgian) level the only institutional body is the National Olympic Committee (BOIC), which mainly facilitates the athletes' participation in the Olympic Games.

The organisation and structure of these 'nations' is discussed in Pillar 2 of the results section.

The 16 sport systems represent a diverse sample when looking at the population and wealth, factors that explain (along with former communism) more than 50% of a nation's success (De Bosscher, 2007). The SPLISS sample nations represent 8.5% of the world population and 10% of global wealth. They won 231 medals in London 2012 (23% of total), produced one-quarter of the London Olympians (26%) and won 99 medals in Sochi 2014 (37%).

Japan and Brazil are the largest countries of the sample. With populations of 127 and 203 million inhabitants, they are the sixth and eleventh largest countries in the world. Estonia and Northern Ireland have the smallest populations. In terms of wealth, Switzerland exceeds all nations, followed by the three medium-sized populated nations (Canada, Australia and the Netherlands). Brazil's GDP per capita is much lower than the other nations.

Table 4: Overview of SPLISS 2.0 nations clustered according to population

Nations with a population of	Population	GDP/cap (PPP)
< 15 million		
Portugal	10,813,834	$ 22,900
Belgium Flanders Wallonia (incl. Brussels)	10,449,361 6,367,963 4,081,398	$ 37,800
Switzerland	8,061,516	$ 54,800
Denmark	5,569,077	$ 37,800
Finland	5,268,799	$ 35,900
Northern Ireland (UK)	1,810,863	$ 36.700
Estonia	1,257,921	$22,400
15-40 million		
Canada	34,834,841	$ 43,100
Australia	22,507,617	$ 43,000
Netherlands	16,877,351	$ 43,300
> 40 million		
Brazil	202,656,788	$ 12,100
Japan	127,103,388	$ 37,100
France	66,259,012	$ 35,700
South Korea	49,039,986	$ 33,200
Spain	47,737,941	$ 30,100
Total SPLISS sample	**620,697,656**	

Source: CIA World Factbook, 2012; GDP/cap in US$

There are many other ways to cluster nations. For example, former communist countries still perform above average during the Olympic Summer Games (De Bosscher, 2007; Stamm and Lamprecht, 2000). Other cultural factors may also explain international sporting success. Little research has been conducted in regard to comparing nations and their approach to elite sport policy. The work by, among others, Bergsgard et al. (2008), Green and Houlihan (2005), Green and Collins (2008) and Houlihan and Green (2008), who explain (at a descriptive level) the evolution of elite sport policies based on historical backgrounds and how policy decisions can influence the path towards elite sport development, has to be recognised in that regard.

3.4 Sample and profiles

3.4.1 Overall sport policy inventory

The overall elite sport policy inventory was a comprehensive research instrument in its own right. Each question allowed for further information or comments leading to an average of 240 pages of information per country (over 3,000 pages in total). In some countries it was hard to collect information for all Pillars. Estonia completed only the Pillar 1 inventory and South Korea did not complete Pillars 3 (participation), 4 (talent), 7 (coaches) or 8 (international competition). Wherever information is incomplete for certain countries, this will be mentioned in the book.

3.4.2 Elite sport climate survey: Athletes', coaches' and performance directors' sample

Athletes, coaches and performance directors were contacted by local researchers in each country through email, phone or social media, such as Facebook in Brazil. The fact that the project was highly dependent on the co-operation of sports authorities and National Olympic Committees, which had not necessarily endorsed the research in all countries, made it challenging to access all three respondent groupings in some countries. For example, there were no performance directors in Estonia and Northern Ireland. France was unable to participate in the surveys due to final approvals arriving after the data collection deadlines. An overview of the response rates is presented in Table 5.

All countries, except Japan, used online surveys. Respondents received reminders by email or by phone. Some countries offered incentives, such as iTunes cards in Canada. The Swiss researchers approached all respondents to complete the surveys immediately after training sessions on iPads, and these iPads could be won by respondents as an incentive to participate. In the Netherlands there was a video message by the Olympic Team chief to stress the importance of partaking in the surveys.

In total 9,258 elite athletes, 2,176 elite coaches and 432 performance directors received the surveys. After data cleaning and omitting respondents that did not fulfil the criteria (e.g., non-Olympic sport disciplines or disabled athletes, or unreliable responses), 3.142 athletes (33.9%), 1.376 coaches (63.2%) and 241 performance directors (55.8%) were included in the final analysis. Of these, 637 elite athletes (6.9%), 193 elite coaches (8.87%) and 27 performance directors (6.3%) did not fully complete the survey. This may be related to the length of the questionnaire

(60 questions, on average 40 minutes to fill out the survey). However, in order to gain insights into all CSFs, this could not be avoided. Some countries chose to modify the questionnaire slightly. For example, the Netherlands did not ask all the questions in order reduce the completion time. Australia also decided–for confidentiality reasons–not to provide specific questions concerning the sport (discipline), age and the wage.

Focus on top 16 athletes and international coaches only when significant differences according to levels occur

The numbers of athletes, coaches and performance directors varied greatly between the countries (Table 5). This is a result of differences in the (population) size of the country and difference in the criteria used by countries to recognise and support athletes and coaches. While in some countries athletes would have to compete in the national level competition to be supported by an elite support programme (e.g., Estonia), in other countries one has to be in the world top 16 or higher (e.g., Netherlands). For coaches, some countries included national youth selection coaches, or 'talent coaches'. These differences between countries will be taken into account throughout this book. When significant differences are likely to influence comparability, the analysis sample has been limited to top 16 level athletes only and international level coaches only. For overall data representation we have weighted the respondents as if each country had an equal number of respondents.

The large sample from Switzerland, with 715 athletes (22.8% of the total sample), 378 coaches (28%) and 40 performance directors (16.6%) is striking. Other big contributors are Brazilian and Korean athletes (13.7% and 11.8%), Estonian and Australian coaches (13.6% and 11.0%) and Korean performance directors (13.3%). Estonia and Northern Ireland did not survey performance directors.

Response rates varied from 71% among Japanese athletes and 82% of the coaches in Flanders, to only 14% of the Brazilian athletes. The targeted response rate was 20%. This target rate was not reached for Brazilian athletes (n = 431), Canadian athletes (n = 157) and coaches (n = 12). We decided to maintain these respondents because of high absolute counts, except for Canadian coaches, where we note that the low response rate requires careful interpretation. Japan had the highest response rates (more than 70%), followed by Switzerland.

Table 5: Number of respondents by nations (response rates in brackets)

Country	Athletes	% of total sample	Coaches	% of total sample	Performance director	% of total sample
AUS	208 (27%)	6.6%	152 (35.2%)	11.0%	9 (30.0%)	3.7%
BRA	431 (14%)	13.7%	57 (51.8%)	4.1%	10 (35.2%)	4.1%
CAN	157 (15%)	5.0%	12 (NA)	0.9%	8 (24.2%)	3.3%
DEN	231 (36%)	7.4%	66 (46.2%)	4.8%	25 (46.3%)	10.4%
ESP	166 (42%)	5.3%	25 (62.5%)	1.8%	13 (43.3%)	5.4%
EST	82 (NA)	2.6%	187 (NA)	13.6%	–	–
FIN	78 (46%)	2.5%	71 (56.3%)	5.2%	17 (48.6%)	7.1%
FLA	168 (57%)	5.3%	137 (82.0%)	10.0%	19 (79.2%)	7.9%
N. IRL	61 (41%)	1.9%	16 (69.6%)	1.2%	–	±
JPN	135 (71%)	4.3%	64 (86.5%)	4.7%	14 (73.7%)	5.8%
S. KOR	370 (NA)	11.8%	62 (NA)	4.5%	32 (NA)	13.3%
NED	153 (20%)	4.9%	81 (33.6%)	5.9%	20 (33.3%)	8.3%
POR	107 (21%)	3.4%	32 (64.0%)	2.3%	24 (85.7%)	10.0%
SUI	715 (62%)	22.8%	378 (55.8%)	27.5%	40 (69.0%)	16.6%
WAL	80 (45%)	2.5%	36 (60.0%)	2.6%	10 (62.5%)	4.1%
Total	**3,142**	**100.0%**	**1,376**	**100.0%**	**241**	**100.0%**

Notes: These responses rates include only Olympic sports; France did not participate in the elite sport climate surveys; Northern Ireland and Estonia did not complete performance directors' surveys.

The next section will introduce the profiles of athletes, coaches and performance directors.

3.4.3 Sample by sport

The sample consisted of 84% elite athletes competing in summer sports (31 different sports), 16% in winter sports (6 different sports) and of 17.5% coaches competing in winter sports, 82.5% in summer sports (Table 6). Of the winter sports, 60% of the athletes and coaches were Swiss (mostly skiing). Similar figures are found among the performance directors.

There was also a significant difference in whether athletes are competing in a team or in an individual sport. On average 77.3% of the athletes are from individual sports and 22.7% are from team sports. For coaches these figures are similar (78.2% and 21.8%, respectively). The percentage of athletes competing in team sports was above 30% in Flanders (36%), Wallonia (33%) and Spain (41%), and was 0% in Japan. In the coaches' sample a higher number of team sports was represented in Portugal and Flanders. These differences can in part be explained by the sports that are recognised as priority sports in each nation.

Table 6: Proportion of summer/winter and individual/team sports in the athletes' and coaches' sample

	Summer sports	Winter sports	Individual sports	Team sports
Athletes	83.8%	16.2%	77.3%	22.7%
Coaches	82.5%	17.5%	78.2%	21.8%
Performance directors	87.2%	12.7%	78.4%	21.6%

Figure 8 shows the 10 summer and 4 winter sports that are most represented in the sample of athletes and coaches. The top five most represented sports represent 35% of the total athletes' sample (aquatics, athletics, skiing, cycling and rowing) and 39% of the coaches' sample (athletics, aquatics, volleyball, gymnastics and handball). The overrepresentation of skiing is a result of the high response rate from Switzerland. This needs to be taken into account in the analysis.

There is a significant difference in the total number of sports per country. The athletes' and coaches' samples of Switzerland represent the highest number of different sports (n = 28): 6 winter sports and 22 summer sports. Japan (n = 12) and Finland (n = 14) for athletes and Canada (n = 10) for coaches have the lowest number of sports represented.

Japan and Canada did not survey winter sports athletes or coaches, irrespective of winter sports being of major importance in these countries. Also in Portugal, Brazil, Flanders, Wallonia, Northern Ireland and Spain, less than 5% are winter sport athletes, whereas 47% of the athletes in Finland and 42% in Switzerland, and one out of three elite coaches in these countries are from winter sports. The average number of sports represented in this survey is 20.5 sports per country (18.2 summer sports and 2.3 winter sports).

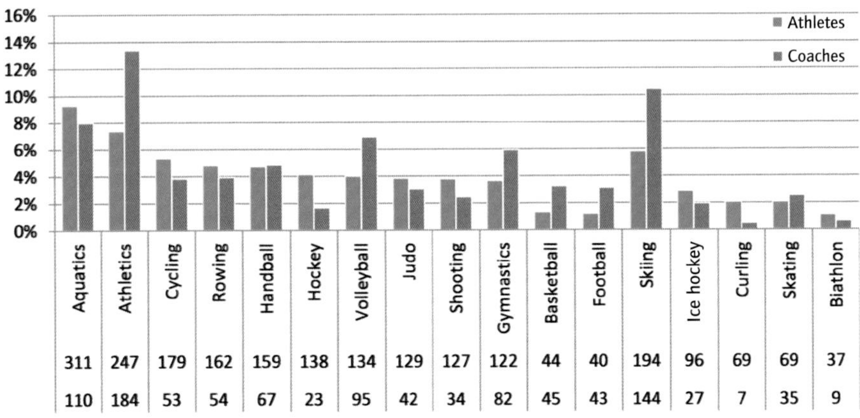

Figure 8: 10 most represented sports in the athletes' and coaches' sample

3.4.4 Athletes' profile

Table 7 presents an overview of the overall sample of athletes. Some differences by nations occur, as will be explained next.

Table 7: Overall athletes' profile

Male	55.46% (n = 1768)
Female	44.41% (n = 1364)
> 25 years	49.27% (n = 1548)
21-25 years	36.31% (n = 1141)
< 21 years	14.42% (n = 453)
Full-time elite athlete	32.23% (n = 1002)
Full-time student	21.55% (n = 670)
Part-time student	19.49% (n = 606)
Employed full-time	8.88% (n = 276)
Employed part-time	11.51% (n = 358)
Other	6.34% (n = 197)

Note: For reasons of confidentiality, some information was not provided by Australia.

Gender

Compared to the average (55.5% male), there were significantly more male athletes in the samples of Brazil, Estonia, Finland, Korea, Portugal, Switzerland and Wallonia. This in contrast with the Netherlands and Northern Ireland where the majority of athletes were female.

Age

The study focused on athletes competing in senior competitions only. The age of athletes is also related to the sport that they compete in which in turn leads to differences between nations. On average, 49.3% of the athletes were older than 25 and 14.4% were younger than 21. Northern Ireland, Wallonia and Denmark have the largest group of under 21 respondents. Spain, Estonia, Finland and the Netherlands have the largest group older than 25. Elite athletes younger than 16 years have been excluded from the sample, mainly from aquatics (n = 29), gymnastics (n = 16) and cycling (n = 12).

Status of employment

Overall, almost one in three athletes is a full-time elite athlete. Two out of three athletes combine their sport career with other duties like a job or studies. Brazil, Northern Ireland, the Netherlands, Switzerland, Wallonia, Spain and Denmark deliver significantly more students (part-time or full-time) than the other countries. The respondents from Spain and Brazil are mainly part-time students (respectively 42.2% and 39.2%). This is in contrast with the samples of Finland, Canada, Korea and Japan which have significantly more full-time elite athletes. Remarkably, in Japan, only 16.3% of the respondents have full-time employment alongside their career as an athlete.

Competition level of the athletes

The level at which athletes compete differs significantly between nations, according to the national criteria for recognition as elite athletes. This means that not all athletes in the sample are international level athletes. As illustrated in Figure 9, on average 26.9% of all athletes are either national-level athletes or have not performed at any of the levels listed in the figure. This is higher than 50% in Denmark, Northern Ireland, Wallonia and Flanders. At the other end of the spectrum more than 70% of the respondents of Japan, the Netherlands, Portugal and Finland are in the world top 16 in their sport. On average 30% of the respondents are in the top 3 of the world, 50% in the top 8 and 60% in the top 16. The performance level of respondents is the highest in Japan, the Netherlands, Australia, Spain and Portugal where approximately 50% or more indicated they have achieved at least in the top eight in the world in an Olympic sport. Japan, the Netherlands, Australia and Spain also have at least 30% world top three level athletes in their sample. This in contrast with Flanders, Brazil and Wallonia, where less than 10% had achieved a world top three ranking. Of course, the presence (or lack) of high performing athletes is assumed to be a function of the level of performance achieved in the various countries.

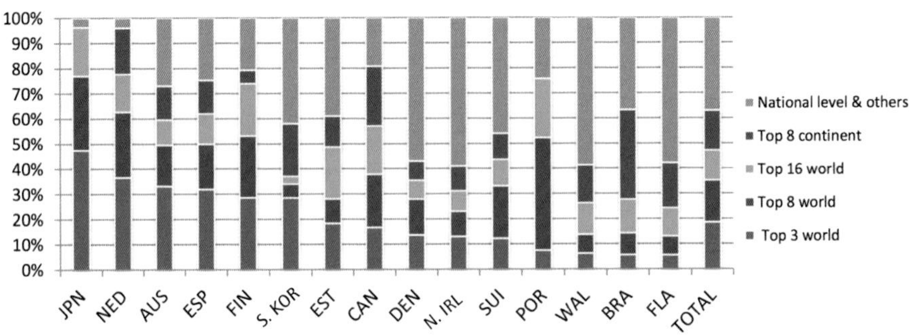

Figure 9: Athletes at the highest level of success they ever achieved as an elite athlete in an Olympic discipline by nation

In some instances—when significant differences were identified—we have focused the analysis on top 16 athletes, again, assuming that the presence, or lack of them, between countries is representative of the country's success in international competition.

3.4.5 Coaches' profile

An overview of the coaches' profile is shown in Table 8.

Table 8: Overall coaches' profile

Male	84.38% (n = 1026)
Female	15.63% (n = 190)
Average age	43.25 (SD ± 17.24)
Coaching experience (years)	9.55 (SD ± 8.28)
Paid by	
National governing body	42.23% (n = 303)
Government/NSA	11.2% (n = 80)
Others	13.11% (n = 94)
None	33.47% (n = 240)
Origin	
Local	88.5% (n = 1047)
International	11.5% (n = 136)
Status	
Full-time coach	57.07% (n = 739)
Full-time working/studying	26.80% (n = 347)
Part-time working/studying	11.51% (n = 149)
Others	4.63% (n = 60)

Note: For reasons of confidentiality, some information was not provided by Australia.

Gender and age

On average 84.4% of the elite coaches were men as illustrated in Table 8. Only in Estonia were more than 30% of the coaches female. Even when limiting the focus to the higher coaching level (= top 16 of the world), females still represent 28% of all Estonian coaches.

The average age of the elite coaches is 43.3 years; in most countries this does not differ a lot from the global average.

Coaching experience

The average coaching experience among international level coaches is 9.6 years, but this number greatly varies between coaches. Flemish coaches have the least experience (4.5 years), whereas the Estonian coaches are the most experienced (15.7 years).

Paying of the coaches

One-third of the coaches indicated that they receive no formal 'coaching' wage. In Brazil, Finland, Portugal and Wallonia, this is the case for more than half of the coaches. When coaches get paid this is mostly through their national governing body. This information was missing for Estonia, the Netherlands and Switzerland.

Coaches' status

57% of the coaches indicated that they were a full-time coach. This varied from 25% in Wallonia and 33% in Denmark to 91% and 74% in South Korea and the Netherlands, respectively. Over one-quarter of the coaches have a full-time job next to their coaching employment. This number is the highest in Flanders, Wallonia and Denmark.

Origin of coaches

On average 11.5% of the coaches are foreign coaches. Only Switzerland has more than 20% foreign coaches (as has Canada, taking into account the small sample, n = 12).

Coaching level

The coaching level indicates the highest level that the coaches have ever coached at during their career. This may differ from their current level of coaching (Figure 11). Figure 10 shows that the highest level coaches come from Spain, Japan and Canada where over 80% once trained world top 16 athletes. The lowest level of coaches comes from Estonia, Wallonia and Flanders where hardly 30% of the elite coaches ever trained top 16 athletes of the world. This corresponds with the level of elite athletes in those countries. Note that in Korea, Japan, and Canada over 50% of the elite coaches have trained top 3 athletes.

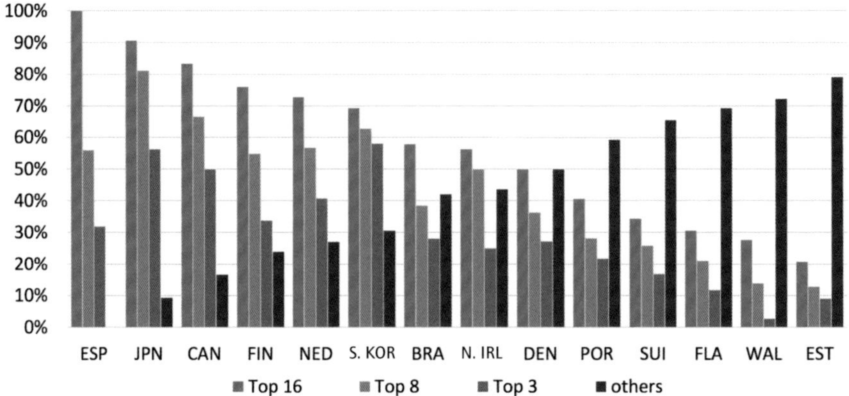

Note: For reasons of confidentiality, information was not provided by Australia.

Figure 10: Highest level at which the coaches ever coached, top 16, top 8 and top 3

The large number of (lower-level) coaches from Estonia (n = 187), Flanders (n = 137) and Switzerland (n = 378), may be explained by the high presence of the national talent coaches (Figure 11). The coaches from Spain, Japan, the Netherlands, Canada and Korea are mainly active at an international senior level.

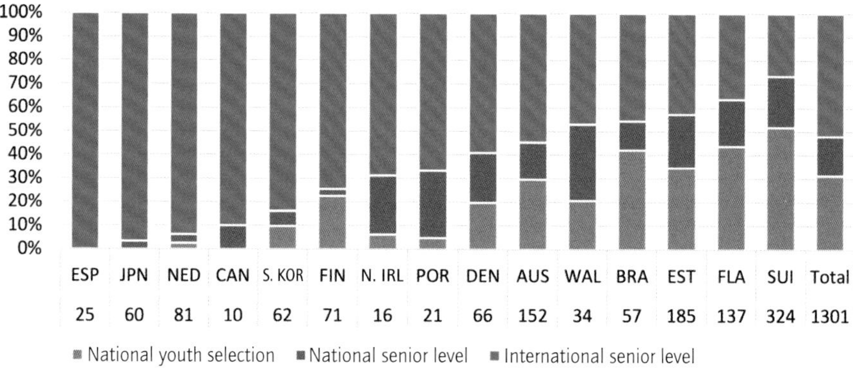

Figure 11: Current level of coaching by country

3.5 Methodological limitations

Data collection and write-up of the results for this project took three years. Very comprehensive and quite complex data collection with limited resources may have contributed to the fact that practice sometimes develops faster than theory. In other words, the outcomes of this research are very much a 'point in time' comparison, and in some of the countries, practice may have moved beyond the facts and figures that are presented here.

Added to that it needs to be reiterated that the project was highly dependent on the co-operation of sports authorities and National Olympic Committees, some being more keen and proactive in their collaboration and access to people and data than others. In summary, Northern Ireland and Estonia did not survey performance directors; France did not participate in the surveys at all. The inventories were not completed in Estonia (except for Pillar 1), South Korea did not complete Pillars 3 (participation), 4 (talent), 7 (coaches) or 8 (international competition). While acknowledging these omissions, we have chosen to separate these nations from the overall scores on these particular components. Data interpretation needs to occur with these missing data components in mind, but with the data available from those countries, valuable comparative interpretations can still be made.

Based on that we would like to note the following limitations:

- Varying response rates, ranging from 14%-82% and variation in sample sizes by country. The three best-represented countries (Switzerland, Brazil and Korea) take up 48% of the athletes' sample. The three least represented countries (Finland, Flanders and Ireland) represent 7% of the athletes' sample. Switzerland is over-represented in the coaches sample, Canada under-represented. Numbers of responding performance directors are relatively low in Brazil, Canada, Australia and Wallonia.
- The average duration to complete the surveys was 40 minutes, which may have led to 'completion fatigue'.
- Canada and Japan did not survey winter sport athletes and coaches; 60% of winter sport respondents are from Switzerland.
- For confidentiality reasons (as stated by Australian sport authorities), Australia's data does not include information concerning the sport (discipline), age and the wage of athletes and coaches.
- A higher performance level of athletes in Japan, the Netherlands, Australia and Spain; and lower levels (national level) in Denmark, Northern Ireland, Wallonia and Flanders.
- While almost one out of three athletes is a full-time elite athlete, the sample in Brazil, Northern Ireland, the Netherlands, Switzerland, Wallonia, Spain and Denmark consists of significantly more part-time athletes or full-time students; Finland, Canada, Korea and Japan have significantly more full-time elite athletes.
- Only 15.5% of the coaches are female.
- Great variation in regard to the full-time status of coaches, varying from 25% (Wallonia) to 91% (South Korea).
- The coaches in Spain, Japan and Canada reported to have coached higher (performance) level athletes (over 80% trained world top 16 athletes).
- Some countries included 'talent coaches' (national youth selection coaches), others did not; in particular Estonia is over-represented in regard to the number of coaches due to a large number of talent coaches in their sample.

Clearly these issues have implications for the degree of like-for-like comparability across surveys. They can skew the sample relative to those nations with a higher number of sports in the sample, more team sports, more winter sports, or higher-level athletes and coaches. In general the results will be considered to reflect some of these issues as follows:

- For athletes, when the level of athletes proves to be significant, the comparative sample will be narrowed down to top 16 level athletes only.

- For coaches, when the level of athletes proves to be significant, the comparative sample will be narrowed down to international level coaches only.
- When overall data are shown, the figures will be weighted by the sample size of the nation.

A further area for consideration is that the surveys have been produced in 12 different languages (English, Dutch, Danish, Estonian, Finnish, French, Portuguese (incl. Brazil), Spanish, Japanese, Italian, German, Korean). This creates only minimal problems when analysing merely quantitative data, assuming that the question is interpreted correctly.

3.6 SWOT of SPLISS

In summary, and in concluding this chapter, we present a SWOT analysis of our research methodology. We believe that the SPLISS methodology, within its limitations and shortcomings, has made some valuable contributions to the field of comparative sport policy studies. As any good research project should do, it has also identified pitfalls and opportunities for future research. We present these various insights in the concluding table (Table 9).

Table 9: SWOT analysis of the SPLISS methodology (adapted from De Bosscher, 2007)

STRENGTHS
General • Reflects economic/management competitiveness measurements; and involves literature from different areas in (elite) sport, effectiveness and strategic management. • Collaboration network with local researchers in each nation and a consortium group with members contributing in different disciplinary expertise. • The use of mixed methods research to address the problems associated with cross-national research, related to operationalisation, comparability, measurement, explanations of causality, validation, reliability, interpretation, moving beyond the descriptive and balancing between global and local factors (Henry et al., 2005) and the lack of standardised and measurable data; 'mixed methods provides strengths that offset the weaknesses of both quantitative and qualitative research and it enabled comprehensiveness and a more reflexive analysis of data' (Creswell & Plano Clark., 2007).
The SPLISS model: • Comprehensive model/data collection, operationalised Pillars into measurable concepts by identifying 96 (first 144 in 2008) critical success factors; based on comprehensive literature analysis, complemented with surveys to address the viewpoints of users (athletes, coaches, performance directors) and experts • Not only 'what' resources are available, but also 'how' these resources can contribute to success; measures of inputs-outputs, throughputs (processes). • Identification of possible relationships between inputs, throughputs and outputs in elite sport; • SPLISS model is being validated in/can be applied to other contexts: sport-specific level as measured in athletics (Truyens, De Bosscher, Heyndels and Westerbeek, 2013), ice skating (Bogerd, 2010), tennis (Brouwers, Sotiriadou and De Bosscher, 2015), canoe (Sotiriadou, Gowthorp and De Bosscher, 2013); at the local/city level (Van Rossum, 2012). • Athlete-centred model (based on a wide range of micro- and meso-level literature, best practices and expert interviews).

Measurement

- Insights into the relationship of Pillars and CSFs with success; clear definition of success, using different methods to measure absolute and relative success.
- Method that goes beyond the descriptive level of comparison using composite indicators. The scoring system is a supportive and tangible way of understanding elite sport policies more broadly in relation to sporting success. It helps (OECD, 2008; Sandelowski et al., 2009)
  - to facilitate pattern recognition in the relationship of inputs and throughputs to outputs.
  - to extract meaning from qualitative data and to verify interpretations.
  - to increase criterion validity.
  - to summarise complex, multi-dimensional realities with a view to supporting decision-makers; thus makes it possible to include more information within the existing size limit.
  - to interpret easier—enable users to compare complex dimensions effectively.
  - to assess progress of countries over time.
  - to facilitate communication with general public and promote accountability.

  Note: Quantitative findings alone are not sufficient to generalise the quality of elite sport systems (De Bosscher et al., 2010).
- Involves key stakeholders in the evaluation of policies to obtain both hard data and perceived data: measurement of data that is difficult to measure.
- Methodology that complements existing comparative elite sport studies.

WEAKNESSES

General

- There is no generic blue print for elite sport policies; the resource configurations of countries differ, countries have different strategies to develop elite athletes (Truyens et al., 2012).
- Practice often develops at a faster pace than theory.
- 'Instant picture': the SPLISS study evaluates elite sport at one moment from a static perspective, while elite sport development is dynamic and changing continuously (Bogerd, 2010).
- SPLISS uses a short-term evaluation, while elite sport is the result of, among other factors, long-term policy evaluation (De Bosscher , 2007), as it takes on average at least 10 years to develop elite athletes (Ericsson, 2003).

SPLISS model

- Limited in taking into account contextual factors and general (sport) culture and political background.
- Model based on and developed for mainly Western capitalist countries; not yet applied to—for example-developing countries.
- Model only applied to able-bodied sports.
- Focus at the overall sports level, without taking into account the specificity of sports: each sport requires specific criteria for evaluation; further validation processes are still required at a sport specific level.
- The environment of elite sport (Pillar 10) is not included: e.g., sponsorship and media, because it is less obvious that these can be directly influenced by policies and also because country-specific information is limited on an international comparable level.
- Limited to focus on government-funded sports, mainly Olympic sports.
- Does not include policy networks and interdependent relationships between different factors and organisations.
- Cause and effect: assumption that elite sport policy contributes to success (but is not a condition); for example, it may be the opposite that success contributes to elite sport policy development.
- The model uses only a functionalistic and rationalistic approach (Bogerd, 2010); the critical success factors are related to success and winning, without taking into account unintentional side effects of these factors (e.g., drop-outs, increased commercialisation, increased gap between elite sport and sport for all), that in turn may have regressive effects on success in a longer term.

Measurement

- Relatively small number of nations (15).
- Construct validity: limited statistical methods to define and confirm the construct and the weights of CSFs; weights could be the subject to subjective dispute.
- Construct validity: partial correlations among the criteria are difficult to avoid, between Pillars, CSFs and sub-factors.
- 'More is better', 1-0 measurements to identify qualitative resources and how these resources are applied is sometimes arbitrary (note: Pillar 1 are relative standardised scores).
- Criterion validity: Spearmans rank correlations with only 15 nations; further statistical confirmation needed.

OPPORTUNITIES

- Contextual factors and long-term evaluation of elite sport policies, including the political and social context of nations and explain 'why' elite sport policy decisions are taken, looking for more evidence based empirical research (Houlihan, 2009).
- Construct validity: factorial analysis and cluster analysis to reduce and cluster the CSFs; criterion validity, involving more countries to improve statistical rigour; construct validation is a continuing process of experimentation and modification leading to the refinement of the instrument that measures the construct (Gliner and Morgan, 2000).
- Provides a methodology that can be further explored at other levels and contexts:
  - sport-by-sport level; sport clusters (e.g., early versus late specialisation sports; team sports versus individual or duo sports; commercialised sports; summer sports versus winter sports, and so forth);
  - local and regional level;
  - private sector sport, commercialised teams and private academies;
  - developing countries;
  - disabled sport/Parasport;
  - sport contexts where government involvement is limited (e.g., United States) or omnipresent (e.g., China).
- SPLISS is based on a resource-based approach (or inside out), focusing on those (production) factors which can be influenced by policies and whereby countries can determine their own competitive position. These methods leave an opportunity for an 'outside-in approach', whereby the market structure (characteristics of the global sporting market) determines the outcome and position of counties in international competition (Truyens et al., 2012).

THREATS/ POINTS OF ATTENTION

- There are many extraneous factors influencing success that cannot be controlled (as they are intangible), such as cultural factors, nationalism or traditions and historical developments.
- Scoring system may not be isolated from the general sports context and historical development, such as path dependency and the general political context (Houlihan & Green, 2008, referring to Kay, 2005);
- There is more than one way to cook an egg: because of country-specific, historical and cultural reasons, nations may find different answers to implement the proposed successful elite sport systems. Is it realistic to develop a theoretical model based on the SPLISS factors? Is the model complete (yet)?
- Dependence on the quality of data (collection and interpretation) delivered by the local researcher
  - Inter-researcher reliability (do researches apply the same scoring method, weight and interpretation)
- Construct validation is never really reached
- Interpretation of the results: elite sport policies does not take part in a closed system; danger of generalizations
- Measurement using composite indicators (OECD, 2008):
  - may send misleading policy messages if poorly constructed or misinterpreted
  - may invite simplistic policy conclusions
  - may be misused, for example, to support a desired policy, if the construction process is not transparent or lacks conceptual/statistical principles
  - may lead to inappropriate policies if dimensions of performance that are difficult to measure are ignored
- Feasibility of comprehensive projects: mixed methods research in an international context is expensive, labour-intensive and time consuming (De Bosscher et al., 2010)
- Organisation: limited co-ordination funding, big differences between nations in regard to accessing local funding

Chapter 3 references

Bergsgard, N. A., Houlihan, B., Mangset, P., Nødland, S. I. and Rommetvedt, H. (2007). *Sport Policy: A comparative analysis of stability and change.* London, UK: Elsevier.

Bogerd, J. (2010). *Twee kanten van de medaille. Sleutelfiguren uit de schaatssport over de gevolgen van de ontwikkeling van de merkenteams voor het topsportklimaat van het langebaanschaatsen en talentontwikkeling in het bijzonder.* (Master sportbeleid en management), Universiteit Utrecht, Utrecht.

Chappelet, J. L. and Emmanuel Bayle, E. (2005). *Strategic and Performance Management of Olympic Sport Organisations.* Champaign, IL: Human Kinetics

Chelladurai, P. (2001). *Managing organisations for sport and physical activity: A systems perspective.* Scottsdale, AZ: Holcomb Hathaway Publishers.

Creswell, J. W. and Plano Clark, V. L. (2007). *Designing and conducting mixed methods research.* SAGE Publications.

De Bosscher, V. (2007). *Sports policy factors leading to international sporting success.* Published doctoral thesis. Brussels: VUBPRESS.

De Bosscher, V., Shibli, S., van Bottenburg, M., De Knop, P. and Truyens, J. (2010). Developing a methodology for comparing the elite sport systems and policies of nations: A mixed research methods approach. *Journal of Sport Management, 24,* 467-600.

De Lancer Julnes, P. (2008). *Performance-based management systems: Effective implementation and maintenance.* New York: CRC Press.

De Pelsmacker, P. and Van Kenhove, P. (1999). *Marktonderzoek: methoden en toepassingen* [Market research: methods and applications] 3rd ed. Leuven Apeldoorn, BE: Garant.

Ericsson, K. A. (2003). Development of elite performance and deliberate practice: An update from the perspective of the expert performance approach. In *Expert performance in sports: Advances in research on sport expertise* (pp. 49-85). K. Starkes and K. A. Ericsson (Eds.). Champaign, IL: Human Kinetics.

Garelli, S. (2002). Competitiveness of Nations: The Fundamentals. http://members.shaw.ca/compilerpress1/Anno%20Garelli%20CN%20Fundamentals.htm

Gliner, J. A. and Morgan, G. A. (2000). *Research methods in applied settings: an integrated approach to design and analysis.* Mahwah, NJ: Lawrence Erlbaum Associates.

Green, M. and Collins, S. (2008). Policy, politics and path dependency: Sport development in Australia and Finland. *Sport Management Review, 11* (3), 225-251.

Green, M. and Houlihan, B. (2005). *Elite Sport Development. Policy learning and political priorities.* New York: Routledge.

Henry, I., Amara, M., Al-Tauqi, M. and Chao Lee, P. (2005). A typology of approaches to comparative analysis of sports policy. *Journal of Sport Management, 19* (4), 480-496.

Hofstede, G. (1998). A case for comparing apples with oranges: International differences in values. *International Journal of Comparative Sociology, 39*, 16-31.

Houlihan, B. (2009). Mechanisms of international influence on domestic elite sport policy. *International Journal of Sport Policy and Politics, 1* (1), 51-69. doi: 10.1080/19406940902739090

Houlihan, B. and Green, M. (2008). *Comparative Elite Sport Development. Systems, structures and public policy.* London, UK: Elsevier.

Kaplan, R. S. and Norton, D. P. (1996). Using the Balanced Scorecard as a strategic management system. *Harvard Business Review, 74* (1), 75-85.

Kloot, L. and Martin, J. (2000). Strategic performance management: A balanced approach to performance management issues in local government. *Management Accounting Research, 11* (2), 231-251. doi: http://dx.doi.org/10.1006/mare.2000.0130

Linssen, G. W. J. M. (1998). Benchmarking. De concurrentietoets 1997: Een voorbeeld van benchmarken [An example of benchmarking]. *Beleidsanalyse, 1*, 14-22.

Mintzberg, H., Lampel, J. and Ahlstrand, B. (2005). *Strategy Safari. A Guided Tour Through the Wilds of Strategic Management.* New York: The Free Press.

Neely, A., Gregory, M. and Platts, K. (2005). Performance measurement system design: A literature review and research agenda. *International Journal of Operations & Production Management, 25* (12), 1228-1263.

Ochel, W. and Röhen, O. (2006). Ranking of countries. The WEF, IMD, Fraser and Heritage Indices. CESifo DICE Report. Research reports.

OECD (Producer). (2008). Handbook on Constructing Composite Indicators: Methodology and user guide. Retrieved from www.oecd.org/std/42495745.pdf

Onsel, Ulengin, Ulusoy, Aktas, Kabak and Topcu (2008). A new perspective on the competitiveness of nations. *Socio-Economic Planning Science, 42*, 221-246.

Papadimitriou, D. and Taylor, P. (2000). Organisational effectiveness of Hellenic national sport organisations: A multiple constituency approach. *Sport Management Review, 3* (1), 23-46. doi: http://dx.doi.org/10.1016/S1441-3523(00)70078-7

Porter, M. E. (1990). *The competitive advantage of nations.* London: The Macmillan Press LTD.

Rosselet, S. (2008). Methodology and principles of analysis. *International Institute for Management Development World Competitiveness Yearbook.* Retreived August 2, 2008 from http://www02.imd.ch/wcc/yearbook

Rudd, A. and Johnson, R. B. (2010). A call for more mixed methods in sport management research. *Sport Management Review, 13* (1), 14-24. doi: http://dx.doi.org/10.1016/j.smr.2009.06.004

Sandelowski, M., Voils, C. I. and Knafl, G. (2009). On quantitizing. *Journal of Mixed Methods Research, 3* (3), 208-222. doi: 10.1177/1558689809334210

Shilbury, D. (2006). A study of organizational effectiveness for national Olympic sporting organizations. *Nonprofit and Voluntary Sector Quarterly, 35* (1), 5-38. doi: 10.1177/0899764005279512

Siggel, E. (2009). *Is intra-industry trade driven by comparative advantage?* Paper prepared for the 2009 congress of the Canadian Society of Economics.

Sledge, S. (2005). Does Porter's diamond hold in the global automotive industry? *Advances in Competitiveness Research Articles, 13* (1), 22-32.

Sotiriadou, P., Gowthorp, L. and De Bosscher, V. (2013). Elite sport culture and policy interrelationships: the case of Sprint Canoe in Australia. *Leisure Studies, 1-20.* doi: 10.1080/02614367.2013.833973

Stamm, H. and Lamprecht, M. (2000). *Der Schweizer Spitzensport im internationalen Vergleich. Eine empirische Analyse der Olympischen Spiele, 1964-1998. GSF-schriften sportwissenschaften* [An international comparison of Swiss high level sport: An empirical analysis of the Olympic Games, 1964-1998]. Zürich: Studendruckerei Uni Zürich.

Truyens, J., De Bosscher, V., Heyndels, B. and Westerbeek, H. (2013). A resource-based perspective on countries' competitive advantage in elite athletics. *International Journal of Sport Policy and Politics, 6* (3), 459-489. doi: 10.1080/19406940.2013.839954

Van Hoecke, J., Schoukens, H. and De Knop, P. (2013). Managing performance in national team sport federations: the importance of controlling and promoting the quality of the distribution network. In *Managing high Performance Sport.* K. Sotiriadou and V. De Bosscher (Eds.). London and New York, UK: Routledge.

van Rossum, F. (2012). Stedelijke topsportondersteuning. Een vergelijking tussen Vlaanderen en Nederland [elite sport support in cities. A comparison between Flanders and the Netherlands]. Masters thesis Vrije Universiteit Brussel.

World Economic Forum (2008). The global competitiveness report 2008. *World Economic Forum.* New York: Palgrave Macmillan.

SPAR
Kanter

4 Chapter 4: Outputs—Measuring the success of elite sport policy

4.1 Introduction

One of the major advances of the SPLISS 2.0 project is that the measurement of success has been built into the research design. This enables us to measure the relationship between independent variables such as scores against the nine Pillars and a dependent variable, namely ‚sporting success'. It is therefore highly important that the dependent variable is justified as an appropriate measure against which to assess the contribution of the independent variables to sporting success. In addition to deriving and justifying our dependent variable for success in both summer and winter sports, this chapter also delves deeper into the nature of success by looking at the types of sports in which nations win medals and the breadth of their medal winning capability. The chapter concludes by looking at 'relative success', that is how nations perform in elite sport on the basis of macro-economic variables such as population and wealth.

4.2 Previous research

There are a variety of methods that can be used to measure performance in elite sport, and these are largely but not exclusively medal-based measures such as:

- medals' table ranking;
- number of gold medals won;
- total number of medals won;
- a points score based on applying weights to the nature of medals won (e.g., gold = 3, silver = 2, bronze = 1);
- market share whereby points won are converted into a percentage score of the points awarded;
- top eight rankings (which is a proxy for producing athletes and teams that reach finals); and
- relative success (controlled for population, GDPcap and (former) communism.

In SPLISS 1.0 we conducted an appraisal of the first five methods and deduced that for measuring the impact of policy on elite sport development systems, market share was the most robust measure of controllable performance that is relevant to policymakers for two key reasons. First, market share is a standardised measure of performance and helps to control for changes in the scale of an event over time. For example, in Seoul 1988 when Korea was the host nation for the Olympic Games, 237 events were contested and Korea achieved a market share of 4.6%. This was a better performance in standardised terms than Korea achieved in London 2012 with a market share of 3.3% from 302 events. Second, changes in market share can be attributed to factors that are within the control of policymakers such as increases or decreases in the number of medals won and increases or decreases in the quality of medals won. The nature of a measure such as medals' table ranking means that it is possible for nations to improve their ranking even if they win fewer medals, which can be caused by other nations becoming more dominant. While this might be a pleasing and fortuitous outcome for some nations, it is not improvement that can be attributed to the effects of policy. As demonstrated in the SPLISS 1.0 research, it is possible for different measures of performance to give conflicting views of a nation's performance. In the case of the UK, a comparison of its performance between Athens 2004 and Sydney 2000 famously showed that depending on the measure selected it was possible to demonstrate that the UK's performance had remained the same (medals' table rank); improved (total medals won); or deteriorated (points and market share %). Thus for the purposes of SPLISS, market share has been adopted as the measure of performance to capture the impact of policy. The concept of market share is explained in detail in De Bosscher et al (2008) and is outlined here as a refresher using data from the London 2012 Olympic Games. In the London 2012 Olympic Games a total of 302 events were contested and 962 medals were awarded as shown in Table 10. If 3 points are awarded for a gold medal, 2 for silver medal, and 1 for a bronze medal, then the total number of points awarded was 1,870, which equates to a total market share of 100%.

Table 10: Market share calculations and performance comparison: An example of London 2012.

Measure	Gold	Silver	Bronze	Total	Market share %
Total medals	302	304	356	962	–
Points awarded	3	2	1	–	–
Total points	906	608	356	1,870	100%
France (7th)	11	11	12	34	–
Points	33	22	12	67	3.6%
South Korea (5th)	13	8	7	28	–
Points	39	16	7	62	3.3%

The principle of market share can now be applied to individual nations to compare their performance against each other as well as themselves over time. South Korea and France were the two most successful nations of the SPLISS 2.0 sample at London 2012, finishing in 5th and 7th place in the medals' table, respectively. However, when we apply market share analysis, a slightly different picture emerges. South Korea was ranked above France in the medals' table by virtue of winning more gold medals (13 compared with 11), but when we examine the totality of achievement by looking at total medals won and the weightings (3-2-1 points) attached to them, we find that France achieved a slightly higher market share (3.6%) than Korea (3.3%) as also shown in Table 10.

Furthermore, when we compare the performance of France and South Korea at London 2012 with their performance at Beijing 2008 we can make a like-for-like time series analysis as shown in Table 11.

Table 11: Market share time series analysis

Measure	South Korea	France
MS% London 2012	3.3%	3.6%
MS% Beijing 2008	3.6%	3.8%
Change in MS%	- 0.3	- 0.2
Percentage change in MS%	- 8%	- 5%

Both South Korea and France performed slightly worse in London 2012 than they did in Beijing 2008 when using market share as an indicator. South Korea won the same number of gold medals (13) on both occasions but fewer medals overall in 2012 (28 compared with 31). Furthermore, even though South Korea won the same number of gold medals in both 2012 and 2008; in 2012 13 gold medals was enough to move Korea two places higher up the medals' table from 7th to 5th. France won more gold medals in London 2012 than Beijing 2008 (11 compared with 7), and this was sufficient to improve France's medals' table ranking from 10th to 7th. However, overall, France won six fewer medals in 2012 compared with 2008 (34 compared with 40) which had the effect of reducing its market share score.

While using data from London 2012 to illustrate the basic thinking behind the concept of market share, we wish to develop our measure of success beyond performance in a one-off event. An acknowledged limitation of our previous research in SPLISS 1.0 is that it relied on measuring performance at a point in time, such as the Olympic Summer Games or Olympic Winter Games, rather than over a period such as a four-year Olympic cycle. To respond to this limitation and to take advantage of improvements in data availability and computer processing power, for SPLISS 2.0 we propose to use an alternative measure of performance based on market share over a period of time rather than a point in time.

4.3 Measures of success

We are aided in the process of taking a longer-term look at sporting performance by the Dutch company Infostrada Sports which maintains a comprehensive record of sporting performance via its Podium Performance database. Using this database enables us to conduct analyses, which would previously have taken weeks to compile, in a matter of minutes. Using Podium Performance we have been able to analyse and summarise the performance of the SPLISS 2.0 nations over a four-year period. Our analysis is based on three key assumptions outlined here.

Timeframe

The cycle under review is the four calendar years from 1 January 2009 up to and including 31 December 2012. The rationale for using this timeframe is that increasingly nations fund their elite sport development systems for an Olympic cycle of four years. By measuring performance over the entire four-year period, we are able to capture all of the outputs associated with a funding cycle, not just performance in the Olympic Games.

Level of competition

The level of competition selected is all world championships and the 2012 Olympic Games results. In practice, the frequency of world championships vary by sport; for example Archery has world championships every two years, whereas in Judo the world championships are an annual event. For winter sports we use the same timeframe to be consistent, which in turn means using the data from world championships 2009-2012 and the results of the 2010 Olympic Winter Games held in Vancouver, Canada.

Events included

The events included in the analysis are the 302 events contested in the Olympic Games at the end of the cycle, in this case London 2012. This is an important consideration because world championships do not necessarily contain the same events as the Olympic programme. For example, in track cycling 10 events were contested at London 2012, whereas in the 2013 world championships 19 events were contested. For our new measure of performance we are concerned solely with performance in the subset of events contested in the Olympic Games. A similar approach is used for winter sports except that the events included in the analysis are those that featured in the Sochi 2014 programme.

The rationale for looking at performance over a four-year cycle is twofold. First, while the Olympic Games is arguably the pinnacle of achievement in most sports, nations which invest in elite sport development systems do not do so solely to perform well in the Olympic Games. The regular diet of elite sport competition outside of the Olympic Games is sufficient for nations to want to perform well in the events that take place between each edition of the Olympic Games, notably world championships. Second, by looking at performance over a period of time rather than a point in time it is possible to smooth out anomalous results that might cause spikes in performance and thereby enable the analysis to focus on consistency instead. The difference in medal winning opportunities between the point in time that is the Olympic Games, and the four-year cycle we have chosen to use, can be seen by comparing the number of medals contested as shown in Table 12.

Table 12: Number of medals: Olympic Games versus four-year cycle 2009-2012 in summer sports

Reference Period	Gold	Silver	Bronze	Total
Olympic Games	302	304	356	962
Four-year cycle	1,065	1,068	1,285	3,418

In the Olympic Games of London 2012, 962 medals were contested and over the four-year cycle when we include results from world championships the number of medals contested in the same 302 events was 3,418. This is more than three and half times the number of medals contested in the Olympic Games and provides a broader base from which to be able to compute consistency of performance in elite sport over a medium term period. The raw data for each of the SPLISS 2.0 nations expressed as market share achieved in the 1,065 events is shown in Table 13.

Table 13: SPLISS 2.0 nations' performance in summer sports 2009-2012

Country	Gold	Silver	Bronze	Totals	Points	M/S %
France	43	50	55	148	284	4.29%
Australia	45	48	39	132	270	4.08%
Japan	41	39	58	138	259	3.91%
South Korea	28	18	38	84	158	2.39%
Netherlands	15	24	25	64	118	1.78%
Spain	13	24	25	62	112	1.69%
Canada	7	26	28	61	101	1.53%
Brazil	15	15	20	50	95	1.44%
Denmark	6	9	12	27	48	0.73%
Switzerland	6	7	5	18	37	0.56%
Belgium	2	3	6	11	18	0.27%
Finland	3	1	6	10	17	0.26%
Estonia	1	2	3	6	10	0.15%
Portugal	0	5	0	5	10	0.15%
Totals	225	271	320	816	1537	23.23%

Different success measurements (top eight-medals) are highly correlated

Overall the SPLISS 2.0 nations account for 23.23% of the market share won in all of the eligible events contested in the four-year period under review. These results are highly consistent with the SPLISS 2.0 nations' performance in London 2012 where they achieved a combined market share of 22.5%. The correlation between performance in the London 2012 Olympic Games and the same events contested in world championships is 0.93, which in turn confirms that both measures have a very strong degree of association with each other, to the point that they are almost the same. The availability of additional data enables more in-depth measures of performance to be calculated. While Table 13 looks at market share based on top three performances it would also be possible to analyse the top eight performances. When we investigate the top eight performances, we find that the correlation between the top three (total medals) and the top eight is 0.98 which means that essentially they are the same measures. Consequently, there is little to be gained at this point by looking beyond actual medal-winning performance. However, it can be seen that all of the measures we have examined are in fact very strong proxies for each other as illustrated in the correlation table shown in Table 14.

Table 14: Correlation table of the relationship between performance measures in summer sports

	Gold medals	Total medals	Medal points	Medal market share %	Top 8 places	Top 8 points	Top 8 market share %
Gold medals							
Total medals	0.98						
Medal points	0.99	1.00					
Medals market share %	0.99	1.00	1.00				
Top 8 places	0.94	0.98	0.98	0.98			
Top 8 points	0.97	1.00	0.99	0.99	1.00		
Top 8 market share %	0.97	1.00	0.99	0.99	1.00	1.00	

Before concluding this section it is important to explain an important adjustment that we made to the data to make it appropriate to the SPLISS 2.0 nations. In the case of Belgium, elite sport policy is not organised at national level and has separate approaches to delivery in the provinces of Flanders and Wallonia. Because of this dual system it is more informative to re-allocate the market share scores for Belgium as a whole to Flanders and Wallonia. This was done by computing the medal winning success by athletes from both provinces separately. Where medals are won by teams combined from both provinces these are allocated on the basis of the number of athletes in each team. For example, if Belgium won a gold medal in the 4x400-metre relay and there were two athletes from each province in the event, the medal would be allocated 50% to Flanders and 50% to Wallonia.

The UK did not take part in the SPLISS 2.0 study, but Northern Ireland which is one of the four nations that comprises the UK did. Generally Northern Ireland competes as a nation in its own right in the Commonwealth Games and in football. In order to include a measure for sporting success for Northern Ireland, we have computed its contribution to success on the basis of medallists from the province who won medals in relevant events during the four-year cycle. The figures we are using for Northern Ireland is 0.3% for summer sports and 0% for winter sports. The final scores for summer sports after adjustments for Belgium and Northern Ireland a shown in Table 15. Note how with the addition of an extra nation in Northern Ireland and its share of the United Kingdom's success, the total market share achieved by the SPLISS 2.0 nations increases from 23.23% in Table 13 to 23.38% in Table 15.

Table 15: Success scores for the SPLISS 2.0 nations in summer sports

Nation	Summer sports 2009-2012
France	4.29%
Australia	4.08%
Japan	3.91%
South Korea	2.39%
Netherlands	1.78%
Spain	1.69%
Canada	1.53%
Brazil	1.44%
Denmark	0.73%
Switzerland	0.56%
Finland	0.26%
Northern Ireland	0.15%
Estonia	0.15%
Flanders	0.18%
Portugal	0.15%
Wallonia	0.09%
Totals	23.38%

The scores in Table 15 are adopted as our dependent variable for summer sports with which we examine the relationship between success and the scores achieved against the nine Pillars throughout the rest of the book.

4.4 Winter sports

In London 2012 a total of 26 different sports involving 39 disciplines were contested (for example the sport of aquatics, involves the four disciplines of swimming, diving, water polo and synchronised swimming). While this is a sufficient number of sports from which to gain an insight into the health of a nation's elite sport system, it does not provide the full picture. In the Olympic Winter Games there are currently 7 sports and 15 disciplines contested, and there are some nations for whom success in these sports is important. Within the SPLISS 2.0 sample there are nations that support and in some cases prioritise winter sports. As winter sports have their own version of the Olympic Games, it is worth considering performance in these sports separate from performance in summer sports. In Pillar 1 (financial support), for example, we distinguish between elite sport expenditure incurred for summer sports and winter sports; and Pillar 6 (training facilities) is a good example of how nations can have a competitive advantage in winter sports.

In Table 16 we show the events contested in Vancouver 2010 and the events contested in the relevant world championship and world cup events over the four-year cycle 2009-2012. The events included are those that featured on the Sochi 2014 programme.

Table 16: Number of medals: Olympic Winter Games versus four-year cycle

Reference Period	Gold	Silver	Bronze	Total
2010 Olympic Games	86	87	85	258
Four-year cycle 2009-2012	331	333	329	993

The key point of note is that the ratio between the *over a period data* and *the point in time data* is 3.8 to 1. This enables any anomalous performance to be smoothed out over time and provides a more consistent insight than Winter Olympic Games data only. The full data for the SPLISS 2.0 sample nations is shown in Table 17.

Table 17: SPLISS 2.0 nations' performance in winter sports 2009-2012

Country	Gold	Silver	Bronze	Total	Points	MS %
Canada	45	37	35	117	244	12.27%
South Korea	25	22	12	59	131	6.59%
Netherlands	17	16	13	46	96	4.83%
France	11	18	18	47	87	4.38%
Switzerland	13	8	9	30	64	3.22%
Finland	7	5	19	31	50	2.52%
Japan	6	6	9	21	39	1.96%
Australia	6	2	2	10	24	1.21%
Belgium (Flanders)	1	0	0	1	3	0.15%
Estonia	1	0	0	1	3	0.15%
Denmark	0	0	1	1	1	0.05%
Totals	132	114	118	364	742	37.32%

Not all of the SPLISS 2.0 nations achieve success in winter sports, notably Brazil, Spain, Portugal and Northern Ireland. In the case of Belgium the single medal won over the four-year period is attributable to the Flanders region and Wallonia has a score of 0%. The Market Share % scores are the values used for the dependent variable 'sporting success' in winter sports.

4.5 The nature of success

In this section we take a closer look at the nature of success for the SPLISS 2.0 nations. This is done in two ways: first, we examine the sports in which the nations win medals; and, second, using London 2012 as a case study we analyse how many sports nations win medals in relative to the number of sports in which they take part.

4.5.1 Medals by sport

In Table 18 we begin this process by reporting the number of medals won in the 2009-2012 cycle by nation and sport. The top performing sports for each nation in terms of total medals won are coloured gold; the second highest performing sports are coloured silver; and the third bronze. As an example in the case of Australia, swimming is its most successful sport with 35 medals, followed by track cycling (30), and rowing (16). At the foot of the table we can see that Australia won medals in 16 different disciplines, and the contribution of the top three sports was 61% of the total medals won during the period.

Table 18: Medals won by nation and by sport at Olympic Games and world championships 2009-2012 in summer sports

Sport	AUS	BEL	BRA	CAN	DEN	EST	FIN	FRA	JAP	S. KOR	NED	POR	ESP	SUI	Total
Archery								2	4	14					20
Athletics	14	2	4	3		3	1	12	4			2	5		50
Badminton					7			1	2	7					17
Basketball	1							1					2		4
Beach volleyball			8												8
BMX	2							8			1				11
Boxing			5	1			1	2	3	3					15
Canoe slalom	1							9					5		15
Canoe sprint	3			7				7	1			1	8		27
Cycling–Road	4	1			2						5		2	3	17
Cycling–Track	30	1		7	3			15			8		1		65
Diving	3			7											10
Equestrian–Dressage											3				3
Equestrian–Eventing				1											1
Equestrian–Jumping		2		1				1			2			1	7
Fencing				1		1		7	3	15	2		1	1	31
Football			1	1					2	1	1		1		7
Gymnastics–Artistic	5		4					4	18	2	3			1	37
Gymnastics–Trampolining				4					3						7
Handball					1			5					3		9
Hockey	2										4				6
Judo		2	13	1				20	47	13	10	2	4		112
Modern pentathlon			1					1		1					3
Mountain bike				1				4					1	7	13
Rowing	16			8	4	1		6			3				38
Sailing	10	2	5		4		6	10	1		11		9	1	59
Shooting	1	1			1		1	4	2	8			2	1	21
Swimming	35		5	8	3			21	19	3	11		4		109
Synchronized swimming													2		2
Table tennis									4	4					8
Taekwondo								2		2			3		7
Tennis								2						1	3
Triathlon	4												5	2	11
Volleyball			4						2						6
Water polo	1			1									2		4
Weightlifting				1				1	1	7					10

Sport	AUS	BEL	BRA	CAN	DEN	EST	FIN	FRA	JAP	S. KOR	NED	POR	ESP	SUI	Total
Wrestling—Freestyle				8				1	20				2		31
Wrestling—Greco-Roman					2	1	1	2	2	4					12
Totals	132	11	50	61	27	6	10	148	138	84	64	5	62	18	816
Count (number of sports)	16	7	10	17	9	4	5	25	18	14	13	3	19	9	
Top 3	61%	100%	72%	80%	78%	100%	100%	46%	60%	50%	50%	100%	52%	70%	

	Most successful sport
	2nd most successful sport
	3rd most successful sport

Table 18 is best analysed vertically and horizontally.

Vertical analysis

There is considerable variation in the breadth of sports that nations win medals in

There is considerable variety in the breadth of sports that nations win medals in and also the extent to which they rely on their top three sports for success. The larger more successful nations such as Australia, France, Japan, South Korea, the Netherlands and Spain achieve medal-winning success in a wide variety of sports (13 to 25) and their top three sports account for between 46% and 61% of their medal winning success, which is a relatively low score within the sample. By contrast, at the other end of the continuum is a cluster of less successful nations, including Brazil, that win medals in fewer sports (3 to 10) and who are heavily reliant on a minority of sports for the majority of their success (72%-100%). Canada is a slightly anomalous case because it has three joint first and joint second place sports which artificially inflates its top three percentage score (80%). It is a nation more in keeping with the successful nations as it won medals in 17 different sports over the period. What this data tell us is that, intentionally or unintentionally, the sample nations seem to take different approaches towards prioritisation and diversification in elite sport. In simple terms, successful nations seem to develop medal-winning capability in a wider range of sports and are less reliant on a minority of sports for their success, whereas less successful nations win medals in relatively few sports and are heavily reliant on these sports for the vast majority of their success.

Horizontal analysis

Swimming and athletics account for 27% of medals

It is perhaps no surprise that athletics and swimming feature as one of the top three sports for six and seven nations, respectively. This is largely attributable to these sports having the most medal-winning opportunities. In the Olympic Summer Games these two sports account for 27% of events and an even higher proportion of medal-winning opportunities. It is therefore quite surprising to see that two sports with relatively few events, judo and sailing, are very important to the sample nations. In the case of judo, seven nations have the sport as one of their top three sports and for five of these it is their most important sport. Although Japan is clearly the most successful nation in judo with 47 medals, it is also the most important sport for France and Brazil with 20 and 13 medals, respectively. Judo is also important to the less successful nations and is also one of the most important sports for Belgium and Portugal. Sailing is a sport with relatively few events (10 in London 2012) and relatively few medal-winning opportunities as nations can qualify one boat only for each event. Thus of the 30 medals available at the Olympic Games a maximum of 10 are contestable by a single nation. Despite these apparent limitations, sailing is a top three most important sports for seven nations of which it is the most important sport for three (Belgium, Finland and Spain). All of the nations that win medals in sailing are relatively wealthy either in terms of GDP or GDP per capita. This perhaps points to a situation whereby access to resources (Pillar 1) and innovation (Pillar 9) are the sources of competitive advantage in this sport.

When similar analysis is applied to winter sports as in Table 19, we find that there are also marked differences in how nations achieve their success. Canada is a good example of a nation that has developed medal-winning capability in a broad range of winter sports. By contrast other nations tend to be more specialised. Finland derives much of its success from cross country skiing; France is successful in biathlon; Japan seems to specialise in figure skating and speed skating; South Korea focuses on short-track speed skating whereas for the Netherlands long-track speed skating delivers virtually all of the nation's winter sport success; finally, Switzerland's strength lies in the traditional Alpine events.

Table 19: Medals won by nation and by sport at Olympic Games and world championships 2009-2012 in winter sports

Sport	AUS	BEL	CAN	DEN	EST	FIN	FRA	JAP	S.KOR	NED	SUI	Total
Alpine skiing			3			2	6				10	21
Biathlon						3	20					23
Bobsleigh			6								1	7
Cross-country skiing			1		1	13						15
Curling			9	1							2	12
Figure skating			11			1	3	11	4			30
Freestyle skiing	5		23			2	6	1			2	39
Ice hockey			6			5					1	12
Luge			2									2
Nordic combined							3	1				4
Short track			25					1	42	2		70
Skeleton			3								1	4
Ski jumping							1	1			5	7
Snowboard	5	1	7			4	8	1		2	8	36
Speed skating			21			1		5	13	42		82
Total	10	1	117	1	1	31	47	21	59	46	30	364
Count (number of sports)	2	1	12	1	1	8	7	7	3	3	8	

	Most successful sport
	2nd most successful sport
	3rd most successful sport

Because there are fewer sports and fewer events in winter sports compared with summer sports, reliance on a minority of sports for the majority of success is more prevalent with top three sports delivering 64% to 100% of all medals for the SPLISS 2.0 nations.

It is an often held discussion in elite sport as to whether nations should pursue a policy that prioritises success in relatively few sports (specialisation) or a policy that aims for success in a wide variety of sports (diversification). A limitation of Table 18 and Table 19 is that it does not tell us how many sports particular nations took part in. To illustrate the basic point, we show in the number of sports that nations contested in London 2012 and the number of these sports in which they actually won medals (Figure 12).

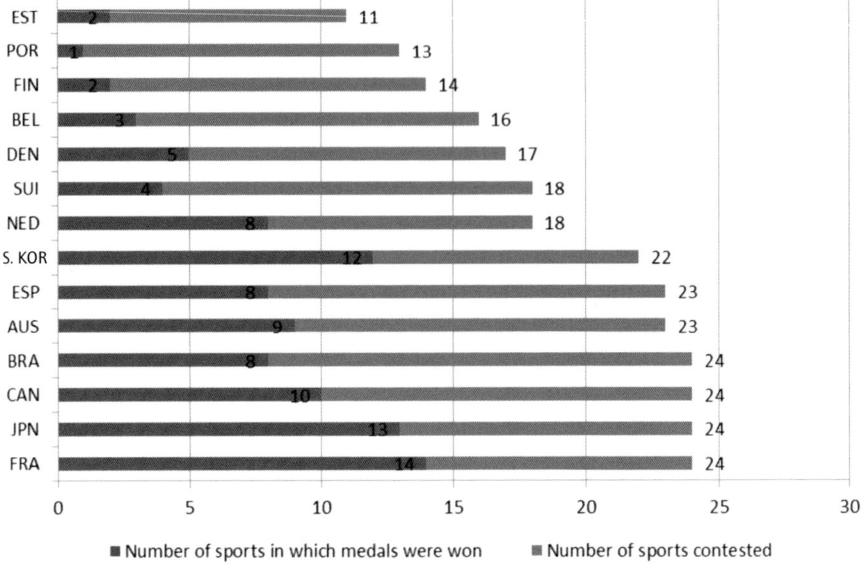

Figure 12: Sports contested and sports in which medals were won at London 2012

> **Population per se does not provide a strong competitive advantage. The breadth of sports in which SPLISS 2.0 nations took part show a modest correlation with population size**

At the London 2012 Olympic Games the programme consisted of 26 sports (39 disciplines, 302 events), and it can be seen in Figure 12 that the majority (12/14) of the SPLISS 2.0 nations contested the majority (14 +) of the sports available. Four nations, France, Brazil, Canada and Brazil, contested 24 of the 26 sports and only Estonia and Portugal contested 50% or fewer of the sports. It is, of course, one thing to take part in a sport and quite another to win a medal in that sport. Only three nations, France, Japan and South Korea won medals in 50% or more of the sports in which they took part. For the SPLISS 2.0 sample as a whole the average was 36%, but this masks some considerable variation in scores notably by Estonia, Portugal and Finland.

The breadth of sports in which the SPLISS 2.0 nations took part in London 2012 shows a modest correlation (0.64) with population size suggesting that a relatively high level of population is positively associated with taking a diversification approach to elite sport. The strength of this relationship diminishes to a correlation of 0.53 when we link the number of sports in which medals are won to population size. This in turn suggests that population per se does not provide a strong competitive advantage when it comes to winning medals, and this is encouraging news to support the idea that proactively managed factors such as policy make a bigger difference than a relatively uncontrollable factor such as population.

Diplomas won (finals)

For athletes who achieve a top eight finish, it is current practice for them to receive an Olympic diploma which is a certificate recognising their achievement (in most cases) in reaching the final of an event. As most nations do not win medals, counting the number of diplomas won therefore provides an alternative measure of performance. Since the 1992 Barcelona Olympic Games at least 50% of nations taking part in each edition have won at least one Diploma. At London 2012 this score was 56%, and the number of medals and diplomas won by the SPLISS 2.0 nations in London 2012 can be seen in Figure 13.

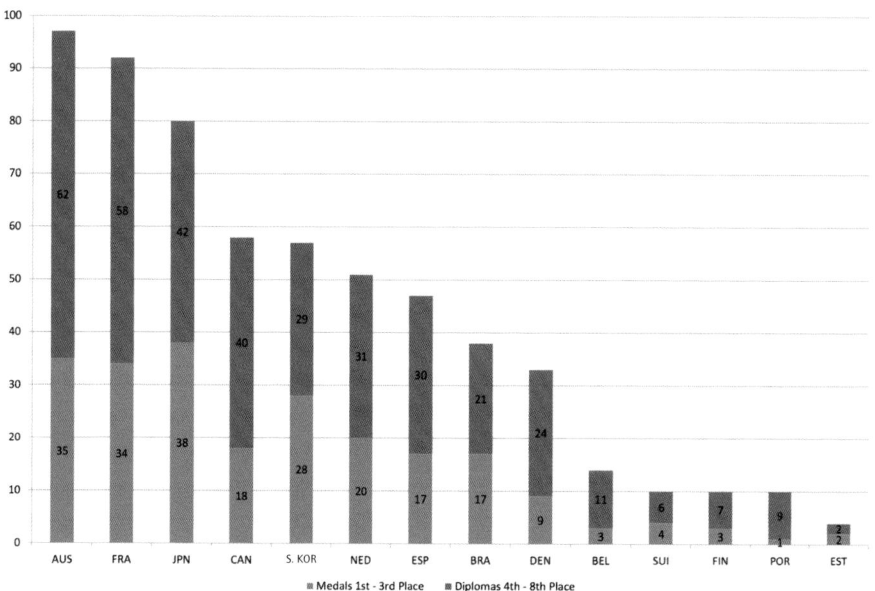

Figure 13: Medals and diplomas won by SPLISS 2.0 nations at London 2012

Australia produced the most top eight performances

In Figure 13 there are three clear clusters of nations that can be seen when reading from left to right. First, there are three nations with 90 or more diplomas (AUS to JPN); second there are six nations (CAN to DEN) with less than 60 but more than 30 diplomas; and, third, five nations (BEL to EST) with fewer than 15 diplomas. There are three performances of particular note here. First, Australia with a population of around 23 million produced the most top eight performances despite what was largely perceived as being a poor performance at London 2012. We can conclude that Australia was highly successful at producing finalists but perhaps less successful at converting these into medallists. Second, it is quite remarkable that a nation such as Denmark with its population of 5.6 million could deliver an overall level of performance that is in the same cluster as Brazil, which has a population of around 200 million. Third, with one medal and 10 top eight places, Portugal has a conversion rate of finalists to medallists of 10%. This score is by some margin the worst in the sample and points to a relative inefficiency in being able to convert competitive athletes into medal winners.

4.6 Relative success

Thus far we have looked at the performance of nations in elite sport without formally considering macro economic variables such as population and wealth. These factors' impact on success and are not controllable by national policy towards elite sport development. Consequently, there are techniques that enable us to examine the concept of relative success by which we mean how nations perform relative to how they would be expected to perform on the basis of exogenous macro economic variables. The effect of this approach is to examine the efficiency of sports systems when the national characteristics of Olympic success are isolated.

Numerous empirical studies show that population and wealth are the most important socio-economic determinants of success (e.g., Bernard and Busse, 2004; De Bosscher, De Knop and Heyndels, 2003a, and b; Jokl, 1964; Johnson and Ali, 2002). These two variables frequently explain over 50% of total medals or medal points. For this reason, success has also sometimes been expressed in terms of medals per head of population or in terms of per capita GDP, as a measurement for wealth.

It is intuitive that the size of a country's population will be a determining factor for sporting success (De Bosscher, 2007). The bigger the population, the larger the pool from which talent can be recruited, and there are greater opportunities to organise training and competitions. When controlled for by population, the Dominican Republic with three medals was the most successful country in London 2012.

There are reasonable explanations for the fact that wealthy countries perform better than poorer countries. Richer countries can invest more in sport and elite sport, individuals may participate in a broader number of sports and having a higher living standard may improve their general fitness and ability to perform at the top level. When we divide the number of medals won in London 2012 by the gross domestic product per head of the population, Ethiopia and China are identified as the most successful nations.

Taking into account just one determinant, population size or wealth is rudimentary in two respects. First, it disregards other potentially important determinants. Second, it assumes an implicit linear relationship between these two factors and success. By dividing medal points by population or wealth (criteria that are sometimes used by the media), the degree to which these factors can influence success is not taken into account. This creates a potentially biased view. After all, a country that has twice as many inhabitants cannot win twice as many Olympic medals. This is the principle of diminishing returns to scale (Glejser, 2002), and in the case of elite sport the principle is demonstrated by the limit that event organisers place on the number of athletes from each country who are allowed to take part. As an example, in the Olympic Games there are 15 weightlifting events which have a combined total of 45 medals available to be won. However, nations are limited to being able to contest a maximum of 10 medals. While from a sporting perspective this is designed to prevent certain nations becoming too dominant in the sport; a secondary impact is that it reduces the potential impact of population size.

To assess whether a particular country or group of countries performs 'well' at the Olympic Games, the literature offers a number of methods. These take the limitations of using single variables such as population and wealth into account by using multiple determinants of success simultaneously and controlling for possible non-linear effects such as qualification criteria. The starting point for our empirical work is a simple OLS (Ordinary Least Squares) estimation of a reduced form model that captures the main macro-determinants of absolute Olympic success. Several studies explored the relationship between international sporting success and the (macro) economic, sociological and political contexts within which sporting talent is developed (e.g., Baimbridge, 1998; Bernard and Busse, 2004; De Bosscher, De Knop and Heyndels, 2003a, and b; De Koning and Olieman, 1996; Den Butter and Van der Tak, 1995; Johnson and Ali, 2002; Tcha and Perchin, 2003). De Bosscher (2007) revealed that among macro-level variables such as population, GDP per capita, area, degree of urbanisation, religion, and the political system, three variables were the main explanatory factors for success: the population, the wealth (GDP/cap) and (former) communism (current or in the last 20 years). The next section explains how these three variables were used in the regression analysis in order to calculate relative success.

Most studies used the total number of medals won as an output measurement. However, in our 2009-2012 performance data for the London 2012 cycle, 106 nations out of the 204 participating nations, did not win any medal. Our analysis measures 'outputs' at three measures:

- the number of Olympians in London 2012;
- the number of top eight places achieved; and,
- the weighted number of Olympic medal points (3 points for gold, 2 for silver and 1 for bronze).

To correct for distributional problems or outliers (Field, 2005), data were transformed logarithmically; the functional form to be estimated is as follows:

Ln (a) Olympians and (b) Medals = $\beta_0 + \beta_1$ Ln (POP) + β_2 Ln (GDPCAP) + β_3 COMM + ϵ

In the equation, Ln (POP) is the (logarithm of the) number of inhabitants that were recorded in millions. Ln (GDPCAP) is the (logarithm of the) gross domestic product per head (recorded as PPP values). COMM is a dummy for (former) communist countries. This dummy is equal to 1 for (former) communist countries and 0 for other countries. β_1 to β_6 are the regression coefficients to be estimated. β is the error term for the regression model, which is the unknown variation (the vertical deviation from the unknown true regression line). When we run the model for the three measures of output, we obtain the result shown in Table 20.

Table 20: Stepwise regression for the three output measures in summer sports

Dependent variable	Independent variables	Coefficients B	SE B	β	Adjusted R²
Model 1 London 2012 Ln (Olympians)	Ln(Population)	–	–	–	.322
	Ln(Population) and Ln(GDP/cap)	–	–	–	.654
	(Constant) Ln(Population) Ln(GDP/cap) Comm	- 10,273 .433 .699 .712	.658 .026 .048 .154	 .680* .587* .183*	.685
London 2009-2012 cycle Ln (top 8 placings)	Ln(Population)	–	–	–	.190
	Ln(Population) and Ln(GDP/cap)	–	–	–	.435
	(Constant) Ln(Population) Ln(GDP/cap) Comm	- 14,316 .585 .932 1.397	1,633 .067 .111 .287	 .546* .527* .300*	.522
Model 3 London 2009-2012 cycle Ln (Medal points 3-2-1)	Ln(Population)	–	–	–	.162
	Ln(Population) and Ln(GDP/cap)	–	–	–	.322
	(Constant) Ln(Population) Ln(GDP/cap) Comm	- 11,066 .472 .646 1,291	1,620 .069 .100 .282	 .537* .490* .323*	.416

*Note: We present the coefficients, standard error (SE) and unstandardised coefficients (β) only for the final model; * $p < .001$.*

A stepwise regression, indicates that the population size explains for 32.2% the number of Olympians that nations send to the summer Olympics. Wealth (GDP/CAP) adds another 33.2%, and together with the political system for (former) communist countries, we end up with a model where 68.5% of the number of Olympians is explained by these three factors.

Population, wealth (GDP/CAP) and (former) communism together predict 52.0% of the top eight placings and (only) 41.6% of the medals

The influence that these factors have, decreases when we consider the top eight places and medal points won. The majority (52.2%) of the total number of top eight places achieved can be explained by these three variables. However, when it comes to actual medal-winning success, the model can only explain 41.6% of this output measure. This is smaller than earlier findings from Stamm and Lamprecht (2001) and De Bosscher (2007) who concluded that these variables predict 50% of Olympic medals. In a way these are encouraging findings for elite sport policymakers because the model suggests that as we move from broad measures of success, such as athletes qualified and top eight places won, to specific measures of success, such as medals won, the impact of exogenous variables decreases. This in turn means that other factors must be becoming more important, of which one of course can be a nation's elite sport development system.

A regression analysis serves two purposes. First it identifies the determinants of international sporting success at the macro-level. Second, under ceteris paribus conditions an analysis of residuals enables comparison between countries and thus diagnosis of their relative success (De Bosscher, 2007). The starting point of our analysis is that the residual represents in part the effects of elite sport policies. In other words, the positive residual of nations is among other factors the result of effective elite sport policies and investments, which is part of the unexplained variance. A residual score in this context is the difference between a nation's actual score and the score that would otherwise be predicted by the regression model. A positive residual score indicates that a nation's actual success is greater than the model forecasts, which in turn points to the possibility of a well developed elite sport development system being in place. By contrast a negative residual score, indicates that a nation might not be using its resources as effectively as it should be.

It should be noted that other factors will, to an unknown extent, also influence the size of the residual. Examples of these other factors can be found at the micro-level (that is, factors that may influence the success of individual athletes), such as genetic qualities or their immediate support network; or at the macro-level (factors that influence success of nations), such as the elite sport culture, the tradition of sport and sporting success in a nation and maybe just 'coincidence'. However, these factors cannot be developed by policies. Although it is not known to what extent the residual can be explained by elite sport policies, these are the only factors that can be developed in the short-term and are called meso-level factors.

Table 21 offers an overview of the SPLISS countries in the order of their residual, or relative success rates, taking the population size, wealth and, where relevant, the (former) communist character of the country into consideration, for each of the three models. In our London 2012 cycle data 98 nations won an Olympic or world championship medal; 128 won a top eight place; and all 204 sent Olympians to London 2012.

Table 21: Residuals for the SPLISS nations in summer sports across the three models

Country	Medal points** (3-2-1) (n = 98)		Top eight placings (n = 128)		Olympians (n = 204)	
	Rank/98	Residual	Rank/128	Residual	Rank/204	Residual
Australia	6	1,802	7	1,858	4	1,498
France	10	1,498	12	1,511	23	,964
Netherlands	15	1,122	18	1,305	38	,812
South Korea	16	1,107	25	1,086	33	,870
Japan	18	1,065	37	0,850	58	,552
Spain	25	,860	24	1,105	13	1,084
Denmark	26	,843	13	1,462	28	,922
Brazil	30	,707	24	0,906	17	1,016
Canada	34	,622	35	0,898	27	,928
Switzerland	48	,131	55	0,362	71	,426
Finland	57	,139	63	0,199	85	,253
Belgium	66	–,460	58	0,278	50	,653
Portugal	70	–,645	45	0,632	51	,633
Estonia	72	–,779	89	–0,331	114	–,037

If we consider Table 21 from right to left all nations except Estonia have a positive residual for the number of Olympians sent to London 2012. This means that they qualified more athletes for 2012 than their population, wealth and broad political nature would otherwise predict. In the case of Estonia, it sent just one athlete less than was predicted by the model, and this should not be seen as serious under-achievement. In terms of top-eight placings Estonia is again the only nation with a negative residual whereas all other nations achieve more than would otherwise be expected. However, when it comes to converting the top eight places into medal points there are four nations, Finland, Belgium, Portugal and Estonia, which underperform. By contrast, at the top of the table Australia, France, Netherlands, South Korea and Japan can be seen to have achieved levels of success that are considerably in excess of what the model forecasts. At face value all nations with a positive residual for any of the output measures can at least argue that this has, in part, been caused by the effectiveness of their elite sport policy systems. For all nations, analysis of their residual scores can provide the basis for non-medal based measures of performance. It is only a minority of nations that achieved medal-winning success in the 2009 to 2012 cycle (98/204). If, however, their residuals are in line with the model, it is possible to make a diagnosis at the broad policy level as to whether or not such nations are producing Olympians and achieving top eight places in line with reasonable estimates. This in turn forms the basis for being able to manage national expectations as to what a nation's elite sport system is reasonably capable of delivering.

4.7 Key points

- Weighted market share percentage is confirmed as being the most appropriate output measure for assessing the impact of elite sport development policy.
- Rather than using performance in the Olympic Games as the basis of our output measure, SPLISS 2.0 uses performance over the four-year cycle 2009 to 2012. Included in the analysis are all performances in world championships and the Olympic Games.
- This technique is replicated for winter sports over the four-year period for the subset of SPLISS 2.0 nations that achieve success in relevant winter sports.
- In practice all medal-based measures of performance such as gold medals won, total medals won, medal points and market share are highly correlated. When we consider the top eight places, which includes non-medal based measures of performance (places 4-8), there is still a very high correlation with the entirely medal-based measures.
- The SPLISS 2.0 nations achieve their successes in a wide variety of different sports and in different concentrations. There are some nations that achieve success in a broad range of sports such as France. By contrast other nations achieve success in a narrower range of sports and are therefore heavily dependent on a minority of sports for most of their success, for example Brazil.
- Innovative analysis of relative success demonstrates that a model based on population, wealth and broad political nature is capable of explaining 68.5% of the number of Olympians produced and 52.2% of top eight places achieved. However, when it comes to explaining medal-winning success, the model is only 41.6% accurate. Over time, this seems to have decreased. This in turn means that other factors must be becoming more important, of which one is the competiveness of a nation's elite sport development system.

While this chapter focussed on the output measures, the next chapters start with the analysis of the nine Pillars, or the inputs (Pillar 1, financial support) and the throughputs (Pillars 2-9).

Chapter 4 references

De Bosscher, V. (2007). *Sports policy factors leading to international sporting success.* Published doctoral thesis. Brussels: VUBPRESS.

5 Pillar 1: Financial support

5.1 Concepts and definition

Pillar 1 examines public expenditure on sport and elite sport at national level by government, lotteries, NOCs and nationally co-ordinated sponsorship

Pillar 1 is concerned with measuring the financial investments made by nations in sport generally and in elite sport specifically. Pillar 1 is the 'input' Pillar as the influx of financial resources into the 'system' enables the remaining eight 'process' Pillars to be implemented. Transnational comparisons of sport expenditure are challenging as expenditure definitions and sport delivery mechanisms vary considerably from nation to nation. As a result, significant adjustment and fine-tuning is required to enable meaningful like-for-like comparisons. An important point to note is that the SPLISS study does not attempt to capture the full picture of financial inputs in elite sport. Within the resources available, the study aims to identify national level policies and how this relates to success. Accordingly, the study focuses only on resources that are nationally co-ordinated and that are used to invest in the other Pillars. This inclusion criterion influences the global picture of elite sport spending as explained next.

To enable meaningful comparisons between nations, Pillar 1 examines public expenditure on sport and elite sport at national level and includes, where relevant, expenditure by central government, national lotteries, National Olympic Committee funding and sponsorship when it is nationally co-ordinated. The vast majority of funding for elite sport at national level tends to come from these sources. We acknowledge that in many countries extensive financial resources allocated to (elite) sport are provided by local government or by the private sector. However, this data is not available in a format that permits transnational comparison. In this regard, an important point of note is that the figures do not include any of the following:

- Sport-by-sport funding, for example from National Governing Bodies (NGBs);
- Sponsorship provided for individual athletes, teams or sports (NGBs);
- Funding that is invested by states or territory governments, or by cities and municipalities, which is an important consideration particularly in larger countries with state academies and trainings centres, such as Australia and France;
- Funding for elite athletes from collaboration with the police and with the military;
- Indirect elite sport funding through tax concessions or the media.

While this excluded funding can have a significant effect on success, a lack of transnationally comparable data prevents our analysis from including such funding sources. For example only a few countries have reliable data on what is spent by commercial sponsors or regional departments and local governments on elite sport. The view taken in the SPLISS study is that this funding is not nationally co-ordinated and, as such, not a measure of national policies. Such funding should therefore be analysed at other levels, for example on a sport-specific basis.

To establish total (summary) scores for Pillar 1, four main areas are taken into account: financial support for sport as a whole; financial support for elite sport; the funding for grassroots and elite sport provided via National Governing Bodies (NGBs); and sport clubs. While the absolute amounts of funding are included in Pillar 1, the strategies on how this funding is spent and prioritised towards different sports are discussed in Pillar 2. In total, eight critical success factors (CSFs) for Pillar 1 were investigated through the inventories, as shown in Table 22.

Table 22: Critical success factors measured in Pillar 1

Critical success factors P1	
I. There is sufficient **national**-level financial support for sport	
CSF 1.1	Total national expenditure on sport (cash terms) (excl. elite sport) national lotteries and central government (overall and per head of population)
CSF 1.2	Total national government expenditure on sport as a proportion of total national government expenditure
CSF 1.3	Increase/decrease in national expenditure on sport during the last four years
II. There is sufficient **national**-level financial support for elite sport	
CSF 1.4	Total national expenditure on elite sport (cash terms) from national lotteries, central government, Olympic Committee and national co-ordinated sponsorship
CSF 1.5	National expenditure on elite sport as a proportion of total national expenditure on sport
CSF 1.6	Increase/decrease in total national elite sport expenditures during the last four years from national lotteries and central government
III. There is sufficient financial support per sport from national collective sources (e.g., national lotteries, central government and NOC), for National Governing Bodies (NGBs) and/or sport clubs	
CSF 1.7	Total funding for NGBs, and/or sport clubs, and/or sport programmes for sport development from national lotteries, central government and NOC (cash terms)
IV. There is sufficient financial support from national lotteries/central government and the National Olympic Committee for specific elite sport (disciplines) for National Governing Bodies (NGBs) and/or sport clubs	
CSF 1.8	Total funding for NGBs, and/or sport clubs and/or programmes for elite sport purposes national lotteries/central government and the National Olympic Committee (cash terms)

Source of information: overall sport inventory;
CSFs that are important to acknowledge and consider but that need to be measured at other levels than this research:
*(a) Total government expenditure on elite sport at the regional and local level: provinces and municipalities**
(b) Total national expenditure on elite sport by sponsors
(c) Total national expenditure on elite sport by the media

5.2 Key findings

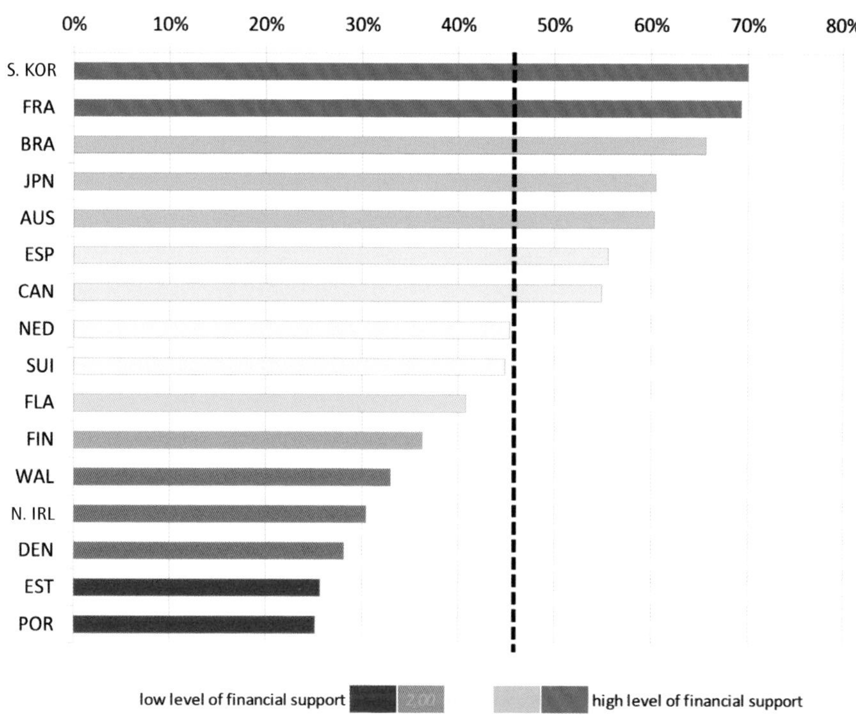

Figure 14: Total scores of the SPLISS sample nations against the eight CSFs of Pillar 1[3]

The key question, of course is, how do nations perform in the global elite sport arena given the financial resources at their disposal? As anticipated, countries with the highest scores on Pillar 1 (Figure 14) generally also perform best in summer and winter Olympic sports. As a reminder, the top

The sample confirms a strong relationship between financial resources available and international sporting success. Elite sport funding is the best predictor of outputs

3 To calculate the overall score, 'Z-scores' were created for each CSF. The calculation of Z-scores standardises the data types on a common scale and allows fair comparisons between different types of data–essential when combining diverse information into a single ranking. Each data point is given a score based on its distance from the mean of the entire data set, where the scale is the standard deviation of the data set. The Z-score is then turned into a 'cumulative probability score' to arrive at the final totals. If country X has a cumulative probability score of 98, for example, then a random country from the same data distribution will fall below that country 98% of the time

four best performing countries in summer sports (ranked in the order of success according to their market shares of Olympic Games and world championships 2009-2012) are France, Australia, Japan and South Korea. In winter sports this is Canada, South Korea, the Netherlands, France and Switzerland. South Korea, Japan, France and Australia provide the most financial support to sport and elite sport; these are also four top 10 nations in summer sports, and the best performing nations of the sample. Brazil is clearly the exception to this general pattern. With the fourth largest (national) elite sport budget in the sample, equal to that of Australia, Brazil's global ranking of 20th is below seven other SPLISS nations: the Netherlands, Spain and Canada along with the four countries mentioned already. Spain and Canada have the same score on Pillar 1, and are ranked 15th and 17th respectively in summer sports (2009-2012). Canada, however, outperforms all other nations in winter sports reflecting the success of its 'Own The Podium' programme. In conclusion, from the data in 16 SPLISS 'sport systems' (13 nations, 3 regions), there appears to be a direct relationship between financial inputs in elite sport and sporting success or outputs.

In our analysis, the relationship between financial resources and elite success in winter sports is less clear. For example, nations with a relatively poor natural 'wintersportscape' (few mountains, warm climate), such as Brazil, Spain and Australia, do not perform well in winter sports relative to their performance in summer sports. Although they are among the biggest spenders on elite sport in general, less than 5% of this funding is invested in winter sports in these nations. The Netherlands is an exception, as it has an average score on Pillar 1 but is ranked above Spain, Canada and Brazil in summer sports and outperforms France, Japan and Australia in winter sports. Rather than interpreting their 'winter sport success' as a result of policy decisions only, it needs to be noted that most of their medals are in speed skating, which in turn is, according to the researchers, a sport that could be described as a national obsession, facilitated by an ubiquitous artificial wintersportscape (400-m speedskating rinks throughout the country). Speed skating is also heavily invested in by the corporate sector, further distorting the interpretation of the data if only national governmental funding is considered.

Grassroots funding is not significantly related to international sporting success

There are a few interesting findings emerging from the analysis of isolated CSFs of Pillar 1. The first concerns grassroots sport funding. Countries that invest more in grassroots sports,[4] do not necessarily also invest highly in elite sport, nor does this seem to influence their performance. Grassroots sport funding by national governments and lotteries is relatively small in successful sporting nations such as Australia, Spain, Canada and Japan. In absolute terms, grassroots sport investments are the highest in Brazil, France and South Korea. There is no relationship with the wealth of the countries (in terms of GDP per capita) and funding for grassroots sport, but there is a correlation with population size. Perhaps somewhat counterintuitively when we compute expenditure per head of population, countries that invest relatively more in grassroots sports tend to be the less successful nations in the sample at world championships and the Olympic Summer Games.[5] Moreover, it appears that the countries which focus on elite sport—countries which invest a higher proportion of national funding for sport in elite sport rather than grassroots sport—tend to perform better.[6] France and the Netherlands are notable exceptions to this observation as they are also relatively high spenders on grassroots sport.

Second, it is not entirely unexpected that the strongest relationship with success in the 16[7] sample nations is determined by the absolute amount of funding allocated to elite sport. This is confirmed by the high Spearman's rank correlations of the scores with summer sports and to a lesser extent with winter sports.[8] In other words, countries that invest more in elite sport, perform better. It was found that 68% of the success in summer sports in the sample nations and (only) 21% in winter sports can be explained by the (scores for) absolute investment in elite sport.[9]

---

4 This is measured using the Spearman's rank correlation. This correlation coefficient expresses the strength of the relationship between the ranking (high to low) regarding grassroots expenditures and the success rankings of nations. The coefficients are not significant, which means that if the ranks of expenditures increase (or decrease), the ranks of success are not more likely to increase (or decrease). The closer the coefficients equals 1, the more likely that 'if one variable increases, the other variable will also increase'. In this case the Spearman's rank coefficients for grassroots sport expenditures (PPP) with success are: $r_{s(summer)} = 0.453$, $p = 0.078$ for summer sports and $r_{s(winter)} = 0.245$, $p = 0.361$ for winter sports.

5 Spearman's rank correlation of international success with grassroots expenditures as a proportion of population is negative: $r_s = -0.628^{**}$, $p = 0.009$; winter sports: $r_s = -0.184$ $p = 0.495$.

6 Spearman's rank correlation of the national expenditure on elite sport as a proportion of total national sport expenditure with success: $r_s = 0.649^{**}$, $p = 0.007$; winter sports: $r_s = 0.441$ $p = 0.088$.

7 13 nations + 3 regions (FLA, WAL, N-IRL).

8 The Spearman's rank correlation between the scores for CSF 1.4, elite expenditures (PPP-values) and international success summer sports are significant at the 0.01 and 0.05 level ($r_{s(summer)} = 0.909^{**}$ $p < 0.01$; winter sports: $r_{s(winter)} = 0.588^{*}$ $p < 0.05$; when we focus on the funding allocated to NGBs or clubs for winter sports only, the relationship in winter sports becomes stronger $r_{s(winter)} = 0.86^{**}$, $p < 0.01$.

9 Applying a linear regression analysis, the adjusted R^2 values are 68.4% ($p < 0.01$) for summer sports and 20.7% $p < 0.05$ for winter sports.

South Korea clearly is an outlier among the sample nations with substantial national funding invested in elite sport but with relatively modest success in terms of market share.[10] South Korea's elite sport expenditures have increased considerably, especially since 2006. These figures are partly distorted by the inclusion of expenditure on international events (Pillar 8) in our analysis, such as the Asian Games, World Student Games and World Athletics Championships. A high proportion of South Korea's 53% elite sport expenditure has been spent on international events, which is not in line with other nations. With regards to its elite sport success, South Korea's market share declined in summer sports from a high of 2.6% in 1997-2000 to a low of 2.1% in the 2001-2004 cycle. Subsequently it has shown two periods of growth to 2.3% and then to 2.4%. In the case of South Korea, it would be reasonable to conclude that extensive investment in staging major sports events does not appear to have had an immediate positive impact on the nation's performance in elite sport.

Another country with noteworthy results is Brazil. Brazilian elite sport expenditure has increased considerably since 2008 (+80%) and is—in absolute terms—among the highest in the sample nations. Given its funding, Brazil under performs: 50 medals, or a market share of 1.4%, is only average compared with the sample overall. Furthermore, while a pre-hosting effect has been quantified for previous Olympic hosts since 1988 at around eight medals, this was not the case for Brazil who actually recorded an increase of just two medals in London 2012 compared with Beijing 2008. This caused Brazil to fall one place in the medals' table from 22nd in Beijing 2008 to 23rd in London 2012.

Elite sport expenditures in the Netherlands are modest compared with the nation's successes. The Netherlands (16.7 million inhabitants) has the stated ambition to be ranked among the 10 best countries in the world in summer sports, which is the position it achieved in Sydney 2000 and was close to in London 2012 (ranked 12th in market share). Furthermore the Netherlands feature regularly in the top 10 nations in winter sports. An annual elite sport allocation of approximately €55 million in 2011 leaves the Netherlands behind other countries in terms of cash spending from public sources and national co-ordinated sponsorship money.

In absolute terms, Switzerland spends a similar amount on elite sport as the Netherlands (€56m). However, when accounting for purchasing power parity (PPP, see later in this chapter), the Swiss budget is much smaller in real terms.[11] With a population of around 8 million (roughly 50% of

10 South Korea as an outlier: This is strengthened when PPP (purchasing power parity) values are taken, which extremely influence South Korea; for example, while elite sport expenditures are comparable to Japan in absolute values, they are almost the double in PPP values.

11 Switzerland i$43m (i$ = 'international dollars') compared with i$67m in the Netherlands.

the Netherlands), Switzerland has been relatively successful over time in winter sports while underperforming in summer sports events (Switzerland was ranked 36th in 2009-2012 which compares unfavourably with the Netherlands ranked 14th). However, as will be presented in the Pillar 2 analysis in the next chapter, Switzerland spends only 50% of its money on Summer sports whereas for the Netherlands this figure is 81%. Another country that performs comparatively well in winter sports, given its limited resources, is Finland, which has been consistently successful at cross-country skiing and ski jumping in the Winter Olympics.

Finally, all other smaller countries (Portugal and Estonia as well as Northern Ireland, Flanders and Wallonia as regions) have low scores on Pillar 1 and moderate to low or even no success in summer or winter sports. One relatively small nation is an exception—Denmark. There has been steady elite sport funding of approximately €34 million per annum since 2003, and Denmark has produced regular success in summer sports. Considering the population of the country (5.5 million inhabitants), Danish elite athletes have consistently delivered top-level international results in sports such as badminton, sailing, rowing and cycling, and the country won nine medals at London 2012. With a moderate elite sport budget Denmark has won six to eight medals in 10 of the 16 Summer Olympic Games since World War II (Storm, 2012). In proportion to its inhabitants, Denmark has consistently been placed among the world's top 20 nations (with the exception of Sydney 2000). Furthermore, despite the fact that, the average total number of Danish medals and top eight places had decreased over time, 2009 and onwards stands out as successful years in Danish elite sport, with an increase of 59% top eight places (Storm, 2012).

Part of this study into the integrated effect of elite sport policies, is to evaluate how (more or less) efficient countries perform against the other eight Pillars as discussed in subsequent chapters. Now that this study has confirmed that absolute spending by nations is a very strong predictor of elite success, it becomes even more important (for countries to achieve a competitive advantage) to determine how these absolute amounts of funding are spent (or can be spent) throughout the system.

The next section continues with the descriptive comparative analysis of Pillar 1.

5.3 Comparative and descriptive analysis

5.3.1 National expenditure on grassroots sport

As noted earlier, comparing national expenditure on sport between nations is a challenging exercise. In many countries, municipalities and cities are the most important source of sport funding. The SPLISS study only looks at the nationally co-ordinated funding. In some countries total sport expenditure figures include physical education in schools (Japan, Korea, Switzerland), sport facilities and events whereas in others it only includes direct expenditure on the sport system. To keep our analysis as consistent as possible, we have chosen to consider national-level public expenditure on sport only, excluding physical education, but including facilities and events. Furthermore, to focus effectively on funding for grassroots sport only, we have excluded elite sport expenditures from the analysis in this section.

Canada is the nation that suffers most from the omission of sub-national expenditure data. National sport expenditures in Canada co-ordinated by Sport Canada are directed primarily to elite sport, whereas grassroots funding is provided by the states and lower levels of local government. Furthermore, at the national level, the distinction between elite sport and grassroots sports funding in Canada is difficult to estimate. For instance, approximately two million Canadian dollars are set aside for LTAD (long-term athlete development) that seems to be focused on grassroots sport development, and as such is excluded from elite sport funding in our analysis.

The most populated countries (not the wealthiest) generally spend the most on grassroots sport

Figure 15 presents an overview of expenditure on grassroots sport only in the sample nations and regions[12]. To facilitate comparability, values were adapted for Purchasing Power Parity[13] (international $) and are shown on the X-axis. Perhaps unsurprisingly expenditure on grassroots sport is positively correlated with the population. From our analysis it appears that the most populous countries, and not the wealthiest countries,[14] generally spend most on grassroots sport. In absolute cash terms, France, Brazil and South Korea exceed the other countries in grassroots sport expenditures. Japan (>127 million inhabitants) is an exception with relatively small grassroots expenditures compared with small countries such as the Netherlands (>16 million inhabitants), Finland (>5 million inhabitants), Flanders (>6.4 million inhabitants), Wallonia (3.5 million, [+ Brussels, 1.1 million inhabitants]) and Switzerland (>7.6 million inhabitants). It should be noted that Japan's expenditure on grassroots sport has increased considerably after the establishment of the Commission on Sport Promotion in 2006, to t155 million in 2011 and has tripled since 2001.

Successful countries in elite sport do not necessarily spend large amounts on grassroots sport

In relative terms (per inhabitant, Figure 16), Finland and Wallonia can be seen as the biggest spenders on sport, followed by Northern Ireland, Flanders, Denmark and Switzerland.

---

12 2011-2012 is used as the reference point, as this was the year which provided the most comprehensive data at the time of the research.

13 (a) Purchasing power parity (PPP) is an economic concept and a technique used to determine the relative value of currencies to be equivalent to (or on par with) each currency's purchasing power. It asks how much money would be needed to purchase the same goods and services in two countries, and uses that to calculate an implicit foreign exchange rate. Using that PPP rate, an amount of money thus has the same purchasing power in different countries. Among other uses, PPP rates facilitate international comparisons of income, as market exchange rates are often volatile, are affected by political and financial factors that do not lead to immediate changes in income and tend to systematically understate the standard of living in poor countries. (b) The values are expressed in international dollars (i$). The international dollar is a hypothetical unit of currency that has the same purchasing power parity that the U.S. dollar had in the United States at a given point in time. Figures expressed in international dollars cannot be converted to another country's currency using current market exchange rates; therefore the figure shows the absolute expenditures in euros. (c) In SPLISS the PPP values are used to develop the scores. This remains however a deliberate choice. While prices of goods and services differ in the sample nations, sport (mainly elite sport) develops at an international level and some prices are equal for all countries (e.g., international competitions, international coaches). Source: Penn World Tables, https://pwt.sas.upenn.edu/php_site/pwt71/pwt71_form.php; Reference: R. Summer and A. Heston, 1991. 'The Penn World Table (Mark 5): An expanded set of international comparisons, 1950-1988' *Quarterly Journal of Economics, 106* (2), pp. 327-368.

14 Spearman's rank correlation between population and grassroots expenditures is r_s=.785; p<.01; linear regression analysis shows that 51% of grassroots sport expenditures is determined by the population (p<.01); although Andreff, Dutoya and Montel (2009) found that richer countries devote a larger share of their GDP to sport financing, this is not the case in the SPLISS sample nations. Here, wealth, measured as GDPCAP, is not significantly related to grassroots expenditures (excluding elite), nor with the share of government funding spent on sport.

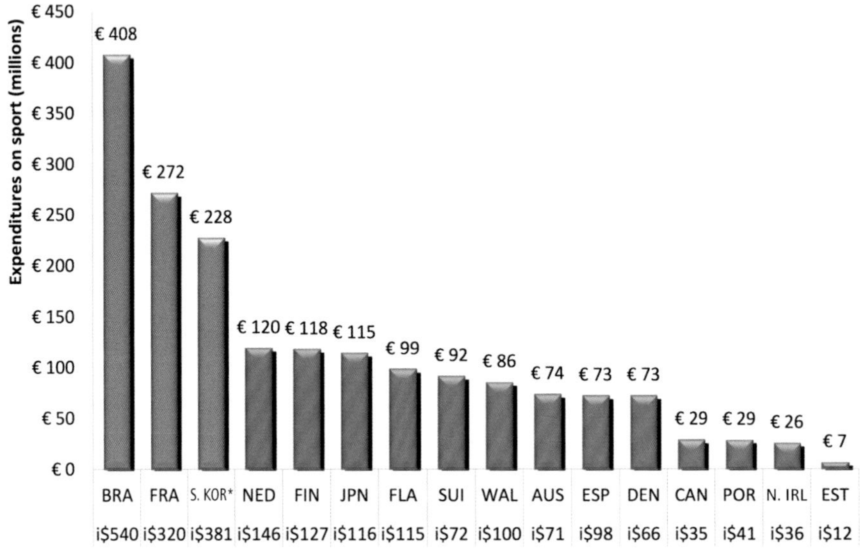

Figure 15: National expenditure on grassroots sport only (lotteries+ government) in the SPLISS nations (in 2011/2012); figure excludes expenditures on physical education and elite sport (X1.000.000 million). Values adapted for PPP in international $ on the x-axis.

Notes with the figure:

1. *The figure excludes budgets on teachers of PE in Japan (€38m), KOR (€17m) and Switzerland (€7.5m).*
2. *The expenditures on sport facilities are included and range from €1.9m in Estonia, to €34m in Japan and €48 m in Wallonia; in Brazil and Portugal these figures were not available. In countries such as the Netherlands and Australia, most sport facility investment takes place at the subnational level (state, province or local).*
3. *In Switzerland, lottery money is distributed mainly at regional level, not at national level; they are therefore not included.*
4. *In Canada an estimation of 20% grassroots sport was made by the Canadian researcher, based on the detailed funding distributions. Furthermore NGBs are funded for sport only at the state level. An estimation is that the total sport expenditure, including state level funding for NGBs, is €186m.*

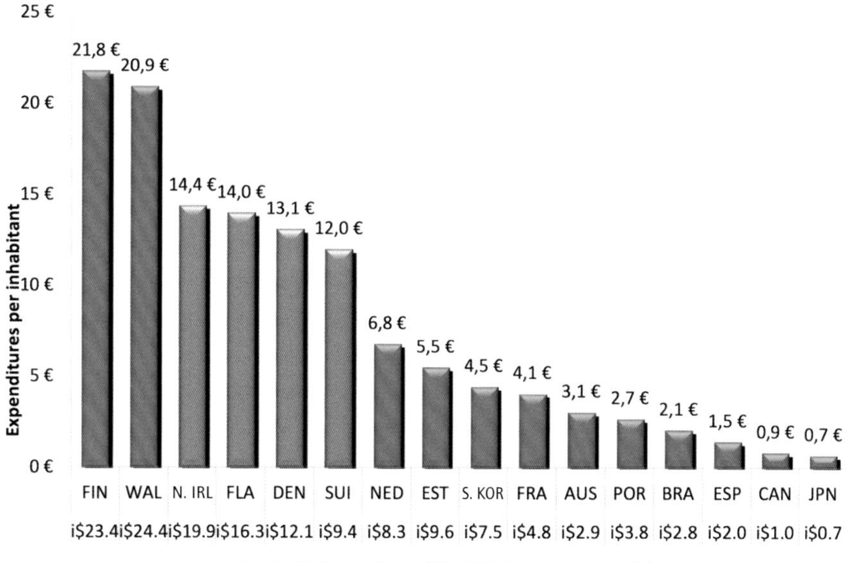

Figure 16: National expenditures on sport per head of population in the SPLISS nations (lotteries + government) (in 2011/2012); Values adapted for PPP in international $ on the x-axis.

5.3.2 National expenditures on elite sport

The nations that spend most on grassroots sport are often not the big spenders on elite sport, which suggests that the decision to invest centrally co-ordinated funding into elite sport is an explicit and separate policy decision from the decisions made about grassroots sport. Elite sport expenditures as presented in Figure 17 includes national government agencies and lotteries, NOC funding and nationally co-ordinated sponsorship money. The latter two are important inclusions as they represent co-ordinated contributions to national elite sport policy development. The NOC budgets, although often consisting of commercial sources, are meaningful in countries such as Japan (€22m, excluding governmental funding), South Korea (€9.6m), and Brazil (€8.2m). Similarly, nationally co-ordinated sponsorship is most significant in the Netherlands, where NOC*NSF collects on average €5.6m a year ('ambition funds') on top of governmental and lottery funding for the preparation of elite athletes for the Olympic Games.

To ensure we adjust for the different wealth of nations, similar to the previous section, the values are adapted for PPP (in international $) and are shown on the x-axis of Figure 17 (in international dollars).

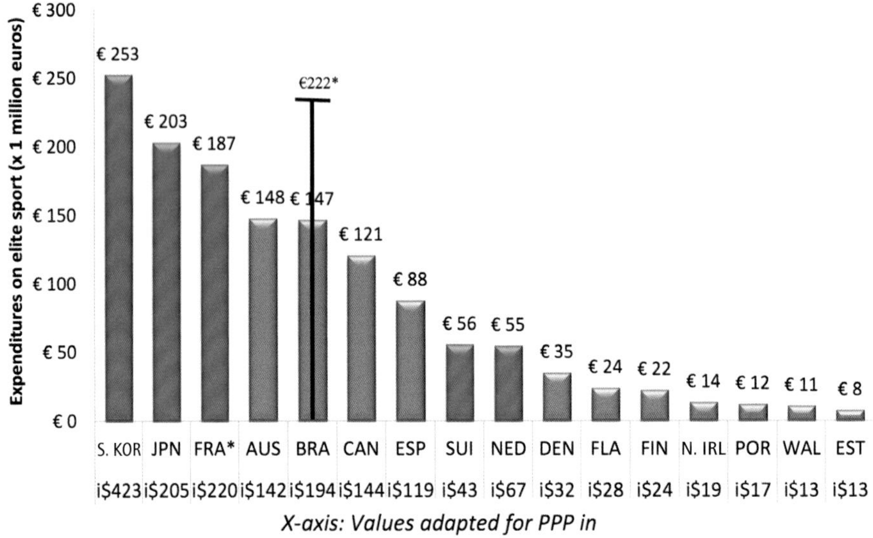

Figure 17: National expenditures on elite sport (only) in the SPLISS nations (lotteries + government + NOC + nationally co-ordinated sponsorship) (x1.000.000 euros) 2011/2012. Values adapted for PPP in international $ on the x-axis.

Notes with the figure:

1. *NOC expenditures (mostly commercial funding) are included as part of national elite sport expenditures: (a) for the part that does not overlap with lottery/government money, (b) only for the part that is used to develop elite sport (develop the Pillars), for example, preparation of athletes for the Olympics.*
   Note that Northern Ireland has no National Olympic Committee. NI athletes can choose to represent either Great Britain and Northern Ireland or the Republic of Ireland and therefore the relevant NOCs are the British Olympic Association and the Olympic Council of Ireland.
2. *Elite sport expenditures exclude funding for paralympic sports in all countries, with the exception of France, where these data are not known. The proportion of Paralympic sports funding varies from 0.3% of total elite sport expenditures in Wallonia to 15.6% in Brazil.*
3. *The figures do not include indirect funding for elite sport from the police (Estonia, France and Japan) and the military (Brazil, Estonia, Finland, Flanders, France, Japan and South Korea) because these amounts cannot be attributed directly to national-level elite sport funding and the policies that are evaluated in this book.*
4. *Sport Canada's expenditure is mainly allocated to elite sport purposes; analysis of the funding led to an estimation of 80% of this funding being spent on elite sport in Canada.*
5. *In Brazil, the data include three sources: (a) transfer from federal government: €28m; (b) Tax Break Act €58m; (c) transfer from Piva Act €52.9m. The data exclude Paralympics (€11.3m). NOC expenditures are approximately €32.9m, of which 75% comes from lotteries (€24.7m) and 25% is additional (from sponsorships, donations and rental income). The total elite sport expenditure in the figure includes lotteries and government (€65.9m) plus an additional €8.2m from the NOC (without lotteries) to avoid overlap. Furthermore the funding data excludes the money provided by the state companies directly to sports (mainly banks), because this is not nationally co-ordinated. Detailed analysis shows an estimation of €75 million provided by the state companies in 2011. Including this, would increase total elite sport expenditure in Brazil to €222 million, as shown by the black line in Figure 17.*

6. *In Australia, €6.2m sponsorship money is not included, as this funding is given directly to NGBs, which is not nationally co-ordinated sponsorship; the total amount is not known in all NGBs.*
7. *In Japan, the figures include €148m from the ministry (MEXT), €26m from Lotteries, €10.5m sport promotion fund (only the element for elite sport is included) and €22.6m NOC (excluding overlap with other sources).*
8. *In Denmark, budgets include 44.1% from the Sports Confederation of Denmark (DIF) for elite sport purposes, Team Denmark funding and SED (Sport Event Denmark, app. €4.0m); Team Denmark (TD) has been the central co-ordinating body for the development of Danish elite sport since 1985.*
9. *Elite sport is not clearly defined in Estonian legislation, therefore the sums stated are based on estimates provided by the SPLISS partner in the National Auditing Office.*
10. *In Finland, the backbone of the sport system is the 11 national and 3 regional institutes that receive a total government funding of €20 million. Among these, there are six high-performance centres. It is not possible to identify the proportion spent solely on elite sport. The Finnish researcher estimated this at €1.6m.*

The best performing countries spend the highest amounts of funding on elite sport

As stated earlier, the absolute amount of funding allocated to elite sport is the best predictor of output (success). In absolute terms, South Korea, Japan and France stand out as the most substantial investors in elite sport, spending more than €200 million each. Transformed into PPP values, striking differences emerge between South Korea and other countries. While in absolute values (euros) South Korean expenditure on elite sport is comparable to France and Japan, in PPP values, this is almost double. Notably 53% of this expenditure is provided for the organisation of international events, such as the Asian Games, IAAF World Championships, the Universiade, and as such these are related to long-term investments in infrastructure.[15] In comparison to this expenditure on events, the proportion of funding for career development of athletes (Pillar 5) and coaches (Pillar 7) is relatively low. Funding for the organisation of international events is intended to promote the country and provide a platform for international performance. Indirectly it leads to more and better (training and competition) infrastructure, which may have a lagged effect on the preparation of South Korean elite athletes in the future.

The next group of countries includes Australia (€148m), Brazil (€147m), Canada (€121m) and Spain (€88m), all with elite sport expenditures between €100-150 million. Australia also spends part of its national elite sport funding (20%) on international events. Australia and Canada are the only nations where national lotteries provide no funding for elite sport. The Brazilian elite sport expenditures are an under-estimation of the real elite sport spending, because of the influence of the state companies which are some of the largest sport sponsors in Brazil (Cunha, 2012). Generally these corporations are legal entities created by the government to undertake commercial activities on behalf of an owner government. In most countries, such entities are commonplace, particularly

15 E.g. in 2010, €48.5m was spent in relation to the 2014 Asian Games, €15.0m for 2011 IAAF World Athletics Championships, and €37.7m for 2015 Summer Universiade. Also, €6.4m was spent on building the Athletics Center in Daegu, the host city of 2011 IAAF World Athletics Championships.

around infrastructure such as railways and telecommunications, strategic goods and services (mail, weapons), natural resources and energy, politically sensitive business, broadcasting, demerit goods (alcohol) and merit goods (health care). In Brazil, however, the impact on sport is different. These state companies are mainly banks that invest considerable amounts of money directly into NGBs (such as judo, tennis, boxing and volleyball), estimated to be around €75 million in 2011. There are no clear criteria, nor is there co-ordination of state company funding, and therefore it was decided not to include the figures in the total expenditures in the SPLISS project. If these investments were included, the total elite sport expenditure in Brazil would then be around €222 million. Another source of income in Brazilian elite sport is derived from the Tax Break Act, established in 2004 and worth around €58 million in 2011 (included in the data). Brazil's commitment to the preparation of the athletes for the Olympic Games of Rio 2016 was already notable in 2011, as demonstrated by a 20% increase compared with 2010; and a 30% increase in 2012 compared with 2011, funded mainly from government sources.

Switzerland and the Netherlands, with total elite sport expenditures of €56 and 55 million, respectively, sit somewhere in between the lower and average spenders on elite sport. As shown in the PPP values in international dollars (Figure 17), the Netherlands has more resources available in real terms (67 i$ versus 43 i$ in Switzerland), which therefore enables more elite sport development activity to take place

The remaining countries are the smaller and less successful countries, with the smallest budgets (< €35m). If Flanders and Wallonia were aggregated, the total amount (€35m) exceeds Denmark and comes close to Switzerland. This, however, would not be an accurate reflection of reality, as both regions have their own governments and policy for elite sport, including ministries, sport associations and NGBs.

Elite sport expenditure (government, lotteries and NOCs) does not relate significantly to the wealth of the countries in the SPLISS sample

An interesting finding is that—as with grassroots funding—there is no significant relationship between elite sport expenditures and GDP per capita.[16] South Korea and Brazil, and also France and Japan, are nations that spend comparatively higher sums on elite sport given their wealth. The strategic choice to invest in elite sport does not seem to be determined by the wealth of countries, but rather by other drivers, where the function of elite sport is associated with a variety of political and societal objectives, some of which may go beyond the immediate context of elite sport success. A case in point is Brazil, the country with the lowest GDP/

16 The correlation between GDP/CAP (PPP, i$) and total elite sport expenditures (PPP) is $r_s = .025$; $p = .899$.

CAP, but driven by the organisation of the 2016 Rio De Janeiro Olympic Games, is investing heavily in its elite sport development system. Another example is presented by Japan where one of the drivers of increased investment was the formation of the Commission on Sport Promotion that produced the Basic Act on Sports (started in 2007 and signed in 2011), which includes a law describing elite sport and international success as a national duty. 2011 was therefore a turning point in Japanese sports promotion legislation, where the Basic Act on Sport positioned sport in the context of achieving broader outcomes, such as stopping a declining birth rate, making positive contributions to an ageing society and reconnecting citizens in an increasingly individualised society.

5.3.3 Source of elite sport funding

National lottery funding

Government and lotteries are balanced as the sources of national elite sport funding

It is accepted practice for (elite) sport to be funded through either national government funding or lottery funding, or a combination of both. In nations where lottery funding is relatively substantial, state funding tends to be relatively low and vice versa (De Bosscher et al., 2008). In most countries–at the national level–the government is still the backbone of the system that fuels elite sport development. Increased government involvement and intervention in sport through funding is a key characteristic of global elite sport policy development. France, in that regard, seems to be moving away from a very state-centred approach dating from the 1980s (Oakley and Green, 2001) towards a more mixed economy with a higher proportion of private engagement and involvement in 2010, both in terms of the national training centre (INSEP) and NGBs. For the first time, the state's sport budget was less than the budget for the National Centre for the Development of Sport (CNDS). However, one of the strengths of the French elite sport system remains that state technical staff working for the sport federations are trained and funded by the ministry.

In some countries, national lottery funding has been the principal driver of elite sport development as illustrated in Table 23. In Denmark, Finland, Portugal and South Korea this represents more than 60% of the funding. In South Korea, 86% of elite sport funding (through the sport promotion fund, and distributed by government) comes from lotteries (sports Toto), which is legalised by the Sport Promotion Act. This act states that *'more than 50% of the profit should be returned to customers, less than 25% used as overhead, and the remaining funds should be collected and invested by the Korea Sport Promotion Foundation for the development of sport'.*

Two countries do not benefit from lottery or gambling money

In Finland the National Lottery (Veikkaus) is a state-owned company, and it has a monopoly position in the betting and lottery market. Two countries, Australia and Canada, do not benefit from lottery or gambling money in the development of sport and elite sport; in Spain and France, data regarding lottery funds for sport were not available. Finally, in Brazil a high fluctuation is noted in the proportion of government funding compared to lotteries (Piva Act), and since 2007 using taxes through the Tax Break Act, varying from less than 10% in 2005 and 2010 to 40% in 2012 (boosted by the Olympic Games 2016) and 72% in 2007 (boosted by the organisation of the Pan American Games).

Table 23: The proportion of funding that comes from government and from lotteries (as compared to total national elite sport expenditures, including NOC and national sponsorship)

	% funding from government	% funding from lotteries	% other sources
AUS	96%	0%	4%
CAN	90%	0%	10%
FLA	87%	7%	6%
WAL	85%	6%	9%
FIN	91%		9%
N. IRL	74%	26%	0%
JPN	64%	11%	25%
SUI	59%	41%	0%
NED	50%	26%	24%
EST	39%	24%	37%
POR	35%	65%	0%
BRA	6%	53%	31%
S. KOR	10%	86%	4%
DEN	8%	78%	14%

Note:

1. *Denmark's figures are based on Team Denmark's funding only.*
2. *In Finland, lottery funding is owned by the state; other funding comes from the NOC; the figures exclude overlap with state/lottery funding and the NOC.*
3. *Other funding sources are for example taxes; sponsorships and television rights; exact data on this are not available.*

Other sources: Taxes, policy and military

There exist varying indirect elite sport expenditures through taxes, the policy and the military

Finally, some countries have indirect elite sport funding through other sources, such as tax relief. Only six nations indicated that they had no specific regulation or reduced taxation for grassroots sport or elite sport. As a few examples, in some countries (e.g., Finland, Flanders), government supports elite athletes directly in the form of elite athlete grants, and these are tax free. The Australian researcher indicates that although there is no specific tax regulation, funding from the Australian Sports Commission to athletes under the Direct Athlete Support Scheme is tax free. As noted earlier, the Tax Break Act in Brazil, as an incentive for the Sport Act since 2007, describes a Federal Tax deduction for enterprises or people that sponsor sport programmes. The Japanese researcher indicated that taxes are not charged on funds that athletes received based on their Olympic results. In South Korea there are reduced taxes for the KSC/KOC (Korea Sports Council/Korea Olympic Committee). The Spanish VAT law states that services provided by public law entities, NGBs, the Spanish Olympic Committee, the Spanish Paralympic Committee, social sport organisations and physical education participants are exempt from paying IVA (which is equivalent to VAT).

Another indirect source of income, not included in the SPLISS elite sport expenditures, is how elite athletes can benefit from collaboration with the police (e.g., Estonia, France and Japan) and with the military (e.g., Brazil, Estonia, Finland [only 5 athletes], Flanders, France, Japan, Switzerland and South Korea). In some countries, such as Brazil and South Korea, this is substantial, because military service is compulsory and is also used explicitly to contribute to the development of elite sport (Nobréga, De Bosscher and Böhme, 2013). In South Korea, currently 405 elite athletes go to the Korean Armed Forces Athletic Corps, also known as *Sangmoo* for their military service.

5.3.4 Grassroots versus elite sport prioritisation

There is a slight pattern that countries which prioritise elite sport expenditures over grassroots are more successful in summer sports (with some exceptions, such as France and the Netherlands)

There remains a philosophical dichotomy between funding elite and grassroots sport. Because so much funding goes to so few elite athletes rather than to the masses at grassroots, elite sport spending always needs to be justified. It seems that elite sport and mass participation sport continue to grow apart, and the logical connection between them is under threat (van Bottenburg, 2002). Some countries have chosen to focus funding primarily on high-performance sport, arguing that elite sport role models drive participation at the grassroots level, through top performance by elite athletes and inspirational elite sport events (De Bosscher, Sotiriadou and van Bottenburg, 2013). As can be seen in Figure 18, Canada, Japan, Australia, Spain, Estonia and South Korea prioritise elite sport as a national investment, with more than 50% of funds for sport invested in this area. In Australia the proportion of funding allocated to elite sport was even higher a decade ago, when only 20% was spent on grassroots sport in 2001.

Belgium (both Flanders and Wallonia), Finland and Brazil tend to focus more on grassroots funding. Across the sample of nations it appears that countries that prioritise elite sport are also more successful in summer sports. France and the Netherlands are an exception, with a higher proportion of funds spent on grassroots sport funding and also very successful elite sport nations.[17]

Government's decision to fucus funding on elite sport does not depend on national wealth

Furthermore, a government's decision to focus funding on elite sport appears not to depend on national wealth. Among the 16 sample nations and regions, the data shows that elite sport expenditure as a proportion of total sport spending is not significantly related to GDP per capita.

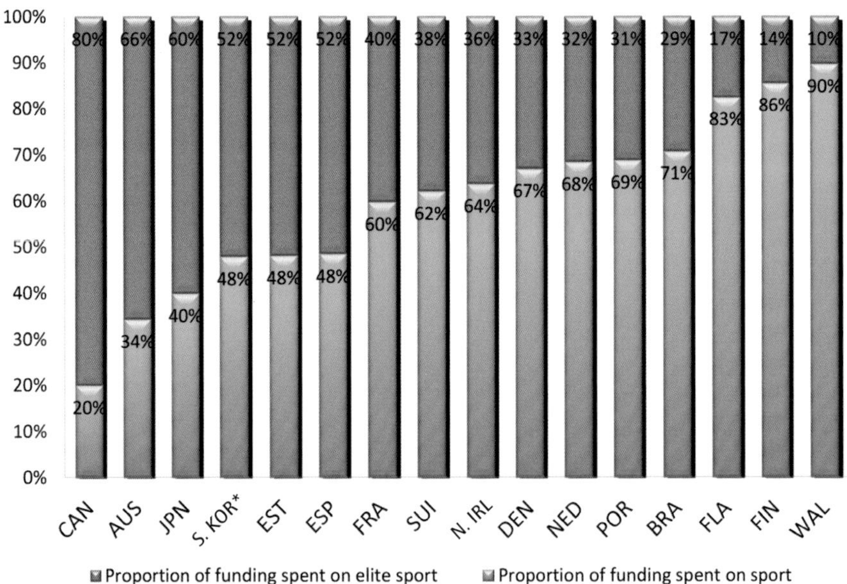

Figure 18: Proportion of national-level public funding for elite sport compared to community/ grassroots sport

17 The Spearman correlation coefficient between the proportion of funds spent on elite sport and success is significant for summer sports only $r_{s(summer\ sports)} = 0.594$, $p = 0.015$; $r_{s(winter\ sports)} = 0.416$, $p = 0.109$.

5.3.5 Changes in national elite sport expenditures: An escalating global sporting arms race?

During the past decade, national elite sport expenditures have continued to increase considerably in all nations, except Spain, Portugal and Denmark

The SPLISS 1.0 study showed that sport expenditure had increased considerably over time in the six sample nations. As can be seen in Figure 19 and Figure 20, this trend continues in the SPLISS 2.0 sample. When comparing expenditure levels in 2012 with those in 2001 (or the earliest point in time where data were available), spending on elite sport increased in most nations. Among the best performing countries the most notable increase was found in South Korea (+143%). South Korea's boost to elite sport funding was marked by a number of mega-events being organised, including future events such as the 2018 Winter Olympic Games in Pyeongchang.

The organisation of Olympic events (has) fuelled the elite sport expenditures in 5 SPLISS nations

It should be noted that of the sample nations, five more have been, or are, driven by the organisation of Olympic events in recent times: France, Japan, Australia, Canada and Brazil. The home advantage effect is a well-known phenomenon in literature and not only 'during' the Games, but also prior to hosting the Olympics (Balmer, Nevill and Williams, 2003). This phenomenon is reflected in the increase in expenditure by these nations. For example the 2009 decision for the 2016 Olympic Summer Games to take place in Rio de Janeiro, Brazil, led to a 96% increase in funding immediately afterwards to €180 million in 2012. Tokyo's (Japan, +57%) bid for the 2020 Olympic Games, fuelled the government's commitment to support elite sport development. SportBusiness International (2014) announced that the 'Brazilian Olympic Committee has pledged to spend a record $600m (€441.1m) in a bid to nearly double the country's medal count at the Rio de Janeiro 2016 Olympic Games.' Australia's boost for increased elite sport funding by government followed the announcement in 1993 that Sydney would host the 2000 Olympic Games. The Australian Government immediately established the Olympic Athlete Programme (OAP) that provided funding of $135m (1994-2000) to ensure Australia's success at its 'home' Games. With a fourth place in the medals' table, the Sydney Olympics were Australia's most successful Games. In Canada the overall funding for Olympic and Paralympic Winter sports in preparation for Vancouver 2010 increased by 70% compared with the 2006 Torino Games. Funding for summer sports increased by 34% from Beijing to London.

While the increase in elite sport expenditure is even higher in some smaller countries, such as in Flanders (+327%), Wallonia (+225%) and Northern Ireland (+209%), these amounts are still low in absolute terms.

Taking inflation into account, in some nations a decrease was observed (Spain: −16%, Portugal: −5%). A possible and likely explanation for decreasing amounts of funding in these countries is the global financial crisis that started in 2007. In the case of Spain, the unsuccessful bid by Madrid to be the host city for the 2020 Games has not led to a boost in elite sport funding. A status quo can also be observed in Denmark. Team Denmark's revenue decreased slightly from 2001 to 2009, having peaked in 2006 and dipped to its lowest point in 2009.

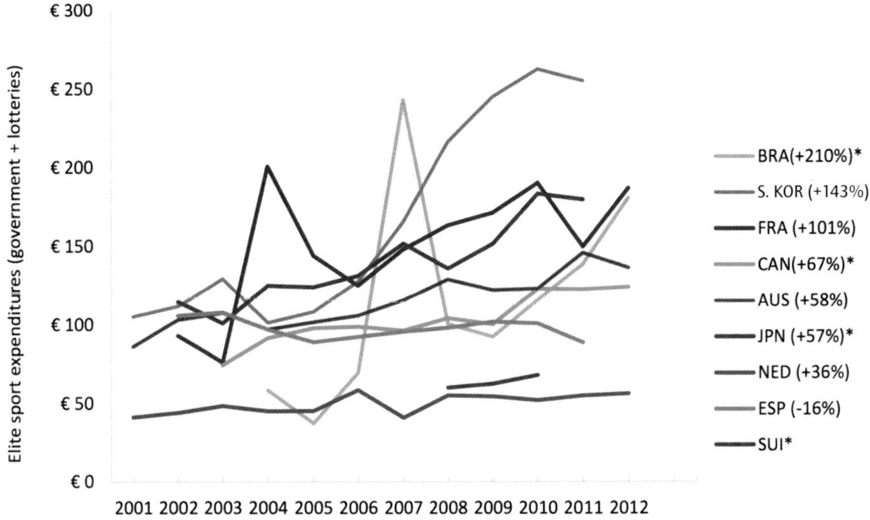

Figure 19: Elite sport expenditures (x million Euros) from government and lotteries by top 20 medal table countries (summer/winter) in 2001-2012, data actualised for inflation (2012)

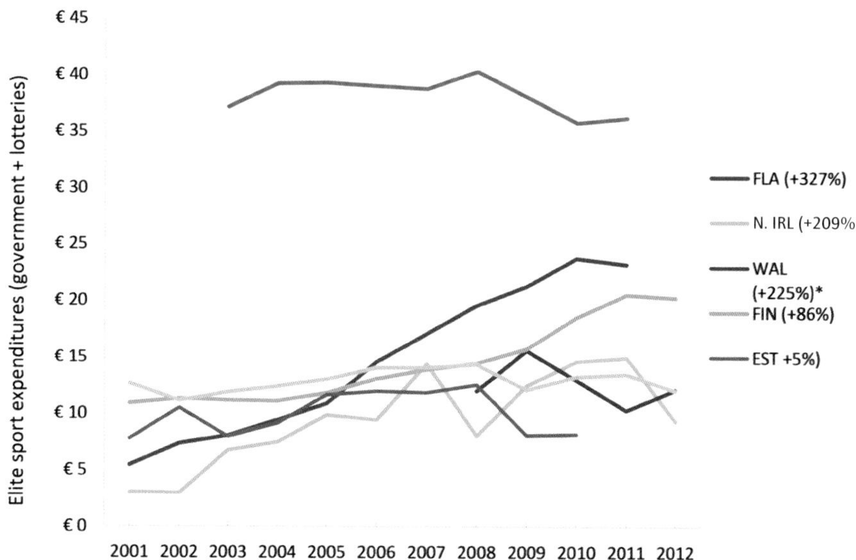

Figure 20: Elite sport expenditures (x million Euros) government and lotteries by smaller countries, 2001-2012; data actualised for inflation (2012)

Notes with the figures:

1. *The percentage illustrates the difference between 2011 and the earliest year where data was available.*
2. *The data exclude the NOCs' budgets; this is particularly important in Japan, where the JOC's additional budget spent on elite sport was around €44m in 2010; this information was not available over a longer period.*
3. *The peak in Brazil during 2007 is explained by the organisation of the Pan American Games, when the total elite sport expenditure was €193,693,066, mainly because of a government funding boost.*
4. *Switzerland's 2008 budget excludes €33.6m in FOSPO expenditure on UEFA Euro 2008; the total elite sport expenditure was €82.2m; without this amount, the total expenditure increased over time; data from 2001-2007 are not comparable to 2008 because of other measurement methods.*
5. *Canada is an estimation based on 80% elite sport expenditures and 20% sport (see earlier).*

5.4 Summary points in Pillar 1

- The evidence consistently indicates that there is a strong positive relationship between the absolute amount of nationally co-ordinated money spent on elite sport and elite sport success. Of all the factors and sub factors included in the SPLISS inventories, elite sport expenditure appears to be the best predictor of success. The important point of note is that expenditure of this type is controllable, and therefore nations can, if they wish, choose to spend money on elite sport. Furthermore, given that there is choice as to how governments spend public money, elite sport expenditure does not depend on the absolute wealth of nations.
- Investment in grassroots sports leads to some interesting findings. First there is no relationship between the amount of money invested in grassroots sport and elite sport. This again points to the notion of nations making choices about the dimensions of sport in which they choose to invest. Second, there is no relationship between investment in grassroots sport and elite sport success. The often cited sports development pyramid whereby talent naturally filters up towards the top is unproven in the SPLISS 2.0 project.
- Nations that prioritise elite sport expenditure over grassroots participation tend to be the more successful nations in elite sport performance.
- The dominant sources of funding for Olympic sports are government funds (Exchequer funding) and the proceeds of lotteries. The proportion of the funding mix from these sources varies considerably from nation to nation. The use of lottery funding enables governments to increase funding for (elite) sport without using taxation and also to insulate themselves from any negative outcomes as a result of this funding being at 'arm's length'.
- There is evidence that as nations invest increasing amounts of money in elite sport over time, there tends to be little or no impact on success over the same time period. In other words there is further evidence of a global sporting arms race as nations spend increasing amounts of money on a relatively fixed supply of success, of which it is difficult to increase their share.

Chapter 5 references

Andreff, Dutoya and Montel (2009). Sport financing in times of global recession. Paper presented at the 'Play the Game' conference, Coventry, June 8-12.

Balmer, N. J., Nevill, A. M. and Williams, A. M. (2003). Modelling home advantage in the Summer Olympic Games. *Journal of Sports Sciences, 21*, 6, 469-478.

De Bosscher, V., Bingham, J., Shibli, S., van Bottenburg, M. and De Knop, P. (2008). *A global sporting arms race. An international comparative study on sports policy factors leading to international sporting success.* Meyer & Meyer, Aachen, Germany.

De Bosscher, V., Sotiriadou, P. and van Bottenburg, M. (2013). Scrutinizing the sport pyramid metaphor: an examination of the relationship between elite success and mass participation in Flanders. *International Journal of Sport Policy and Politics, 5* (3), 319-339. doi: 10.1080/19406940.2013.806340

Cunha, V. (2012). Jogada de craque? fatores críticos que levam. empresas públicas a patrocinarem o esporte. Master thesis from fundação getulio vargas escola brasileira de administração pública e de empresas. Document retrieved July 6th 2013 from http://bibliotecadigital.fgv.br/dspace/bitstream/handle/10438/9914/Dissertação_Vinicius_Cunha.pdf?sequence=1.

Nobréga, L. F., De Bosscher, V. and Böhme, M.T. (2013). The elite sport and military participation in international sporting success. In *Elite Sport Success: Society Boost or not? Proceedings of the first SPLISS conference*, p 50-51. V. De Bosscher (Ed.). Brussels: VUB. Antwerp, 13 – 14/11. ISBN 978-90-5472-261-8

Oakley, B., & Green, M. (2001). The production of Olympic champions: International perspectives on elite sport development system. European journal for sport management, 8, 83-105.

Sport Business International (2014). Brazil to increase investment for Rio Games medal bid. Retrieved, 29/07/2014 http://www.sportbusiness.com/sportbusiness-international/search?search_api_views_fulltext=brazil&=Apply

Storm (2012) Danish elite sport and Team Denmark: new trends? In *Nordic Elite Sport. Same ambitions, different tracks.* S. Andersen and L. Tore Ronglan (Eds.). Norway: AIT Otta AS.

van Bottenburg (2002). Sport for all and elite sport: Do they benefit one another? In NOC*NSF (Ed.), proceedings of the 9th World Sport for All Congress, 'Sport for all and elite sport: Rivals or partners?' p. 25, NOC*NSF, Ahrnem, NL.

GER
London 2012

6 Pillar 2: Governance, organisation and structure of (elite) sport policies: An integrated approach to policy development

6.1 Concepts and definition

Pillar 2 is the most comprehensive Pillar. The elements dealt with, concern the national co-ordination, long-term planning, stakeholder involvement, staff, communication, decision making and collaboration with commercial partners

Pillar 2 concerns the governance, organisation and structure of elite sport. Of all Pillars, this one is the most complicated to evaluate due to the significant differences between national elite sporting systems, how they are structured and organised and how elite sport is embedded in the overall policy system. There is no consensus amongst sport managers or academics about the best practice approach to developing and implementing elite sport policies and governance. Andersen and Ronglan (2012), for example, found different pathways towards excellence among Nordic elite sport systems, with a centralised strategy in cycling in Denmark and a decentralised model in tennis and golf in Sweden. The authors argue that both can be seen as efficient and well suited to the particular organisational situation in a specific period of time, which is in effect a contingency approach to building elite sport systems. As argued by many authors (e.g., De Bosscher et al., 2008; Digel et al., 2006; Houlihan and Green, 2008), there is no magic formula for elite sport success, but there is room for different approaches within and between countries and within and between individual sports.

On the other hand, Green (2009) indicated that the need for control and co-ordination is more pronounced in elite sport than in other sport settings, which is in line with Mintzberg's (1994) early organisational theories that illustrate the preference for centralisation when a high degree of specialisation is required (such as in elite sport). It is reasonable to say that the SPLISS study adopts the perspective that for nations to maximise their chances of elite sporting success, government or National Sport Associations (NSAs) need to take charge of developing policy and governance structures strategically. National co-ordination could be concerned with steering, guiding, shaping and leading, whether sporting competitions are organised in a centralised or decentralised manner. Operationally, a coherent and holistic structure is a prerequisite for the efficient use of resources. Oakley and Green (2001) and Clumpner (1994), in that regard, state that it is especially important to delineate clearly the responsibilities of different agencies; to ensure there is effective communication between them; and to simplify administration. Pillar 2 deals with these issues.

Furthermore, research shows the importance of engaging stakeholders, in this case elite athletes and coaches, in decision-making processes and the evaluation of elite sport policies prior to and after decision making (Dooms, 2009; Thibault, Kihl and Babiak, 2010).

Pillar 2 is the most comprehensive Pillar, with 18 CSFs that are investigated in this Pillar, including 119 subfactors. Data collected for Pillar 2 from all 15 sample nations (13 nations and 3 regions: Flanders, Wallonia, Northern Ireland) contained over 500 pages. Additionally, some critical success factors were explored in greater depth by seeking the views of the main stakeholders (athletes, coaches, performance directors) using the elite sport climate survey.

6.2 Key findings

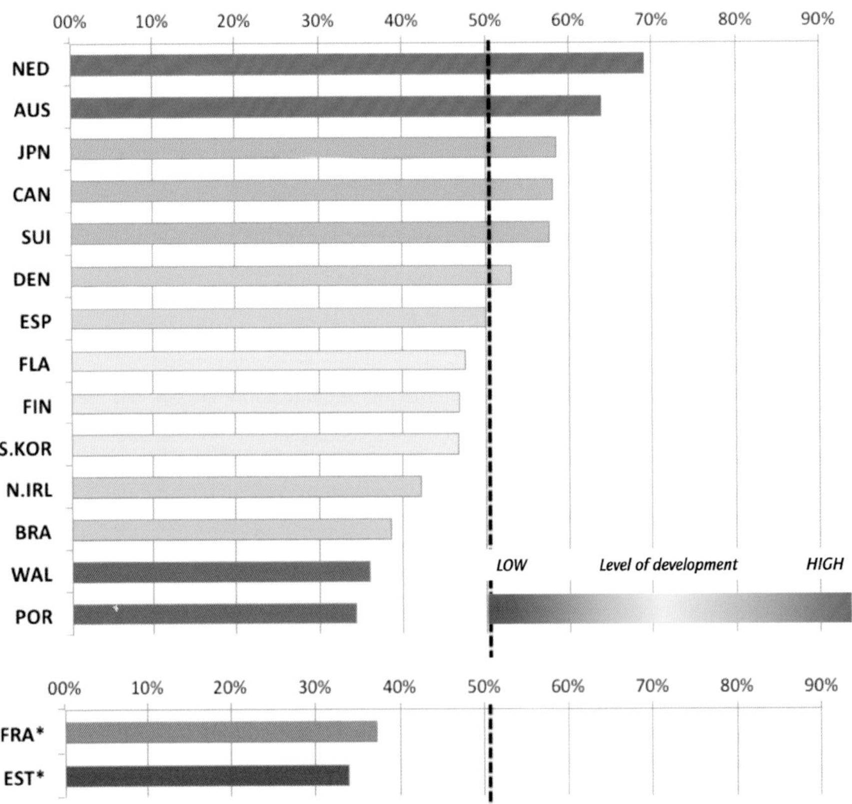

* *Note: 13 nations + 3 regions (FLA, WAL, N-IRL). Only partial data available in France (no elite sport climate survey); South Korea and Estonia (no inventory). Caution is therefore needed when interpreting the scores.*

Figure 21: Total scores of the SPLISS sample nations against the 18 CSFs of Pillar 2

The score on Pillar 2 (organisation, structure, governance) is a reflection of the success of nations in summer sports or in winter sports

For most countries, the score on Pillar 2 is a reflection of their success in summer sports or in winter sports, which is confirmed by the significant correlation between medal performance and the Pillar 2 scores.[18] In other words, within the sample there is a positive association between the governance, organisation and structure of elite sport policies and medal-winning success. The findings show that National Sport Associations (NSAs) of the best performing nations in the sample, all have full-time management staff for the continuous support of elite athletes, coaches and performance directors. This factor has the strongest relationship with success, both in winter and summer sports, and is indirectly related to the financial resources available to countries (Pillar 1). Management staff are responsible for dissemination of important information, the delivery of consultancy and storage (centralisation) of expertise including well-developed support services and consultancy for NGBs. Furthermore it appears that high performing nations have strong national co-ordination of activities and financial inputs with clear task descriptions and deliverables. One key finding is that it is not the countries with the most centralised approach that perform best, but rather those who best co-ordinate activities and collaborate with different partners. NGBs are heavily dependent on government funding, and governments therefore set targets for NGBs to achieve against the funding provided, using the principle of 'earned autonomy' (Goodwin and Grix, 2011). This system of governance allows governments to intervene when NGBs do not deliver on targets. In some countries it seems that elite sport systems are emerging (such as Australia) where 'sport runs sport' and where government devolves the strategic responsibility to NSAs. Principles of 'new public management' practised in the public sector, where decentralisation, collaboration and accountability principles have been more prominent, are also embedded in elite sport. In high performing nations such as Australia and the Netherlands, governance of the governing bodies is carefully planned and monitored by government and a strong service-oriented approach is advocated underpinned by setting clear objectives, and using key performance indicators to make NGBs accountable for the funding they receive. Successful nations also seem significantly more likely to involve athletes and coaches in policy evaluation and to give them a voice in the decision making process of the NSA.

The SPLISS results show no straightforward link between a strategy seeking to prioritise funding for certain sports over others and success

A key finding regarding Pillar 2 concerns the prioritisation strategy that many nations have implemented over the past decade targeting funding at those sports that have medal-winning potential. Improving efficiency by doing more with fewer resources is one possible answer in response

18 $r_s = .720$ $\rho < 0.01$ for summer sports and $r_s = .685$ $\rho < 0.01$ for winter sports.

to an escalating global sporting arms race. Even though absolute funding has increased for most nations, more nations have entered the medal race, and most of the existing competitors have increased funding. In that context, the SPLISS results show no straightforward link between a strategy seeking to prioritise funding for certain sports and success. For example, at one end of the continuum is Australia, one of the early adopters of a prioritised funding strategy, and at the other end is France with the most diverse approach (investing in many sports), yet these are also the two most successful countries in the sample. Other examples of successful countries that invest in a diverse number of sports are Canada, the Netherlands, South Korea, Spain and Brazil. Furthermore, there is some evidence to suggest that countries that invest in a higher number of sports, such as France and Canada, are also successful in more sports.

Scores on Pillar 2 vary from 34% (least developed/integrated) in Portugal to 69% (most developed/integrated) in the Netherlands.

Figure 21, the overall score against 18 CSFs, reveals that the Netherlands and Australia have the most integrated approach to elite sport policy development. Both countries' approach can be characterised by strong national co-ordination, long-term policy planning and NSA policies that are regularly evaluated by athletes and coaches. Furthermore both NOC*NSF (Netherlands) and the Australian Institute of Sports have sufficient full-time staff; they provide a range of services to their NGBs and other stakeholders and the quality of the communication and decision-making structure is evaluated positively in the elite sport climate survey. Interestingly both countries have a different funding approach–priority funding in Australia and diversity funding in the Netherlands (concepts that will be discussed in greater depth later in the chapter).

Countries score well on different blends of CSFs

A second group of countries is formed by Canada, Switzerland, Japan and Denmark that perform above the average of all sample nations. Their situation can be characterised by having full-time management staff at the NSA level along with a range of elite level services offered to NGBs. In regard to some CSFs elite sport development approaches are less homogeneous. In Canada and Denmark most elite sport decisions are made by one or a small number of organisations, whereas in Switzerland and Japan there appears to be greater plurality of involvement in elite sport decision making. Co-ordination of regional elite sport activities is well the developed in Denmark. An important strength of the Japanese and Swiss elite sport policies is their focus on long-term planning, which is less developed in Denmark. Canada shows especially strong involvement of stakeholders in the policy decision-making process. Switzerland and Japan are quite unique in their development of a national strategy in collaboration with commercial partners. An interesting point needs noting in the Danish elite sport policy. Since the revised Act on elite sport in 2004, there exists collaboration between 18 elite sport municipalities, which was identified as a key to success after 2009 by Storm (2012), because it has released financial and organisational resources focussed at elite sport development not previously seen in Denmark at municipal level.

With the exception of South Korea, the remaining countries suffer from a lack of national co-ordination and lack of support services through the NSA. Stakeholder involvement is most problematic in Northern Ireland, Brazil and South Korea.

In conclusion, Pillar 2 shows evidence that countries' score is composed of different blends of CSFs. France, in many ways, seems to be an outlier on Pillar 2 compared with other high performing nations. The results reveal remarkably low scores that fail to explain France's success when considering the scores of other nations on this Pillar. This is shown in the separate results for the inventory only in Figure 22 (France did not complete the elite sport climate survey). France was the best performing nation in the sample in absolute terms in summer sports and was also relatively successful in winter sports. France has the most region/provincially-centred elite sport policies of all nations, and it has staff appointed at the national sport institute INSEP who lead on programmes for elite sport and the organisational development of NGBs. On the other hand, limited co-ordination exists between the 16 regional training centres, called CREPS (Centres de Resource, d'Expertise et de Performance Sportive) and the 115 local departments. There is less long-term planning and stakeholder involvement in policy evaluations. It seems that France is moving from a strong state-centred policy approach towards more decentralised elite sport development with room for collaboration with the private sector.

Neither the elite sport climate survey (as perceived by athletes, coaches, performance directors) nor the inventory (the Pillar objective data as collected by the researcher) independently correlate significantly with summer or winter sport success. However, when combining both scores there is a significant correlation, implying that absolute and perceived reflection in combination provide a more complete picture of reality. This is further explained by looking at the case of Flanders', which is a politically autonomous (Northern) region of Belgium. When looking solely at the elite sport climate survey evaluation by athletes, coaches and performance directors (Figure 22), scores are generally low, with the highest score (59%) achieved by Flanders. Despite the lack of Belgian success in international competition, the positive evaluation by athletes, coaches and performance directors can possibly be explained by the fact that Flanders' elite sport budgets have more than tripled over the past decade, and a range of additional services were provided to stakeholders. As such, the first evaluation of the elite sport climate conducted in 2004 improved from 'average' to 'good' in the 'third measurement' in 2011 (De Bosscher and De Croock, 2012).

In the next part of the chapter we continue with a detailed comparative analysis and discussion of each cluster of CSFs.

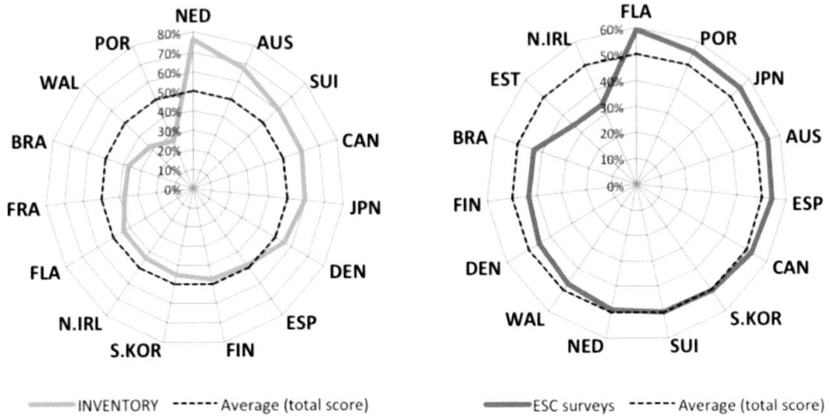

Figure 22: Separate scores of the SPLISS sample nations for the overall inventory (left) and the elite sport climate survey (right) on Pillar 2 (sorted from largest to smallest)

6.3 Comparative and descriptive analysis

6.3.1 National co-ordination of elite sport policies

Critical success factors P2		INVENTORY	SURVEY		
I. There is strong co-ordination of all agencies involved in elite sport, with clear task descriptions, no overlap of different tasks and political recognition		O	A	C	PD
CSF 2.1	There is national co-ordination of activities and financial inputs (horizontal) and a clear decision making structure: there is (only) one organisation at the national level that makes the major decisions on elite sport only and that co-ordinates and records expenditures and activities centrally so that no overlap takes place.	X	No survey evaluation on these CSFs		
CSF 2.2	There is co-ordination of financial inputs (vertical direction) and activities: allocation of funding and management of activities in regard to elite sport at regional/district level: if there is any significant financial input of this type it is recorded and co-ordinated nationally.	X			
CSF 2.3	Elite sport is recognised as a valuable component of a politician's portfolio of responsibilities.	X			

Source of information: O: overall sport inventory; A: athletes' survey, C: coaches' survey; PD: performance directors' survey

Governments set goals but autonomy is provided to the NSA to identify how the goals should be reached

Elite sport development in many countries has been characterised by increasing 'governmentalisation' and institutionalisation over the past 20-30 years. Governmentalisation refers to *'the development of a state apparatus for the delivery and management of services that were previously the primary role of responsibility of organisation of civil society'* (Houlihan, 2009, p. 55). Sport policy studies have noted increasing government intervention to establish and refine elite sport policy objectives, alongside the provision of substantial investment of public and lottery funds in elite athletes' development (e.g., Green and Houlihan, 2005; Bergsgard et al., 2007). While former communist countries have a long history of state direction of elite sport, a similar approach to elite sport development emerged much later in many non-communist countries.

Among the sample nations, strong government involvement can still be observed in South Korea, Australia and Spain. An interesting finding is that countries such as Australia and, to a lesser degree, France seem to be moving away from significant government involvement, with the emphasis now being more on a 'sport runs sport' approach with funded organisations held more accountable for delivering agreed objectives. Based on the view that 'strategy' requires a 'macro' perspective but that implementation may require a 'micro' lens, it seems logical for governments to be engaged with setting strategic goals but not necessarily driving the process by which these goals should be reached.

Horizontal co-ordination at the national level

In successful nations, only one national co-ordinating body takes the major strategic decisions in elite sport

A key finding from the SPLISS 1.0 study was that countries with only one national co-ordinating elite sport body responsible for elite sport (and not sport for all), such as UK Sport or Olympiatoppen in Norway, have an advantage over countries where decision-making responsibilities are split between different organisations. Such a structure reduces transaction costs and avoids strategic disagreement, and reduces internal competition between elite sport and grassroots sport. This 'level of horizontal co-ordination' as a critical success factor is confirmed by the results in the sample countries. The National Sport Associations (NSA) in Australia (Australian Sports Commission via the Australian Institute of Sport), Canada (Sport Canada), France (the Sports Ministry via INSEP), Spain (the Consejo Superior de Deportes (CSD), South Korea (Korea Sports Council/Korea Olympic Committee) and the Netherlands (NOC*NSF) take the lead in the elite sport decision-making process. In other countries elite sport is co-ordinated by at least two organisations, and sometimes by three in Japan and Wallonia or even more in Flanders (see Table 24). As a partial solution, some countries have a department that co-ordinates the operations of the different agencies and institutions so that expenditures and activities are recorded and co-ordinated (Flanders, Japan) or they have formulated an agreement to ensure collaboration and task description (such as in Switzerland). Interestingly, in South Korea, a separate body was established by the government in 2007 for the development of young talents: NEST, Next Generation Sport Talent Foundation.

Table 24: Level of horizontal national co-ordination of elite sport activities and expenditures

	Number of decision-making organisations for elite sport development	Level of national co-ordination
AUS	1	High
BRA	2	Low
CAN	1	High
DEN	2[4]	High
FIN	2	Low
FRA	1	High
JPN	3	Medium
NED	1	High
S. KOR	1	High
POR	1	High
ESP	1	High
SUI	2	Medium
N. IRL	2	Low
FLA	5[2]	Medium
WAL	3[3]	Medium

Notes:

1 In Finland the organisations responsible for elite sport are the NOC and the Ministry of Education and Culture. The NSA is excluded, because it has a very limited role in elite sport despite the fact that they do participate in elite sport strategy processes. There is no clear co-ordination for elite sport. Organisation of Finnish elite sport is very fragmented like the whole sport movement in Finland.

2 As a solution to the dispersion of responsibilities in Flanders, a task force in elite sport has been set up as a co-ordinated meeting where the main decisions in elite sport are taken. This task force consists of five organisations that meet once a month: Ministry of Sport, Department CJSM (culture-youth-sports-media), Bloso (the national sports administration), BOIC (National Olympic Committee), VSF (Flemish Sports Federation). Bloso (as a governmental organisation, responsible at operational level) takes most of the final decisions, however, this always happens in consultation with the task force.

3 In Wallonia, it needs to be noted that most athletes from the German community are affiliated with a French-speaking federation and that the Ministry of the German Community (only 70,000 inhabitants) and French-speaking community organise meetings to co-ordinate their activities.

4 In Denmark, Team Denmark is in charge of most top elite sport, but it is still DIF (merged with NOC) which announces the team for the Olympics (in co-operation with Team Denmark).

The NSA and NOC are merged in two nations

Only in Switzerland (since 1997), South Korea (since its establishment) and the Netherlands (since 1993) is the National Sports Association (NSA) merged with the National Olympic Committee (NOC). This can be seen as strengthening the national co-ordination and decision making-process in elite sport.

While the NOCs have the most decision-making power for elite sport in Brazil, Finland and Japan, NOC influence on elite sport policy is limited in most other countries. In many countries there exists tension between the NOC and the NSA because of the limited power the NOC has in regard to determining elite sport policies, mainly resulting from their limited elite sport funding role—with the exception of South Korea (€100m), Japan (€41m) and to a lesser extent Canada (€11.6m). Their influence reaches as far as athletes' preparation for the Olympic Games. In Japan the governmental role of the NAASH (National Agency for the Advancement of Sports and Health) has significantly increased over the past years since they established the Japanese Institute of Sport Science (JISS) in 2001 and the National Training Centre in Tokyo in 2008, mainly with governmental funding. This was reported by the Japanese researcher as one of the keys to Japan's increased success in recent editions of the Olympic Games.

Flanders, Wallonia and Northern Ireland have separate elite sport systems and are seen as distinct nations in SPLISS

National co-ordination challenges are unique in Belgium, quite different from all the other countries in the sample. Because of the complex state structure, responsibility for sport is delegated to the independent regions (Dutch-speaking Flanders, French-speaking Wallonia and German-speaking community). Consequently there is no national sport policy driver other than the National Olympic Committee (BOIC), which only has limited funding. There are three ministries of sport, for which the law (i.e., decree) determines that they cannot fund another region or a federal (Belgian) sport structure; accordingly there are three national sports administrations and also national governing bodies, although for Wallonia and the German-speaking community many NGBs are merged. Limited collaboration at the federal (Belgian) level exists. NGBs only co-operate for the selection of athletes for international competitions, and even this process often creates tension. A Belgian virtual co-operation exists, called the ABCD commission. This is a meeting, assembled once a year between Adeps (Sports administration in Wallonia) Bloso (Sports administration in Flanders), BOIC (National Olympic committee, called COIB in French) and D (Deutschsprachige Gemeinschaft, sports administration in the German-speaking part of Belgium). For these reasons, Flanders and Wallonia are seen as two distinct nations in this study. Apart from this complex state structure, different organisations influence elite sport policies even within Flanders and Wallonia (governments, NSA, BOIC, umbrella of the sport federations), which does not foster straightforward decision-making. Clearly, the situation in Belgium is less than ideal compared with nations in the sample that have less complex political and operating environments.

Compared to the above, the situation in Northern Ireland (NI) and the UK is different. With UK Sport as the co-ordinating authority, there is a relatively centralised structure. In Northern Ireland, DCAL (government Department of Culture, Art and Leisure) sets the policy direction and Sport NI puts it into practice. Some sports are supported at UK level; others are supported at the home nation level of Northern Ireland. Northern Ireland competes as a nation in its own right in football and sports contested in the Commonwealth Games, and as such it has no separate National Olympic Committee. Athletes from Northern Ireland can choose to represent either Great Britain and Northern Ireland or the Republic of Ireland and therefore the relevant NOCs are the British Olympic Association and the Olympic Council of Ireland.

Vertical co-ordination between regions

Good collaboration with and co-ordination between regional training activities is critical in large countries

Another level of vertical co-ordination deemed a critical success factor happens at the level of regional training departments and training centres. Co-ordination and collaboration appears to be more critical in larger countries where this is more difficult to get organised. For example, in France, where the 16 regional CREPS (Centres de Ressource, d'Expertise et de Performance Sportive) depend on the national ministry and where also six partnerships centres exist with local governments, the need for national co-ordination between them and collaboration with the national trainings institute INSEP is seen as a key area for improvement. In Australia, a National Institutes System Intergovernmental Agreement (NISIA) was recently developed (in 2011) which aims to generate a structured co-operative agreement between the eight (independent) state (provincial) institutes and academies of sport. However, they are not compelled to deliver programmes against NGB plans and there remain disagreements on who should pay for working towards achieving outcomes required at national level. In the Netherlands, NOC*NSF has developed an accreditation system, for which regional centres receive funding. In this way activities are nationally instigated and standardised documentation has been developed to be completed by each region. In the South Korean system the 16 regional sport councils are funded by the KSC/KOC (albeit only with €142,800) in order to prepare for participation in the National Sports Festival, the biggest national sporting event held every year. This is seen by the South Korean researcher as a unique system strength, because of the engagement it creates at the regional level between sport organisations.

Elite sport municipalities as stakeholders for local elite sport development exists in Denmark and to a lesser extent the Netherlands

Finally, also of note is the existing collaboration between Team Denmark (TD) and 18 recognised elite municipalities (21 since 2014) who are responsible for talent development in collaboration with the NGBs and local clubs. Each municipality delivers on a number of focus sports. Six professionals are appointed within TD with the specific responsibility to develop these elite municipalities and elite facilities across Denmark. This strategy facilitates elite sport investments at local level and is part of the national elite sport strategy. It was identified by Storm (2012) as one of the explanations for Danish success after 2009. It facilitated the co-ordination of local efforts and raised sponsorship revenue for local elite sport projects. Such local development increased following the 2004 elite sport act revision. To some extent such local involvement in elite sport policies also exists in the Netherlands, through seven regional Olympic networks, recognised by NOC*NSF as partners in elite sport development. The strength of these networks is that they create collaboration and involvement of municipalities, NGBs, educational institutions, and local industries in sport and elite sport development, which in turn has an indirect effect on the local community as a whole. In some support centres, over 45 staff members are appointed on a full-time basis.

6.3.2 Long-term planning regarding elite sport policies

Critical success factors P2		INVENTORY	SURVEY			
II. There is (evidence of) long-term planning for elite sport development with the commitment of subsidies for elite sport		O	A	C	PD	
CSF 2.4	Long-term policy plans are developed (at least on a 4-8-year period) specifically for elite sport and are communicated in public, regularly evaluated and supported with financial resourcing	X				
CSF 2.5	NGBs are subsidised for (at least) a four-year cycle	X				P1
CSF 2.6	Long-term policy plans are required for governing bodies in order to receive funding, including requirements regarding the development of elite sport	X			X	

Source of information: O: overall sport inventory; A: athletes' survey; C: coaches' survey; PD: performance directors' survey. Right column shows if the CSFs are interlinked with other Pillars.

Long-term national policy planning (at least four years) is a key characteristic of successful national elite sport policies

All countries, except Wallonia (and to a lesser extent Denmark and Portugal), develop elite sport policy plans for at least a four-year cycle, and some countries, like Australia, Canada, Japan, Northern Ireland, the Netherlands and Switzerland develop even longer term policy plans of up to eight years into the future. The Dutch policy is a notable example in this regard, with the Olympic Plan 2028 that started in 2006, driving planning more than 20 years ahead. The first stage of this plan runs up to 2016, with the aim to 'advance the Netherlands to a higher Olympic level, from participation to elite sport'. The original plan was to work towards a bid for the 2028 Olympics and the go/no-go decision was to be made in 2016. The plan had significant budget commitments and involved different levels of policy involvement from local to provincial to national, and it included a range of different stakeholders such as sport clubs, NGBs and media partners. The strong Dutch strategic planning process has appeared to be successful in London, where the Netherlands (±17 million inhabitants) won 20 medals in 11 disciplines. However, as a result of the global financial crisis, the newly elected Dutch government decided in 2013 to terminate the Olympic Plan, to the disillusionment of many Dutch sports stakeholders. This example probably highlights one of the few disadvantages of extreme long-term planning—that contextual circumstances can change beyond the control of the policymakers and to the extent that ambitious objectives become unrealistic and unachievable.

NGBs are not necessarily funded on a long-term basis in order to increase accountability

While four-year funding cycles for NGBs are seen as an advantage in the SPLISS study because they allow coaches and NGBs to develop a long-term athlete career planning, some countries deliberately allocate funding on an annual basis. This is the case in Australia, Brazil, Canada, Denmark, Japan, Finland and Portugal. In Canada and Denmark, however, major funding is provided annually, but the funding decisions are set every four years (based on the SFAF, Sport Funding and Accountability Framework). In Australia funding is provided on an on-going basis subject to the outcomes of the Annual Sport Performance Review that is undertaken by the Australian Sports Commission. The reason for this as explained by the Australian researcher is to develop accountability for NGBs in regard to their performance. The planning cycle will vary from sport to sport, as stated here:

'If a NGB does not meet their required/stated key performance indicators (KPIs) then it is discussed with key stakeholders as part of the Annual Sport Performance Review assessment process. Only in extreme situations will funding be withheld or withdrawn from a sport.' (Australian researcher)

6.3.3 Stakeholders' involvement

Critical success factors P2		INVENTORY	SURVEY		
III. Athletes, coaches and other important key stakeholders are involved in the policy development		O	A	C	PD
CSF 2.7	Policy is regularly evaluated with athletes, coaches, performance directors who are formally invited to be involved in the evaluation process PRIOR and AFTER policy takes place	X	X	X	X
CSF 2.8	Athletes and coaches are represented within national governing bodies	X	X	X	X
CSF 2.9	Athletes and coaches are represented in the decision making process of the NSA and are consulted about their specific needs	X	X	X	

Source of information: O: overall sport inventory; A: athletes' survey, C: coaches' survey; PD: performance directors' survey

In recent years, important stakeholder groupings such as athletes and coaches, have started to play an increasingly influential role in the development of sport policies and in the decisions that impact policy (Thibault and Babiak, 2005). Freeman (1984) stated that planning from a technocratic, top-down perspective is not enough. Operational stakeholders need to be involved. Leaders of national and international sport organisations increasingly recognise this with the establishment of commissions of athletes or coaches taking part in the governance process or in the evaluation of policies. Their participation in the policy-making and/or decision-making process can enhance the quality of these policies/decisions (Thibault et al., 2010; Walters, 2011), and according to Freeman (2006), they become important to the value creation process of an organisation.

Stakeholder involvement is still limited in regard to elite sport governance

The relevant CSFs are largely measured by the elite sport climate survey. Figure 23 shows the total scores of the sample nations regarding the assessment by athletes and coaches on the extent to which they are sufficiently involved in the development of national-level elite sports policies (by the NSA and the NGB), *prior* to these policies being written and communicated and in the evaluation process *after* policy plans have been implemented. This distinction was made because literature shows that taking into account aspects of stakeholder management during the strategy formulation *(ex ante)* and during evaluation phases *(ex-post)* of long-term planning processes can contribute to the quality of decision-making and the effective implementation of specific projects (Dooms, 2010). Our results reveal that stakeholder involvement remains limited in elite sport policy governance. Athletes and coaches in none of the nations report a high level of involvement (score above 0.5). There is a significant difference in scores of these CSFs between the top 16 elite athletes and the others (including national-level athletes): top 16 athletes give higher scores for their involvement in the policy development and evaluation process of NGBs and NSAs relative to the rest of the elite athletes. This is also the case for international elite coaches versus the rest. Athletes in Japan, South Korea and the Netherlands and coaches in Canada and the Netherlands generally evaluated policy involvement better than other countries. This is also confirmed as a strategy that characterises Canadian elite sport policy (Thibault et al., 2010). The lowest scores were found in Switzerland and Wallonia.

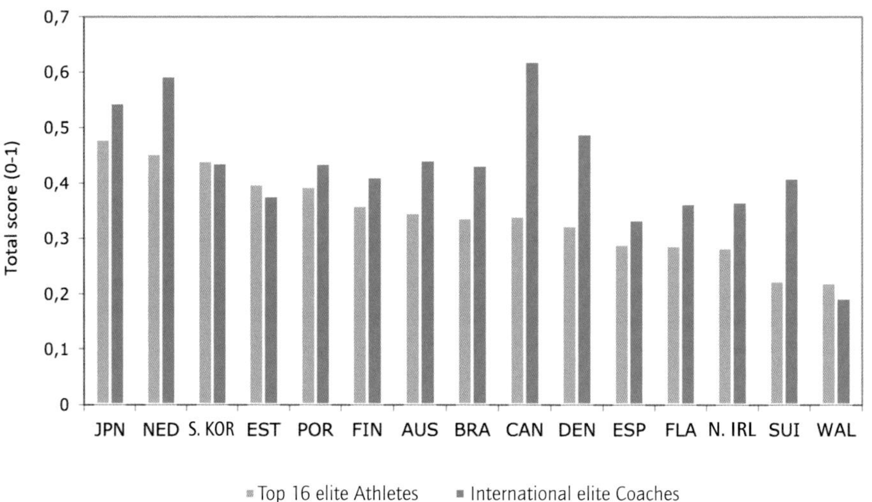

Figure 23: Sum of net scores regarding the extent of involvement in the policy development and evaluation process of NGBs and NSAs, according the top 16 elite athletes and the coaches at international level (except for Australia which includes all coaches)

Most NOCs have an athletes' commission; in the NSA this type of involvement still remains limited

One way of involving stakeholders is through a commission for athletes or coaches. In most countries athletes are represented in the NOCs to a greater or lesser extent on commission of this type. In the NSA this is less common and only six countries (AUS, BRA, CAN, JPN, NED, S. KOR, SUI, including the countries where the NSA and NOC are merged [SUI, S. KOR, NED]) report such a commission. In Finland the NOC and the NSA take the main decisions in elite sport. Only in Denmark and Switzerland do athletes have voting rights. Coaches are generally not represented in the formal decision-making process of NSAs.

In the NGBs, results of the elite sport climate survey revealed that an average of 43% of all athletes in the sample nations, indicated that the NGB has an athletes' commission (Figure 24). This is highest in Canada, Australia and Spain. The top 16 athletes are significantly more aware of the existence of an athletes' commission than the other athletes.[19] In Canada NGBs must demonstrate that athletes have the opportunity to be informed about matters affecting them, particularly in the area of national team programming. This must be planned and announced and not determined on an ad hoc basis. Elite coaches at the international level are significantly more aware of their NGB's coaches' commission than the total coaches' sample. Over 70% of the coaches in Portugal and Estonia indicated that their NGB has a coaches' commission.

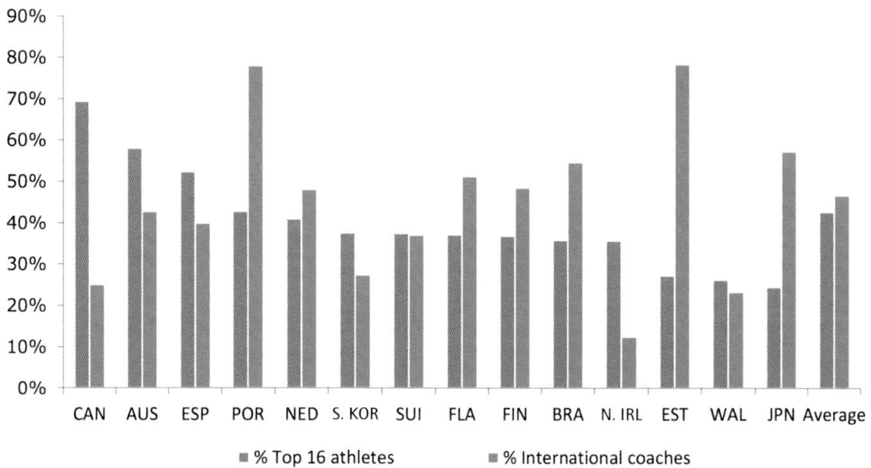

Figure 24: NGB athletes' commission (blue) and coaches' commission (green) (percentages according to top 16 elite athletes and international-level coaches [except Australia which includes all coaches]) (remark: Denmark is excluded because the question was interpreted differently after translation and included both NGB and DIF/Team Denmark)

19 Note: All athletes versus top 16 athletes: $X^2 = 81{,}7$, $p < 0.000$, d.f. = 2; all coaches versus international level coaches: $X^2 = 14{,}09$, $p < 0.000$, d.f. = 2, chi-square test).

6.3.4 Staff at the NSA and the professional development of NGBs

Critical success factors P2		INVENTORY	SURVEY			
IV. Full-time management staff in the NSA are responsible for the elite sport development process and the professional support of NGBs		O	A	C	PD	
CSF 2.10	The government/NSA has implemented a series of programmes and organisational requirements on the NGBs/clubs/sports regarding the development of elite sport	X				
CSF 2.11	There is a formal objective measurement instrument to evaluate the NGB funding criteria, undertaken by an independent organisation	X				
CSF 2.12	Full-time management staff in the NSA are responsible for the specific purpose of the development and support of elite coaches, elite athletes and other areas such as sport science, marketing and communication	X				P1
CSF 2.13	NGBs receive information and support services (other than financial) on different aspects of elite sport development	X			X	

Source of information: O: overall sport inventory; A: athletes' survey, C: coaches' survey; PD: performance directors' survey. Right column shows if the CSFs are possibly on the interface with other Pillars.

Full-time professional staff at the NSA is a key characteristic of world-class elite sport systems and is positively associated with higher levels of funding

The CSF that appears to have the strongest relationship with success in Pillar 2 concerns the number of staff the National Sport Association has (CSF 2.12, see Table 25). There is an obvious relationship with components of Pillar 1 in that availability of monetary resources allows nations to employ more elite sport professionals in the NSA. NSAs have professionalised in recent years in most countries, with specific departments for coach development, athlete assistance, talent development, communication of sport science, and marketing staff all dedicated to servicing elite sport. This pattern is least evident in Portugal, Flanders and Wallonia, Brazil and Finland. At the other end of the spectrum sits the highly structured Australian Institute of Sport with 220 staff members working in elite sport. Of these, approximately 82 are responsible for the sports programmes, which include support for NGBs. A further 61 people are specifically appointed within six departments in sport science support (performance psychology, recovery, sports nutrition, movement science, aquatic testing, training and research); and 35 FTEs work across sports medicine, physical therapies and strength and conditioning. Five people are responsible for the high-performance coaching and leadership (HPCL) team, with five more responsible for career and education. INSEP in France and KSC/KOC (Korean Sports Council/Korean Olympic Committee) work in a similar way.

> **High-performance managers in the NSA are appointed as service providers to increase NGB expertise and with increasing accountability for NGBs**

With more funding to win medals, elite sport development has been characterised by increasing government involvement, intervention and control over NGBs. In recent years principles of new public management have been introduced in elite sport governance, such as accountability, the use of key performance indicators (KPIs), prioritising output over process and the principles of 'earned autonomy' as indicated by Houlihan and Green (2008). The results in this study confirm this evolution towards increased accountability, in which NGBs are assisted to improve their capabilities and self-governing capacity. The NSAs have developed and implemented core services, programmes and set organisational requirements for NGBs, to ensure continuity of training and athlete development. This accountability has become a key characteristic of Australian NGB funding. Under the principle of 'sport runs sport', NGBs can determine the ways in which funding is spent, and also make use of the support services offered by the Australian Sports Commission, but funding needs to be accounted for in elite performances and/or elite sport developments.

In five countries the NSA has appointed high-performance managers to assist athletes and coaches and who also regularly visit NGBs. In Australia 45 coaches are employed in the Australian Institute of Sport through the ASC (Australian Sports Commission), working across 14 sports and 6 additional consultants work across 34 sports. Team Denmark (TD) has employed 17 consultants, covering 55 NGBs, and all of these professionals are, besides their role as NGB consultants, part of one or more of the six teams in TD. In Switzerland and the Netherlands five NGB consultants cover 82 and 60 sports, respectively, making regular visits in the field.

Table 25: Number of staff members working at the NSA only for elite sport and personnel responsible for NGB consultancy as their main task

	FTE at NSA solely responsible for elite sport development	NGB consultants (main task)
AUS	220	45 (+ 6)
BRA	± 15	NA
CAN	NA	NA
DEN	40	17
ESP	± 33	NA
FIN	6*	2
FLA	8	NA
FRA	162*	18
N. IRL	20	NA
JPN	40	None
S. KOR	140	NA
NED	27	5
POR	0	NA
SUI	14	5
WAL	3	NA

FTE (full-time equivalent); NA: data not available

* *Note: in addition to the 162 staff working at INSEP in France, called 'Elite Sport Mission' the staff numbers at the ministry are unknown. In Finland, the figures only concern NOC staff (who takes the main decisions in elite sport).*

A few countries make use of external monitoring systems to evaluate NGBs' management

Some countries make use of external monitoring systems as a process evaluation to assess performance management of NGBs. This happens in Canada, Denmark, Switzerland and the Netherlands where scientific research is the means of process evaluation. In the Netherlands, the quality of (a structured and strategic approach to) management of NGBs is also increasingly used as a criterion for funding. In Canada the Sport Funding Accountability Framework (SFAF) is a quality evaluation system that represents industry best practice. The sport industry is not as advanced as other industries where quality benchmarks such as ISO standards have been developed.

'The Sport Funding Accountability Framework (SFAF) is the tool used by Canadian Heritage since 1996 to identify which organisations are eligible to receive Sport Canada contributions under the Sport Support Programme–in what areas, at what level and under what conditions. There are four stages to the SFAF process: Eligibility, Assessment, Funding and Accountability. Once organisations have completed the SFAF process, they are advised of their results in the form of a score and a

reference level which assists in planning for funding. Once organisations receive funding from Sport Canada, there is continual active assessment and evaluation to ensure the NSOs are fulfilling the policy plans.' (Canadian researcher)

Globally, NGB funding criteria show a similar pattern across nations

Finally, although NGB funding criteria are not included in the CSFs and hence the scores for each nations, they are useful insights to nations' approaches to elite sport and interesting to compare informally. An overview is shown in **Appendix 1**. There appears to be some similarities in the funding criteria, mainly across three levels: performance based; popularity of the sport within a nation; and the management structure. While performance is the sole funding criterion in Spain, the other two criteria are taken into account in the other countries. The popularity of the sport is evaluated in eight countries (AUS, BRA, CAN, DEN, FIN, FLA, JPN and NED), based on national and international exposure, number of club members, and scale of the sport (number of countries that participate internationally in championships). Most countries also include the professional management of the NGB (such as programmes for athlete and talent development) as a criterion for funding, although this might not always be evaluated in a transparent manner. Finally, some countries provided data on the number of part-time or full-time funded NGB staff members (both technical and administrative staff), amounting to 106 in Northern Ireland, 138 in Switzerland, 140 in Wallonia, 697 in Japan and 835 in France. In Portugal and Spain the scale of funding does not allow NGBs to appoint staff specifically for elite sport.

6.3.5 Communication and decision-making structure

Critical success factors P2		INVENTORY	SURVEY		
V. There is an effective communication and punctual decision-making structure through all levels of sport agencies		O	A	C	PD
CSF 2.14	The board of NGBs is composed of professionals who make decisions on elite sport	X			X
CSF 2.15	There is a board within the NSA that is comprised of professionals who make decisions on elite sport, with relatively small management committees so that quick decisions can be made	X			
CSF 2.16	Athletes, coaches and performance directors are well informed about national policies, support services and other aspects		X	X	X

Source of information: O: overall sport inventory; A: athletes' survey, C: coaches' survey; PD: performance directors' survey

The boards of NGBs often hinder effective decision-making, because of conflicts of interest and tensions between volunteers and professionals

From a governance perspective, NGBs of sport are typically nonprofit organisations, managing both professional and amateur sports and administering the allocation of considerable amounts of funding, especially public funds. Generally research on board governance in NGBs in sport remains underdeveloped (Ferkins, Shilbury and McDonald, 2005). A primary objective of recent governance reforms, adopted from the private sector, has been ensuring that organisations are run in the interest of their shareholders (Taylor and O'Sullivan, 2009). NGBs increasingly appoint a board of directors to decide on the organisation's strategy and to ensure that management pursue the formulated strategy appropriately. The SPLISS sample nations all report that boards of directors represent NGBs. Similar challenges within this system are identified in the countries with regard to the composition of NGB boards. Research shows that the board characteristics may influence organisational effectiveness (Taylor and O'Sullivan, 2009). Board members often have different interests and tend to defend the interest of the structure from which they come (Bayle and Robinson, 2007). This issue is also relevant to the context of the potential for conflict between the objectives of elite sport and the objectives of community sport. Apart from South Korea where separate grassroots and elite NGBs have been set up, and the Netherlands, where the Dutch Royal Football Association has an amateur football and professional football board, there seem to be no split boards in other sample countries. Consequently, board members (often elected members from community sport clubs) typically are not familiar with the quite different demands of elite sport. Sub-committees for elite sport exist in some countries, depending on the type of sport (AUS, FLA-WAL, DEN, FIN, FRA, N. IRL, SUI), but these are mainly advisory and more often than not they have no decision-making authority. The CEO or performance director often is excluded from voting. This creates tension between elite sport and community sport on the one hand and between professional staff (e.g., the high-performance director) and voluntary board members on the other. Although the type of board member (skills and capabilities) differs across sports, in general the board of the NGBs is usually comprised of (non-paid) volunteers. Consistent with this point in the SPLISS sample the scores are low (few professionals on boards) on this critical success factor (CSF 2.14). Even though NSA funding for NGBs has increased in many countries, they can exert only a limited influence on NGB board composition with regard to elite sport, as NGBs are empowered to run their own businesses. While there is a legal statute in general, board composition in most countries is quite sport-specific. Australia's system seems to be the most advanced in the way the Australian Sports Commission (ASC) tries to advocate NGB governance. Since 2007 NGBs are required to follow the ASC's guidelines on good governance in order to be considered for funding; this includes board composition, roles and powers, governance systems, board processes and reporting. For example, one principle states that each board should be structured to reflect the knowledge of the sport and sports industry; the board should be broadly reflective of the organisation's key stakeholders but not at the expense of the mix of skills available to boards.

Table 26 provides an overview of the main strengths and weaknesses in the decision-making structure of NGB boards that were identified through the overall sport policy inventory of the SPLISS sample.

Table 26: Strengths and weaknesses in the decision-making structure of NGB boards in the SPLISS sample

Strengths	Weaknesses
• NGBs are the **sport owners;** they can operate **independently** and run their own businesses; this way each NGB can make decisions that are in the best interest of their own sport utilising specialisation and expert knowledge • **Democratic** and broadly-based decision-making structure • The board can be composed of (independent) *professional experts* from other fields, for example from the sport industry	• **Conflict** of interest: NGB boards are comprised of representatives from both **grassroots** and **elite sport**; elite sport is therefore not (always) a top priority for NGBs; important decisions (e.g., financial) can be taken that are not in the best interests of elite sport • The level of **expertise and the skills** of board members for specific high-performance decision-making can be substandard • **Tensions** between **voluntary** board members and professional technical staff of NGBs • **Compromise** approach • No **competitive threat** for board members (they remain elected) • **Continuity** in decision making (e.g., when there is a high turnover of members on NGB boards–AUS) • The resistance to **'change'** (especially with voluntary board members); lack of innovation in some NGBs

NAS governance

In most countries, the NSA is also governed by a board of directors. Only in Canada, Flanders, France, and Portugal is this not the case, and in Spain the board consists of internal (paid) staff. In Flanders there is a steering committee, composed of external members, but they only meet around twice a year and have no voting and decision-making powers. In order for boards to be efficient and effective they cannot be too large. Taylor and O'Sullivan (2009), in that regard, advise a maximum of 12 members. The number of NSA board members differs across the SPLISS sample: Wallonia has 10 representatives, Australia 12, Finland 13, Spain 24 and Japan 33. In Australia, Denmark, France the NSA board members are paid.

NSA-Communication and dissemination of information towards athletes and coaches is generally well developed

Finally, with regard to communication with athletes, coaches and performance directors, the last CSF of this section, we draw solely on the data collected by the elite sport climate survey. Most respondents score the quality of communication from average to high in all countries, with the best scores in Canada, Japan and Estonia, Denmark and Switzerland. The stakeholders also assessed the communication with different organisations such as clubs, NGBs, government, NOC and NSA. Northern Ireland's athletes are most negative about this factor and their scores compare unfavourably with Japanese athletes and Danish coaches who gave the most positive responses.

6.3.6 Co-operation with commercial partners

Critical success factors P2		INVENTORY	SURVEY		
VI. There is a structured co-operation and communication strategy with commercial partners		O	A	C	PD
CSF 2.17	There is a structured co-operation and communication strategy with the media and sponsors	X			

Source of information: O: overall sport inventory; A: athletes' survey, C: coaches' survey; PD: performance directors' survey

Nationally co-ordinated communication and collaboration with commercial partners is not yet considered as an important national elite sport development strategy

One of the basic assumptions in the SPLISS model (De Bosscher et al., 2006) is the distinction between factors that, through human intervention, can be influenced by policies on the one hand and those factors that cannot be influenced on the other hand. In between there is a grey zone of factors referred to by Digel et al. (2006) as 'the environment of elite sport as a resource of world class performance in sport'. Under this dimension, De Bosscher (2007) recognised a general elite sports *culture*, the *tradition* of success and the *private sector* as an investor in elite sport as important grey zone factors. These factors were also confirmed to be important by other researchers (e.g., Brouwers et al., in press; Sotiriadou et al., 2013; Truyens et al., 2013). We have considered how the NSA or ministry have actively developed a national strategy for collaboration with sponsors and media partners and negotiate an agreement that facilitates the co-operation with NGBs. Although this does not constitute 'direct' policy influence, it considers how drivers of elite sport policy enhance and facilitate an environment in which elite sport can be advanced. This can also be considered a responsive strategy in regard to the ever-increasing professionalisation in the sport industry, and the influence of commercial teams, media and sponsors on athletic career development. The professional athlete is driven by economic interests and is therefore exposed to a number of risks (Westerbeek and Hahn, 2013).

A structured communication strategy with both sponsors and media is most strongly developed in Denmark, where Team Denmark and the Sport Confederation of Denmark own an official sponsorship company 'sport one Denmark' and a 'Sports Media Committee', jointly created by Team Denmark, the Danish Sports Confederation and the NGBs. Their main objective is to negotiate the property rights for sport in the numerous electronic media.

Furthermore a structured national co-operation with sponsors exists only in Finland, Japan, Spain and the Netherlands, and only in Spain and the Netherlands does the NSA closely align its strategies with media partners. It is reasonable to conclude that the most intense and strategic collaboration between commercial and media partners continues to take place at the level of individual sports.

In the near future, the relative importance of investigating this critical success factor further will increase. A simple explanation for this is the ongoing commercial development of sport, and its resulting heightened attractiveness for non-governmental organisations—both for profit and not-for-profit. For example, in Brazil the involvement of commercial (semi-state owned) organisations in funding sport already blurs the boundaries between the influence of government and non-government organisations on sport policy.

6.3.7 Prioritisation of elite sport policies

Critical success factors P2		INVENTORY	SURVEY			
VII. Resources are targeted at relatively few sports through identifying those that have a real chance of success at world level (see Pillar 1)		O	A	C	PD	
CSF2.18	Resources are targeted at relatively few sports through identifying those that have a real chance of success at world level (see Pillar 1)	X				P1

Source of information: O: overall sport inventory; A: athletes' survey; C: coaches' survey; PD: performance directors' survey. Right column shows if the CSFs are possibly interlinked with other Pillars.

As a result of the global sporting arms race, national elite sport associations are looking to maximise the return on their investments, and one way to do this is to increase efficiencies (achieving more with the same resources or maintaining position with less resources). An often used approach is to 'target the resources on only a relatively small number of sports through identifying those that have a real chance of success at world level' (Oakley and Green, 2001, p. 91). This strategy has already been proven successful by former communist countries during the late 1980s and early 1990s. In the preparation for Rio 2016, policy plans in some countries (e.g., the Netherlands, Flanders) have introduced a focus on 10 sports or less. In another example, in 2010-2011 50 Australian NGBs received direct funding for elite sport development. In 2011, 25 sports were prioritised within the Australian system, including the Paralympic sports and the Olympic Winter Institute.[20] In the Netherlands the prioritisation approach was sharpened for 2013, with 75% of the elite sport funding allocated to just 10 sports instead of the 25% that these sports received previously. Also Flanders' elite sport action plan 2009-2013 has shown a clear focus on only 10 priority Olympic summer sports. Some countries fund elite sports programmes fully through the NGBs; others also fund individual sport programmes (without involvement of the NGBs) or a combination of both. In this section we analyse to what extent a wide range of sports is funded (i.e., diversity approach) versus a small number (i.e., priority approach), and we also look at the amount of funding these sports receive. An overview of these funding principles per nation is provided in **Appendix 2**.

6.3.7.1 Number of sports funded

Most countries prioritise Olympic sports; non-Olympic sports receive less than 10% of all funding

What can be derived from Figure 25 is that prioritisation firstly relates to the amount of funding delivered to Olympic versus non-Olympic sports and secondly within the Olympic sports, the funding distribution between winter and summer sports. Most countries spend more than 70% of elite sport funding on Olympic summer sports. Switzerland (33%) and Canada (31%) are the biggest spenders on winter sports followed by countries such as Estonia (18%) and Japan (13%). Seven countries spend less than 3% on winter sports.

Several countries provide limited support to a wide range of non-Olympic sports, up to 45 different sports in Switzerland. Two countries (Brazil and Estonia) do not invest in non-Olympic sports and four countries invest less than 10% of the funding in these sports: Japan (28 sports), Portugal (3 sports), Canada (9 sports) and Flanders (6 sports). Budgets for non-Olympic sports are remarkably high in Northern Ireland (35%, which is allocated to sports that are considered to be 'culturally significant', for example sports under the umbrella of the Gaelic Athletic Association [GAA]).

---

20 The Olympic Winter Institute in Australia manages most of Australia's elite winter sport programmes (i.e., aerial skiing, alpine skiing, curling, figure skating, mogul skiing, ski cross, snowboarding, short track speed skating and skeleton).

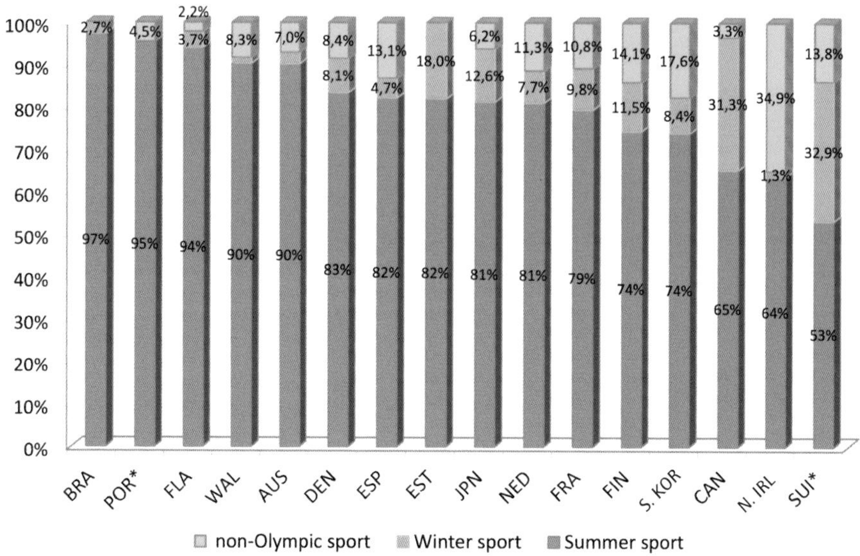

Notes with the figure: In Portugal and Switzerland national sport club funding for elite sport purposes is included in these figures (respectively €0.06m and €5.6m).

Figure 25: proportion of funding divided over Olympic summer sports, winter sports and non-Olympic sports (2010)

A wide range of funded NGBs is not necessarily an indicator of a diversity approach

One key characteristic of prioritisation, and a trend of recent elite sport development is the number of national governing bodies that are funded for elite sport programmes. As can be seen in Tables 27 and 28, this is very focused in Flanders (26) and Brazil (28), whereas a wide range of different sports receive funding in Switzerland (82), Finland (74), Spain (64), Japan (63), France (58), the Netherlands (56, of which 23 are non-Olympic sports) and Australia (50). It could be argued that these nations have a more diverse approach regarding the funding of elite sport. In the Netherlands, the funding strategy changed from structurally developed elite sports funding through the NGBs, towards direct funding for elite sport programmes, independent of NGBs. For example, 94 elite sport programmes are funded in the Netherlands within Olympic sports (of which 76 are in summer sports, and 18 are in winter sports). In these sports, 33 NGBs receive funding (28 summer, 5 winter).

Table 27: Number of funded NGBs for sport and elite sport purposes in Olympic and non-Olympic sports (excluding Paralympics)

	AUS	BRA	CAN	DEN	ESP	EST	FIN	FLA	FRA	N. IRL	JPN	NED	POR	SUI	WAL	S. KOR
Number of NGBs funded for sport	54	28	61	61	64	58	74	64	136	42	68	82	57	82	56	–
Number of NGBs funded for elite sport	50	28	42	35	64	–	74	26	58	28	63	56*	28	82	45	55

** 56 NGBs are funded in the Netherlands, of which 33 in Olympic sports (28 summer, 5 winter), 23 in non-Olympic sports.*

Table 28: Number of summer sports, winter sports and non-Olympic sports that are funded (excluding Paralympics)

	AUS	BRA	CAN	DEN	ESP	EST	FIN	FLA	FRA	N. IRL	JPN	NED*	POR*	SUI*	WAL	S. KOR
Summer sports (incl. rugby and golf)	27	26	27	23	29	26	30	24	28	26	30	30	24	27	23	30
Winter sports	2	2*	6	3	2	5	5	5	3	2	7	6	0	7	2	7
Non-Olympic sports	19	0	9	9	28	0	41	6	25	12	28	23	3	45	16	20

Note: Funding in the Netherlands is based on elite sport programmes: 94 elite sport programmes in Olympic sports (76 summer + 18 winter) in 36 sports; 46 non-olympic programmes.

However, this does not answer the key question of prioritisation. It appears from the data that some sports receive extremely small amounts of funding, sometimes negligible, indicating that the funding provided is more a strategy of recognition of the (elite) sport than one of prioritisation. For example, in Switzerland while 82 NGBs are funded, only 45 are classified under the best funded categories 1-3, and the amount of funding to the other 37 sports represents only 5% of total funding.

All countries prioritise: 50% of funding goes to less than 10 sports (O1 and O3 in Figure 26)

A more specific and appropriate way of investigating prioritisation, is the extent to which a wide or small range of sports receive more or less funding. We have done this by creating four equal quartiles (Figure 26), each constituting 25% of the total funding. For example, while 56 sports are funded in the Netherlands, 25% of the funding goes to just four sports and 50% to just nine. One observation that can be made based on this information is that, despite the high number of funded sports in some countries, virtually all countries prioritise: 50% of the funding is allocated to 10 or less sports. South Korea is the only exception to this point, where a 50% of the funding is allocated to 14 sports. The number of sports that receive 75% of total funding allocation rises to 27 in South Korea, 24 in Switzerland, and 20 in both Spain and France. These countries can be seen as having the most diverse approach to resource allocation. On the other side of the spectrum, this number drops to less than or equal to 12 sports in six nations: Denmark, Flanders, Australia, Wallonia, Portugal and Estonia. A methodological conundrum arises here as some countries cluster sports differently. For example, while the sport of 'aquatics' is seen by the International Olympic Committee and the SPLISS study as only one sport, in practice it is comprised of four disciplines, namely swimming, diving, synchronised swimming and water polo. In Australia each of these disciplines are all separate, independent NGBs. Furthermore, although only two winter sports receive direct funding the Olympic Winter Institute in Australia manages most of Australia's elite winter sport programmes (e.g., aerial skiing, alpine skiing, curling, figure skating, mogul skiing, ski cross, snowboarding, short track speed skating and skeleton). These issues mean that it is difficult to define what a sport actually is when trying to analyse prioritisation and diversification of funding.

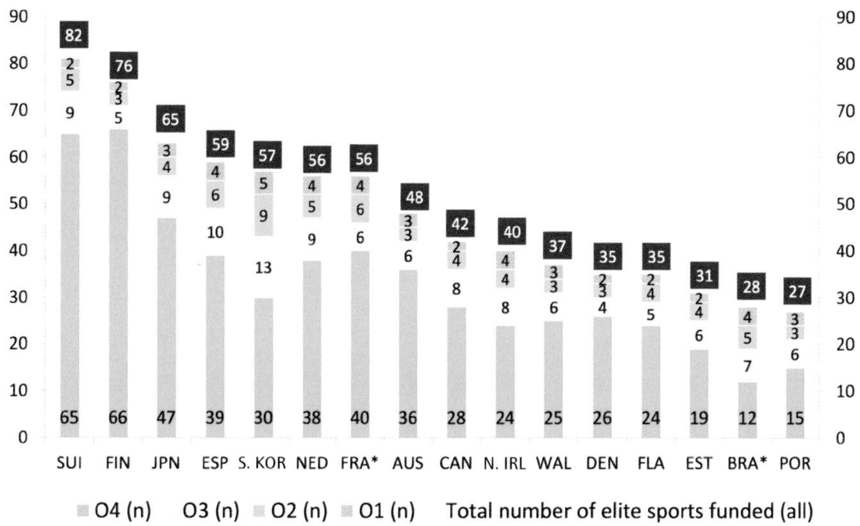

Figure 26: Number of sports funded in four quartiles (25% of the funding in each quartile) (all sports: Olympic summer, winter and non-Olympic sports; excluding Paralympics)

Note: The figure uses the IOC classification for Olympic sports; for example, skiing is identified as one sport (including snowboard, ski jumping, alpine skiing, freestyle skiing, Nordic combined, cross-country skiing); Brazil and Spain fund 'snow sports and ice sports', seen as two different sports in the figures; in Australia, swimming, diving, sync swimming and water polo are all separate, independent NGBs. In Japan, the data include government funding to NGBs through JOC and the amount of subsidy from lottery and 'Sport Promotion Fund' for elite sport purposes.

6.3.7.2 Concentration ratios

An alternative way of looking at prioritisation strategies is to consider concentration ratios CR4 and CR8.[21] In economic research, concentration ratios are usually used to show the extent of market control of the largest firms in the industry and to illustrate the degree to which an industry is oligopolistic. Following traditional industrial economics, it is most common to focus on the market shares of the four and eight largest firms/countries, or in this case 'sports' (or market leaders) (Clarke and Davies, 1983; Deutsch and Silber, 1995). For our purposes, the concentration ratio CR4 signifies market share of the four best funded sports where the lower the concentration ratio reflects a more modest concentration of funding. When the maximum value equals 1 (or expressed as a percentage, 100%), it means that all funding goes to four sports (De Bosscher, Du Bois and Heyndels, 2011). Similar calculations are made for CR8, which is the share of funding to eight sports. The results are presented in Figure 27.

In most countries, more than 30% of the funding goes to (less than) four sports and 50% to less than eight sports

Our results show that all nations prioritise except France and South Korea, as more than 50% of total elite sports funding is invested in eight sports or less, and for half of the nations 40% of the funding goes to four sports or less.

Australia, Denmark, Estonia and Belgium (both Flanders and Wallonia) have the most prioritised funding strategies, and South Korea and France, along with the Brazil, Spain and Netherlands have the most diverse approach to funding distribution. Note that despite the strong focus on only funding Olympic sports in Brazil, the country still applies a diverse funding model. Denmark is a good example (50% of the funding goes to (less than) eight sports) illustrating a move towards increased prioritisation, following a change of strategy by Team Denmark (TD) resulting from the performance contract they had signed with the Ministry of Culture in 2006. There was a reduction of NGB funding following the period 2001-2004, when 16 NGBs lost their financial support from TD and in the 2005-2008 period a further 17 NGBs; 16 other NGBs received more support than they did before. This continued in the preparation for the London Olympic Games (Storm, 2012).

It is important to note here, that we have calculated concentration ratios based on the total number of sports that receive funding. In some countries such as Australia this is a significantly higher number of sports (50) than others; for example, only 27 sports receive funding in Brazil. In a way it could be argued that this represents an early prioritisation decision. However, as we are mainly interested in determining prioritisation in the context of limited resources, we have excluded those sports that have not received any funding.

---

21 The scoring is based on these CR4 and CR8 figures.

Countries that target their funding towards fewer sports are not more successful

The key question underlying the existence of prioritisation funding strategies is whether or not the focus of funding provided leads to more success. Although our initial dataset remains rudimentary, acknowledging a time lag effect and only one funding data point (2010 funding related to 2009-2012 success measurement) the data does provide first insights into the effects of prioritisation of funding on outputs. As noted by Oakley and Green (2001), one would expect that nations that are more successful adopt a priority approach over a diversity approach.

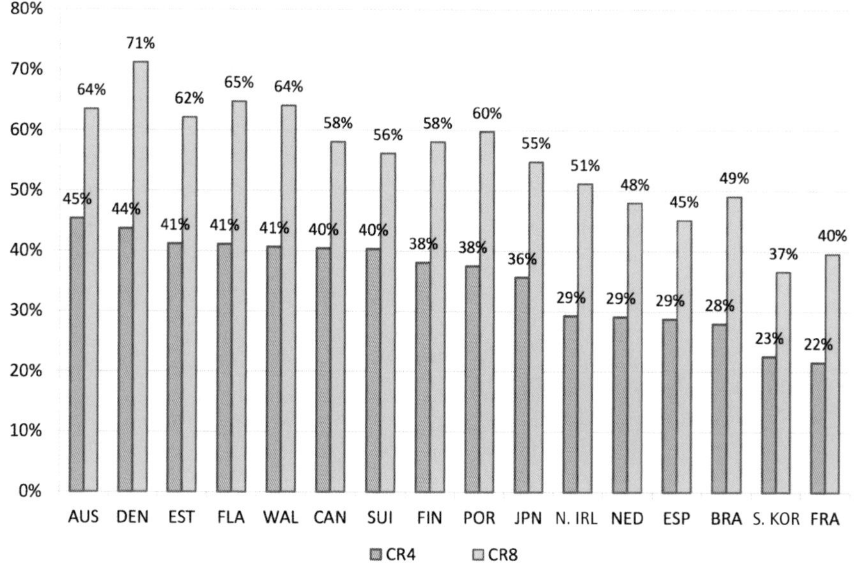

Figure 27: Concentration ratios CR4 and CR8 of the sports funded in the sample nations (2010) (excluding Paralympics)

However, based on concentration ratios, the results revealed a slight trend that countries that prioritise more tend to be less successful. The correlation between the scores on CSF 2.18 and the market share figures from 2009-2012, is negative but not significant for either summer or winter sports ($r_s = -.459$, $\rho = 0.073$ for summer sports and $r_s = -.253$, $\rho = 0.345$). This means that we cannot (dis)confirm that nations that target their funding more, win more or less medals at the Olympic Games and world championships. What we can conclude is that nations with a more diverse funding approach are also successful. Australia and France exemplify these findings; as the two most successful countries of the sample they also are on opposite ends of the concentration ratio spectrum–Australia is the country that targets the most and France the least. This is also illustrated in the scatter plots in figure 28. South Korea, Brazil, the Netherlands and Spain are all countries with a diverse funding model which performs relatively well. In winter sports, Canada was the most successful country with no explicit evidence of adopting either a prioritisation or diversification strategy .

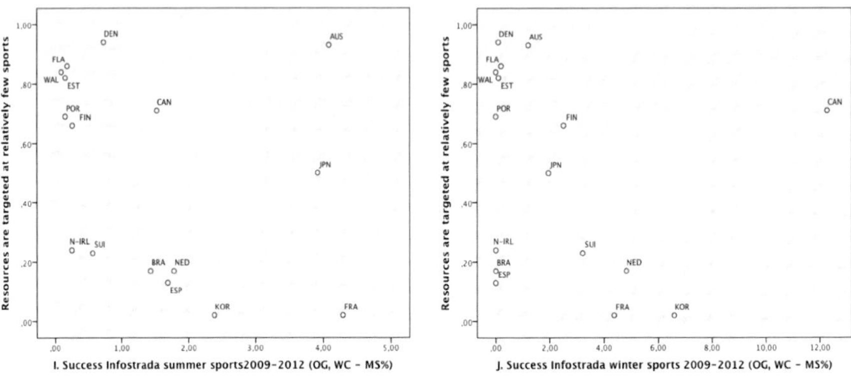

Figure 28: Scatter plots of nations that target their resources at a few number of sports against the outputs (market shares 2009-2012) in summer sports (left) and winter sports (right)

There is a pattern that countries that target their funding to a wide number of sports, win medals in more sports

Finally, a quite logical outcome is that nations that invest a minimum amount of funding in many sports, will win medals in more sports than those nations that invest in fewer. Table 29 provides an overview of the number of disciplines nations won medals in at world championships and Olympic Games from 2009-2012. CN 75% (concentration number) represents the number of sports in which 75% of all funding is invested. For example, in Switzerland, 75% of the funding allocation is invested in 24 sports. There is some evidence that nations that spread their funding most widely (a higher CN75), win medals in more sports. This correlation is positive but not significant ($r_s = .403$, $\rho = 0.123$ for summer sports and $r_s = -.293$, $\rho = 0.271$). CN75 is the highest in Switzerland, France, South Korea and Spain. Switzerland and France also won medals in the highest number of sports disciplines. On the other hand Canada won medals in 29 different sports, while 75% of the funding is invested in just 14 sports. Also the Netherlands has shown a diverse approach to elite sports funding, but has won medals in only 16 sports. We would argue that there is no clear evidence that either prioritisation or diversification of funding leads to more success in elite sport.

Table 29: Number of sports the country won medals in from 2009-2012 in summer and winter Olympic sports, at Olympic Games and world championships and the number of sports that receive 75% of the funding (CN75%)

	SUI	FRA	CAN	JPN	ESP	AUS	S. KOR	NED	FIN	DEN	BRA	FLA	EST	WAL	POR
Total number of disciplines medalled in	39	32	29	25	19	18	17	16	13	10	10	6	5	4	3
Number of SUMMER sports	9	25	17	18	19	16	14	13	5	9	10	5	4	4	3
Number of WINTER sports	30	7	12	7	0	2	3	3	8	1	0	1	1	0	0
CN75%	24	20	14	16	20	11	27	18	14	10	16	11	12	12	12

Note: No output data available from Northern Ireland.

In conclusion, for the countries in our relatively small SPLISS sample, it can be assumed that funding strategies are more dependent on the specific national context and systems rather than based on a generic success principle that favors prioritisation over diversification.

6.4 Summary points in Pillar 2

There is a strong relationship between Pillar 1 and 2, but no generic blueprint

While this section has identified that there is a strong positive relationship between Pillar 1 (financial inputs) and Pillar 2 (governance, organisation and structure of elite sport policies), it is also clear that there is no generic blueprint that can be transferred into any national context with the guarantee of delivering success. There is evidence that comparable outcomes are being achieved by the use of different methods in different nations. None of these are necessarily right or wrong, and it is simply a case of finding a set of ingredients that work effectively in a given context. Factors that are specific to nations such as geography, cultural context and path dependency, ensure that the underpinning concepts are contingency theory and localisation.

The most appropriate role for governments is one of enabling rather than delivering

One noticeable pattern that is apparent is that despite the level of funding provided by governments and other public sources such as national lotteries, the most appropriate role for governments is one of enabling rather than delivering. Sport is a highly specialised and dynamic environment that does not lend itself well to bureaucracy. The compromise approach is for governments to provide funding but with strings attached in the form of agreed objectives and outputs that must be achieved to maintain the relationship. In this respect modernised national governing bodies with a proven track record of delivery and positive future prospects operate within an environment of 'earned autonomy' in which there is an implicit understanding of the notions of sanction and reward.

There are some outline ingredients that effective elite sport policies seem to have

There are elements of elite sport development systems that are positively associated with success, but we have not found what might be regarded as the causal factors of success. At various points we find situations where some nations seem to prove a particular point and others contradict it. These are not disappointing findings, but merely a recognition that results can be achieved in different ways and that social science research exists within the fluctuating whims of real life. There are, however, some outline ingredients that effective elite sport policies seem to have and the more successful nations seem to be able to tick more of the boxes than unsuccessful nations. These include:

- Sufficient funding for the management of elite sport
- Nationally co-ordinated and clear strategy
- Simplicity of governance and communication between strategic bodies
- Governments as enablers and sports professionals as deliverers
- Clear performance targets and accountability via sanction and reward
- A focus on outputs and outcomes (producing medals and Olympians) rather than process (producing good Pillar scores)
- Planning horizons that are long-term, consistent with Olympic cycles
- Involvement of key stakeholders in the process
- The recruitment of professionals to provide leadership at national level and the realisation that there is a global market for the best talent
- Suitably modernised NGBs that are fit for purpose
- Co-operation with the private sector as an integral part of policy delivery
- Allocation of funding to where it is most likely to make a difference regardless of whether this is through a priority or diversity approach
- Realisation that the only way to maintain current performance or indeed to improve is through commitment to continuous improvement in all aspects of the system
- Long-term sustainability lies in the ability of a system to innovate in order to achieve competitive advantage rather than imitating what others are already doing

Chapter 6 references

Andersen, S. and Tore Ronglan, L. (2012). *Nordic Elite Sport. Same ambitions, different tracks.* Norway: AIT Otta AS.

Bergsgard, N. A., Houlihan, B., Mangset, P., Nødland, S. I. and Rommetvedt, H. (2007). *Sport Policy: A comparative analysis of stability and change.* London, UK: Elsevier.

Bayle, E. and Robinson, L. (2007). A framework for understanding the performance of national governing bodies of sport. *European Sport Management Quarterly, 7* (3). 249-268. doi: 10.1080/16184740701511037

Brouwers, J., Sotiriadou, P. and De Bosscher, V. (in press). An examination of the sport specific policies and factors that lead to international success: The case of tennis. *Sport Management Review*

Clarke, R. and Davies, S. W. (1983). Aggregate Concentration, Market Concentration and Diversification. *The Economic Journal, 93* (369), 182-192. doi: 10.2307/2232172

Clumpner, R. A. (1994). 21st century success in international competition. In *Sport in the global village* (pp.298-303). R. Wilcox (Ed.). Morgantown, WV: Fitness Information Technology.

De Bosscher, V. (2007). *Sports policy factors leading to international sporting success.* Published doctoral thesis. Brussels: VUBPRESS.

De Bosscher, V., Bingham, J., Shibli, S., van Bottenburg, M. and De Knop, P. (2008). *The global sporting arms race. An international comparative study on sports policy factors leading to international sporting success.* Aachen: Meyer & Meyer.

De Bosscher, V. & De Croock, S. (2012). Trends in het Vlaams topsportklimaat. Evaluatie volgens topsporters, trainers en topsportcoördinatoren: 2-meting (2003-2007-2011) [Trends in the elite sport climate in Flanders. Evaluation according to elite athletes, coaches and high performance directors]. Brussel: VUB. ISBN: 9789090272788

De Bosscher, V., Du Bois, C. and Heyndels, B. (2011). Internationalization, competitiveness and performance in athletics (1984–2006). *Sport in Society, 15* (1), 88-102. doi: 10.1080/03031853.2011.625280

Deutsch, J. and Silber, J. (1995). Static versus Dynamic Measures of Aggregate Concentration: The Case of Fortune's 500. *Southern Economic Journal, 62* (1), 192-209. doi: 10.2307/1061385

Digel, H., Burk, V. and Fahrner, M. (2006). High-performance sport. An international comparison. *Edition Sports International, 9.* Weilheim/Teck, Tubingen, DE: Bräuer.

Dooms (2010). Crafting the integrative value proposition for large scale transport infrastructure hubs: a stakeholder management approach. Brussels: VUBPRESS

Ferkins, L., Shilbury, D. and McDonald, G (2005). The role of the board in building strategic capability: Towards an integrated model of sport governance research. *Sport Management Review, 8* (3), 195-225.

Freeman, R. (1984). *Strategic Management: A stakeholder Approach.* Boston, MA: Pitman.

Freeman, R. (2006). The Wal-Mart effect and business, ethics and society. *Academy of Management Perspectives, 20* (3), 38-40.

Goodwin, JM. and Grix, J. (2011). Bringing structures back in: the governance narrative, the decentred approach and asymmetrical network governance in the education and sport policy communities. *Public Administration, 89* (2), 537-556.

Green, M. (2009). Podium or participation? Analysing policy priorities under changing modes of sport governance in the United Kingdom. *International Journal of Sport Policy*, 121-144.

Green, M. and Houlihan, B. (2005). *Elite sport development. Policy learning and political priorities.* London and New York: Routledge.

Houlihan, B. (2009). Mechanisms of international influence on domestic elite sport policy. *International Journal of Sport Policy and Politics, 1* (1), 51-69. doi: 10.1080/19406940902739090

Houlihan, B. and Green, M (2008). *Comparative elite sport development. Systems, structures and public policy.* London: Elsevier.

Houlihan, B., Bloyce, D. and Smith, A. (2009). Developing the research agenda in sport policy. *International Journal of Sport Policy,* 1-12.

Mintzberg, H. (1994). *Organisatiestructuren [Organisational structures].* Schoonhoven: Academic Service.

Oakley B. and Green, M. (2001). The production of Olympic champions: International perspectives on elite sport development system. *European Journal for Sport Management, 8*, 83-105.

Sotiriadou, P. and De Bosscher, V. (2013). Elite sport culture and policy interrelationships: The case of Sprint Canoe in Australia. *Leisure Studies, 32*, 6. http://dx.doi.org/10.1080/02614367.2013.833973. ISSN 0261-4367

Storm (2012) Danish elite sport and Team Denmark: new trends? In *Nordic Elite Sport. Same ambitions, different tracks.* S. Andersen and L. Tore Ronglan (Eds).Norway: AIT Otta AS.

Taylor, M. and O'Sullivan, N. (2009). How should national governing bodies of sport be governed in the UK? An exploratory study of board structure. Corporate Governance: *An International Review, 17* (6), 681-693. doi: 10.1111/j.1467-8683.2009.00767.

Thibault, L. and Babiak, K. (2005). Organizational changes in Canada's sport system: Toward an athlete-centred approach. *European Sport Management Quarterly, 5*, 105-122.

Thibault, L., Kihlb, L. K. and Babiak, K. (2010). Democratisation and governance in international sport: addressing issues with athlete involvement in organisational policy. *International Journal of Sport Policy, 2* (3), 275–302.

Truyens, J., De Bosscher, V., Heyndels, B. and Westerbeek, H. (2013). A Resource-Based Perspective on Countries' Competitive Advantage in Elite Athletics. *International Journal of Sport policy and Politics.* http://dx.doi.org/10.1080/19406940.2013.839954. ISSN: 1940-6940

Walters, G. (2011). The implementation of a stakeholder management strategy during stadium development: a case study of Arsenal Football club and the Emrates Stadium. *Managing Leisure* (16), 49-64.

Westerbeek, H., & Hahn, H. (2013). The influence of commercialisation and globalisation on high performance sport. In *Managing High Performance Sport* (pp. 239-255). P. Sotiriadou and V. De Bosscher (Eds). London: Routledge.

Appendix 1: Overview of NGB funding criteria for each country

COUNTRY	Subsidisation framework for NGBs	Priority
AUSTRALIA	The ASC reviews all recognised NSOs (funded and unfunded) as part of the **Annual Sport Performance Review** which is based on the priorities outlined in the National Sport and Active Recreation Policy Framework (NSARPF). • Six key principles underpin the funding of all NSOs. • Six key stages to determine NSO funding (grassroots and high performance funding).	Australia is currently evaluating its method for categorising and funding elite sports. While not finalised, it's likely funding priorities will focus on specific disciplines/events and HP investment will be allocated in three broad categories to reflect: • Sports where Australia has traditionally won medals or championships • Sports where Australia has proven some ability to win, but inconsistently • Sports where Australia has growing success or new opportunities
BRAZIL	In 2009, general criteria were established by the NOC for NGB funding, mainly based on the technical results during the OS cycle, the structural development of the sport and its popularity (COB, 2010).	No formal priority.
CANADA	The **Sport Funding and Accountability Framework (SFAF)** is the tool used by Canadian Heritage to identify which organisations are eligible to receive Sport Canada contributions under the Sport Support Programme (in what areas, at what level and under what conditions). The SFAF has been divided to follow the Summer and Winter Olympic Cycles. There are four stages in the SFAF process: Eligibility, Assessment, Funding and Accountability.	Based on the assessment score, NGBs receive a certain amount of funding (60% based on the Excellence programme, for 40% reflecting sport participation and development issues). Additionally, initiatives such as **'Own the Podium'** allocated additional funding based on past success and popularity (ice hockey and track speed skating).
DENMARK	NGBs are categorised in three different groups for elite sport funding: **elite NGBs, individual NGBs and development projects.** The amount of athletes performing at an international level is the decisive determinator.	Yes, based on the categorisations of NGBs (elite, individual or development projects) and the categorisation of elite athletes (world class, elite or Team Denmark).
FINLAND	Governmental support for NGBs is based on the evaluation of quality and scale of actions. The total amount of subsidies is directed to NGBs based on percentage scores for specific purposes: 50% based on results in children and youth sports, 25% based on their results in adult recreational sports and 25% based on their results in elite sport. Additionally, the NOC provides structural support to successful sports described as 'system support', based on 11 criteria.	Success (and the actions to achieve success) are the main criteria for governmental and NOC support for NGBs elite funding. The NOC redirects subsidies to NGBs for elite sport purposes. This support is called the system support (see Pillar 1, question 20). Even though the system support is directed to NGBs it is allocated to improve coaching of specific elite athletes who have real chances to succeed in international competitions.

Based on performance?	Based on popularity?	Based on management structure?
Yes, but not in formula-based approach. Sporting Excellence (i.e., performance at senior benchmark events), sporting relevance (sport participation figures in Australia) and sporting effectiveness (i.e., governance, management and financial viability of the NSO).	Yes, as the sporting relevance is measured (the sport participation figures in Australia)	Yes, as the sporting effectiveness is measured (the governance, management and financial viability of the NSO)
Yes, funding for NGBs is based on results during the Olympic cycle (technical level, South American, Pan American, world championships, and Olympics).	Yes, the level of funding refers to the number of athletes enrolled or registered officially.	Yes, the level of funding refers to technical infrastructure and administration for sport development.
Yes, performance is part of the assessment in the SFAF. Performance at the three last Olympic Games (2000-2008) and world championships count for 40% of the total assessment.	Yes, within the SFAF framework, there are different characteristics which determine a percentage score in the assessment weighting grid: membership (10%), sport participation (5%).	Yes, within the SFAF framework, 20% of the score is determined by the high-performance system of the NSO.
Yes. In order to receive funding, NGBs must meet performance criteria as stipulated in a yearly contract with Team Denmark.	No.	Yes, as a part of the annual overall evaluation.
Success in international competition is used as a criterion for evaluating elite sport results.	Yes, it takes into account • Quantity of member clubs, • Quantity of individual members in member clubs, • Regular participants that take part in actions of governing bodies, • Quantity of campaigns, programmes and events, • Quantity of paid staff in clubs.	A qualitative evaluation is made of • the organisational actions, • the educational system • the practice and coaching system and • the competition system and sport events.

COUNTRY	Subsidisation framework for NGBs	Priority
FLANDERS	NGBs are categorised based on four different criteria to be subsidised for elite funding: • The elite sport structure within the NGB • International performances of elite athletes and promising youth • National exposure of the sport • International exposure of the sport	For each Olympiad, there is a list of recognised and subsidised elite sports. In the period 2009-2012, there are 26 sports, subdivided into four different categories with a maximum level of financial support for each category.
FRANCE	All NGB's are funded no matter if there are formal objectives of elite sports. A contract is signed between the ministry and the NGB about formal, and specific objectives in order to have subsidies. But there is a general system of recognition for high-performance sport.	–
JAPAN	Member organisations of the Japan Sport Associations are subsidised for grassroots-level sport based on the rules determined by the NAASH. For elite sport, member organisations of JOC are subsidised based on the evaluation of performance and performance enhancement strategy plan.	All NGBs receive performance-enhancement funding. However to get more funding NGBs have to achieve excellent competition results in Olympics, world championship and Asian Games (continental competition). Performance is affected to 70% of the evaluation of NGBs rank. (30%: TID system, coach development, information strategy, medical, science activity, etc).
SOUTH KOREA	A sport is recognised as elite sport and subsidised if the sport has a NGB recognised by KSC/KOC. There are written criteria to be recognised as NGB.	For the 42 sports that are included Olympic or Asian Games, summer sports are categorised according to three levels of performance: (a) core sport, (b) strategic sport, and (c) general sport.
PORTUGAL	For both grassroots and elite sport funding, an analysis is made of the Plan of Activities. For the Olympic Preparation Programme (only supporting the very best athletes) the sport is subsidised based on international results (medals, finalists, semi-finalists and selected athletes for the OG).	No.
SPAIN	For elite sport funding, Olympic Sports receive funding from the NOC in the 'ADO Programme', based on three main dimensions regarding sporting excellence: • Aid to athletes with Olympic chance to get results of interest. • Incentives to technicians responsible for the preparation of athletes. • The development of special plans to improve the preparation of athletes within the programme.	No.

Based on performance?	Based on popularity?	Based on management structure?
Yes. There are specific performance criteria for individual (Olympic/non-Olympic) and Olympic team sports.	Yes, although the objective criteria to measure the national exposure of a sport are not clear.	Yes.
Yes.	–	Yes.
Yes, the NGBs' funding depends for 70% on the performances of athletes during the last two years at various competitions.	No.	Yes, 30% of the evaluation is based on the elite sport system of NGBs (long-term development, coach development, international competency, anti-doping, training base, information strategy, medical, science and co-operation with JOC).
Yes.	No.	No.
Yes, depending on results at the last Olympic Games and present Olympiad.	No.	No.
Yes, participation at international competitions (Olympics, world or European championships) is required.	No.	No.

COUNTRY	Subsidisation framework for NGBs	Priority
NETHERLANDS	Elite sport disciplines are recognised if (in summary) they are Olympic and/or there exits a world championship in which a minimum number of countries participate (minimum competitive level). If a world championship does not exsits, comparable events can be chosen, where a global top eight position is required. The policy in the years to come (2013-2016) will be as follows. The total amount of funding for the NGBs' elite sport programmes will depend on four criteria: (1) The number of countries participating at the world championship in the sport discipline concerned; (2) The scale of the national training programme in the sport discipline concerned; (3) The achievements in the sport discipline concerned; (4) The commitment of the NGB, i.e., at least 30% of the overall costs of the sport discipline's trainings programme funded by NGBs' own means.	Currently (2009-2012), there is a segmentation between all NGBs regarding their potential to develop international success, based on a one to three star ranking. Later on (2013-1016) priority will be given to 8-10 successful sports.
SWITZERLAND	The different criateria for NGBs to be funded by the SOA include the popularity of the sport, the establishment of the NGB, the objectives, management and membership; these criteria concern grassroots funding mainly. With regard to elite sport, the sport-specific ranking (from 1-5) is the most important criterion. This ranking is related to the NGBs' global budget for elite sport.	Ranking in five categories
WALLONIA	There are some general criteria for NGBS to recognised and to receive elite-level support.	–

Based on performance?	Based on popularity?	Based on management structure?
Yes.	Yes.	Yes.
Yes.	No, not for elite sport.	Yes (as for grassroots sport).
Not officially, but it is requested that athletes of NGBs perform at world top 8-12 levels and European top 6-8.	No. However, big and Olympic federations receive more funding.	Yes, the quality of the strategic plan and professional development of the sport is taken into account.

Appendix 2: Overview of NGB funding for each country

COUNTRY	Total NGBs' COUNTRY directly funded (elite sport)	Total elite sport funding NGBs only	Elite sports programmes funded*	Total funding for elite sport disciplines (NGBs or clubs)
AUSTRALIA	50	€ 60.9	35	€ 84.2
BRAZIL	28	€ 23.4	–	€ 23.4
CANADA	42	€ 64.5	–	€ 64.5
	(Note: An estimation of € 186m is made when including state funding to NGBs.)			
DENMARK	35/33	€ 11.6	35	€ 11.6
	(Note: 33 NGBs receive direct funding; the NGBs do not receive funding for from DIF solely for the purpose of developing elite sport; however the funding NGBs receive from Team Denmark is specifically targeted to elite sport; the € 11.6m is only Team Denmark funding for elite sport.)			
FINLAND	74*	€ 8.7	46	€ 9.8
	(Note: The ministry finances basically all NGBs for elite sport purposes (and many non-Olympic sports receive a small funding amount). However, there are approximately 23 NGBs with quite low level of investment.)			

I. TOTAL funding 2010 summer + winter + non-Olympic sports		II. Olympic summer sports only (+ rugby/golf)	III. Olympic winter sports only	IV. Non-Olympic sports
(a) Top 4 and top 8 sports	(c) Total funding top 4/top 8 sports (d) CR4/CR8 (*)	TOTAL funding % of the total funding	TOTAL funding % of the total funding	(a) Total funding 2012 (n) % non- Olympic sports of total
1. Aquatics 2. Cycling 3. Rowing 4. Football 5. Athletics 6. Ice hockey 7. Sailing 8. Basketball	Top 4: t 33.0 CR4: 47.3% Top 8: € 55.8 CR8: 66.25%	€ 77.4 (n=27) 91.9%	€ 0.83 (n=2) 2.7%	€ 6.0 (n=6) 7.1%
1. Athletics 2. Gymnastics 3. Sailing 4. Judo 5. Aquatics 6. Handball 7. Volleyball 8. Canoe	Top 4: € 6.6 CR4: 28.0% Top 8: € 11.5 CR8: 49.1%	€ 22.8 (n=25) 97.3%	€ 0.63 (2*) 2,7% (*snow and ice sports)	€ 0 0% (Rugby, Olympic in 2016 included in summer sports)
1. Aquatics 2. Skiing 3. Skating 4. Rowing 5. Athletics 6. Basketball 7. Canoe 8. Ice hockey	Top 4: € 26.0 CR4: 41.8% Top 8: € 37.5 CR8: 60.1%	€ 42.1 (n=27) 65.3%	€ 20.2 (n=6) 31.3%	€ 0.22 (n=9) 3.3%
1. Handball 2. Rowing 3. Football 4. Sailling 5. Badminton 6. Aquatics 7. Ice hockey 8. Cycling	Top 4: € 5.0 CR4: 43.71% Top 8: € 8.1 CR8: 71.22%	€ 9.5 (n=23) 83.5%	€ 0.92 (n=3) 8.9%	€ 0.96 (n=9) 8.1%
1. Skiing 2. Athletics 3. Ice hockey 4. Football 5. Shooting 6. Gymnastics 7. Volleyball 8. Skating	Top 4: € 3,7 CR4: 38.08% Top 8: € 5,7 CR8: 58.07%	€ 7.3 (n=30) 74.3%	€ 1.1 (n=5+2 (non olympic)) 14.5%	€ 1.4 (n=41) 14.1%

COUNTRY	Total NGBs' COUNTRY directly funded (elite sport)	Total elite sport funding NGBs only	Elite sports programmes funded*	Total funding for elite sport disciplines (NGBs or clubs)
FLANDERS*	26	€ 13.4	35	€ 18.2
FRANCE	58	€ 76.8	88	€ 68.7
	(Note: 55 Olympic, 33 non-Olympic; furthermore, there are 22 Paralympic disciplines.)			
JAPAN	63	€ 30.8	13* *multi-support project: not a direct funding to NGBs to support	€ 47.8 *this includes € 17m for the multi-support project
NORTHERN IRELAND	28	€ 3.1	40	€ 4.2
PORTUGAL	28	€ 8.3	24	€ 12.7

(a) Top 4 and top 8 sports	(c) Total funding top 4/top 8 sports (d) CR4/CR8 (*)	TOTAL funding % of the total funding	TOTAL funding % of the total funding	(a) Total funding 2012 (n) % non- Olympic sports of total
1. Cycling 2. Athletics 3. Football 4. Gymnastics 5. Aquatics 6. Volleyball 7. Judo 8. Tennis	Incl. lottery/ excl. lottery (Bloso+CJSM) Top 4: € 7.5/€ 6.8 CR4: 41.1%/37.1 Top 8: € 11.8/€	€ 10,9 (n=22) 96,1%	€ 0,38 (n=3) 3,4%	€ 0,065 (n=4) 0,6%
	(FLA: As national lotteries are federal, the figures include (only) lottery money for the Flemish community [only subsidies, no sponsorship; however, it is discussable to what extent the lotery money is part of policy outcomes].)			
1. Skiing* 2. Athletics 3. Handball 4. Aquatics 5. Cycling 6. Sailing 7. Judo 8. Canoe	Top 4: € 16.6 CR4: 21.6% Top 8: € 30.4 CR8: 39.6	€ 61.1 (n=28) 79.5%	€ 7.6 (n=3) 9.8%	€ 8.1 (n=25) 10.8%
1. Judo 2. Football 3. Aquatics 4. Athletics 5. Skating 6. Wrestling 7. Gymnastics 8. Skiing	Top 4: € 10.4 CR4: 35.8% Top 8: € 16.0 CR8: 55.0%	€ 25.0 (n=30) 81.3%	€ 3.9 (n=7) 12.6%	€ 1.9 (n=28) 6.2%
1. Hockey 2. Football 3. Rugby 4. Sailing 5. Cycling 6. Aquatics 7. Canoe 8. Athletics	Top 4: € 1,2 CR4: 37.1% Top 8: € 1,8 CR8: 63.2%	€ 2.9 (n=24) 63.7%	€ 0.6 (n=2) 1.3%	€ 1.6 (n=14) 34.9%
1. Athletics 2. Judo 3. Handball 4. Basketball 5. Aquatics 6. Volleyball 7. Football 8. Canoe	Top 4: € 4,4 CR4: 37.5% Top 8: € 7,0 CR8: 59.8%	€ 11.2 (n=24) 95.5%	€ 0 0%	€ 0.527 (n=3) 4.5%

COUNTRY	Total NGBs' COUNTRY directly funded (elite sport)	Total elite sport funding NGBs only	Elite sports programmes funded*	Total funding for elite sport disciplines (NGBs or clubs)
SPAIN	64	€ 76.5	NA	€ 86.6
NETHERLANDS	56	€ 29.0	140	€ 28.8
SWITZERLAND	82	€ 16.1	–	€ 22.0
	(Note: 82 NGBs are priorised from 1-5 and funded. The prioritised 1-3 receive a total of € 13.0m; the remaining part goes to the NGBs ranked 4 and 5.)			
WALLONIA	45	€ 7.9	25	€ 8.6 45
	(Note: 45 are eligible; in 2010, not all received funding for elite sport activities (e.g., boxing and wrestling.)			

(a) Top 4 and top 8 sports	(c) Total funding top 4/top 8 sports (d) CR4/CR8 (*)	TOTAL funding % of the total funding	TOTAL funding % of the total funding	(a) Total funding 2012 (n) % non- Olympic sports of total
1. Athletics 2. Basketball 3. Aquatics 4. Canoe 5. Sailing 6. Cycling 7. Handball 8. Football	Top 4: € 24.9 CR4: 28.7% Top 8: € 39.1 CR8: 45.1%	€ 71.2 (n=29) 82.5%	€ 4.0 (n=2*) 4.7% *snowsports and ice sports	€ 11.4 (n=28) 13.1%
1. Aquatics 2. Cycling 3. Volleybal 4. Sailing 5. Rowing 6. Athletics 7. Judo 8. Equestrian	Top 4: € 8.43 CR4: 29.1% Top 8: € 13.99 CR8: 48.0%	26.47 (n=29)	€ 2.22	€ 3.27
1. Skiing (6 dsc) 2. Gymnastics (3 dsc) 3. Aquatics 4. Ice hockey 5. Tennis 6. Cycling (4 dsc) 7. Athletics 8. Volleyball	Top 4: € 6.5 CR4: 40.0% Top 8: € 9.0 CR8: 56.1%	€ 8.5 (n=27) 53.3%	€ 5.30 (n=7) 32.9%	€ 2.22 (n=45) 13.8%
1. Tennis 2. Athletics 3. Rugby 4. Basketball 5. Table tennis 6. Judo 7. Aquatics 8. Gymnastics	Top 4: € 3.0 CR4: 40.7% Top 8: € 4,7 CR8: 67.1%	€ 6.6 (n=23) 90.3%	€ 0.10 (n=2) 1.4%	€ 0.60 (n=16) 8.3%

Joma
ESP
Divina
Pastora
SPAR

7 Pillar 3: Sport participation

7.1 Concepts and definition

It is often argued that elite sport policy and grassroots sport policy are complementary in the quest for elite sport success. This link, however, is not that apparent in most countries. In Pillar 3, the main question is to establish the extent to which national sport participation and physical education policies contribute to the nation's elite sporting success.

It has often been argued in the past that building a broad-based pyramid of participation is crucial for creating a successful elite sports programme. This pyramid assumption is debatable. From a top-down perspective, the evidence of a relationship between elite sport success and mass participation, often called the trickle-down effect, is fragmented, and previous studies have mostly failed to demonstrate any connection between the two variables (De Bosscher, Sotiriadou and van Bottenburg, 2013; Hanstad and Skille 2010; Veal and Frawley 2009; Weed, 2009; Feddersen, Jacobsen, and Maennig, 2009; Sotiriadou, Shilbury and Quick, 2008; van Bottenburg, 2002). A recent study (De Bosscher et al., 2013) revealed that there is no consistent relationship between membership levels in sport clubs and sporting success across 20 sports in Flanders and the Netherlands. However there does appear to be sport-specific trends and other variables on which this relationship depends, such as media attention and the quality of management of the NGB in regard to its success and its role models.

Although a direct impact of sport for all on elite sport is hard to determine, most elite athletes have their roots in sport for all (van Bottenburg, 2002). We can hypothesise, therefore, that a broad sport participation base is neither a necessary nor sufficient condition for success, but that it may influence success to some extent because of the continuous supply of young talent and the filtration of talent to progressively higher levels of performance.

Sports participation is evaluated at three levels: (a) sport opportunities at school, (b) sport participation rates and (c) management to improve quality

Comparing sport participation internationally is a tremendously difficult task, because of the different standards of defining sport and determining frequency and intensity (Gratton, Rowe and Veal, 2011). Most of Pillar 3 should be evaluated at a sport-by-sport level. To test if sport participation policy—at a national level—has had an impact on elite sport success in our sample nations we narrowed our focus down to three levels of analysis.

- Children have opportunities to participate in sports at school, during physical education (PE) or extra-curricular activities.
- There is a high general level of participation in sport within the country; and
- There is a national policy towards promoting the implementation of the principles of (total) quality management in sport clubs, at the level of mass participation and talent development.

These three levels are the subtotals of the scores for 10 different critical success factors (CSFs) (and 28 sub-factors), that are measured with the inventory only. There are no questions about Pillar 3 in the surveys of athletes, coaches and performance directors and as such there is no score for Estonia.

7.2 Key findings

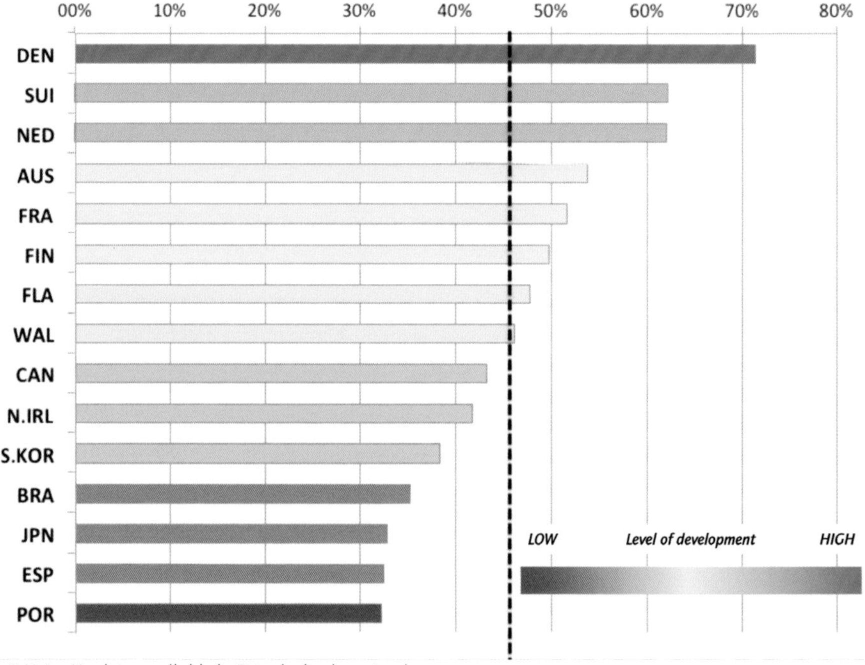

Figure 29: Total scores of the SPLISS sample nations against the 10 CSFs of Pillar 3

When we look at the total scores on Pillar 3 in the participating countries, Figure 29 shows the highest scores for Denmark, Switzerland and the Netherlands. By contrast, Spain, Japan, Wallonia and Brazil have the lowest scores. It is quite striking that the three best scoring countries in Pillar 3, have high general sport participation rates (60-70 %) for people aged 18 and over; a high number of sport club members; and, a reasonably high number of people participating in sport competition. Denmark outperforms other nations with the best scores on these CSFs. The SPLISS study takes the view that–if a link between sport participation and success exists–this occurs mainly through organised sport participation, because most athletes find their roots in sport clubs and through sporting competitions (van Bottenburg, 2002). Therefore, as sport participation rates represent 3 of the 10 critical success factors measured in Pillar 3, their weight on the overall score for Pillar 3 is relatively high.

There is room for improvement for the countries in general, the national policy towards the implementation of quality management in sport clubs and improving the quality of talent development in sport clubs, with only the Netherlands performing well. The surveys revealed that most athletes received dedicated attention as an emerging talent at a relatively late age from their club and national governing bodies. This finding is interesting as most (basic and sport-specific) skills can be accelerated at a young age and (early) quality coaching/education in sport clubs/school may be an important element in the long-term career development of elite athletes.

The countries that perform the best at the Olympic Games and world championships (in summer sports) are typically not the same countries who have the highest scores on Pillar 3. Australia performs well in elite sport but only has average scores at grassroots level. Australia has low scores, the opportunities for children to play sport at school and Japan, as another good performing country in elite sport, scores low on the general participation rate factors (CSF 3.6-3.8).

There is a long way to go from sport practitioner to being an elite athlete; therefore a link between sport participation and success is hard to determine. Nations invest in grassroots sport for other reasons than international sporting success

A correlation between sport participation and elite sport success is hard to find. None of the critical success factors was found to be significant with success in summer and winter sports, and most of them correlate marginally, varying from between −0.2 and +0.2, meaning that the association between Pillar 3 and success is weak.[22] The highest correlation is found in CSF 3.6 ('a high percentage of people who participate in sport') in relation to winter sports success, although it is weak in summer sports and as such hard to conclude that sport participation is positively linked to elite sport success. In contrast with sport participation, the correlation coefficients of success and PE in schools are mostly negative.

---

22 The Spearman's rank correlation of the Pillar scores with success: $r_{s(\text{summer sports})} = .093$, $\rho = 0.742$ and $r_{s(\text{winter sports})} = .267$, $\rho = 0.377$. The correlation of CSF 3.6 is $r_{s(\text{summer sports})} = -.11$, $\rho = 0.974$ and $r_{s(\text{winter sports})} = .519$, $\rho = 0.084$.

The fact that we did not find significant correlations might be a problem of measurement (comparable data) or due to the fact that our sample nations do not differ greatly. For comparability reasons, we used existing sources from the Eurobarometer surveys (EB) and the International Social Survey Programme (ISSP). Ten out of the 15 nations that we compared are European countries with a relatively high sport participation rate. If we had compared nations with huge differences in sport participation, we might have found different results; countries with weak performances in elite sport can score well on Pillar 3 and thus the scores do not depend on the success of nations in elite sport (or vice versa). Logically, the choice of countries to invest in sport for all is independent of any success in high-performance sport.

We can nonetheless conclude from our data that there is at least a strong indication that sport participation and physical education policy is not a crucial factor for increasing the chance of elite sporting success, in the short term. These findings should not come as a surprise. There is a big difference between being physically active in school and being an elite athlete. Talent recognition and development programmes (Pillar 4), the support in being an elite athlete (Pillar 5) and Pillars 6 to 9 have a far more direct and immediate impact on elite sporting success. The link between levels of sport participation and elite sport success is not as direct as is often implied or suggested in sport policy texts.

7.3 Comparative and descriptive analysis

7.3.1 Sport at school, during physical education (PE) and extra-curricular activities

Critical success factors		INVENTORY	SURVEY			
I. Children have opportunities to participate in sport at school, during physical education (PE) or extra curricular activities		O	A	C	PD	
CSF 3.1	There is a sufficiently high weekly average amount of time for PE at school (in minutes per week, at least 100 min.)	X	No survey evaluation exists on Pillar 3			
CSF 3.2	Physical education lessons are delivered by a certified PE teacher in all grades.	X				
CSF 3.3	There are regular extra-curricular (extra mural) school sport competitions at school (at least 2 times/month)	X				
CSF 3.4	There is an organisation/staff responsible for regular organisation and co-ordination of extra-curricular school sport competitions	X				P8
CSF 3.5	School is finished early so that children get opportunities to sport during the day (or sport after school is included in the school curriculum)	X				P4

Source of information: O: overall sport inventory; A: athletes' survey; C: coaches' survey; PD: performance directors' survey; the right column shows where the CSFs are possible on the interface with other Pillars.

Physical education in school

It can be argued that countries where children get more opportunities to practice sport during the day are in a better position to achieve elite success, because in the end, these countries will have a larger pool of talent from which to identify their future elite athletes. An important political and academic discussion in that regard is about the role of physical education (PE) in schools and how often (per week) children get exposed to it. In relation to elite sport, insufficient sport opportunities at school is often blamed when nations are perceived to have underachieved. Development of actual and perceived movement competence, metacognitive skills and the optimum bio-psychosocial balance must be nurtured and deployed effectively within the primary and secondary school system (Collins, Richard, Ford, MacNamara, Toms and Pearce, 2011).

In most countries, PE is made compulsory in the primary education curriculum. There are exceptions in the cases of France, Flanders and Wallonia where it is compulsory in nursery education and in the Netherlands where it only becomes compulsory in secondary education. In Australia, Brazil and Northern Ireland there is no national statutory minimum number of hours of PE at any level of education.

PE is mostly compulsory from primary education. The amount of time for PE is on average 120 minutes (not statutorily determined)

The average amount of time per week for PE is 133 minutes in nursery education (France, Flanders and Wallonia) and around 120 minutes in primary and secondary education. This varies from only 45 minutes in primary education in Portugal (but 135 minutes in secondary education) to 160 minutes in France and 180 minutes in secondary education in South Korea (150 minutes for primary education). In Denmark, there exists a different school system from most other countries, through the public 'Folkeskolen', that cannot be divided into the same levels of education as other countries and which run only until lower secondary education (approximately 15 years of age). After 'Folkeskolen' during the 'Ungdomsuddannelser', time for PE decreases. Minimum guidelines are determined by the Danish Ministry of Culture but each municipality can set its own standards which allows for some degree of freedom at local level.

PE lessons are only taught by certified PE teachers in primary education in four countries (Denmark, Portugal, Spain and Wallonia). In secondary education, it is a legal requirement that PE is taught by appropriately qualified teachers (12 of the 15 countries). In Australia, Brazil and the Netherlands, it is not a legal requirement that qualified PE teachers are employed at any level of education. Only in Wallonia are PE lessons delivered by qualified PE teachers in all grades.

Extracurricular (extra mural) school sport

Most countries have an association responsible for co-ordination of extracurricular sport activities

Extracurricular competitions–both at primary and secondary education level–take place on a regular basis in all countries except for the Netherlands and only partly in South Korea. Consequently, there is a specific association responsible for the organisation and co-ordination of regular extracurricular sport activities in these countries. Countries vary in the way that extracurricular sport is delivered mainly in collaboration with schools, or in collaboration with/or organised by sport clubs and NGBs who take the lead in organising school sport competitions (e.g., Australia, Brazil, Denmark, Japan and Switzerland).

Extra-curricular school competition is largely not a compulsory part of PE teachers' job description

In South Korea there have been extracurricular competitions in some schools, but there was no formal structure of extramural competitions. The government (MCST and MEST) has pushed forward the 'School Sport Clubs Promotion' policy since 2009, as a part of its 'primary and secondary school physical education promotion plan'. It includes registration of school sport clubs at Education Offices and competitions within and between schools. One interesting point of note is that PE teachers' involvement in extracurricular school sport is mentioned explicitly in the job descriptions of PE teachers in France and Portugal only. In all other sample countries their involvement is more or less voluntary.

A relevant issue in regard to the need for more sport participation during school time is the finishing time for schools and the number of half days on which children have no school. There are no big differences between the sample nations, with the exception of Brazil, where school is not a full-time activity, and where children only go to school for five half days a week (as well as some school during the weekends). School times finishes on average at 3pm in primary education (the earliest finishing times are in Brazil and South Korea), and in secondary education at around 3:45pm. In Spain, school lasts until 5pm; as pupils have free time between 1-3pm for lunch and rest because of the high temperatures, and as such this does not represent an additional opportunity for sport activities.

7.3.2 General sport participation rates

Critical success factors		INVENTORY	SURVEY			
II. There is a high general sport participation rate		O	A	C	PD	
CSF 3.6	There is a high percentage of people who participate in sport (on a non-organised or organised basis).	X	No survey evaluation exists on Pillar 3			
CSF 3.7	There is a high number of (registered) sport club members (=participation on an organised basis) (overall and per inhabitant)	X				
CSF 3.8	There is a high number of people that participate in sport competition	X				P8

Source of information: O: overall sport inventory; A: athletes' survey; C: coaches' survey; PD: performance directors' survey; the right column shows where the CSFs are possible on the interface with other Pillars.

Sports participation is hardly comparable; there is a pattern that countries in Northern Europe have higher sports participation rates than Southern Europe

It is widely recognised in sports research that comparability of sport participation surveys is problematic, if the methodology and questionnaires have not been standardised. Surveys on sport participation in different nations are generally developed and conducted independently of one another, which, from a comparative perspective, leads to problematic like-for-like comparisons. Issues range from the use of different questionnaires, research designs, methodology to the varying definitions of the subject matter, such as which sports are included, the place of physical education in schools, other possible activities considered for inclusion (such as gardening) and the frequency and intensity of participation (van Bottenburg, Rijnen and van Sterkenburg, 2005). Some cross-national surveys on sport participation were launched in the 1970s and 1980s through a unique project attempting to harmonise data at the end of the 20th century, called 'the COMPASS project' (the CO-ordinated Monitoring of Participation in Sports) (Gratton, Rowe and Veal, 2011). Some international surveys exist, which do not focus exclusively on sport but include some sport-related questions. The various Eurobarometer surveys (EB) and the International Social Survey Programme (ISSP) are perhaps the most obvious examples (Scheerder, Vandermeerschen, Van Tuyckom, Hoekman, Breedveld and Vos, 2011). In the SPLISS study, we make use of these two surveys in order to determine the general sport participation data[23] in some nations. Still, comparison remains problematic, as data are not available for Brazil, Canada, Northern Ireland and Wallonia. In the ISSP (ASEP, 2007), data are available for nine SPLISS countries, in the EB (European Commission, 2010) for three additional countries (Denmark, Spain and Portugal). For the purpose of this study, these studies were considered and compared with the study of Scheerder et al. (2011). We only looked

23 The data obtained from the SPLISS researchers showed diverse definitions of sports participation; therefore we referred to existing comparative sports participation studies from ISSP and EB for adults.

at 'the percentage of people participating in sport at least once a week'. Within this criterion, the highest sport participation rates for adults are found in Denmark, Finland and Switzerland (over 60%-70% that take part at least once a week). These are followed by the Netherlands and South Korea. This is partly confirmed by previous studies that state that sport participation rates tend to be higher in Nordic countries and lower in Southern European countries (van Bottenburg et al., 2005; Scheerder et al., 2011). Lower participation rates in the SPLISS sample–taking part in sport at least once a week–are found in Japan, Portugal and Brazil. Sport participation among young people is higher in all countries, with on average 71% of the population participating.

As most elite athletes find their roots in sport clubs, organised sports members is the main criterion in Pillar 3

Van Bottenburg (2002) showed that elite sporting success is only significantly correlated with sport participation when the sport is intensive and competitive. Even in sports where talents are identified outside a sport's participation base, or where governments invest in talent transfer from one sport to another (e.g., diving from gymnastics; bobsleigh from track and field), most athletes still find their roots in sport clubs. With van Bottenburg's evidence in mind, we looked at the number of organised sport club members per head of population, based on data delivered in the inventories. In Australia and Canada, such data is not available, even at the state government level.

The European SPLISS countries have a higher proportion of sport club members than the European average

Denmark exceeds all other sample nations, with over 40% of the population being a member of a sport club. This finding is consistent with Scheerder et al. (2011), although in the European Social Survey the Netherlands narrowly surpassed Denmark. Club life appears to be strong in Denmark, with approximately 15,000 registered sport clubs. However van Bottenburg et al. (2005) states that–although sport clubs members increased in absolute terms in Denmark–they have lost market share over the past decades, due to other sporting environments being offered, notably in the private sector. In Flanders, Brazil, France and Switzerland the proportion of sport clubs members is relatively high (over 20% of the population). This is higher than the European average of 13% in the 28 states measured in the Eurobarometer (European Commission, 2010). In France the total amount has increased with approximately 3,600,000 new members in the past 10 years (growth of 26%). Sport club members have also increased considerably in Portugal, whereas in Switzerland a decrease has been recorded. In the Netherlands the total number of registered sport club members has increased by 10% during the last 15 years even though there has been a slight decrease recently in the 18+ age group.

Data on the number of competitive sport participants (CSF 3.8) were not available in most countries. Scheerder et al. (2011) provided an overview for European countries that can be applied to nine of the SPLISS countries. In this research, Denmark and the Netherlands, followed by Northern Ireland, have the highest share of the population active in competitive sports. In these countries, more than one out of four people (aged 15-64) takes part in competitive sport. The lowest figures are found in Finland and Spain.

7.3.3 Quality management in sport clubs

<table>
<tr><th colspan="2">Critical success factors</th><th>INVENTORY</th><th colspan="3">SURVEY</th><th></th></tr>
<tr><td colspan="2">III. There is a national policy towards promoting the implementation of the principles of (total) quality management in sport clubs, at the level of mass participation and talent development</td><td>O</td><td>A</td><td>C</td><td>PD</td><td></td></tr>
<tr><td>CSF 3.9</td><td>There is a national policy (including funding) implemented by the government and/or NOC, NSA towards the improvement of quality in sport clubs</td><td>X</td><td colspan="3" rowspan="2">No survey evaluation exists on Pillar 3</td><td></td></tr>
<tr><td>CSF 3.10</td><td>There is a national policy and funding towards improving the quality of talent development in sport clubs</td><td>X</td><td>P4</td></tr>
</table>

Source of information: O: overall sport inventory; A: athletes' survey; C: coaches' survey; PD: performance directors' survey; the right column shows where the CSFs are possible on the interface with other Pillars.

7.3.3.1 Ages at which extra attention is received from club or national governing body

As most athletes have their roots in sport clubs, Pillar 3 refers not only to the number of sport participants but also to the quality of the sporting experience delivered at club level. As stated by Tihanyi (2001, cited by Green and Houlihan, 2005):

'It is much too late to develop Olympians at the level of the training centres. This process must be incubated, nurtured and brought to fruition at the club level.' (2001, p. 29)

Athletes were therefore asked at what age they first received extra attention as an emerging talented athlete, from their NGB and from their club. Figure 30 shows that on average athletes first received extra attention at the age of 17.0 years old (SD ±3.6 years). At club level, this was 1.4 years earlier, at the age of 15.6 years old (SD ±3.8 years). There are only slight differences between individual sports and team sports and results obviously differ between different sports as can be observed in Figure 31.

Sport clubs are important in athlete development: Top-level athletes first received extra attention as an emerging talent relatively late (±17 years from NGBs and ±15.6 years from sport clubs)

In Canada, Korea and Brazil. dedicated attention from NGBs was provided after the age of 18 and after 16 years of age in South Korea, Brazil, Portugal, Flanders, Japan, Canada and Australia. Talented athletes have already been in their sport for about 4.5 years, before they receive dedicated attention from the club to develop their talent further, and it takes 6 years before any specific support is provided to them by the NGB. These data are an indicator that sport clubs play a significant role in the athlete development at younger ages, as many skills are best trainable before the age of 12. Policymakers rarely include the role of sport clubs in their athlete development policy plans, and the quality of sport club management is often underdeveloped as well (Van Hoecke, 2000). In this respect, the last two CSFs (3.9 and 3.10) look at the national policy co-ordination relative to the implementation of quality management and talent management systems in sport clubs.

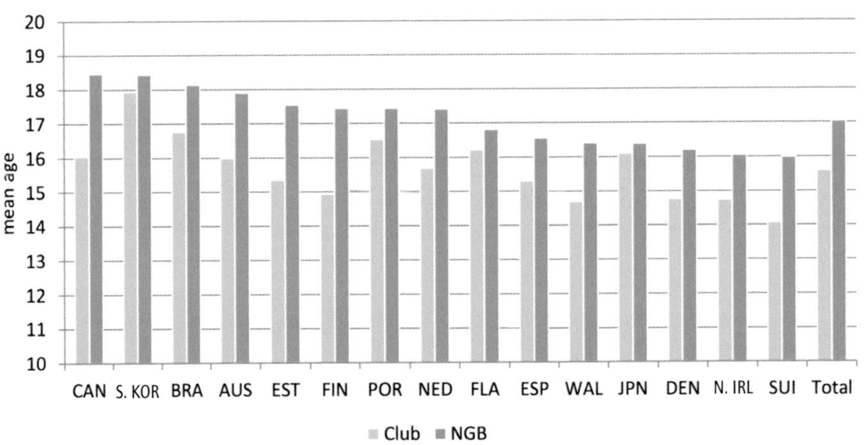

Figure 30: Overview by country; at what age did you first receive extra attention and extra provisions as an emerging talented athlete? (n=2423)

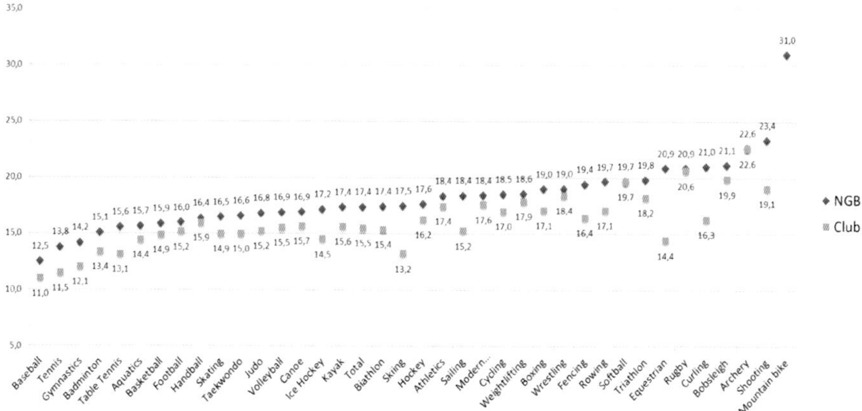

Figure 31: Overview by sport; at what age did you first receive extra attention and extra provisions as an emerging talented athlete? (n=2423)

7.3.3.2 Quality management and talent management

Although quality (of management) in sport clubs is a criterion that certainly needs to be explored in greater depth on a sport-by-sport basis, some nations have set up national projects to stimulate total quality management (TQM) in sport clubs (Van Hoecke, 2000). In the sample nations, this is most highly developed in Australia, Canada, Flanders, Japan, Northern Ireland and the Netherlands. A co-ordinated programme to improve the quality of club support during the fundamental stages of an athletic career exists only in Flanders, Japan and Switzerland.

In Japan attempts to implement TQM within sport clubs are related to the club manager development programme, which is an accredited programme to develop the human resource capabilities of the clubs. In Brazil, Denmark, France and Wallonia, the researchers indicated that there is neither a national policy for TQM nor general talent development services for sport clubs.

In Switzerland the Y+S Kids is FOSPO's sport development programme, aimed at 5- to 10-year-old children it seeks to improve talent development in sport clubs. Any club wishing to offer sporting opportunities to this age group must first complete five to six days of training. Clubs and NGBs subsequently receive financial support for the courses they run. Y+S currently funds two training sessions a week. Clubs providing Y+S, kids receive funding totaling around CHF 20 million (app. €25 million) a year.

In Flanders, Bloso, the Flemish sports administration, funds NGBs for the development of quality management projects in sport clubs–specifically in relation to youth sport development. As a result, some NGBs have developed monitoring systems in collaboration with an independent (private) company to evaluate quality objectively. This operational quality system is now being used in several sports by NGBs for the certification of clubs that are managed and operated well (Van Hoecke, De Knop and Schoukens, 2009). However, this system is not specifically developed for talent development.

Despite the efforts from national governments to co-ordinate, steer or fund initiatives to improve quality and talent management in sport clubs in different countries, holistic quality of sport clubs (management) has not been investigated in this study, and it is therefore recommended as a subject of investigation in the future. What we may derive from our findings is that sport clubs are not considered high on the list of priorities of national policymakers as a means of developing long-term success and succession in elite sport.

7.4 Key points in Pillar 3

- There appears to be no link between elite sport success and grassroots participation using the variables included in this Pillar.
- There is considerable variation in the way in which physical education and sport is delivered in schools in terms of the amount of time allocated to the subject; the qualifications of those who deliver it; and the approach to extracurricular provision. The organisation and delivery of school sport differs greatly between the sample nations.
- Like-for-like comparisons of how many people take part in sport in each nation do not exist. The most promising indicator appears to be the proportion of people who take part in competitive sport, but reliable data for this indicator are generally not available.
- Young talented athletes tend to be identified initially through their clubs and begin to receive dedicated attention at around 15.4 years of age before coming under the umbrella of their sport's NGB 18 months later. At what age young talents are selected varies per sport, adding to the argument that sport clubs as a key stakeholder in developing athletic pathways, may benefit from a national approach to developing quality management in clubs.
- Few countries recognise the opportunity that lies in early talent detection and development through their established sport club systems. For those nations investing in this, there may be short term competitive advantage in doing so.

Chapter 7 references

ASEP. (2007). International Social Survey Programme–Study documentation: ISSP 2007–Leisure Time and Sports.http.://www.jdsurvey.net/jds/jdsurveyAnalisis.jsp?ES_COL=127&Idioma=I&SeccionCol=01&ESID=502

Collins, D., Richard B., Ford, P. A., MacNamara, A., Toms, M. and Pearce, E. (2011). Three Worlds: new directions in participant development in sport and physical activity. *Sport, Education and Society, 17* (2):225-243. doi: 10.1080/13573322.2011.607951.

De Bosscher, V., Sotiriadou, P. and van Bottenburg, M. (2013). Scrutinizing the sport pyramid metaphor: an examination of the relationship between elite success and mass participation in Flanders. *International Journal of Sport Policy and Politics, 5* (3), 319-339. doi: 10.1080/19406940.2013.806340

European Commission. (2010). Sport and physical activity. Special Eurobarometer 334/Wave 72.3. Brussels: directorate-general Education and Culture

Feddersen, A., Jacobsen, S. and Maening, W. (2009). Sports heroes and mass sport participation–The (Double) paradox of the 'German Tennis Boom'. Retrieved 26 January 2012, from http://ssrn.com/abstract=1544320

Gratton, C. Rowe, N. and Veal, A. (2011). International comparisons of sport participation in European countries. An Update of the COMPASS project. *European Journal for Sport and Society,* 8 (1-2), 99-116.

Green, M. and Houlihan, B. (2005). *Elite Sport Development. Policy learning and political priorities.* New York: Routledge.

Hanstad, D. V. and Skille, E., A. (2010). Does elite sport develop mass sport? A Norwegian Case Study. *Scandinavian Sport Studies Forum, 1,* 51-68.

ISSP Research Group. (2009). International Social Survey Programme: Leisure Time and Sports–ISSP 2007. GESIS Data Archive, Cologne. ZA4850 Data file Version 2.0.0, doi:10.4232/1.10079

Scheerder, J., Vandermeerschen, H., Van Tuyckom, C., Hoekman, R., Breedveld, K. and Vos, S. (2011). *Understanding the game sport participation in Europe: Facts, reflections and recommendations.* K.U. Leuven.

Sotiriadou, P., Shilbury, D. and Quick, S. (2008). The Attraction, Retention/Transition and Nurturing Process of Sport Development: Some Australian Evidence. *Journal of Sport Management, 22* (3), 247-272.

van Bottenburg, M. (2002). *Sport for all and elite sport: Do they benefit one another?* Paper presented at the 9th World Sport for All Congress, 'Sport for all and elite sport: Rivals or partners?' Ahrnem, NL.

van Bottenburg, M., Rijnen, B. and van Sterkenburg, J. (2005). *Sport participation in the European Union: Trends and differences.* Nieuwegein, The Netherlands: Arko Sports Media.

Van Hoecke, J. (2000). De ontwikkeling van IKGym: een relevante toepassing van de principes van integrale kwaliteitszorg en servicemanagement binnen de (traditioneel) georganiseerde sport, [the development of IKGym: a relevant application of the principles of total quality management and service management within the (traditional) organised sport] Doctoral dissertation, Vrije Universiteit Brussel). Ghent, BE: PVLO.

Van Hoecke, J., De Knop, P. and Schoukens, H. (2009). A decade of quality and performance management in Flemish organised sport. *International Journal of Sport Management and Marketing, 6* (3), 308-329. doi: 10.1504/IJSMM.2009.029091

Veal, A. J. and Frawley, S. (2009). *'Sport for All' and Major Sporting Events: Trends in Sport Participation and the Sydney 2000 Olympic Games, the 2003 Rugby World Cup and the Melbourne 2006 Commonwealth Games.*

Weed, M. (2009). The potential of the demonstration effect to grow and sustain participation in sport: Centre for Sport, Physical Education & Activity Research (SPEAR), Canterbury Christ Church University.

FRANCE
AREVA

8 Pillar 4: Talent identification and development

8.1 Concepts and definition

Once young people have chosen to participate in a sport on a regular basis, it is an important part of NGBs' planning processes to ensure young talents can be identified and developed further. The international 'battle for medals' requires a high-performance system that not only allows for a sustained level of superior performance but also for the continued development of talented athletes to the elite level (De Bosscher et al., 2008). The '10-year rule', first applied to chess (Simon and Chase, 1973) and later to other areas, like sport, stipulates that an average 10-year commitment to deliberate practice is the minimum requirement to reach the expert level (Ericsson, 2003). Research in the past decade has shown that this timeframe has increased as athletes start ever younger with their sport (van Bottenburg, 2009); they train more hours, and more national and international championships are organised for younger age categories (Gullich et al., 2004). Responding to the increasing performance pressure for athletes, several countries have set up programmes to support talent identification and talent development. Without support services during talent development, athletes are unlikely to reach their performance potential as outlined by Bloom three decades ago:

'The study has provided strong evidence that no matter what the initial characteristics (or gifts) of the individuals, unless there is a long and intensive process of encouragement, nurturance, education and training, the individuals will not attain extreme levels of capability in these particular fields.' (1985, p. 3)

The increasing competition between nations, has further spurred the professionalisation of talent development programmes. The progression of the athletic career cannot be seen as separate from athletes' development in other domains, such as the psychological, psychosocial and the academic/vocational level (Wylleman and Lavallee, 2004). In the context of Pillar 4, young talents will make the transition from the local sport clubs to formal competitive sport with a view to improve performance, as a first selection process and eventually be selected into a regional or national youth team (De Knop, Wylleman, Van Hoecke, De Martelaer and Bollaert, 1999). Significant time is spent on training with a shift from emphasising fun (during the initiation), to more focus on skill development during talent development (Bloom, 1985). Furthermore, as athletic performance increases, an athlete will move from competing at regional and national competitions to international events. Meanwhile, at the level of *psychological* development, young talents move from childhood to adolescence. At the *psychosocial* development level other individuals are perceived by athletes as becoming more significant (peers, the coach and parents) (Wylleman and Lavallee, 2004). Athletes are also confronted with *academic* transitions. As most countries have compulsory education up until the age of 16 or 17, athletes will face the challenge of balancing their academic and athletic development (De Knop et al., 1999). This dual role of being a student and athlete puts individuals in a situation where they need to invest their available time and energy into developing potential in two areas of achievement (De Knop et al., 1999), which has been offered as an explanation as to why talented athletes terminate their sport careers (Bussmann and Alfermann, 1994).

Pillar 4 looks at national strategies towards the identification of young talents, how talent development is facilitated and what services are delivered. This Pillar needs to be analysed further on a sport-specific basis

Taking into account the outlined aspects to talent development (psychological, psychosocial and academic), Pillar 4 is concerned with the national strategies towards the identification of young talents and how talent development is facilitated in the different nations. Once young people have chosen to participate in a sport on a regular basis, it is an important part of the relevant NGBs planning processes to ensure young talents can be identified and developed. In this pillar we look at 12 CSFs including 169 sub-factors. The majority of Pillar 4's issues need to be analysed on a sport-specific basis as talents are usually recruited from within the existing participation base of a sport. In the SPLISS project we only looked at sport-specific data through the surveys completed by the performance directors from each sport, but in some countries response rates were low.

8.2 Key findings

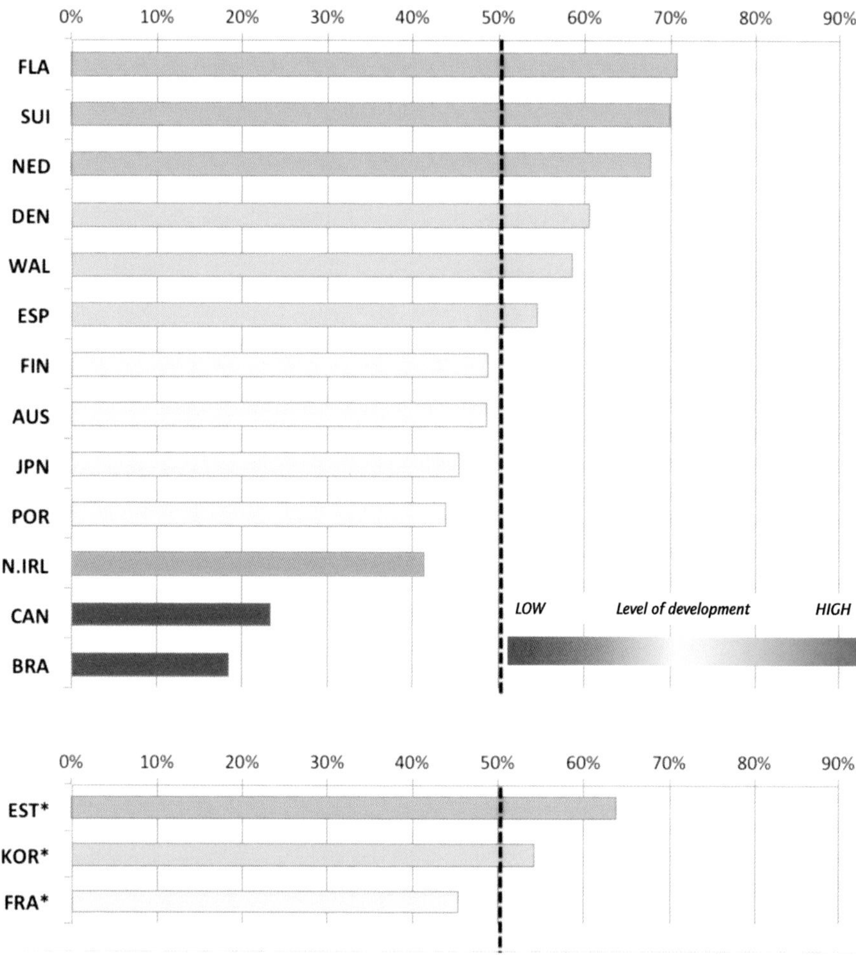

* *Note: 13 nations + 3 regions (FLA, WAL, N. IRL). Only partial data available in France (no elite sport climate survey); Korea and Estonia (no inventory). Caution is therefore needed with the interpretation of scores.*

Figure 32: Total scores of the SPLISS sample nations against the 12 CSFs of Pillar 4

While the SPLISS 1.0 study concluded that Pillar 4 was generally under-developed in the six sample nations, it seems that the SPLISS 2.0 nations were more advanced, with an average score of 54% (similar to other Pillars). Some countries have average to high scores, with the best level of development in Flanders, Switzerland and the Netherlands. These countries are characterised by comprehensive planning in regard to talent identification and development. According to the performance directors much of this consists of support of and involvement by sport scientists; multidimensional support services appropriate to the age and level of young athletes; and nationally co-ordinated support for the combination of sports development and academic study. The NSAs in Flanders and the Netherlands stood out in the development of sophisticated systems in that regard.

Pillar 4 is developed better in smaller nations. Nations have low scores specifically for talent identification strategies at the national level

Concentrating on talent identification only, for which the average score is only 33% across six critical success factors, the study reveals an area offering scope for significant improvement across a number of nations. According to the high-performance directors, the general planning of talent identification by the NGBs is still limited. One possible explanation for these low scores may be that, the majority of talent identification systems are developed at a sport-specific level. Despite the fact that NSAs and governments have increasingly sought to take control over elite sport identification processes, for example by copying best practices from the former Eastern bloc countries, it appears to be difficult to develop reliable criteria for the generic recognition of young talents, and particularly with a national system spread across all sports. This makes talent identification an expensive element of national policy development. It is likely that return on investment and time taken to realise benefits are less predictable than for other Pillars and therefore countries do not prioritise it. Switzerland and Japan are the most advanced nations in talent identification in the SPLISS 2.0 sample.

Countries have different approaches of dual career programmes. Most countries provide a strong national co-ordination but with a decentralised system, or provide both (centralised and decentralised) talent development

In talent development, countries have developed systems to facilitate the combination of elite sport and studies, both in secondary and tertiary education. An interesting point of discussion emerging from our analysis is the extent to which parts of talent development systems need to be more centralised, decentralised or both. Countries are moving away from 'government/NSA-run talent programmes' only. Most countries organise talent development, and career and education support in particular, on a decentralised basis. Countries with nationally co-ordinated and centralised training centres such as Australia, France, and Spain have moved to a combination with decentralised systems for the development of young talents, allowing young people to train more in their home environment, with their personal coaches. Only 30% of the athletes surveyed indicated they attended a specialised school for training and education; nevertheless, most athletes were satisfied with the support they had received to combine elite sport and study. It appears that the effectiveness of initial and costly centralised elite sport and study systems has been balanced with more regionalised systems, where the 'state or NSO' empowers and facilitates, with sufficient room for local implementation and quite often lower dropout rates.

No CSF correlates significantly with success in Pillar 4

One key point emerging from the results of this Pillar—perhaps not unexpectedly—is that the total scores correlate negatively with success, mainly in summer sports.[24] This is stronger in the elite sport climate surveys. In other words, countries with better scores on Pillar 4 generally win less medals. Furthermore, no CSF correlates significantly with success but the strongest relationship exists between success and the support that NGBs receive for the development of a TID monitoring system (CSF 4.4); how it is informed by scientific research (CSF 4.5); and a nationally co-ordinated system to combine elite sport and study in higher education, as it was perceived by athletes and coaches (CSF 4.12). A range of CSFs correlate negatively: in the best performing countries, NGBs have less coherent planning towards talent identification and development. The question remains, however, to what extent is talent identification and development an essential ingredient of success? The answer is not straightforward, but may be found when taking a closer look at the data. The analysis shows that mainly smaller nations, both in terms of 'surface area' and to a lesser extent 'population', score better on Pillar 4.[25] This is an interesting finding, and it may derive from the fact that in larger countries the co-ordination of talent identification and development is more complex and expensive to organise. Smaller-sized countries have capitalised on their 'small size' competitive advantage in this Pillar over other countries. Of course, smaller population pools (of talent) are less likely to deliver success, and this may explain the direction of the (non-significant) correlation. As such it can be argued that when large countries also start investing in maximising their potential talent development, the future prospects of smaller nations may diminish further.

---

24 The total scores correlate weakly with success: $r_{s(summer)} = -.148$ ($p = 0.629$) and $r_{s(winter)} = .237$ ($p = 0.435$). For the elite sport climate survey only: $r_{s(summer)} = -.486$ ($p = 0.066$) and $r_{s(winter)} = -.254$ ($p = 0.362$).
The correlation of CSF 4.4 with success is: $r_{s(summer)} = .350$ ($p = 0.220$) and $r_{s(winter)} = .187$ ($p = 0.522$); CSF 4.5: $r_{s(summer)} = .299$ ($p = 0.298$) and $r_{s(winter)} = .346$ ($p = 0.226$); A negative relationship is found in CSF 4.2 (NGB funding for TID), CSF 4.5 (covered by scientific research according to NGBs), CSF 4.9 (multidementional support services according to athletes); it is remarkably highly significant in CSF 4.3 (NGB comprehensive planning, according to the surveys) $r_{s(summer)} = -0.427$ ($p = 0.146$) and $r_{s(winter)} = -0.775^{**}$ ($p = 0.002$).

25 The correlation of the Pillar 4 scores with population is: $r_s = -0.368$ ($p = 0.216$); with land mass $r_s = -0.626^{**}$ ($p = 0.022$); the negative correlation with the inventory and surveys is even stronger.

8.3 Comparative and descriptive analysis

8.3.1 Planning of talent identification (TID) and talent development (TD)

Critical success factors		INVENTORY	SURVEY			
I. TID planning: There is an effective system for the identification of young talented athletes, so that the maximum number of potential top-level athletes are reached at the right time (age)		O	A	C	PD	
CSF 4.1	There is a systematic talent selection process to identify potential elite athletes from outside a sport's participant base or by talent transfer	X				
CSF 4.2	NGBs can receive funding for the identification (recognition and scouting) of young talented athletes in their sport	X			X	P1
CSF 4.3	There is comprehensive planning for talent identification: NGBs are encouraged to have (and have) detailed long-term policy plans describing how talents in their sport are recognised, identified and selected in order to receive funding	X			X	P2
CSF 4.4	NGBs receive sport specific support to develop a testing system (tests for the recognition of young talents) and monitoring system with clear criteria for the identification of young talents in each sport	X			X	P2
CSF 4.5	The talent identification system is informed and covered by scientific research (including the socio-psychological development of children and the development of a stage-specific, individualised and balanced approach)	X			X	P9
CSF 4.6	There is a national framework on how the talent identification and selection process has to look like (or different frameworks as guidelines for different sports)	X				P2
II. TD planning: There is nationally co-ordinated planning for NGBs in order to develop an effective system for the development of young talents in their sports		O	A	C	PD	
CSF 4.7	NGBs or sport clubs can receive funding specifically for talent development and receive information, knowledge and support services (other than financial) in order to develop their talent development programmes	X			X	P1
CSF 4.8	NGBs have a co-ordinated long-term and short-term planning for talent development (how talents in their sport are developed from club level to regional level to national level in order to receive funding), that is covered by scientific research	X			X	P2

Source of information: O: overall sport inventory; A: athletes' survey; C: coaches' survey; PD: performance directors' survey; right column shows where the CSFs are possible on the interface with other Pillars.

The countries generally score weak on TID

From a talent identification process perspective, the influence of Pillar 4 begins when a talented athlete is discovered and starts to receive special attention. In order to detect talent, monitoring systems to identify talent characteristics, robust talent detection systems that minimise drop out, and well-organised scouting systems (Rowe, 1994) are required. Talent identification is concerned with different phases of talent recognition (i.e., monitoring systems based on criteria that recognise young talent), talent scouting (i.e., the processes undertaken to recruit young talents) and selection processes (i.e., the process of selecting young talents for specific purposes (such as competitions and training activities).

Financial pressure and increasing competition have motivated sport teams and organisations to identify future stars at a very early age. Logically longer lead times decrease the reliability of TID models (Vaeyens et al., 2008). The success ratio of TID depends on the sport in three ways: (a) sports where specialisation occurs early (e.g., soccer) or those where peak performance occurs at young age (e.g., gymnastics) require a different approach compared to sports that emphasise late specialisation (e.g., rowing) or when peak performance is achieved at a later age (e.g., triathlon); (b) sports where one or two (skill) variables have a high predictive value will be more suitable for effective TID in contrast to multi-skilled disciplines; (c) the prediction of success is likely to be easier in more 'closed' rather than 'open' sports because in the former movements are less affected by the environment and fewer components are likely to impact on performance. These constraints most likely explain why national governing bodies (NGBs) have invested more resources in TID models for closed sports (e.g., rowing, cycling, athletics, canoeing and weightlifting) and are now recruiting potential medal winners at later stages (e.g., talent transfer or sporting giants) (Vaeyens et al., 2008).

Generally, the SPLISS results show that across the sample nations there is a low level of development regarding talent identification, with the exceptions of Switzerland, Northern Ireland and Japan. Flanders and Spain are in the middle band, and all other countries produce weak scores. This is not only true for nationally co-ordinated planning processes, but also at sport-specific level as perceived by the NGBs in the surveys.

Systematic talent selection: Outside the existing sport participation

The development of a generic talent identification system, which aims to identify potential elite athletes from outside a country's known sport participation base, predominantly through schools, known as a 'system-related scientific selection process' (Fischer and Borms, 1990) was typical in the former communist countries (Riordan, 1994). As one of the early adopters of such systems, the Australian Sports Commission established between 1994-2010 multiple sophisticated, evidence-based and scientifically underpinned systems and initiatives focusing on national talent detection and mass screening programmes. Examples include Sports Search, Talent Search, the electronic talent identification (eTID) system and the Talent Assessment Centre (TAC) network. These programmes were phased out after a significant change in Australia's national sports funding model in 2011.

A lack of evidence on reliable criteria and ethical aspects are barriers to develop a talent selection process, that aims to identify potential elite athletes from outside a sport's participant base. None of the countries have developed such a system-related talent selection programme

Currently none of the countries in this project reported having a systematic talent selection process to identify potential elite athletes from outside a sport's participant base. In six countries (Australia, Canada, Denmark, Japan, Northern Ireland and Portugal) talent selection/scouting was the responsibility of the NGBs, and some sports are better at it than others. Only one country, Switzerland, reported having a national initiative for providing children with early exposure to different sports, followed by testing and trials to identify sports that best suited their abilities. Switzerland operates two complementary national programmes in this area—(1) a multi-sport participation-focused programme known as 'Y+S Kids' *(Youth + Sport Kids,* for all 5- to 10-year-olds) run by the Federal Office of Sports (FOSPO) and the NGBs, and (2) a multi-sport-focused programme for potential future elite athletes called 'Talent Eye', which is run by the Swiss Olympic Association. The latter has a selective entry policy that uses science-based admission tests (balancing backwards, standing long jump, target throwing, sideways jumping, sit-ups, 20-metre sprint, tapping [arm speed], 20-metre shuttle run, anthropometry). However, on completion of the tests, no recommendations are made regarding suitability for any specific sport, and according to the Swiss researchers the programme is not yet very accurate. Talent Eye is not run nation-wide, at the time of writing, only six cities in four Cantons (out of 26) were involved. A similar scientific project/testing battery was financed by the government in Flanders since 2006, called 'Sport Compass' (Lenoir, Philippaerts and Pion, 2010). This project originally aimed to direct children towards the sport that best suited their abilities, based on their scores in three categories, varying from orientation for healthy lifestyles to orientation for elite sport. 10,000 6- to 12-year-old children have been tested, and furthermore the 10% 'best movers' were identified. The results also showed that one out of three of the 10% best scoring children was not a member of a sport club (De Clercq and Labath, 2010). Currently the project is further developed for talent identification in elite sport schools, as such it only involves children who are already members of sport clubs.

In conclusion, it can be argued that several reasons are hindering countries from talent selection procedures outside a sport's existing participation base. For example, there are ethical issues concerned with early talent selection and directing children towards sports based on their talent characteristics (Bergsgard et al., 2007). Probably a more important reason is that little evidence exists of the predictive value of early and generic (overall sports) testing batteries, which makes the return on investment of such testing questionable.

NGB funding for talent identification (TID) and development (TD)

Not all countries provide NGB funding specifically for the identification and development of talents

Half of the participating countries provide discrete funding to NGBs for talent identification processes (Flanders, Japan, Northern Ireland, Portugal, Spain, Switzerland and Wallonia) and nine countries (Denmark, Finland and the Netherlands in addition to the aforementioned) for talent development. Funding is either the result of national policy/law/decree (Switzerland, Wallonia), merit-based project funding (Japan, Northern Ireland, Portugal, Spain), or a combination of both (Flanders). These countries also require NGBs to have written policy plans (as part of an NGB's annual sport plans) on talent identification in order to receive the funding and often programmes are monitored through annual NGB performance reviews. These reviews take the form of NGBs submitting self-evaluations, progress reports and interviews between NGB and NOC/NSA personnel. Only in Switzerland do sport clubs receive government funding for talent development programmes/initiatives.

Australia, Canada, Denmark and France are four (of seven) countries that do not require NGBs to submit a policy plan on talent identification or development processes largely because funding is not allocated to NGBs directly for this activity. However, these countries do expect that talent identification and development are considered to be elements in NGBs' broader sport planning frameworks (i.e., 'whole of sport development', 'path to sporting excellence', 'discipline analysis', 'as part of the annual plan') even though such planning is usually general in nature and focused on holistic development of the athletes. In Denmark it was reported that many NGBs were not particularly advanced with this element of planning.

France does not directly fund NGBs for talent development; however NGBs are provided with lump sum funding based on their 'path of sporting excellence' annual plan by the NSA (INSEP). The talent development plan is contracted between NGBs through regional training centres or associated centres (i.e., academies of sport) where 'pôle' are implemented (i.e., the term used for a collective of identified elite athletes in a sport). Such athletes have been identified and given a category in the French elite athlete system. Athletes are organised into 'Pôles Espoirs' (structure for young talents), or 'Pôle France' (structure for senior elite athletes).

Nationally co-ordinated NGB support services for effective TID and TD systems

Australia, Japan, Spain, Switzerland and the Netherlands provide the most comprehensive and co-ordinated support to NGBs for talent identification programming and planning. Interestingly, of these top five countries, as indicated in the previous section, Australia does not directly fund NGBs for TID and TD. For talent development Australia, Brazil, Canada, France, Portugal, Spain and Wallonia reported that they do not provide NGBs with nationally co-ordinated support services to develop their talent development programmes. As the Canadian researcher explained: *'the only support given to NGBs is in conjunction with (preparation of) the Long Term Athlete Development (LTAD) model'.*

The services are provided at different levels in different nations; for example, one-on-one consultation with specialist sport scientists (Australia, Northern Ireland, Switzerland, Netherlands); programme assistance via planning with sport consultants to enhance development pathways (Denmark, Finland, Northern Ireland, Switzerland, Australia); access to research and best practice principles in the science of talent identification (Australia, Japan, Switzerland, Netherlands); desktop evaluation tools such as TID questionnaires, strength/weakness analyses (Flanders); talent identification/profiling conferences and workshops (Japan, Northern Ireland, Spain, Switzerland); and co-ordinated initiatives that facilitate knowledge sharing across NGBs (Denmark, Northern Ireland).

Some countries develop national frameworks for TID as funding criteria and mainly as guiding tools for NGBs to improve their TID

Despite TID and TD needing to be developed at a sport-specific level and sometimes athlete-specific level, Japan, Northern Ireland, Switzerland and the Netherlands provide NGBs with a detailed national framework to develop their talent selection processes. Of the four countries, Switzerland's Prognostic Integrative Systematic Trainer Evaluation (PISTE) system can be considered the most advanced and detailed talent selection system. It provides assessment criteria for selecting young athletes based on coaching science. Criteria include: competition results, performance tests, performance development, athlete motivation, athlete biography, and biological development assessment. Talent 'cards' and subsequent funding by the Swiss Olympic Association (SOA) are allocated based on the PISTE criteria and rankings provided by each sport. The Swiss researchers believe the strength of its talent identification and development programmes lies with *'the ability of NGBs to adapt talent scouting and selection processes specifically to their own needs and the fact that the PISTE system has a relatively high degree of acceptance among the NGBs as a financially effective instrument'.* Switzerland and Japan also required the most sophisticated frameworks for the development of talented athletes that includes a clear 'step-by-step' plan on the different processes of talent development. For example details about the age young talents can move up the talent pyramid, long-term planning, final attainment levels and the holistic development of young talents are required to be recorded.

Appendix 1 provides an overview of national policy processes for talent development.

Another interesting example of national talent identification co-ordination can be found in Japan. Here the National Sport Festival (NSF) is a national sport competition in which representatives from 47 local government districts (called prefectures) compete. JISS and JOC support the TID and athlete development systems of these local governments (e.g., funding, scientific support) aimed to produce elite athletes for the National Sport Festival.

Talent identification plans are still of limited development in NGBs; a lack of specialised talent coaches is the most often cited problem in TID according to performance directors

While acknowledging that the majority of the sample countries require, or at least expect, their NGBs to have well-written policy plans for talent identification, on average, only half of the NGB performance directors (PDs) surveyed (n=192), believed that the system of talent identification in their country (for their sport) was well developed; 28% disagreed. When the PDs were asked about the problems impacting the success of their talent identification systems, the most cited concerns were the lack of specialised coaches for young talents (71%), improving the development pathway from talent to elite athlete (61%), and establishing quality educational programmes with sufficient hours for training (56%).

Scientific research for TID

Less than 40% of the performance directors (NGBs) reported that their TID systems are based on scientific knowledge of the sport

Australia, France and Switzerland offer NGBs access to scientific personnel and project funds for the development of sport-specific talent identification testing systems. NGBs must apply for access to research funds, which are awarded based on merit. There is usually no automatic process of scientific support for identification and testing. The fact that only a few countries offer access to scientific personnel and research funds for the development of sport-specific talent identification testing systems, might explain why only 39% (on average) of the sports surveyed (n=187) reported that their talent identification systems were based on scientific research/knowledge about the sport. Denmark, Flanders and Portugal scored the highest, with Canada and Wallonia having the least confidence in the scientific rigour of their talent identification plans.

8.3.2 Talent development: Nationally co-ordinated, multi-dimensional support services

Critical success factors		INVENTORY	SURVEY			
III. Young talents receive multidimensional support services that are needed to develop them as young athletes at the highest level		O	A	C	PD	
CSF 4.9	Young talents receive age-level appropriate multidimensional support services at different levels, including training and competition support, medical/paramedical support and lifestyle support.	X	X	X	X	

Source of information: O: overall sport inventory; A: athletes' survey; C: coaches' survey; PD: performance directors' survey; right column shows where the CSFs are possible on the interface with other Pillars.

During the talent development phase, athletes become highly committed to their sport, train more and become more specialised. Athletes face a number of transitions during this stage. Talented junior athletes start to receive dedicated attention and extra benefits from their sport club (or personal coach) and governing bodies. This CSF was measured by 44 different objective and subjective criteria that have retrospectively been evaluated by athletes and confirmed by coaches and performance directors. In summary, the support services that athletes had received, such as extra training opportunities, training schedules, access to international competitions, equipment, reimbursement of expenses, medical support services, mental coaching, nutrition and biomechanics, were assessed as quite reasonable across the sample nations, with on average 47% of all athletes receiving these kind of services as an 'emerging talent' from their respective NGBs and/or clubs. The scores were the highest in Spain (60%), Estonia (55%) and Denmark (55%) and the lowest in Japan (34%), South Korea (37%) and Canada (39%).

63% of the coaches and 32% of the athletes rated NGB support during talent development as insufficient

However, an assessment of the quality of service provision showed that only 27% of the coaches (n=1144) and 39% of the athletes (n=2932) rated the support they/their athletes received as an emerging talent from their NGB as sufficient (Figure 33); 32% of athletes and 63% of coaches found it insufficient. There were no significant differences between the performance levels of athletes. With the exception of the Netherlands, coaches generally tend to give lower ratings than the athletes. Only 1 coach out of 19 in Spain gave a positive rating to the sufficiency of services that talents receive. In Canada, Finland, South Korea, Estonia and Brazil less than 30% of athletes and coaches find the level of talent development support sufficient. Coaches may give lower ratings than athletes because they are more experienced and have a greater appreciation of what is taking place in rival nations relative to the situation in their own sport. The highest score across all nations was found in Japan, with 58% of the Japanese athletes rating the level of support from their NGB as (very) sufficient. Coaches did not take this view, with just 34% of the Japanese coaches finding it sufficient. In the Netherlands this was the highest with 55% rating it as sufficient.

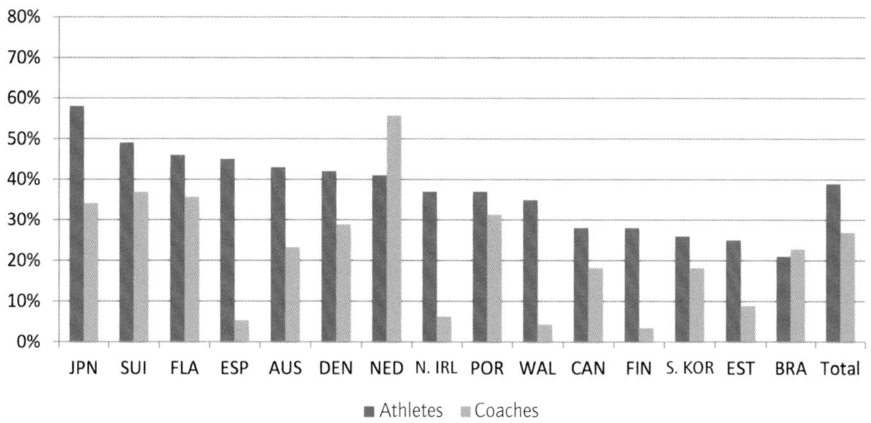

Figure 33: Percentages of all athletes and coaches rating the amount of support that athletes received as an emerging talented athlete from their NGB as (very) sufficient to develop at the highest possible level

In those countries where support services by the NGBs are perceived as insufficient, athletes tend to assign higher levels of expertise to their club coaches than NGB coaches

Athletes also rated the expertise of their NGB and club coaches who trained them as emerging athletes, as shown in Figure 34. Interestingly, maybe not surprisingly, in those countries where support services received lower ratings from athletes (Brazil, Estonia, South Korea, Finland and Canada), club coaches were rated better than NGB coaches. This was also the case in Portugal and Spain.

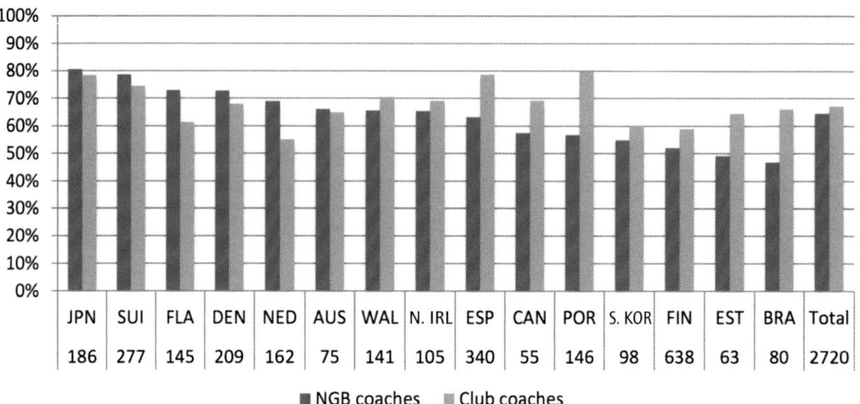

Figure 34: Percentages of all athletes rating the expertise of the coaches who trained them as an emerging talent from their club and NGB in order to develop at the highest possible level as (very) sufficient

8.4 Dual career support: Nationally co-ordinated support for combining sport training and academic studies in secondary and primary education

Critical success factors		INVENTORY	SURVEY			
IV. Young talents receive nationally co-ordinated support for the combination of sports development and academic study during secondary education (12-16/18 years) and where relevant primary education (for early specialisation sports where such a system is required)		O	A	C	PD	
CSF 4.10	There is a legal framework (whereby young talents have their elite sport status recognised contractually by the sports and education ministries at an age appropriate to their sport) and governments/ NSA recognise the cost involved with elite sport and study in secondary education	X				P1-2
CSF 4.11	There is a nationally co-ordinated system that facilitates the combination of elite sport and studies during secondary and primary education.	X	X	X	X	P2

Source of information: O: overall sport inventory; A: athletes' survey; C: coaches' survey; PD: performance directors' survey; right column shows where the CSFs are possible on the interface with other Pillars.

The expanding commercialisation and professionalisation of high-performance sport and increasing funding by national sport organisations and governments (De Bosscher et al., 2008) accompanied with growing pressure on the athletes to perform, impairs the educational and vocational career of the athletes (Conzelmann and Nagel, 2003; Gullich et al., 2004; Weber, 2009). It is almost impossible for athletes to combine an average of 15-25 hours training a week with regular schooling, without losing potential development in either one or both and with high dropout levels as a result (Wylleman, De Knop and Sillen, 1998). The demands of elite sports make it difficult to balance the demands of school and sport. Apart from the pressure from coaches to perform well, talented athletes will have to deal with national educational laws and pressure from parents to perform well in school (Van Rens, Elling and Reijgersberg, 2012). Some athletes choose to invest fully in their sport, disregarding education and as such they jeopardise their long-term future. Many European athletes eventually chose education and as such are lost to sport. This is partly explained by the fact that in Europe there is no elite sport pathway through primary school or intercollegiate sports such as in North America. As a result of this, elite sport and study programmes developed in many countries since the 1990s aim to provide athletes with a balanced and flexible approach to academic and sporting commitments (De Knop et al., 1999). Among the SPLISS nations, nine countries have set up national regulations for the combination of elite sport and study, of which Australia (1981), France (1974), Wallonia (1984) and Finland (1986) are among the prime movers. Other countries have only recently set up such programmes such as Switzerland (2005) and Japan (2008).

The extent to which the state or NSA run and co-ordinate these programmes, differs between countries. In secondary education, some countries have set up specific schools, with programmes for talented athletes, allowing them to: train during the day; participate in international competitions; have distance learning guided by a study co-ordinator; as well as other tailored support. For the purposes of this analysis, an 'elite sport school (ESS)' is considered to be either a type of 'sports-orientated' school (educational institution) that offers athletes flexible study options, or a sports training centre/academy which is linked with one or more 'normal' schools that offers athletes flexible study options. Nine countries (Australia, Denmark, Finland, Flanders, France, Japan, Switzerland, Netherlands and Wallonia) operate some kind of nationally co-ordinated system for the flexible combination of elite sport activities and secondary education.

The key point of dual career support is that (young) athletes are protected from not having to choose between training and education. National co-ordination means that they do not depend on individual initiatives for flexible educational arrangements

The key questions regarding elite sport and study systems are concerned with two levels of discussion: the level of national co-ordination and the level of centralisation versus decentralisation.

4 levels of coordination:
• State/NSA centric
• State/NSA as a facilitator
• NGBs as intermediary
• Laissez-Faire

With regard to co-ordination, the level of state/NSA intervention ranges from a strong 'hands on' approach to virtual 'laissez-faire'. As secondary (and primary) education is compulsory in most countries, a national statute can ensure that flexible educational arrangements for athletes are co-ordinated. Aquilina and Henry (2010) provided a typology of four approaches for higher education that we have applied to secondary education to classify the ESS systems of the SPLISS nations. The different levels of co-ordination are outlined next. In essence, the key point of co-ordination concerns the issue where athletes may or may not be dependent on the decisions and flexibility offered by their educational institutes in order to receive support services.

Centralisation: athletes train, live and go to school at one place; Decentralisation: athletes train in their home environment

The degree of co-ordination was then cross tabulated against the level of centralisation of these ESSs (see Figure 35). A high level of centralisation is present when athletes train, live and go to school at one place and when there are a limited number of elite sport schools; decentralisation is present when athletes mainly train in their home environment. It seems that countries with a long tradition of having national training centres, such as Australia (AIS) and France (INSEP) have moved on from centralised provision to a combined centralised and decentralised talent development support system.

- In a *state/NSA-centric regulation*, there is a directive towards the schools, to provide flexible opportunities for student-athletes typically through legislation, statutory requirement or government regulation (usually in collaboration with the NSA). For example, two countries, Flanders and the Netherlands, have a national law/covenant in partnership with both the Ministry of Education and the Ministry of Sports, and both ministries contribute financially to the ESS system. Entry requirements, curriculum, location, adapted programmes are all nationally determined.
- State/NSA as *a sponsor/facilitator*, is an approach where by the state promotes formal agreements to ensure that student-athletes' needs are being met, for example through permissive legislation (rather than statutory requirement). The state or NSA plays a less direct interventionist role, enabling rather than regulating responses to the specific needs of the student-athlete (for example with regard to entry requirements, flexible timetables, distance learning, and scholarships). Denmark, Finland, Portugal, Wallonia, Australia, Switzerland, Spain and France all have been classified under this category. In these countries the governments either provide legislation that allows student-athletes to have flexible

arrangements (e.g., Portugal, Wallonia, Spain, France), or the NSA develops a network of recognised schools with which some agreements are set up and where funding is provided (Australia, Switzerland). The level of co-ordination is determined by regions or Cantons. These countries all tend to facilitate decentralised systems of elite sport and study, where athletes can live and train in their home environments, apart from the national training centres in Australia, Spain and France (which admit athletes from the age of 17). All these nations (except for Australia) also have an agreement with the Ministry of Education, although in France (where school education is compulsory up to the age of 16), these covenants ('double project') are made on a local basis, with decentralised agencies of the Ministry of Education (called 'académies' and 'rectorat'). Finland is a good example where there are 13 official sport primary schools and 11 vocational schools, which receive extra funding from the state and where the Ministry of Education has provided a special provision for athlete education. However, the municipalities and schools have the autonomy to decide on the implementation; this network is co-ordinated by the NOC which plays the role of facilitator.

- *National governing bodies/institutes as Intermediaries* is an approach in which there is an established system of recognised channels for sporting advocates (usually national governing bodies) to act on behalf of the student to negotiate flexible educational provision with schools and where staff may advise and act on behalf of the student-athlete. Here there are no national regulations and athletes are dependent on their NGBs as a facilitator. Although there exists national funding for elite sport and study in Japan, there is no national regulation, for example, with regard to absence from school.
- In the laissez-faire approach there are no formal structures in place and arrangements rely on individually negotiated agreements. Brazil, Northern Ireland and Canada are typical examples of this. In Canada the educational system is run by the provincial Ministries/ Departments of Education and is directed by the District School Boards who decide what flexibilities they provide. There are some individual initiatives, for instance the National Sport School in Calgary (provincial level), the Edge School (a private school, with relatively high tuition fees).

Figure 35 shows a typology of the levels of co-ordination and centralisation in the sample countries.

Degree of co-ordination			Highly decentralised	(partly, through NTC)	Highly centralised
	High	State/NSA -centric	–	NED	FLA
	↑	State/NSA as facilitator	DEN FIN POR WAL SUI	AUS* ESP* FRA*	–
		NGB as intermediary (no state/NSA involvement)	–	JPN	–
	Low	**Laissez-Faire** (no formal structures)	BRA N. IRL CAN	–	–
			Degree of centralisation →		

*Note: * The systems are generally decentralised except for the national training centres*

Figure 35: Typology of state co-ordination (Aquilina and Henry, 2010) (usually in collaboration with the NSA) and centralisation of elite sport and study systems in secondary education in the SPLISS nations

Another level of discussion faced by policymakers and NGBs, is concerned with the level of centralisation (i.e., where best athletes train together in one training centre) or decentralisation (where best athletes train in their home environments). This discussion should also be seen in the light of academic views on early specialisation (therefore often requiring centralisation) versus early diversification. Early specialisation assumes that expert athletes need to limit their childhood sport participation to one single sport, with a deliberate focus on training and development in that sport (Côté, Fraser and Thomas, 2007). Early diversification on the other hand favors a focus on involvement in different sports through which an athlete develops multilateral physical, social and psychological skills, before specialising at later stages of development (Wiersma, 2000; Baker, 2003). Centralised systems require earlier specialisation (i.e., deliberate practice–effortful practice done with the sole purpose of improving current levels of performance; Ericsson, 2003), which is especially necessary in sports for which peak performance is achieved before adulthood (e.g., gymnastics, figure skating). In response to growing criticism regarding the downside of early talent identification and the accompanying performance targets that come with it, a number of researchers have emphasised the need for deliberate play (maximising fun, intrinsic motivation and enjoyment) with adapted sport rules, in order to decrease dropout rates (from sport in general and from young talents in particular), reduce injuries, and to improve long-term sport participation, personal development and the achievement of expertise (e.g., Côté, 1999; Wiersma, 2008; Vaeyens et al., 2008). With that in mind NGBs need to balance their policies between 'centralising in order to increase specialisation opportunities' (usually co-ordinated by NGBs) or decentralising in order to encourage a more diversified talent development.

Countries search for a balance between central/national co-ordination and a high flexibility for local negotiation and implementation of elite sport schools

In the SPLISS project, most of the countries with a high level of national co-ordination (state-centric/ as a facilitator) apply a decentralised approach to the development of ESS, or a mixed centralised/ decentralised approach, which means that central co-ordination is combined with high flexibility for local negotiation and implementation. As such, ESSs are regionally spread (sports-orientated schools) or 'normal' schools can agree to provide flexible study (status benefits). For example in Denmark, the concept for elite (sport) schools is covered by the 18 existing 'elite municipalities' with recognised schools where young athletes can train during school time. Team Denmark employs a staff member who develops flexible systems for primary/secondary/higher education as well as assisting athletes individually. In Switzerland education is the responsibility of the 26 Cantons that use quite different procedures and are, together with the NGBs, the main facilitators. Despite this decentralisation, there is national co-ordination by the Swiss Olympic Committee of 43 Swiss Olympic Partner Schools and 5 Swiss Olympic Sport Schools (May, 2011). The latter schools are specifically geared towards gifted young sportsmen and women and receive financial support for Swiss Olympic Talent Card holders in accordance with PISTE. This is where Switzerland differs from Canada, where the provinces are also facilitators, but where there is no national co-ordination by Sport Canada.

Combined centralised and decentralised systems seem to be most appropriate to reach all athletes

While there is a nationally co-ordinated and centralised training centre (including national agreements with local schools) in Australia, France, and Spain, the system of educating elite athletes is considered to take place in a decentralised manner by all the contributing researchers. For example the Australian researcher reported that:

'Whilst there is a nationally co-ordinated athlete career & education programme (NACE) that offers essential advice and training services to AIS/SIS/SAS scholarship athletes, ultimately athletes have the choice as to where they live and train (and study). With the exception of the national development sports programmes at the AIS where the majority of athletes have re-located to Canberra and attend one of 3 or so schools, all other elite student athletes are spread around the country, attending different schools (i.e., most athletes live and train in their home environment). The AIS ACE programme funds Liaison Teachers and for a few athletes distance education through both the public and private school system.' (Australian researcher)

This is similar to France. Athletes in the national training centre INSEP need to be at least 17 years old. In some sports younger athletes also train at INSEP (like gymnastics), that has an agreement with local secondary schools, and teachers in and outside INSEP. Athletes can be prepared for their 'baccalaureat', which is the exam they need to pass in order to go to the university. In secondary education, schooling is organised by the NGBs, but there exists a national regulation through the 'double project' mentioned earlier. It can be argued that a culturally appropriate combination of centralised and decentralised systems seems most appropriate.

In the Netherlands there are 29 regional LOOT-schools (assisting talents to combine sport and school, since 1991), and at the national level, there are four centralised Centres for Elite sport and Education (CTOs), since 2008 and 5 national training centres (NTCs), that all provide services for talents and elite athletes. They are directly or indirectly funded by the Dutch Ministry of Health, Welfare and Sport, the Dutch Ministry of Education, Culture and Science, and NOC*NSF. The Danish researcher reported that Team Denmark is currently moving towards a more centralised approach.

The cost of state-centred and centralised systems should be balanced against the benefits compared to decentralised, local systems where the state acts as a facilitator

Of all SPLISS 2.0 countries, Flanders takes the most state-centric (nationally co-ordinated) and centralised approach to elite sport and study. Elite sport schools (ESS) are developed as national training centres for specific sports and therefore are as seen as the main pathway to develop young talents in Flemish elite sport policies. An agreement between the Ministry of Sport and Education states that students have 12 hours a week available for training during school time and are entitled to a number of half days off school for competitions and training camps (varying from 40-130 half days according to the A/B status and grade of the student-athlete). There are six ESS for 17 sports. Schools are funded by the Ministry of Education to appoint a study co-ordinator and create special classes for sport athletes only. NGBs are funded by the NSA (Bloso, through the ministry) to develop the training and competition programmes of ESS. Talent development is mainly developed through these ESS, as illustrated also by the highest amount of funding of all countries provided for the ESS through the NGBs, a total of €2.4 million (2009); these figures exclude the extra cost for the Ministry of Education (calculated as teaching hours per pupil). In comparison, the cost in Australia is €0.16m, €0.12m by Team Denmark, €0.56m by the Finnish government, €0.62m for the Japanese Olympic Committee elite academy, and €0.26m in Switzerland.

In summary, it seems that national talent programmes have moved away from early developed centralised approaches in the late 1990s (and in countries with national training centres) towards more decentralised approaches where athletes can train in their home environments. So far, research has not confirmed the effectiveness of systems where athletes can live, train and go to school in one place (De Bosscher and De Croock, 2010). The advantages of both programmes are shown in Table 30.

Table 30: Advantages of centralised versus decentralised systems for training and study (De Bosscher and De Croock, 2010)

Advantages of decentralised systems	Advantages of centralised systems
• Athletes sleep in their home environments, train with club coach • Avoid early drop-out and burnout • Invest in a broader talent development pyramid, more potential athletes • Individual approach • Motivation of sport clubs who are involved in talent development process; room for local implementation	• Athletes live, study and train in one place • Cheaper cost per athlete; efficient inputs • Allows more 'all-inclusive' services • Time efficiency (travelling time) • 'Better athletes make athletes better' • Centralisation of expertise: best coaches, sport science and • Quality and services for talent development in sport clubs are often under developed

Despite the fact that less than 30% of the elite athletes had attended a specialised school that offerd facilities for elite sport and study, 68% of the athletes were satisfied with the support they received during secondary education

The extent to which elite sport and study systems require a high level of centralisation and national co-ordination can also be debated based on some evidence from the surveys. Less than 30% of all athletes in the sample (n=2603) indicated that they had attended 'a specialised secondary school in their country that offers specific facilities to support elite sport and academic study (other than a regular school/institute).' This proportion is considerably higher in Finland (69%) (Figure 36). As some systems have been implemented quite recently, such as in Switzerland (2005) and the Netherlands (2008), athletes surveyed may not have been able to make much use of it and as such the data that we present needs to be seen in that light.

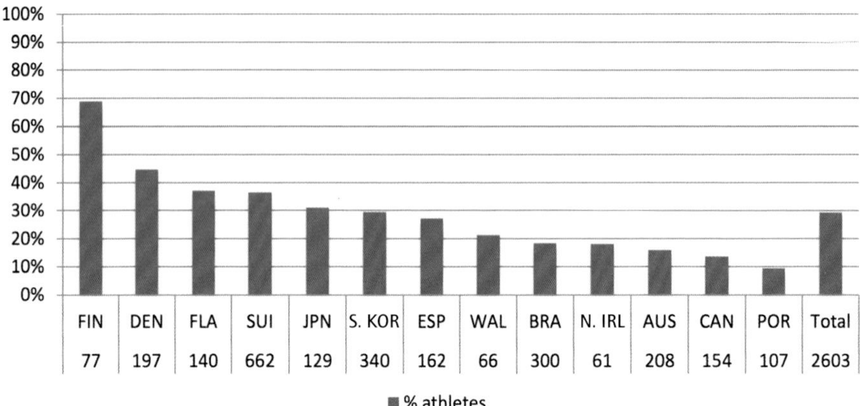

Figure 36: Percentages of athletes that indicated they went to a specialised secondary school that offered specific facilities to support elite sport and academic study (other than a regular school/ institute) (ALL athletes surveyed)

Despite this fact, 68% of the athletes were satisfied with the support they had received during their secondary education (Figure 37). It seems that there is no great desire by athletes to be supported centrally in that regard; a decentralised system based on local agreements can in some cases deliver better on the athletes' personal preference, as long as the NSA (or state) plays a facilitating role. Higher dissatisfaction ratings can be observed in the countries with a laissez-faire approach (Portugal, Brazil, Northern Ireland). Despite the facilitating role of the state in Spain (through legislation), there is a decentralised approach (apart from the 10 schools related to national training centres) that apparently does not fulfill the young talents' needs. Athletes and coaches are most satisfied in Australia, Finland and the Netherlands. All these countries have decentralised views, where athletes can train in their home environment, although the Netherlands recently (2008) has started to become more centralised.

In conclusion, lessons can be learned from centralised and decentralised systems. There is seemingly no single best approach, and this finding endorses the notion that elite sport development systems have broad homogeneity with local variations on the central theme.

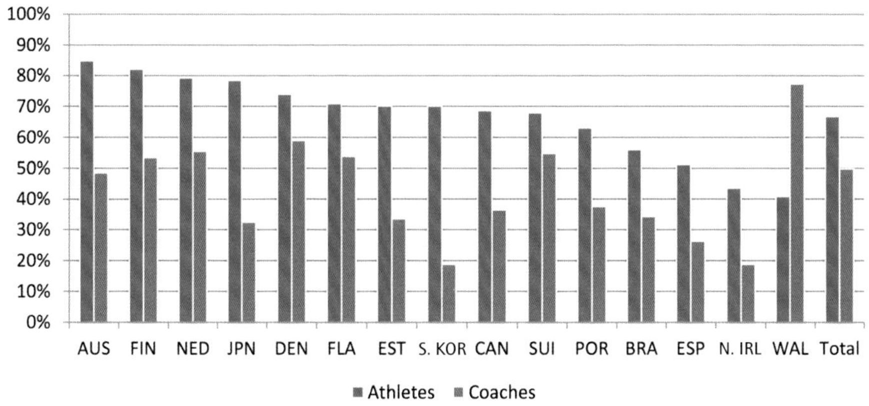

Figure 37: Percentage of athletes and coaches that rate the general support to combine elite sport training activities with studies as sufficiently good

8.5 Dual career support: Nationally co-ordinated support for combining sport training and academic studies in tertiary education (university/college)

Critical success factors		INVENTORY	SURVEY			
V. Young talents receive nationally co-ordinated support for the combination of sports development and academic study during higher education (university/college level)		O	A	C	PD	
CSF 4.12	There is a nationally co-ordinated system that facilitates the combination of elite sport and academic studies in higher education and governments/NSA recognise the cost involved with it.	X	X	X	X	P1-2

Source of information: O: overall sport inventory; A: athletes' survey; C: coaches' survey; PD: performance directors' survey; right column shows where the CSFs are possible on the interface with other Pillars.

Co-ordination for student-athletes aged 18 and older means that the NSA/state facilitates and the athletes are not dependent on the individual decisions of the higher educational institutes with regard to flexible arrangements for elite sport and study

As tertiary education is not compulsory, support at the national level does not require legislation that allows athletes to train during the day. This CSF is concerned with the flexibility that individual athletes, their coaches, clubs and preferably NGBs can negotiate on an athlete's behalf. The state or the NSA can facilitate in that process. A summary overview is provided in Figure 38.

Degree of co-ordination			
	High	State/NSA -centric	Spain,** Portugal*
	↑	State/NSA/NOC as facilitator	France,* Australia*, Denmark*, Finland*, Flanders and Wallonia
		NGB as intermediary	In the countries with*, the NGB makes the arrangements with educational institutions
	Low	Laissez-Faire (no formal structures)	Brazil, Canada, Netherlands, Japan, Northern Ireland, Switzerland and countries with**

*Note: * The systems are generally decentralised except for the national training centres*

Figure 38: Typology of state/NSA co-ordination (Aquilina & Henry, 2010) in higher education in the SPLISS nations

While not nationally co-ordinated, Portugal and Spain provide athletes with 'legal elite athlete' status which has associated benefits when studying at universities such as, placement quotas for elite athletes (who meet entry criteria), timetable flexibility, permitted absences and access to study tutors. According to Aquilina and Henry (2010), these countries could be classified as 'state/NSA-centric' for this reason. In Spain universities are compelled by law to reserve 3% of the total places available for elite athletes accredited as such and who meet general university entry requirements. However, although legislation providing a statutory requirement to support access to higher education may be in place, the researchers from Spain and Portugal report that the implementation is still weak and specific arrangements need to be made by individual athletes, sometimes in collaboration with the NGBs. This explains the (*) and (**) in Figure 38.

> **Higher education is less institutionalised than secondary education elite sport and study support because it is not compulsory. National co-ordination developed later and is still in an early development stage in most countries. Most nations have a mix of NGBs as intermediaries and state as a facilitator**

In higher education, combining elite sport and study support is less 'institutionalised' than in secondary education. In most nations the NGBs are the intermediaries to organise elite sport and study. One way to facilitate and co-ordinate elite sport and study in higher education, is by the development of agreements with (a selection of) higher education institutes/universities, that allow their student-athletes to organise their study requirements around training and competition obligations. This is the case in only five (Australia, Denmark, Finland, Flanders, and Wallonia) of the 14 countries. For most of them this system was developed on the back of establishing a system for athletes in secondary education. Australia, Denmark and Finland have systems that facilitate agreements between the NSA/NOC (as a facilitator) and universities for the provision of flexible study options for elite athlete students. For example Team Denmark made four bilateral agreements with Syddansk Universitet, Aarhus Universitet, Aalborg Universitet and UC Nordjylland. These universities receive funding per student enrolled (approximately t200 a year) which allows the universities to provide special support systems. Other universities can also receive funding from Team Denmark if they provide flexible study options for TD athletes. In Australia, the Australian Institute of Sport (AIS) co-ordinates the 'Elite Athlete Friendly University (EAFU)' network. This network involves 38 of the 42 Australian universities and includes flexible study options for elite student athletes (flexibility with assessments, enrolment, attendance, and examinations) where each university has a dedicated liaison officer to assist elite athletes. In Finland there are 19 sport academies of which 10 have an official elite sport academy status, audited by the NOC, and supporting the training and coaching needs of student athletes. Each elite sport academy has agreements with universities on behalf of their athletes. Study support services include intensified guidance, remedial instruction, flexible exam timetables, and possibilities to sit exams during training camps, distance learning and extra time for studies. The costs involved are paid by the universities. The system in Flanders and Wallonia is probably more advanced. In the whole of Belgium a covenant signed by the education sector (universities) and sport organisations (Bloso and Adeps) provides athletes with legally recognised 'elite' status and as such enables them to qualify for NSA funding. Funding is provided at two levels: (a) to athletes for extending their studies over a longer period and (b) to universities to appoint an elite sport and study co-ordinator (e.g., for flexible time tables, athletes being abroad, e-learning services) up to €3,000 per student-athlete. Different approaches exist in the nations with large national training institutes, that are usually facilitated and funded by the state (e.g., INSEP, AIS). For example in France, apart from the national legislation since 1987, the state also operates five state-run national sport institutes to accommodate elite athletes (Aquilina and Henry, 2010): the National Institute of Sport and Physical Education (INSEP); the National School of Ski and Mountaineering (ENSA); the National School of Sailing (ENV); the National Equestrian School (ENE); and the National School of Cross-Country Skiing and Ski Jumping (ENSF). At INSEP, there are opportunities to combine elite sport with a whole range of academic programmes. Rather than providing access to existing university courses, in the INSEP system, teaching staff come to the sport sites to teach the student-athletes. However, the French researcher reports that–during the past decade–how to combine elite sport and tertiary education has moved from being state centred to a situation whereby NGBs have more autonomy and become responsible for collaboration with educational institutes. In France, the NSA or state is a facilitator for Olympic sports, but in professional sports NGBs are the intermediaries (e.g., football, rugby).

Many countries reported that the 'systems' for supporting athletes attending higher education institutions were still based on a 'laissez-faire approach' (Brazil, Canada, Finland, Japan, the Netherlands, Northern Ireland, Switzerland). In the Netherlands NOC*NSF provides a list of the services and facilities that universities/primary schools offer, but there is no national co-ordination, legislation or regulation, nor finance to facilitate this. There are some private initiatives, such as the Johan Cruyff University and Randstad Topsport Academy; however these only reach a few elite athletes and provide only a narrow range of study options.

Only four countries provide specific funding to assist athletes in higher education/university by:

1. appointing specialist/liaison teachers (Finland and Flanders);
2. direct athlete funding/grants (Denmark, Finland, Flanders and France); or
3. funding NGBs for extra coaching (Finland and Flanders).

8.6 Summary points in Pillar 4

- There appears to be a degree of ambivalence towards talent identification and development in many of the sample nations. This is likely to be the result of three key problems: first, the return on investment is uncertain; second, the time lag between making investment and seeing rewards may be perceived as too long to be worthwhile; and third, it is difficult to attribute causality between elite sport success and talent identification and development work.
- For all nations in the sample, funding is more or less dependent on providing funding agents with business plans as to how investment will be used. Talent identification and development are explicit components of such plans in some nations and implicit components in other nations.
- Talent identification is increasingly seen as a specialist area within elite sport development systems. A challenge reported consistently by all nations is that there is a lack of suitably qualified professionals in this field.
- Coaches are more critical of the provision of talent identification and development than athletes. This may be because coaches are more experienced and have greater knowledge of what is recognised as best practice globally. They are therefore in a stronger position to make informed judgements and comparisons.
- There are various methods for integrating academic and sporting careers ranging from highly centralised state-controlled systems to much more informal approaches, facilitated by NGBs. There is seemingly no single best approach, and this finding endorses the notion that elite sport development systems have broad homogeneity with local variations on the central theme. What is important, is that athletes do not depend on the individual decisions and flexibility of their educational institutes in order to receive support services. In secondary education, mixed centralised and decentralised systems appear to be most appropriate, offering nationally centralised training opportunities, but meanwhile applying an individual approach to the different needs of young talents, within different sports. In higher education, national co-ordination developed later and is still in its infancy in most countries, and as such is a potential cause of drop-out.
- The presence or absence of a nationally co-ordinated talent identification and development system does not correlate highly with success. Future research should focus on sport-specific talent identification and development systems.

Chapter 8 references

Aquilina, D. and Henry, I. (2010). Elite athletes and university education in Europe: A review of policy and practice in higher education in the European Union Member States. *International Journal of Sport Policy, 2* (1), 25-47.

Baker, J. (2003). Early specialization in youth sport: A requirement for adult expertise? *High Ability Studies, 14* (1), 85-94.

Bergsgard, N. A., Houlihan, B., Mangset, P., Nødland, S. I. and Rommetvedt, H. (2007). *Sport Policy: A comparative analysis of stability and change.* London, UK: Elsevier.

Bloom, B. (1985). *Developing talent in young people.* New York: Ballantine

Bussmann, G. and Alfermann, D. (1994). Drop-out and the female athlete: A study with track-and-field athletes. In *Psycho-social issues and interventions in elite sport* (pp. 89-128). D. Hackfort (Ed.). Frankfurt: Lang.

Conzelmann, A. and Nagel, S. (2003). Professional careers of the German Olympic athletes. *International Review for the Sociology of Sport, 38* (3), 259-280. doi: 10.1177/10126902030383001

Côté, J. and Fraser-Thomas, J. (2007). Play, practice, and athlete development. In *Developing sport exercise: Researchers and coaches put theory into practice.* D. Farrow, J. Baker and C. Macmahon (Eds.). New York: Routledge.

De Bosscher, V. and De Croock, S. (2010). *Effectiviteit van de Topsportscholen in Vlaanderen [Effectiveness of the elite sport schools in Flanders].* Research report for the department CJSM, Flemish government. Brussel: Vrije Universiteit Brussel.

De Bosscher, V., Bingham, J., Shibli, S., van Bottenburg, M. and De Knop, P. (2008). *The global Sporting Arms Race. An international comparative study on sports policy factors leading to international sporting success.* Aachen: Meyer & Meyer.

De Clercq, K. and Labath, J. (2010). *Onderzoek naar het onderscheidend vermogen van het Vlaams Sport Kompas bij lagere schoolkinderen, in teken van talentdetectie.* Master thesis, University of Ghent. Document retrieved October 14, 2013 from http://lib.ugent.be/fulltxt/RUG01/001/459/035/RUG01-001459035_2011_0001_AC.pdf

De Knop, P., Wylleman, P., Van Hoecke, J. and Bollaert, L. (1999). Sports management—A European approach to the management of the combination of academics and elite-level sport. In *Perspectives—The interdisciplinary series of physical education and sport science. Vol.1 School sport and competition* (pp. 49-62). S. Bailey (Ed.). Oxford: Meyer & Meyer Sport.

Ericsson, K. A. (2003). Development of elite performance and deliberate practice: An update from the perspective of the expert performance approach. In *Expert performance in sports: Advances in research on sport expertise* (pp. 49-85). K. Starkes and K. A. Ericsson (Eds). Champaign, IL: Human Kinetics.

Fisher, R. J. and Borms, J. (1990). The search for sporting excellence. *Sport Science Studies, 3*, 5-89.

Gullich, A., Emrich, E., Espwall, S., Olyslager, M., Parker, R. and Rus, V. (2004). *Cooperation between elite sport and education in Europe.* Brussels: European Commission.

Lenoir M., Philippaerts, R. and Pion J. (2010). Talentdetectie en–identificatie: het Vlaams Sport Kompas. During conference 'Topsport en Wetenschap', Brussels, October 12.

Riordan, J. (1994). Communist sports policy: the end of an Era. In *Sport in the global village* (pp.89-115). R. Wilcox (Ed.). Morgantown, WV: Fitness Information Technology.

Rowe (1994). *Talentdetectie in basketbal [Talent detection in basketball].* Unpublished doctoral dissertation, Catholic University of Leuven, BE.

Simon, H. and Chase, W. (1973). Skill in chess. *American Scientist, 61*, 394-403.

Vaeyens, R., Lenoir, M., Williams, A. M. and Philippaerts, R. (2008). Talent identification and development programmes in sport: Current models and future directions. *Sports Medicine, 38* (9), 703-714.

van Bottenburg, M. (2009). *Op jacht naar goud. Het topsportklimaat in Nederland, 1998-2008. [the hunt for gold. The elite sport climate in the Netherlands, 1998-2008].* Niewegein, Netherlands: Arko Sports Media.

van Rens, F. E., Elling, A. and Reijgersberg, N. (2012). Topsport Talent Schools in the Netherlands: A retrospective analysis of the effect on performance in sport and education. *International Review for the Sociology of Sport.* doi: 10.1177/1012690212468585

Weber, R. (2009). Protection of Children in Competitive Sport: Some Critical Questions for London 2012. *International Review for the Sociology of Sport, 44* (1), 55-69. doi: 10.1177/1012690208101485

Wiersma, L. D. (2000). Risks and benefits of youth sport specialization: perspectives and recommendations. *Pediatric exercise science, 12* (1), 13-22.

Wylleman, P. and Lavallee, D. (2004). A developmental perspective on transitions faced by athletes. In *Developmental sport and exercise psychology: A lifespan perspective* (pp. 507-527). M. Weiss (Ed.). Morgantown, WV: Fitness Information Technology.

Appendix 1: National policy towards talent development

COUNTRY	National talent development plans
AUSTRALIA	NGBs are only required to present a strategic overlay of their talent development plans. The NSA is focused on 'partnering' with sports to assist them with their planning. The emphasis is on good practice, not compliance planning and reporting.
BRAZIL	–
CANADA	NGBs only have to complete and present the LTAD plan. This plan does include key objectives for TID/development, but this would not necessarily constitute the sport's talent development plan.

Services available to young talents	Support services for NGBs
n Australia, co-ordinated support services for elite athletes are based on an athlete having a scholarship at one of the National Institutes of Sport (i.e., AIS, SIS/SAS). The SIS/SAS are primarily focused on providing the daily training environment for elite athletes, not developing or pre-elite athletes (i.e., below 'Potential International' evel). And because Australia does not have a talent roster system, such as the 'carded athletes' in the United Kingdom, this means that pre-elite athletes receive next to no nationally co-ordinated support services i.e., support services for athletes lower than a 'PI' level, s solely at the discretion of the NSO). The only exception (for a minority of pre-elite athletes classed as being 'Potential International' athletes) is for sports that have chosen to invest in a pre-elite/development programme at the AIS. As these athletes would be on scholarship they would have access to almost all of the services at AIS.	'Young talents' is not a definitive category across sports. In general, NGBs do not receive nationally co-ordinated support services from the NSA for talent development (i.e., ancillary services); however it does depend on the sport. That said, National TID scientists work closely with some NGBs to assist them with national co-ordination of talent development (implementing innovative pathway approaches to elite athlete development). Past years (prior to funding cuts in this area) NTID provided more co-ordination to more sports than they currently do now.
–	–
Support services are only offered (on a nationally co-ordinated level) for 'carded' athletes: top elite athletes n each sport. The Canadian Sport Centres throughout Canada, offer such support services. http://www.canadiansportcentre.com/en/services Recently, Provincial and regional development centres (ex: Alberta- www.asdc.ca) have been implemented to provide imilar support to young developing athletes. Not all provinces have these centres. There may be some privately funded support service programmes, but this is not nationally governed and would be funded privately such as corporations, parents, port supporters, etc.	The only 'support' given to NGBs is in conjunction to the LTAD Model.

COUNTRY	National talent development plans
DENMARK	NGBs categorised as 'elite' have to complete a plan for 'discipline analysis'. As part of the discipline analysis, the ATK (age-related training concept) needs to be a major part and the conditions of this concept need to be strictly followed. It is expected that the coaches have a high-level coaching education (at least level 3), but a talent identification plan is not a compulsory part of this. Within the discipline analysis, under 'talent recruitment and development' required elements include description of: (1) performance level, (2) daily training programme within a club, (3) technical/tactical/movement development, (4) secondary discipline and tests, (5) performance attitude, (6) athlete mental health, (7) participation in championships/national games.
FINLAND	Funding support is directly to the athlete, therefore the prerequisites for support are athlete specific. For the NOC Challenger Programme, athletes must submit the following documents to the NOC and NGB—annual training plan, long-term athletic and civil career plans, and an annual training budget.
FLANDERS	Many NGBs provide detailed talent development plans, but there is no evidence that such a plan is required, nor that it should be used as a guiding tool. Only with regard to elite sport schools, the NGB have to show weekly plans, monthly plans and yearly plans of talented athletes; they do not have to show how these elite sport schools fit in the overall talent ID and development process.
FRANCE	The 'Path of Sporting Excellence' contains the plan for young talented athlete development. This plan is contracted between NGBs' through Regional Training Centre or associated structures (like academies) where 'pôle' are implemented. Sports ministry and scholar/ training institutions can participate in the process.

Services available to young talents	Support services for NGBs
Team Denmark has a carded system–world-class athletes, elite athletes and TD athletes, who can receive co-ordinated support services (albeit at different levels of access). Regarding services for young talents Team Denmark can provide support in the following ways (as part of the concept 2009-2012): (1) physical training; (2) career and education; (3) sports nutrition; (4) sports medicine; (5) testing; (6) psychological advice. However talents who haven't yet proven their abilities at the top level won't get access to these services	NGBs need to have a 'plan for talent development' as part of their overall plan. NGBs receive talent development funding from TD (discipline analysis) and DIF through Fordelingsnøglen (regulation tool for NGB grant funding). Amount of funding depends on activities of NGB. Plans evaluated by TD discipline analysis provide a 'picture of prospects'. If sport is deemed eligble for talent development funding, a contract agreement is created between NGB and TD. Talent development is supported with funding and services relating to (1) performance level, (2) daily training programme within a club, (3) technical/tactical/movement development, (4) secondary discipline and tests, (5) performance attitude, (6) athlete mental health, (7) participation in championships/ national games. In addition, TD focuses on improving national talent development by investing project funds relating to (1) support for NGBs, (2) elite municipalities, (3) knowledge sharing and communication.
NOC organises the elite sport system development project. The NOC works with NGBs (19 to date) to develop or enhance each sport's athlete development pathway. In terms of co-ordination of ancillary services for young talents, this seems to be the responsibility of the NGB or club (although these services are predominantly funded by the NOC).	Four major initiatives for talent development. (1) NOCs 'Challenger Programme' (NGBs nominate athletes with high potential for future world/Olympic success). In 2010, €365,000 supported 132 athletes. (2) Grants from Ministry of Education and Culture (45 athletes in 2010, €7,500 per athlete). (3) In 2006, NOC started subsiding NGBs to employ full-time Olympic coaches for talented young athletes. In 2010, NOC subsided 58 youth Olympic coaches in 22 sports (€750,237 from NOC). However NGBs cover 60-70% of wages. (4) NOCs elite sport development programme assists NGBs created better talent development programmes (10 NGBs have already completed the programme).
–	NSA has a questionnaire for NGBs to assess the status of their talent detection and development systems. A strength/weakness analysis is done on answers from 175 questions. Guidelines and remedies are then composed to enhance the NGBs planning in this area. The NSA is also developing an elite sport tracking system for NGBs to record development of elite athletes. Eventually this system could be used to identify and track young talents much sooner. The government (dept. CJSM) is also working to create an instrument for measuring co-ordination skills of young children between 6 and 11 years of age. This could also be used as a tool to show which basic development is needed for young talents.
There isn't a nationally co-ordinated system to provide support services to young talents. If young talents are identified and selected to be in a regional training centre they can have the access of the support services provided (depending on the centre).	–

COUNTRY	National talent development plans
JAPAN	Very comprehensive talent development plans are required. Elements include: (1) annual plan in accordance to attainment target of each time (level); (2) short-, medium-, long-term plan; (3) target competition of each time (level); (4) provision of opportunity to participate in international competition; (5) setting of step-by-step clear goal; (6) TID base, coach and system of each time (level) and area; (7) curriculum in order to acquire technique and physical level which is necessary for each time (level) (e.g., instructional book, video material, etc.) (8) sport education curriculum which is necessary for each time (level); (9) programme for Olympic movement and career education; (10) co-operation with other sport (organisation) and intercommunication programme; (11) co-operation with foreign development programme; (12) follow-up programme; (13) provision of science support system and service; (14) co-operation organisation (university, research centre, etc.); (15) employment of full-time professional staff.
NETHERLANDS	The NOC*NSF make an assessment of the sport's talent development, resources and facilities people and programme, and results. On the basis of this assessment, each federation is certified with a number of stars, with 1 being the lowest and 5 the highest (and best). The number of stars determines the height of the funding received.
Northern Ireland	Basic overview required (i.e., planning and preparation; profiling and recruitment; talent confirmation; and talent development).
PORTUGAL	–
SPAIN	Required elements include: (1) contextualisation of the project; (2) technical programme description (measurable objectives); (3) technical staff requirements; (4) athlete characteristics/ explanation of selection criteria; (5) summary of training programme, competition schedule, evaluation/monitoring tools; (6) detailed budget; (7) programme location information/ facility requirements; (8) indicators for programme evaluation.
SWITZERLAND	NGBs need to complete a detailed youth development strategy which is derived from the 12 basics for success–'the key to youth sports development in Switzerland': (1) environment conducive to physical activity; (2) elite sport and school education; (3) talent scouting, talent selection, talent development; (4) coaches: elementary and continued training; (5) social support, career planning; (6) medical, therapeutic, social and psychological counselling and support; (7) regionalisation, regional centres; (8) squad-based structures for long-term performance development; (9) competition structures to enhance competitiveness; (10) long-term training plan, training analysis and training management; (11) critical analysis and theoretical research; (12) funding–development measures.
WALLONIA	NGBs are required to provide an annual plan for detecting and preparing future elite athletes. Requirements for this plan include outlining preparatory periods, recovery periods, evaluating periods, selected competitions, as well as information concerning the selection criteria for talented athletes and testing protocols.

Services available to young talents	Support services for NGBs
–	–
Each registered talent has the possibility to receive support services in almost each imaginable area. This does not mean the service is free, but they will get help in getting the best support they need.	Funding can be provided for Talent Coaches and for the talent development programme.
SINI support three Performer Development Centres. Here confirmed talents receive strength and conditioning and physiotherapy as core services; other services (e.g., lifestyle) are provided on as-needs basis. 'Performance planning' is also a kind of support service that is offered to talented athletes and their coaches. Currently about 75 athletes in this category.	NGBs receive support through the SINI talent ID officers, and through investments made via the Athlete Investment Programme. SINI also fosters a 'network' of representatives from NGBs, clubs and other stakeholders who embrace the principles of TID. The network meet occasionally for updates and to exchange ideas on good practice.
–	–
–	21.5% of NGB funding is allocated to 'evaluation/tests and following'. This funding supports: (1) activities related to the evaluation/testing of athletes, (2) training to improve quality of sport practice, (3) academic training, (4) participation in relevant competitions, (5) other activity (e.g., communication/dissemination of the National Programme for Talent Development).
–	–
NGBs are provided with funding for elite and future-elite athlete development. Elite athletes and future elite athletes can train at elite sport centres, and they're also eligible for free scientific and medical tests of their abilities. Support services for coaches and NGBs are provided by Adeps (since 2011) (assist with identifying evaluation tests and programing for elite athletes).	Elite athletes and future elite athletes do receive support service from the NSA (but not via the NGBs). NGBs receive funding to develop elite sport (most for participation in competitions, stages, training, sport trainers and sport directors, activities to detect, anti-doping campaigns etc.) and may receive informal advice from NSA.

9 Pillar 5: Athletic career and post-career support

9.1 Concepts and definition

The fifth Pillar concerns athletic career and post-career support, when athletes reach their highest level of athletic proficiency (Bloom, 1985). Many young athletes have visions of becoming professional athletes, but the chances of turning these visions into reality are quite low (Coakley, 2001). In addition professional sport opportunities are extremely short term. What this means is that after an athlete's sport career ends, they still have about 40 more working years ahead of them. Media exposure to the public often portrays athletes as wealthy individuals with unlimited income. Generous publicity is given to those athletes who sign the 'super contracts.' However, in reality, salaries vary widely within professional sport. The super contract athletes are the exception; most participants in a professional sport sign for the league minimum and are often forced out of their career for various reasons before they can cash in on fame and fortune. Despite these facts, the dream of becoming a professional athlete is still very prevalent for some people (Coakley, 2001; Lotysz and Short, 2004).

From talent development to senior-level, athletes face changes in the transition from junior to senior competition; structural and organisational changes of competitive sport (e.g., from regional to national and continental competitions); greater sports specialisation; more intensive training; and, change from being an amateur to being a professional (Stambulova, 2000). At a strategic level it is our view that for nations to have a realistic chance of elite sporting success, appropriate support can make the difference between success or failure, especially with regard to Olympic sports on which the SPLISS study focusses. During the past decade an increasingly holistic approach to the athletic career development of athletes can be observed. During each stage of their career athletes face different challenges. These challenges should be understood from a 'beginning-to-end' or a life-span perspective and need to take into account the transitions faced by athletes in other domains of their development (Wylleman and Lavallee, 2004). At the psychological level athletes face transitions from adolescence to adulthood (e.g., self-identity, identity foreclosure, cognitive development). The psychosocial development concerns changes in social networks (e.g., athletes-parents-coach-peers relationship and roles). Finally the academic/vocational level concerns the transition into higher education and/or a professional occupation and/or transition into a postgraduate lifelong learning phase. This stage is often accompanied by an athlete's increased efforts to secure greater financial and personal security (Reints, 2011).

Pillar 5 deals with the support services athletes receive once they start to perform at senior level and how they are prepared for life after sport

In this Pillar we aim to achieve a better understanding of how policies are developed to deal with these issues and get insights into the support that athletes receive to develop their career. We also investigate how athletes combine their sporting career with an academic/vocational career. and ultimately, how they can or cannot progress beyond their professional sport career. In addition Pillar 5 is concerned with the retirement of athletes and their transition out of top-level sport. While this Pillar contains only six CSFs that are measured, it includes 120 subfactors.

9.2 Key findings

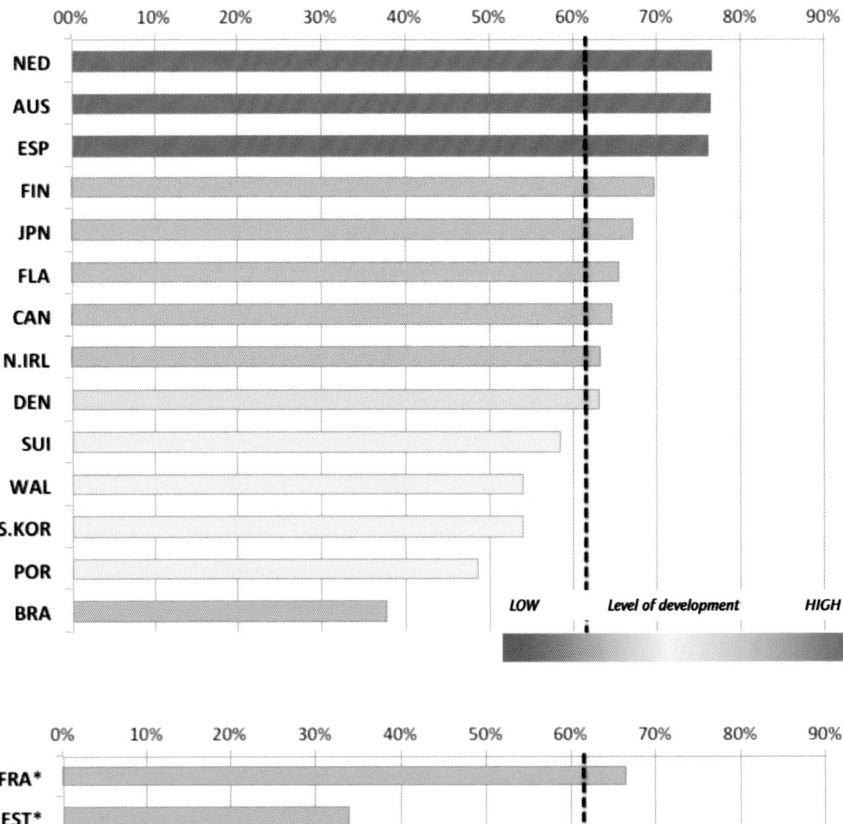

Figure 39: Total scores of the SPLISS sample nations against the 5 CSFs of Pillar 5[26]

26 These figures exclude France (no elite sport climate survey) and Estonia (no inventory). One CSF (5.6) was not measured due to a lack of sufficiently detailed data: a co-ordinated support programme to support the transition form junior to senior athlete.

The average Pillar 5 scores are the highest of all Pillars and have the least variation between countries. Nations are increasingly recognising the need for a holistic approach to athletic career development

Compared with the other Pillars, the degree of variation between countries is noticeably smaller in Pillar 5. Apart from Brazil with a score of less than 40%, the overall Pillar 5 scores range from 49% (Portugal) to 78% (the Netherlands). The average score of 61% is quite high relative to other Pillars. Based on these findings it can be argued that national sport organisations are increasingly recognising the need for an holistic approach for developing and supporting athletic careers. Athletes pursuing success in their sport are increasingly recognised and treated as employees, where resources to support the cost of training, competition and the cost of maintaining a certain lifestyle are linked to reasonable living costs and access to other support services. In the athletes' survey, almost 70% of the top 16 athletes reported that they received a monthly salary for their elite sport activities. Meanwhile, training as an elite athlete at the highest level still remains a personal devotion and investment by the athletes themselves, as one-third of all full-time top 16 athletes reported that they earned less than approximately €10,000 a year. One clear point emerging from our analysis is that respondents have different views on how and for what purpose athletes should be funded. In Australia, Canada, Japan, Switzerland and France athletes receive direct funding to assist with their training and living costs rather than receiving a wage for full-time training, as is the case in the Netherlands, Finland, and Belgium (Flanders and Wallonia).

The importance of the Pillar 5 CSFs in relation to success in summer and winter sports is less explicit compared to some of the other Pillars.[27] This is partly explained by the fact that there is less variation between the countries. Stakeholders (athletes, coaches and performance directors) in the Netherlands and Flanders were of the opinion that support during and after the athletic career was less impactful on sporting success than some of the other Pillars. From our analysis, the only CSF that correlated significantly with success (summer sport only) was concerned with athletes' average income (CSF 5.1)[28] and contains subfactors related to their monthly income, income from their own resources resulting from their elite sport activities, and whether the income was sufficient to train on a full-time or part-time basis. These results differ between the performance levels of athletes, as well as between males and females. Generally, men earn more than women and higher level athletes earn more money to re-invest in their careers, hence the more pronounced link with success. In a way it can be argued that the income of athletes is a more direct financial resource

---

27 The correlation of the Pillar 5 scores with success is: $r_{s(summer)} = 0.483$ ($p = 0.08$) and $r_{s(winter)} = 0.322$ ($p = 0.261$).

28 The correlation CSF 5.1 with success is: $r_{s(summer)} = 0.587$ ($p = 0.027$); for winter sports the Spearman's rank correlation was much lower: $r_{s(winter)} = 0.209$ ($p = 0473$).

measure than money invested by the national government (Pillar 1). Higher income allows athletes to 'buy' more time and support services to be invested in perfecting their sporting trade. This will be further explored in the next sections. Other CSFs that are related to success (r_s>0.4) are employers' support for athletes' careers (CSF 5.2) and the evaluation of the support programme by athletes and coaches (CSF 5.4). Again, caution must be exercised with the interpretation of data from a small sample where the scores on Pillar 5 are generally high in most cases.

The high scores achieved by Spain on Pillar 5 are quite surprising. Spain scores well on every CSF, and ranks fifth in the elite sport climate survey, just above the average (see Figure 40). In Spain there are 16 staff members at the three CARD (Centro de Alto Rendimiento Deportivo) centres dedicated to look after the support programmes for elite athletes, including career coaching, legal advice, media training, coaching support, training and competition support, sports science and sports medicine support. Also post-career support programmes in Spain are reasonably well developed. In Brazil we found the opposite, with an almost complete lack of service delivery to support athletic careers. More than half of the top 16 Brazilian elite athletes reported that they earned less than €10,000 per annum from their sport, yet spent relatively large amounts of their own money on their sport activities. Similar results are found in Portugal, Northern Ireland and Wallonia, compared with less than 30% of all athletes earning less than €10,000 in Australia, Denmark, Spain, Flanders, Japan, South Korea and the Netherlands (after correcting for student athletes in the dataset). Scores on the income subfactors are also lower in Canada, which explains in part why the nation achieved only an 'average' level of development score on Pillar 5.

Throughout the sample, the lowest average scores are on the post-career support sub factors. Lifestyle support services, career coaching, legal and financial advice are among the least-developed services in all the countries as also confirmed by the perceptions current athletes have on being prepared for life after their athletic career. Furthermore one-third of the athletes indicated that concerns about future prospects outside sport have negatively affected their ability to focus fully on being an elite athlete.

More detailed analysis of Pillar 5 reveals that discrepancies between scores on the inventory and scores on the surveys are apparent. Separate scores for each country are shown in Figure 40. The average inventory scores are higher than the elite sport climate survey, with the exception of Brazil and Portugal. It seems that from an overall national perspective, policymakers perceive themselves as being more supportive of athletes than is perceived by the athletes themselves (apart from Brazil and Portugal). Furthermore this finding indicates that triangulation of results through the use of different sources of data is required to improve the reliability and validity of the findings. It is also noteworthy that success is mainly explained by the scores on the elite sport climate survey data,[29] where there is a positive relationship between the personal living and training circumstances of athletes and national success.

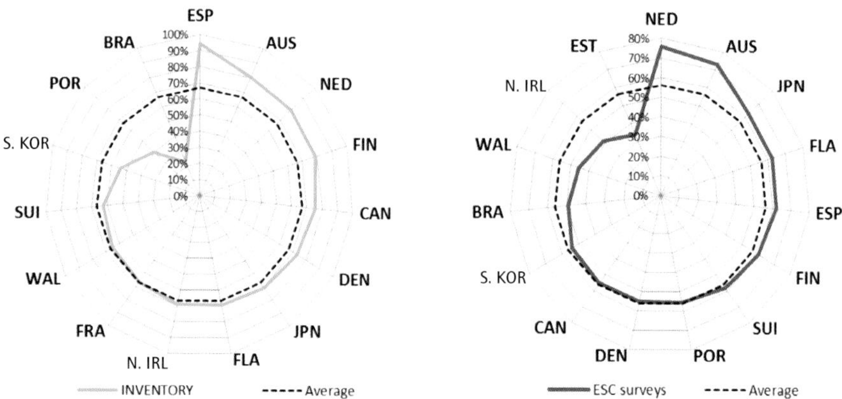

Figure 40: Separate scores of the SPLISS sample nations for the overall inventory (left) and the elite sport climate survey (right) on Pillar 5 (sorted from largest to smallest)

Overall it can be concluded that in successful countries, athletes are supported during and after their careers more than in less successful countries, but the variance between the countries is relatively small compared to other Pillars. Therefore, in future research, a more diverse sample of nations may offer more conclusive evidence of the impact of Pillar 5 on national sporting success. In the next part of this chapter we will present a more descriptive comparison of different CSFs within Pillar 5.

29 The correlation of the total scores on the elite sport climate survey with success is: $r_{s(summer)} = 0.582^{*}$ ($p = 0.023$) and $r_{s(winter)} = 0.280$ ($p = 0.313$); for the inventory: $r_{s(summer)} = 0.282$ ($p = 0.308$) and $r_{s(winter)} = 0.182$ ($p = 0.517$).

9.3 Comparative and descriptive analysis

9.3.1 Time spent on training activities

Full-time athletes, higher level athletes and athletes from individual sports on average train more

With an increasing number of athletes focusing on their sport on a full-time basis, the average time spent on training has also increased over time. This item was not scored as a criterion, but nonetheless has been evaluated to provide some additional context.

As a starting point, Table 31 shows the number of full-time athletes by nation. On average 32% of all athletes are angaged in their sport on a full-time basis. This is higher for top 16 athletes (40%). The key question then is to what extent being a full-time athlete influences the training activities of elite athletes?

Table 31: Number of athletes that indicated to be full-time athlete only

Country (n)	AUS (208)	BRA (431)	CAN (157)	DEN (231)	ESP (166)	EST (82)	FIN (78)	FLA (168)	JPN (135)	S. KOR (370)	NED (153)	N. IRL (61)	POR (107)	SUI (715)	WAL (80)	TOT (3142)
All athletes	18%	22%	44%	18%	29%	49%	52%	40%	39%	45%	27%	21%	29%	35%	27%	32%
Top 16 athletes	18%	31%	54%	23%	35%	68%	53%	63%	36%	50%	28%	50%	34%	47%	40%	40%
Top 3 athletes	23%	33%	65%	26%	42%	87%	64%	89%	45%	54%	29%	25%	50%	51%	50%	45%

On average an elite athlete trains 22.4 hours on a weekly basis (including sport-specific training, strength and conditioning and other relevant training activities). Compared with the sample from the SPLISS 1.0 study in 2004-2008, the SPLISS 2.0 data reveals an increase of almost two hours per week.

In the sample of athletes, it appears that higher ranked athletes also train longer, with average scores rising to 24 hours a week for top three elite athletes. More than 60% of all athletes train for more than 20 hours a week and 30% train for more than 25 hours per week. Not unexpectedly this is related to the status of athletes: full-time athletes on average train more (75% exceed 20 hours a week), athletes in full-time employment train less (on average 17 hours/week, with only 39% training for more than 20 hours a week) and also full-time students train less (53% train for more than 20 hours a week). Finally, athletes from individual sports train significantly more than athletes from team sports: 68% of these athletes train more than 20 hours per week compared with 42% in team sports.

The relationship between the level of support services received and the level of sporting achievement largely remains a black box. Higher level athletes will receive more support and as a result will be able to train more. In the context of Pillar 5 this means that if and when policymakers consider support services delivered to athletes to be in the interest of improving performance, support services should also be targeted strategically to those who do not yet have the time and resources to train.

Table 32: Overview of training hours/week of elite athletes

		Average (h)	<20 hrs	>20 hrs
Level	All Athletes (n=2794)	22.4	38.5%	61.5%
	Top 16*(n=1345)	23.2	34.1%	66.0%
	Top 3* (n=528)	24.0	31.6%	68.4%
Status	Full-time*(n=882)	24.9	25.2%	74.8%
	Full-time student*(n=609)	21.3	46.4%	53.6%
	Full-time employed*(n=236)	17.4	39.1%	60.9%
Gender	Male (n=1557)	22.1	37.8%	62.2%
	Female (n=1218)	22.8	39.4%	60.6%
Ind/Team	Individual*	23.5	31.7%	68.3%
	Team	18.5	57.9%	42.1%

*Note: *= significant difference of this group of athletes (training less/more) compared with the athletes not belonging to this group.*

Some differences are also identified between sports and between countries. Of all top 16 athletes, training hours appear to be the highest in Canada (on average 29 hours/week), Korea (29 hours/week) and Japan (28 hours/week), and in the sports of modern pentathlon and softball (approximately 35 hours/week), skating, aquatics, and athletics (approximately 30 hours/week). The lowest numbers are found in Denmark (16 hours/week) and Switzerland (19 hours/week), and in sports like curling, kayak, bobsled and ice hockey (approximately 16 hours/week). Differences between nations are only useful if they can be assessed on a sport-by-sport basis, which goes beyond the scope of this analysis. It is clear that the requirement for athletes to be able to train full-time depends on the sport in particular, and that a non-discriminatory approach to offering such support will be suboptimal. In order to prepare for maximum performance, some sports are simply less time-intensive than others. Furthermore, in some sports recovery is an integral part of the training process that should not be compromised by additional physical demands.

9.3.2 National elite athletes support programme: Financial support

Critical success factors		INVENTORY	SURVEY			
I. The individual living circumstances of athletes are sufficient so that they can concentrate on their sport full-time		O	A	C	PD	
CSF 5.1	Athletes' monthly income (total gross annual income) in general and income from their sport activities is sufficient		X			P1
CSF 5.2	Employers are supportive towards athletes' careers		X			
CSF 5.3	Athletes can receive financial support that allows them to dedicate themselves sufficiently to their sport (sustain a living while preparing for and competing in elite sport)	X	X			P1

Source of information: O: overall sport inventory; A: athletes' survey; C: coaches' survey; PD: performance directors' survey; right column shows where the CSFs are possible on the interface with other Pillars.

Total income of elite athletes

The scores are generally high on factors that focus on the individual living circumstances and related financial support of athletes, with Brazil, Northern Ireland, and Wallonia scoring lower than the sample overall. Athletes in the Netherlands, Spain, Australia and Finland have the highest scores, with South Korean athletes' income from sport activities identified as being the highest of all countries in the sample.

25% of the elite athletes rate the support they receive from their employers as poor. Higher level athletes are more satisfied

Athletes often face challenges when trying to combine their sporting career with work. In the survey sample, it was described earlier that 32% of the athletes trained on a full-time basis, 9% were employed full-time and 12% were in part-time employment. Others are students, either part-time (19%) or full-time (22%). Athletes working part-time or full-time were asked how they rate the support of their employer towards their elite sporting career. Generally higher level athletes (top 16 level, n=546) were more satisfied with this support from their employer compared with the overall sample; 56% found the support sufficient, but 25% perceived this support to be poor. In Northern Ireland, particularly, but also in South Korea and Flanders, these scores were low.

69% of the top 16 elite athletes receive a monthly salary. Two out of three elite athletes find the support they receive reasonable to sufficient. A substantial number of athletes are employed in full-time or part-time jobs other than sport

A recent development in various countries has been policies designed to enable athletes to become full-time. However, a substantial number of elite athletes still require part-time or full-time employment to supplement their sport-related funding. From the athletes' survey data, on average 69% of all top 16 athletes reported that they received a monthly salary for their elite sport activities. This statistic is significantly lower in Denmark (43%) and Switzerland (41%). For two out of three athletes the support they receive is perceived to be reasonable or sufficient relative to the time they require to prepare for peak performance. The most positive evaluations are reported (in descending order) in Flanders, Spain, Estonia, Japan and Australia, as can be seen in Figure 41.

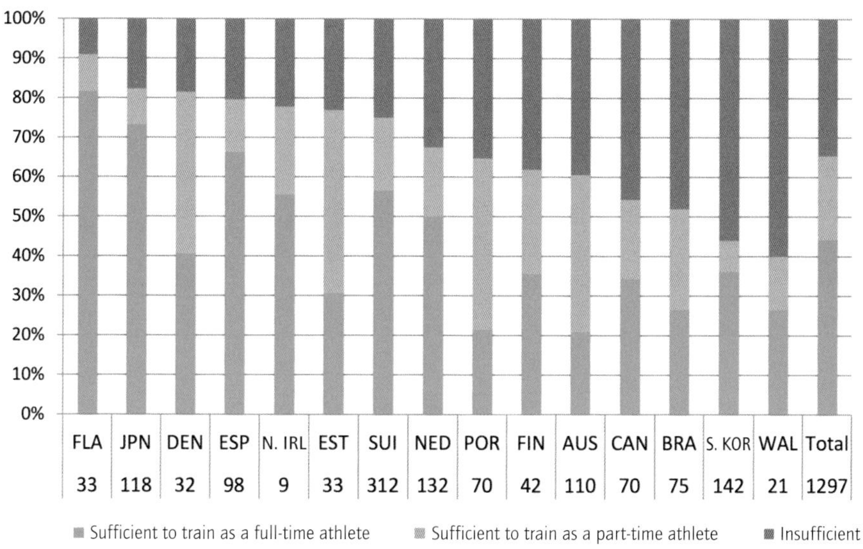

Figure 41: Perceived adequacy of the monthly financial support to pay for living and training costs as a full-time/part-time elite athlete (top 16 athletes)

Countries have different views on how to use financial support that is required to become a full-time elite athlete and on how this support is generated

Countries appear to have different views on the financial support that should be provided to elite athletes. In eight countries, the direct financial support for athletes is meant to enable full-time commitment to their sport as a professional elite athlete. This is not the case in Australia, Canada, Japan, Switzerland, France, Brazil and Portugal. In some of these countries the support is perceived to be insufficient (POR, BRA), and the state's objective for the payments is to 'assist athletes with their training needs as they prepare for upcoming benchmark competitions', but not to become full-time state-funded athletes only. In Northern Ireland athletes are mainly home national-level athletes and not team GB (UK), where UK Sport considers Athlete Personal Awards to be an 'award' to be used as a contribution towards living and sport-related costs and not a 'reward' for being an elite athlete or for winning medals.

Income of elite athletes from their elite sport activities

The higher the standard of athletes, the more they earn. However, 32% of the full-time athletes (non-students) earn less than 12,000 international dollars a year

In only a few sports can athletes make a living from their earnings and pay for all the costs they incur. This is also shown in Table 33; athletes were asked to estimate their gross annual income from their elite sport activities (separated by direct payment [salaries], prize money and reimbursements). For comparability reasons, similar as explained in Pillar 1, figures are presented in PPP (Purchasing Power Parity) values. Of all athletes responding to this question (n=2213), 61% reported that they earned less than i$12,000 (as a reference point, for Belgium this corresponds with €10,300), 16% earned between i$12,000-26,000 (i.e., €10,300-22,360 in Belgium). Athletes performing at higher levels earn more, however, looking only at top 16 athletes, 48% of them earned less than i$12,000. Similar figures are found when students are excluded from this sample. There are no significant differences between top 16 and top 3 athletes. The sports in which athletes were most likely to receive less than i$12,000 per annum are aquatics (11%), athletics (6%), skiing (5.9%) and gymnastics (5.4%). Interestingly, 32% of the top 16 athletes who classified themselves as being full-time athletes only, reported that they earned less than i$12,000. These include some commercial sports, like skiing (9.4%), cycling (9.3%), athletics (7.6%) and volleyball (7.4%). For many of these athletes supporting their career financially is a big challenge. Of all the full-time elite athletes, only 18% reported earing more than i$42,000 (corresponds with €36,000 in Belgium).

Table 33: Annual income of elite athletes from their elite sport activities (in PPP values)

	All athletes *(n=2213)*	**Top 16 athletes*** *(n=987)*	**Full-time athletes only (top 16)** *(n=743)*
<i$1,000	27.7%	20.1%	18.3%
i$ 1,001-12,000	33.7%	28.1%	13.6%
i$ 12,001–26,000	15.6%	18.8%	17.3%
i$ 26,001–42,000	9.8%	12.7%	12.6%
i$ 42,001-57,000	7.0%	9.7%	8%
i$ >57,000	7.0%	10.6%	10%

**Note: Similar figures for top three athletes; the figures exclude Australia, because the Australian researcher did not provide these data.*
In comparison, i$12,000 corresponds in Belgium to €10,300; i$26,000; with €22,360; i$42,000 with €36,000.

Sources of elite athletes' income from elite sport activities

When analysing the source of income more broadly, the results reveal that there is considerable variation in how athletes receive financial support, as is also indicated by the European Union (EU expert group, 2012).

As Figure 42 shows the direct payment in the form of salary, grants and funding make up almost half of the total income from elite sport activities, received by 1,202 elite athletes. This is followed by sponsorship (23%, n=715), prize money (17%, n=627) and reimbursements (13%, n=746). While relative sources of income do not differ between top 16 and top 3 athletes, the absolute amounts received do. As can be derived from Figure 43, the total income from elite sport activities, is much higher for top 3 athletes, compared to top 16 and all other athletes from the sample.

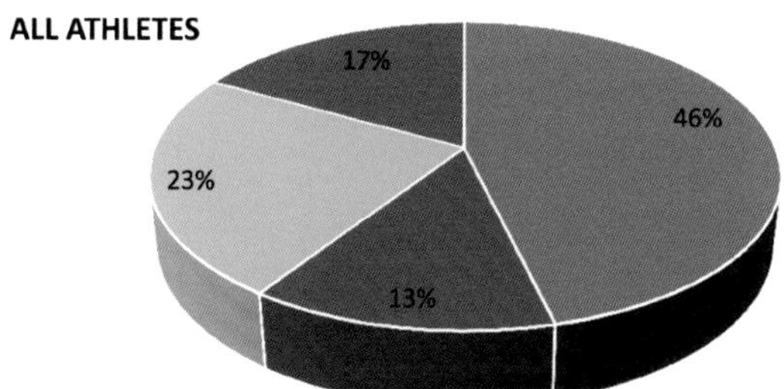

Figure 42: Division of the financial support from elite sport activities of all elite athletes by source of income (weighted for sample differences)

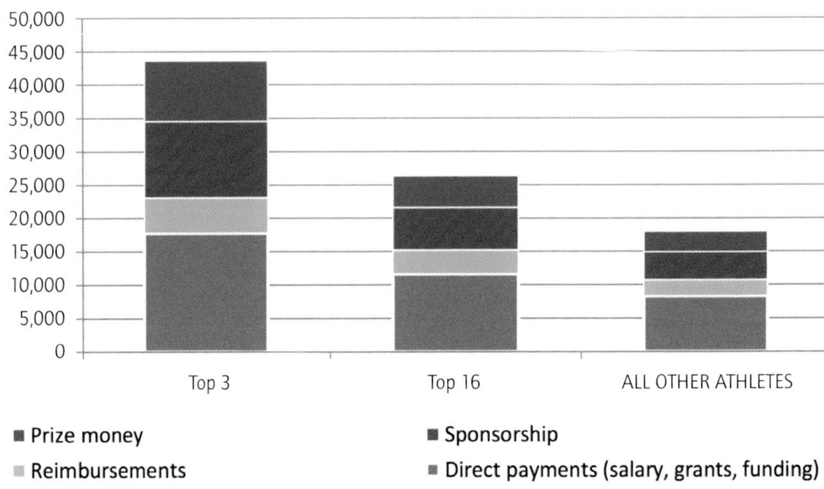

Figure 43: Financial support from elite sport activities according to the level of elite athletes, by source of income

Comparison by sport

A breakdown by sport (Figure 44) highlights that more than 50% of all elite athletes earns less than i$12,000 in most of the sports. A higher number of athletes in badminton, tennis, triathlon and skiing earn more than i$57,000 a year (corresponds to €49,000 in Belgium). This is, however, country-specific, as a higher number of these athletes come from South Korea (n=50, including 8 badminton players) and Japan (n=22, including 7 judokas) and Switzerland (n=31, including 14 skiers).

An independent t-test generally does not reveal significant differences between individual sports and team sports; in winter sports athletes' income is slightly higher than in summer sports Surprisingly also among top 16 athletes only (23 sports), there are many sports where elite athletes do not earn more than i$12,000.

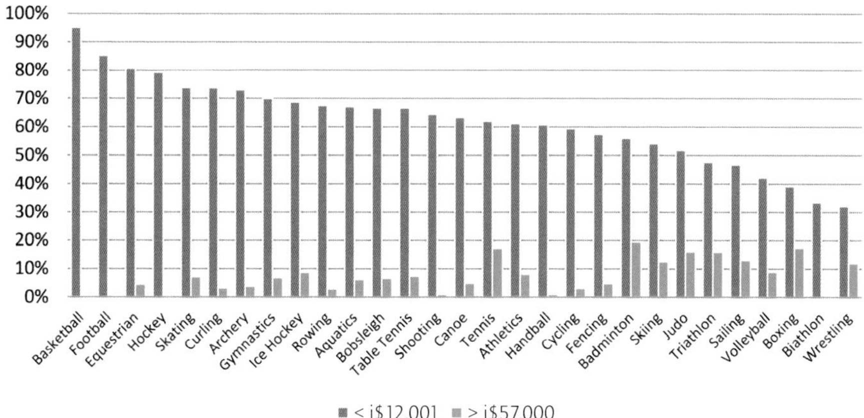

Figure 44: Breakdown by sport of the number of athletes that earn respectively below €10,000 and above €50,000 with their elite sport activities

Country comparison (in PPP values)

Comparisons by country are not straightforward, because of the variation in popular sport, athlete status and different costs of living. The analysis in Figure 45 uses PPP values expressed in international dollars, and is limited to top 16 athletes only. The results presented in this graph might be a distortion of what athletes really earn, as 25% of the athletes did not respond to this question (top 16, n=987). 50 athletes that earn more than i$220,000 on a yearly basis have been omitted from the analysis as outliers, because of their influence on the average values. Most of these athletes were Swiss (n=33), 6 were from Japan, 3 from Japan, 3 from Brazil and the others from Spain (2), Flanders (2), Finland (2), Estonia (1) and Denmark (1).

The most secure source of income that athletes have through their elite sport activities is direct wage payments, which are the highest in South Korea, Japan, Spain and Flanders. The total average income (from all sources) is the highest in South Korea of which 67% of the income comes from direct payments for wages and reimbursements. South Korea's athletes' income exceeds all other countries, and it has the most normally distributed income curve, with the least number of extreme values and with the highest values all below €100,000 per annum. In comparable terms (PPP values), in Wallonia, Brazil, Northern Ireland, Denmark, Portugal and Canada the average income of top 16 elite athletes is much lower than the sample average. In Northern Ireland these athletes are mainly home national-level athletes and not Team GB (UK) athletes. If they were to get onto UK Sport-funded pathways, Podium-level athletes can receive up to £28,000 per year as well as access to services worth around £70,000 per year; this explains why reimbursements are almost the only financial support athletes receive. It also needs to be noted that only 18 top 16 athletes in Northern Ireland completed this question.

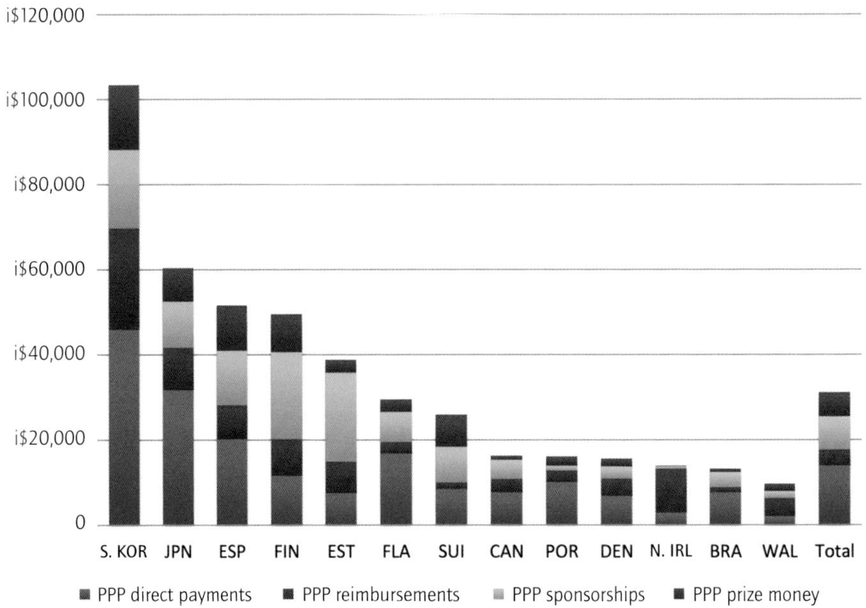

Figure 45: Overview of the average global financial income by elite athletes (top 16, n=987) per country through their elite sport activities, of top 16 athletes (in i$ for PPP-values) (Note: this question was not included in the Netherlands, and was not made available to SPLISS by Australia.)[30]

As there is also a large number of athletes earning less than i$1,000, the next graph presents the data in five categories. In these categories, the athletes earning more than i$220,000 are included. Significant differences between countries exist, with the highest number of athletes earning less than i$12,000 in Wallonia, Denmark, Switzerland and Northern Ireland. A higher number of athletes earn more in South Korea and Japan.

30 The Australian researcher used other data intervals, these data intervals were allocated to the general data intervals: 1-15,599 AUS$ equals <€10,000; AUS$ 15,600-31,199 equals €10,000-35,000; AUS$ 32,200+ equals €35,001-50,000.

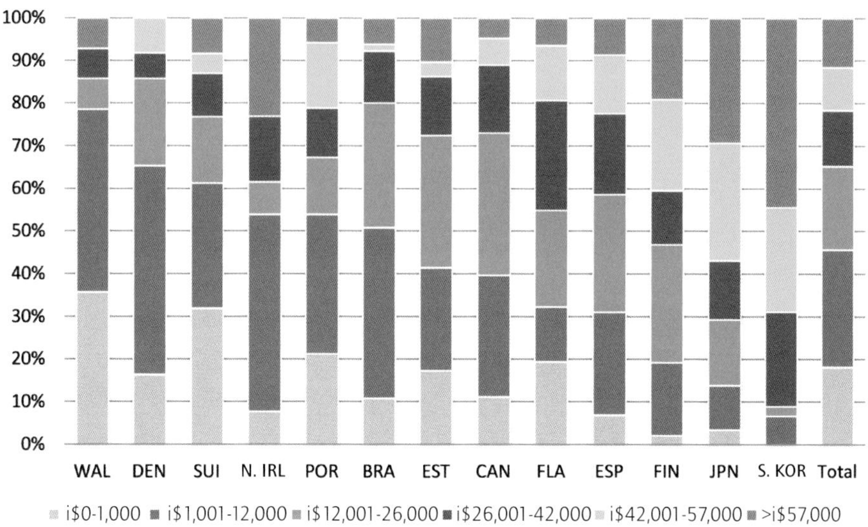

Figure 46: Overview of the average global financial income by top 16 elite athletes per country (excluding full-time students) (n=800) through their elite sport activities, breakdown by category (in PPP values) (Note: This question was not included in the Netherlands, and was not made available to SPLISS by Australia.)

Not unexpectedly, there are also income differences between men and women. In general male elite athletes are paid 40% more compared to their female counterparts.

In general male elite athletes are paid more in direct payments than female elite athletes

Overall it can be concluded that the amount of total income received by athletes differs greatly within countries and between countries. This is not an unexpected finding as it is clear that both the level of elite performance and the market attractiveness of specific sports drive the value that is derived from the sporting performance. In other words, athletes who excel in sports that are popular among mass (international) audiences will find it easier to attract substantial direct and indirect income through their sport than those participating in less popular sports. As the sports practiced differ greatly between countries in the sample, so, too, can big differences in amounts and sources of income be observed. The range of support services delivered by governments or national governing bodies is discussed in the next section.

9.3.3 National co-ordinated support programme for elite athletes

Critical success factors		INVENTORY	SURVEY			
II. There is a co-ordinated support programme for elite athletes		O	A	C	PD	
CSF 5.4	There is a co-ordinated support programme for elite athletes (apart from financial support) including career coaching, legal advice, media training, coaching support (specialist coaches), training and competition support (training facilities, training camps), sports science support (strength and conditioning, nutrition, mental coaching), sports medicine support (medical specialists, physiotherapists, etc)	X	X	X	X	
CSF 5.5	Specific personnel are appointed at the NSA/NOC to guide and help athletes during their career	X			X	P2
CSF 5.6	There is a co-ordinated support programme to support the transition from junior to senior athlete	Not measured				

Source of information: O: overall sport inventory; A: athletes' survey; C: coaches' survey; PD: performance directors' survey; right column shows where the CSFs are possible on the interface with other Pillars.

Research shows that the peak performance of elite athletes in most sports is not achieved until well into adulthood. Furthermore, performance analysis reveals that the age at which peak performance is achieved has increased over time. For example, compared to the 1980s, male elite athletes in 2008 were on average 3.5 years older in sailing and 3 (men) to 5 (women) years older in swimming (Sweetenham, 2009). As stated earlier, there is also a tendency that elite athletes prolong their elite career in order to maximise their performance and the related returns on this investment (van Bottenburg et al., 2012). Over time, this career extension has been underpinned by an increasingly professional approach and a holistic developmental perspective to building a career in and after sport. In line with this, national and regional sport institutes have set up support programmes that contribute to athlete development in a high-performance environment in the areas of sport science, sports medicine and counselling. These include sport and exercise medicine, physiotherapy, soft tissue therapy, strength and conditioning, recovery, nutrition and dietetics, physiology, biomechanics, performance analysis, skill acquisition and decision-making, psychology, vocational guidance and support and information management and data mining (Fricker, 2013). All countries in this study reported that they had a support programme of this type that was co-ordinated nationally; for example Australia has its Direct Athlete Support Scheme (DAS, for living costs) which is combined with AIS and/or state institutes (SIS/SAS) support services. In Brazil there is the Brazilian Athlete Grant Program; Sport Canada offers an Athlete Assistance programme and all other sample nations have their own variations on the theme. However what is actually delivered through these programmes differs greatly. In this study we looked at the issue from two perspectives. First what support services National Sport Associations deliver (as assessed through the overall inventory) and second what kind of support services athletes have received over the past year, as well as how athletes, coaches and performance directors perceive these support services (through the elite sport climate surveys). These two perspectives do not always align with each other. For example, in Brazil, the services delivered by the NSA/NGB are limited (giving Brazil the weakest score on CSF 5.4), but the majority of the top 16 athletes (80%) indicate that they did receive a wide variety of services over the past 12 months. Of those receiving services, 41% perceive the services to be of fair or lower quality. In other words, in Brazil most services are not delivered or co-ordinated primarily by the NSA and by centralising these services in the future, the overall perceived quality of support in Brazil could improve.

Most support services are sufficiently available in most countries, the assessment of the quality of these services is only average

The overall availability of support services as shown in Figure 47 (which provides the sum of 11 different services) reveals that there are only slight differences between countries in regard to the availability of support services. Coaches' perceptions generally agree with the perceptions of athletes. Most athletes in all countries (over 95%) received sports medicine support from specialised sports doctors, physiotherapy and massage, mental coaching (by a psychologist) and psychology support. Also strength and conditioning training (82%) seems to be widely available and taken up by elite athletes in general. The services that are the least available to top 16 athletes are related to lifestyle support: career coaching (advice regarding the athletic career, elite sport lifestyle management), legal and financial advice and media training. Average scores on these are below 65% and with only minor differences between countries. An expected finding is that services are significantly more available to top 3/top 16 athletes compared with lower ranked athletes, except for strength and conditioning, physiotherapy and psychology support, which seem to be the most common services available to all elite athletes.

Top three athletes receive more services than lower level athletes

Figure 48 presents the quality that the different services are rated at by the athletes and coaches. Services are rated highest in Japan, Northern Ireland and Flanders and considered to be worst in Wallonia and Estonia. It can be seen that athletes and coaches differ somewhat in their views about the standard of support services in their countries. On average 42% of the athletes perceive the quality of the support services to be fairly high to very high. With the exception of Brazil and Northern Ireland, athletes generally rate services received more highly than coaches.

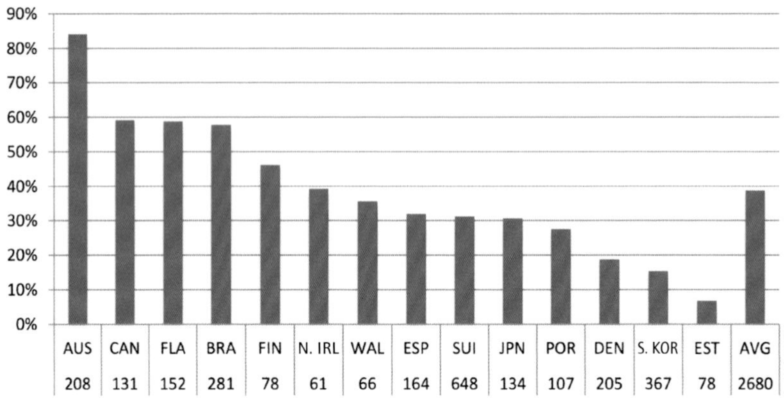

Figure 47: Average percentage scores on the availability of 11 services (e.g., sport science, medicine, and performance lifestyle support services) that athletes received over the past 12 months (according to top 16 athletes and coaches)

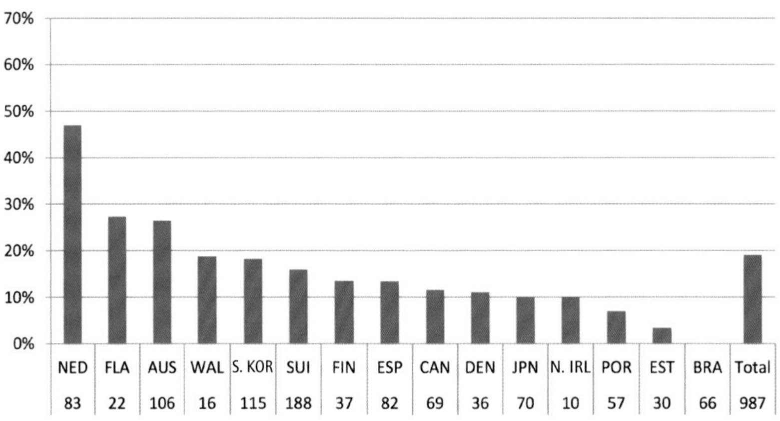

Figure 48: Average scores on the quality ratings given by top 16 athletes and coaches on 11 services (e.g., sport science, medicine, and performance lifestyle support services) that athletes have received (Note: data not available in the Netherlands)

Finally, research shows that athletes face particular challenges during the transition from junior to senior competitions, not only at athletic level, but also at the psychological, psychosocial, academic/vocational, and financial levels (Rosier and Wylleman, 2013). Only one junior athlete in three makes a successful transition into the elite senior ranks (Reints and Wylleman, 2011). This transition therefore requires specific support to minimise the unnecessary loss of athletic talent.

The results from the inventory illustrate that most countries do not specifically run programmes that address this issue. The researchers in the sample nations, considered this role to be the responsibility of the NGBs, as transitions tend to be sport-specific. If there is any attention paid to this stage, such as in the Netherlands and Japan, it happens through lifestyle management support, or through education. For example, seminars organised by the Japanese Olympic Committee allowed athletes to be connected to former Olympic athletes who became mentors. Further research is required to explain the kind of support services that are appropriate and most effective during this junior-senior transition.

9.3.4 Post-athletic career support

Critical success factors		INVENTORY	SURVEY			
II. There is a co-ordinated support programme for elite athletes		O	A	C	PD	
CSF5.7	Government/national sports bodies offer a post-career support programme to prepare and assist athletes for life after sports, such as: financial support (in the early stages) after their sports career, study support (for athletes who want to start studying or to finish their studies), job offers, advice and personal assistance (in the early stages) to find a suitable job after their sports career, lifestyle coaching, psychological support and partnerships with consultancy agencies	X	X	X	X	

Source of information: O: overall sport inventory; A: athletes' survey; C: coaches' survey; PD: performance directors' survey; right column shows where the CSFs are possible on the interface with other Pillars.

Due to the demands of an elite sporting career, such as the significant physical, psychological, emotional, financial and social commitments that are required, athletes are left with little time to engage in the self-development and self-exploration needed to make responsible and effective life choices beyond sport (Gordon and Lavallee, 2004). As a result, athletes may not be prepared for their post-athletic career and experience distressful reactions upon athletic retirement (Lally, 2007; Lavallee and Robinson, 2007). In their overview of career termination research, Taylor and Ogilvie (1994) formulated four main reasons which bring about the end of an athletic career, namely (a) injury, (b) age, (c) deselection and (d) free choice. These reasons influence the transition into employment outside sport. Furthermore the athletic career of elite athletes usually ends at a relatively young age compared with those in mainstream employment. Accordingly, research shows that to maximise performance during a career and to minimise adjustment problems after an elite career, athletes should start preparing for life after sport during their sporting career (Wyllemann and Lavallee, 2004; Stambulova, Stephan and Jäphag, 2007). In general, career development programmes on offer include three broad areas of service provision namely (a) career management, (b) education management, and (c) life-skills training (Reints and Wylleman, 2011).

> **There is an increasing awareness of the need of post-career support programmes, during and after an athlete's career but the supply of such progammes is limited**

While there exists a growing awareness of the need for post-athletic career support in most SPLISS countries, post-career programmes are in limited supply.

Spain, Switzerland, Canada and Australia seem to be the most developed nations in this regard. The worst scoring countries are Brazil, Portugal, South Korea and Denmark. Some interesting best practice can be noticed. Preparation for the post-athletic career **'during'** the athletic career exists mainly through athletes and education programmes and with specific staff appointed for career counselling. For example, in Australia, the Athlete Career and Education (ACE) programme includes: career counselling and planning, personal development training courses, educational guidance, employment preparation, career referral networks, transitional support, online services, referrals (to other services such as psychologists, financial advisors, relationship counselling, etc.), and lifestyle management. Also in Switzerland dedicated attention is paid to training in life skills. Here athletes can attend courses concerned with seeking sponsorship, developing media skills, mental strength development, professional marketing and time management.

> **The support services 'after' athletic retirement are limited**

In terms of services provided **'after'** retirement, the support is more limited. The most interesting cases are found in Canada, the Netherlands and South Korea. In South Korea the post-career support includes the opportunity of a pension for medallists, prize money for coaches of medallists, a pension for athletes who retire after injuries and a welfare fund for athletes. Furthermore Olympic medallists can apply for 'study abroad support' of up to €2,150 per semester over two years and short-term training programmes for up to one year. Sport Canada also supports athletes with post-secondary tuition that they can defer until retirement and through the Athlete Assistance Programme (AAP). In the Netherlands consultants are available for elite athletes for two years after retirement. They facilitate a career-coaching programme (by Randstad), study advice, job searching, interview training, and improving networking skills. There is also a programme called 'Gold in the company' in which athletes are supported to get a job during or after their career. In addition many countries collaborate with human resource companies, such as Adecco, that have developed programmes to help athletes find a job and develop job-related skills. To date, 10,000 athletes have benefited from career-training and job placement support in over 30 countries (Athlete Career Programme, 2013). For example in Spain, the PROAD programme (from the Consejo Superior de Deportes), engages with more than 50 companies and institutions for post-career athletes (such as Adidas, IKEA, NH Hoteles, Randstand, Telefónica España and Unipost).

Athletes have concerns about their future career prospects. The importance of post-career support is still not fully recognised by administrators

There still seems to be a discrepancy between what NSAs/NOCs say that they deliver (as shown by the inventory) and the services that athletes say they receive (as shown by the surveys). For example in Japan most elite athletes reported that they received only a limited number of support services that can prepare them for their post careers (Figure 49), which is not in line with the inventory evaluation. Estonian, South Korean and Danish elite athletes rate these services much lower than their counterparts in Australia, Canada and Flanders. We could argue that governments have not fully grasped the importance of offering post-career support services as less than 40% of the top 16 athletes agreed that post-career support is well developed in their country (see Figure 50). The highest scores are found in the Netherlands.

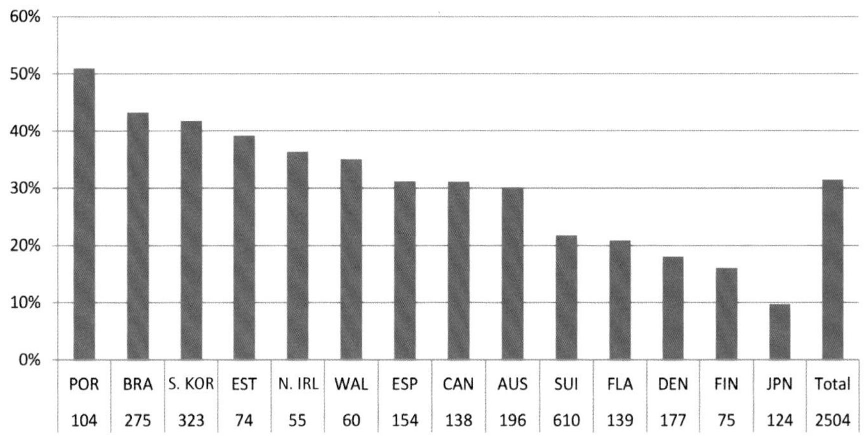

Note: The Netherlands did not include this specific question in their surveys.

Figure 49: Total percentage scores on the different post-career support services (8 items) according to elite athletes (specific programmes to prepare for the end of the career; sport psychologist; building a social network; building a professional network; adapted curriculum for education; career coaching; financial support; financial advice) (ALL athletes)

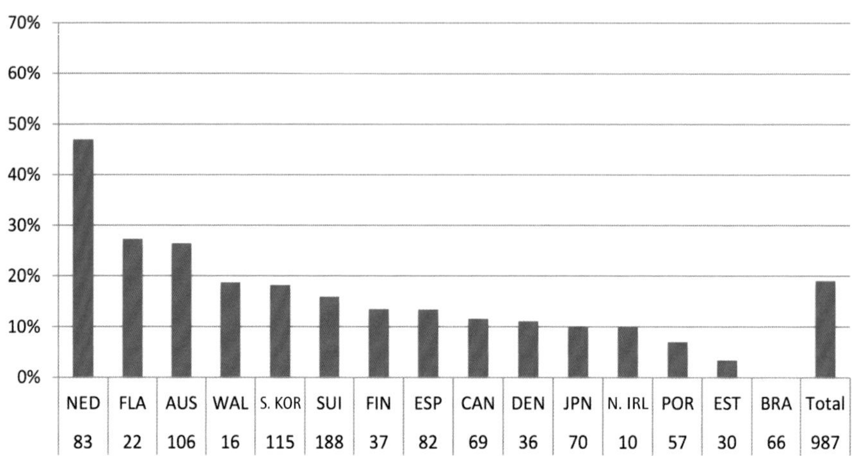

Figure 50: Top 16 athletes' opinion on the statement, 'the post-athletic career support is well developed in my country'

It seems that most government agencies can benefit from obtaining a better understanding about the during and post-career needs of athletes. Our results show that a significant number of athletes feel sufficiently affected by insecurity about their future to let it negatively influence their ability to focus on their sporting career. As an elite sporting career is nothing like a regular professional career, and most athletes retire from their sporting job at a time when many young adults start their first of second job, employer or government support is required. Even the few athletes who make substantial amounts of money during their career (the exceptions to the rule) require help in preparing for a life after sport (when significant earning capacity may dry up quite rapidly).

Finally, athletes were asked to give their opinion 'if concerns about future prospects outside sports affects their ability to focus fully on being an elite athlete'. About one-third of the elite athletes seem to be concerned enough about their future after sport to let this affect their career during sport. There are no significant differences between athletes at different levels of performance. Athletes in Northern Ireland, Brazil, Estonia and South Korea though, are more concerned about their future than athletes in other countries.

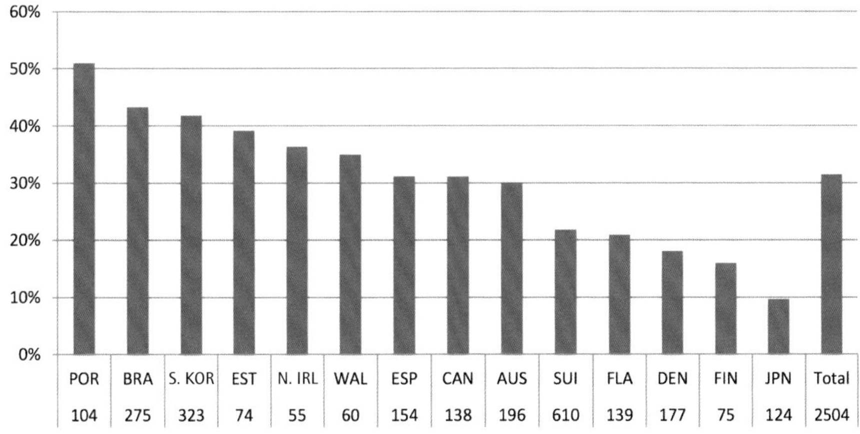

Figure 51: (ALL) elite athletes that (fully) agree with the statement, 'concerns about my future prospects outside sport negatively affect my ability to focus fully on being an elite athlete'

9.4 Summary points in Pillar 5

- Pillar 5 provides evidence that respondents consider elite sport success is best achieved as a planned intervention rather than through passive reliance on macroeconomic variables such as population and wealth.
- There is relatively little variation between nations' scores on Pillar 5 and success because in broad terms nations are doing essentially the same things. Therefore assessing effectiveness should be concerned more with measuring how well nations perform particular functions rather than measuring whether or not these functions are present.
- There are two basic ingredients to Pillar 5. First, provide athletes with the time to be able to train in their sport. Second, provide athletes with the necessary financial resources so that they do not have to spend time earning money required to pay for their sporting expenses. Despite these points, many top 16 and even full-time athletes earn less than i$12,000 a year. Many athletes work part-time or full-time, as they are unable to sustain themselves from their sport earnings.
- There is considerable variation in national-level policies regarding the amount and purpose of providing direct athlete funding. In some nations funding is seen as an 'award' linked to the cost of doing business; in others it is used as a 'reward' for achieving international sporting success. It provides further evidence that although elite sport systems can be compared at the level of implementation there remains great variation.
- Evidence has shown that full-time athletes, higher level athletes and athletes from individual sports on average train more than other athletes. This is possibly a 'chicken and egg' scenario as there are two possible explanations. Providing the necessary support to enable their sport to be a full-time activity might create the conditions for success because athletes can train more. Alternatively, it may be the case that successful athletes receive more support and thus have the opportunity to spend more time on training.
- There appear to be differences of opinion between what policymakers report on their inventories about the provision of services to athletes, coaches and performance directors and how these key stakeholders perceive such services. This is an important finding that justifies the use of different research methods to investigate the subject.

- The more enlightened nations see an elite sport career holistically as concerned with the development and wellbeing of athletes from the identification of their talent, the conversion of talent into elite level performance and the ultimate withdrawal from competitive sport. By putting in measures at the various transition points to prevent athletes from dropping out and to minimise the perceived risks of a sporting career, nations can maximise the amount of talent that achieves its full potential.
- Although there exists a growing awareness of the need to develop post-career support programmes, this remains an area for further improvement, especially after the career ends.

Chapter 9 references

Athlete Career Programme. (2013). About the programme coverage. Retrieved July 28, 2013, from http://athlete.adecco.com/Pages/Home.aspx

Bloom, B. (1985). *Developing talent in young people.* New York: Ballantine

Coakley, J. (2001). *Sport in Society: Issues and Controversies, 7th Ed.* New York, NY: McGraw-Hill.

De Bosscher, V. and De Croock, S. (2012). Trends in het Vlaams topsportklimaat. Evaluatie volgens topsporters, trainers en topsportcoördinatoren: 2-meting (2003-2007-2011) [Trends in the elite sport climate in Flanders. Evaluation according to elite athletes, coaches and high performance directors]. Brussel: VUB.

EU expert group. (2012). *EU Guideline on Dual Careers of Athletes, Brussels, European Union.* http://ec.europa.eu/sport/library/documents/c3/dual-career-guidelines-final.pdf

Fricker, P. (2013). Support services in athletic development. Good practices from the field. In *Managing high Performance Sport*, pp. 183-203. P. Sotiriadou and V. De Bosscher (Eds.). London and New York, UK: Routledge. ISBN: 978-0-415-67195-8

Gordon, S. and Lavallee, D. (2004). Career transitions in competitive sport. In *Sport psychology: Theory, applications and issues* (2nd ed., pp. 584-610). T. Morris and J. Summer (Eds.). Brisbane, Australia: Wiley.

Lally, A. (2007). Identity and athletic retirement: A prospective study. *Psychology of Sport and Exercise, 8*, 85-99.

Lavallee, D. and Robinson, H. K (2007). In pursuit of an identity: A qualitative exploration of retirement from women's artistic gymnastics. *Psychology of Sport and Exercise, 8*, 119-141.

Lotysz, G.J., Short, S.E. (2004). 'What Ever Happened To...' The Effects of Career Termination from the National Football League. Athletic insight. *The online journal of Sport Psychology, 6* (3), 47-66.

Reints, A. and Wylleman, P. (2011). Managing athletes' post-athletic careers. In *Managing High Performance Sport*, pp. 221-236. P. Sotiriadou and V. De Bosscher (Eds.). London and New York: Routledge.

Reints, A. (2011). *'Validation of the holistic athletic career model and the identification of variables related to athletic reteriment' PhD thesis.* Vrije Universiteit Brussel.

Rosier, N. and Wylleman, P. (2013) The transition from junior to senior athlete: a high performance directors' perspective. In *Elite Sport Success: Society Boost or not? Proceedings of the first SPLISS conference*, p. 2-13. V. De Bosscher (Ed.). Nieuwegein: Arko Sports media & VUB. Antwerp, 13-14/11. ISBN 978-90-5472-261-8

Stambulova, N., Stephan, Y. and Jäphag, U. (2007). Athletic retirement: A cross-national comparison of elite

French and Swedish athletes. *Psychology of Sport and Exercise, 8* (1), 101-118.

Stambulova, N. B. (2000). Athlete's crises: A developmental perspective. *International Journal of Sport Psychology, 31*, 584-601.

Sweetenham (2009). *Age of Olympic swimmers and sailors.* Internal document received from Australian/British Coach.

Taylor, J. and Ogilvie, B. C. (1994). A conceptual model of adaptation to retirement among athletes. *Journal of Applied Sport Psychology, 6*, 1-20.

van Bottenburg, M., Dijk, B., Elling, A. and Reijgersberg, N. (2012). *Bloed, Zweet en tranen. En een moment van glorie. 3-meting topsportklimaat in Nederland. [Blood, sweat and tears. And a moment of glory. 3-measurement elite sport climate in the Netherlands].* Nieuwegein: Arko Sports Media.

Wylleman, P. and Lavallee, D. (2004). A developmental perspective on transitions faced by athletes. In *Developmental sport and exercise psychology: A lifespan perspective* (pp. 507-527). M. Weiss (Ed.). Morgantown, WV: FIT.

BRASIL
LIVE YOUR GOALS
10
10

10 Pillar 6: Training facilities

10.1 Concepts and definition

The sixth Pillar is concerned with elite sport facilities and infrastructure. In many countries, the most significant providers of sport facilities are at sub-national levels of government (local authorities). Facility planning and development is an element of the sport delivery system traditionally located within the remit of local authorities (Green and Houlihan, 2005). National elite sport development has often been hampered by the fact that local authorities identify their own priorities, and there are often conflicting demands between members of grassroots sport clubs and elite athletes regarding access and the specification of training and competition facilities (Green and Houlihan, 2005). Elite sport facilities are expensive and used by only a small number of athletes. For example, elite level swimmers have often trained in pools owned by local authorities, where lane hire is costly and access restricted primarily to time slots in the early morning or late at night. Increasingly authorities have built 50-metre pools and general public access is made available around training times for elite swimmers. With the emergence of full-time athletes and opportunities for athletes to compete and train on a full-time basis, the need for athletes to have facilities available at any time of the day has increased. Over time, several countries have built multi-functional indoor and outdoor training facilities specifically for elite sport.

These facilities house several sports and elite level athletes can have full-time access to them, and enjoy centralised services, such as hotel facilities (for athletes to live and train at one location), sport science and sport medicine support, lifestyle and performance planning services and close links with schools or universities. Some of the early adopters of elite sport facility centralisation were INSEP (Institut National du Sport, de l'Expertise et de la Performance, founded in 1975) in Paris (France) and the AIS (Australian Institute of Sport, founded in 1981) in Australia. Central facilities such as these were built, among other things, to reduce duplication costs, to encourage the exchange of knowledge between sports, and to reduce travel time for athletes between their homes and training venues. INSEP and the AIS have been powerful examples for other countries to emulate. France and Australia have subsequently developed their facility infrastructure from large centralised locations to regionally located networks, in part to reduce athlete drop-out because of 'homesickness' (especially among younger athletes) (Oakley and Green, 2001). The SPLISS 1.0 project in 2008 suggested that smaller nations (geographically) may have a competitive advantage in Pillar 6, as there is less need for centralisation because athletes and coaches are not required to travel as much to training locations (De Bosscher et al., 2008).

Pillar 6 is concerned with national co-ordination and planning of elite sport facilities and the network of high-quality national and regional facilities

In this Pillar we identify seven CSFs, situated at two levels: (1) national co-ordination and planning of elite sport facilities and (2) the network of high-quality national and regional training facilities. While many previous elite sport studies have recognised Pillar 6 as a key component for achieving success (Andersen and Ronglan, 2012; Bersgard et al., 2007; Green and Houlihan, 2005; Houlihan and Green, 2008), none of these studies considered the views of athletes and coaches in regard to the quality and availability of training facilities. Pillar 6 consists of 84 sub-factors, of which 34 are measured by means of the elite sport climate survey.

10.2 Key findings

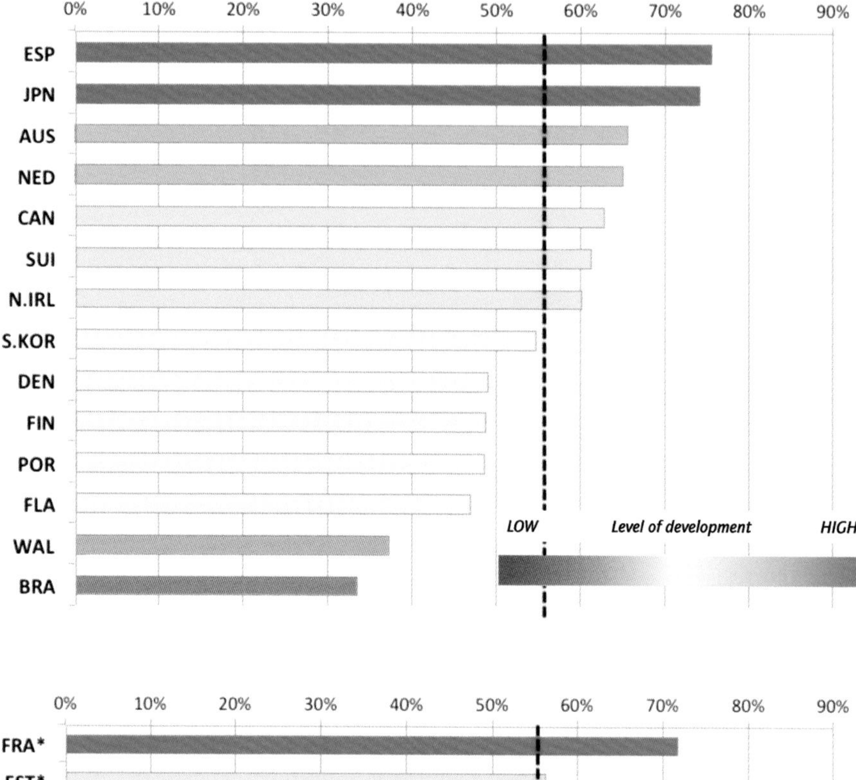

** Note: 13 nations + 3 regions (FLA, WAL, N-IRL). Only partial data are available in France (no elite sport climate survey); Estonia (no inventory). Caution is therefore needed with the interpretation of scores.*

Figure 52: Total scores of the SPLISS sample nations against the 7 CSFs of Pillar 6

Larger, more populated countries have higher scores on Pillar 6. A high-quality national training centre with all facilities and services available is the most important CSF

A high score on Pillar 6 correlates significantly with international sporting success in summer sports and moderately in winter sports; in other words, medal success is associated with the availability of a network of national and regional training facilities.[31] Generally, larger and more populated countries tend

31 Correlation between Pillar 6 scores for summer sports: $r_s = 0.704$ ($p = 0.005$) and winter sports: $r_s = 0.354$ ($p = 0.214$).

to score higher. In this Pillar, responses from the inventory and from the elite sport climate survey also display a pattern of agreement. The link to high performance on this Pillar is mainly explained by one CSF: a high-quality national training centre with all facilities and services available on site (CSF 6.5). CSF 6.6–a network of high-quality regional training facilities–correlates positively with success in summer sports, but negatively with winter sports[32]. However, neither of these correlations are significant. Having identified that there is an association between facilities and success, the direction of this correlation needs to be explored further.

On first inspection, it may seem surprising that Spain has the best score on Pillar 6 along with Japan and France. Spain does not have such well-known national trainings centres like the Australian Institute of Sport or INSEP in France, which have been studied and copied all over the world, but it does have a range of world-class training facilities distributed all over the country and considered by the athletes, coaches and performance directors to be of excellent quality. Japan scores well not only on the quality and services of the national training centre, but also on the network of high-quality regional elite sport facilities, where athletes can train in an elite environment at any time of day. In these countries, athletes and coaches rated the facilities better than most other countries against the criteria: world-class facilities and also community facilities of high quality, available at any time of the day and with a full suite of elite support services on site. Switzerland, in that regard, achieved the highest score on the elite sport climate surveys for Pillar 6, as can be seen in Figure 53. Scores are about average in Australia, Canada, South Korea, the Netherlands, Estonia and Portugal, whereas Flanders and Wallonia, Finland and Brazil have lower scores.

The overall elite sport facility score is also well developed in Australia, the Netherlands, Canada, Switzerland and Northern Ireland, which all score above the average of 56%. In many countries facility planning and development falls within the jurisdiction of local authorities and is therefore out of the national body's control. In Australia national strategy is particularly hampered by this distribution of power between various jurisdictions within sports, where the Australian State authorities identify their own priorities. These observations point to a high degree of organisational complexity that has perhaps been masked by the success of Australian elite swimming in the past. Consequently a lack of national co-ordination has impacted negatively on the scores of Australia and also Canada. Moreover, local authorities' priorities are often shaped by successful bids to host major events that have initiated the need for new facilities and the upgrading of existing facilities in order to provide the infrastructure for world-class events. Sustainable and 'sport for all' facilities are often used as a legacy argument to win the event for a city or nation. For example, in Australia the 'Sydney Olympic legacy', 'Melbourne Commonwealth Games legacy', and the Gold

---

32 The correlation of CSF 6.6 with summer sports: $r_s = 0.352$ ($p = 0.217$) and winter sports: $r_s = -0.302$ ($p = 0.293$).

Coast Commonwealth Games are major events for which the infrastructure investment has been rationalised on having a positive impact on elite sport as well as on community sport. Similar examples exist in Canada, after the 2010 Olympic Winter Games and the Pan American Games of 2015. On the other side, the Brazil's low scores can be explained by the lack of a national planning strategy on the use of facilities for elite athletes and talent development. Despite the fact that several sport facilities have been built or upgraded in relation to the hosting of international events over the past decade, there is no national training centre and elite facilities are used more often for events and entertainment than for their primary purpose. There is little collaboration between different NGBs on facilities, nor any national co-ordination. At grassroots level, facilities in Brazil are also underdeveloped. These findings are confirmed by Brazil scoring lowest on the elite sport climate survey (Figure 53).

Another point emerging from the data is the increased interest from governments to collaborate with private partners in developing and running the sport infrastructure on a commercial basis. In Australia and Canada, public-private sport facility partnerships are seen as an area that can strengthen overall infrastructure planning. There is an increasing realisation in Australia that when elite sport infrastructure is developed in the heart of dense urban growth areas, it will come with great community benefits if facilities also offer full community access and usage.

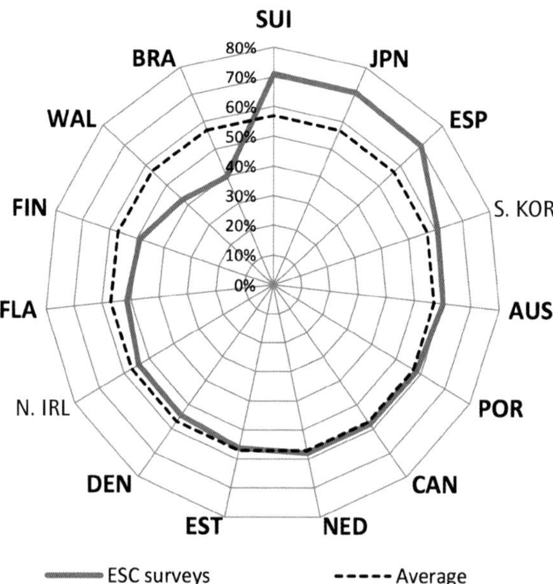

Figure 53: Scores on Pillar 6 in the elite sport climate survey (according to athletes, coaches and performance directors)

10.3 Comparative and descriptive analysis

10.3.1 Co-ordination of elite sport facilities

Critical success factors		INVENTORY	SURVEY			
I. Nationally co-ordinated planning: sport facilities and elite sport facilities throughout the country are recorded and the needs of athletes and coaches are known and clearly mapped out		O	A	C	PD	
CSF 6.1	There is a database available of sport for all and elite sport facilities in the country and this database is frequently updated	X				P2
CSF 6.2	There is an inventory of the needs of elite athletes and coaches with regard to training facilities and travelling times of elite athletes and coaches	X				P2
CSF 6.3	Time spent on travelling for athletes and coaches is kept to a minimum.		X	X		

Source of information: O: overall sport inventory; A: athletes' survey; C: coaches' survey; PD: performance directors' survey; right column shows where the CSFs are possibe on the interface with other Pillars.

At the national level, government can influence policies regarding training facilities in several ways. Most fundamental to effective influence is to make it a statutory requirement that a database of the location and type of each elite sport facility is maintained. Mapped against this are the requirements and needs of athletes at national level. France, Japan, Northern Ireland and Switzerland are the five countries that have a national strategy when it comes to the co-ordination and location of elite sport facilities but only six of all participating countries have a national elite sport facility database. Of these countries, the Flemish, Spanish and Dutch databases contain relevant details for elite athletes regarding the characteristics, availability and quality of the sport facilities, whereas the Finnish, Japanese and Swiss databases are less specific. At the time of the research, Denmark was working on establishing an elite sport facilities' database. Some nations (Australia, Canada, Flanders, Japan, Northern Ireland, the Netherlands and Wallonia) collect data on the needs of elite athletes and coaches with regards to training and competition facilities, on a sport-by-sport basis. Such information provides insight into training conditions and on the travelling time of athletes and coaches which is a starting point for more efficient training facility planning and construction.

Athletes and coaches spend on average between 5-6 hours per week on travelling. Travel times are higher in big countries

The perceived benefit of centralised training facilities is often discussed in the context of time spent travelling to and from training. Generally, in most countries, travel times seem to be acceptable. For 2,627 athletes answering this question from 15 countries, the average weekly commute time was 5.65 (±5.27) hours, and the 1,139 international elite coaches surveyed reported an average weekly commute of 5.39 (standard deviation ±5.39) hours. These values differ significantly according to the size of countries; in general, travel times are higher in bigger countries, but it seems that Finland, Japan and Spain are an exception in this regard, as can be seen in Figure 54. The average travel times reported by athletes are relatively high in the Brazil, the Netherlands, Portugal, Canada, Australia and Wallonia and for coaches they are particularly high in Flanders, with an average of 8.1 hours of travel a week.

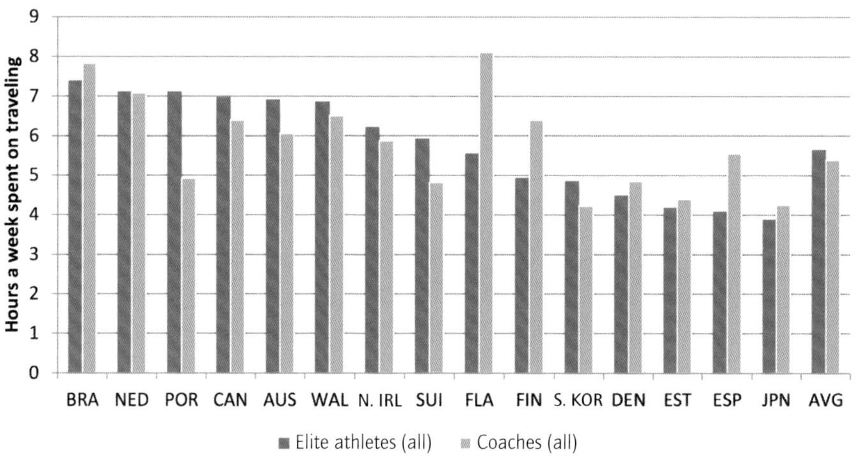

Figure 54: Total time per week spent on travelling to and from training by elite athletes (n=2627) and elite coaches (n=1139)

10.3.2 High-quality national and regional elite sport facilities

Critical success factors		INVENTORY	SURVEY			
II. There is a network of high-quality national/regional elite sports centre (s)/ facilities, where athletes can train in appropriate conditions at any time of day		O	A	C	PD	
CSF 6.4	There is a sufficient number of high-quality sport facilities either exclusively for, or with, prioritised use for elite sports.		X	X	X	
CSF 6.5	There is a high-quality national elite sport centre(s) including: an administrative headquarters; hotel facilities/overnight accommodation; available sports medics, sports scientists; a close link with universities and the education of younger athletes	X	X	X	X	P5
CSF 6.6	There is a network of high-quality regional elite sports facilities, specifically for elite sport purposes (only), including: an administrative headquarters; overnight accommodation; a close link with sports medics; a close link with sports scientists/co-operation with universities; and a close link with the education of younger athletes	X	X	X	X	P2 P5
CSF 6.7	Athletes can have full-time access to high-level training facilities		X			

Source of information: O: overall sport inventory; A: athletes' survey; C: coaches' survey; PD: performance directors' survey; right column shows where the CSFs are possible on the interface with other Pillars.

National training centre (NTC)

Three levels of centralisation:
(1) 1 all in NTC
(2) different multi-sport NTCs distributed
(3) one NTC per sport/NGB

As stated in the introduction, since the 1970s many countries have built multifunctional and sophisticated training infrastructure where all facilities are centralised in one location. This is a first level of full centralisation (see Table 34, option *a)*. Reasons to centralise are related to the increase of expertise and knowledge in one location, efficient information exchange between sports, and the economies of scale created by avoiding the duplication of costs. A second level, less centralised, exists when different national training centres are distributed over different regions, hosting several sports centralised in one location (see Table 34, option *b)*. Most of these centres are funded by the (national) government/public services. A third way in which countries develop facilities, is when each sport, usually operated by the NGB, has its own national training centre (NTC); in some cases, multiple sports are clustered in one centre. The latter centres are often less sophisticated than option (a) or (b) centres, and sometimes are designated for community or other use as well (e.g., Finland) such that athletes cannot have full-time access (see Table 34, option *c*).

Australia (AIS), France (INSEP) and Japan (JISS) have the most comprehensive national training centres

Based on these three categories, an overview of countries' facilities is provided in Table 33. From the available data and the services identified by the researchers, it is difficult to differentiate between quality levels of the facilities. We consider the opportunity to train at any time of the day and whether athletes can access elite level training conditions and support services as being the key quality indicators. Australia (AIS), France (INSEP) and Japan (JISS) have the most comprehensive national training centres, including several indoor and outdoor training halls, a climate room, cameras and laboratories, onsite medical services, psychological support, scientific services and athlete accommodation. Compared with Australia and France, Japan is a recent starter, with the National Training Centre established in 2008, by MEXT (the ministry) and owned by the National Agency for the Advancement of Sport and Health (NAASH). Some 17 sports use this centre as their national training facility. It is interesting to note that Japan also reported the highest number of indoor facilities (approximately 50,000), outdoor facilities (approximately 84,000) and swimming pools (approximately 35,000) for community use. Spain was second to Japan but with a significantly lower number of community facilities: indoor (approximately 4,000), outdoor (approximately 25,000) and swimming facilities (approximately 2,500).

Generally, in the context of developing facilities for elite sport purposes, it seems that the sample nations have created unique local solutions particularly when searching for cost-effective outcomes.

Canada takes a decentralised view, with a network of seven national training centres

Canada has applied a decentralised approach to elite sport facility development. The CSC, Canadian Sport Centres Network, consists of seven national trainings centres, regionally distributed, hosting over 1,500 senior elite athletes. Many facilities are a result of the Calgary 1988 Olympic legacy. The four largest are situated in Pacific (Victoria), Calgary, Ontario and Montreal. These facilities operate independently and in practice there is limited real national co-ordination. All these facilities service a number of sports in collaboration with the NGBs. In most centres, partnerships are developed with universities. The Canadian researcher reported there was a need to develop elite world-class facilities further to ensure athletes do not have to travel to other countries to train and to bring athletes, coaches, high-performance support personnel and administrators together under one roof.

Many countries have less expensive/ sophisticated training centres and build a network of several services regionally spread

In the other countries, the number of national training centres ranges from two (Korea, Denmark) to nine (the Netherlands) (see Table 34). Some of these centres are run by the NGB in countries such as Flanders (partly in collaboration with Bloso, the national sports administration, for some sports), Portugal, Spain, Switzerland and the Netherlands. In the Netherlands, four centres are developed for education and training (multisports), where elite athletes can live, train and study in one location. The Dutch national training centre, Papendal, can be seen as the major elite sport facility, and it also provides headquarters for NOC*NSF (the National Olympic Committee/National Sport Federation). An accreditation system is used to identify the centres that fulfill world-class elite criteria. Despite the fact that one of the accreditation criteria for elite facilities is related to the (limited) travel times of athletes, actual travel times appeared to be relatively high in the Netherlands compared to other countries (see Figure 54). The situation in Denmark is different, as apart from the two national training facilities in Århus and Brøndby (Copenhagen), where expertise and support services are delivered by Team Denmark, many sports have their national training centre located elsewhere. These are not necessarily run by NGBs, but by clubs (supported by NGBs and Team Denmark). Consequently, these training centres are not used exclusively for elite sport purposes. However, dependent on the discipline, elite athletes have priority access.

In Flanders there are no multisport national trainings centres. Each NGB usually has one national training centre, where they organise and aim to deliver all of the services required for their athletes. However in reality, it is difficult for all world-class services to be available in one centre. Furthermore, the NSA (Bloso) owns 13 sports centres that mainly offer sport for all services such as sports camps but where elite athletes can be provided with priority access.

It was found that Finland has no nationally co-ordinated training centre, and the facility structure for elite sport is complicated. Sport institutes (14), are the traditional centres in rural areas, established between the years 1925-1970. They are mainly used for short-term training camps (Mäkinen, 2012) and not solely for elite sport purposes (comparable to the Bloso centres in Flanders). The Finnish Olympic Committee argued in 1987 that four institutes should be recognised as elite sport training centres, but only in 2013 did the Ministry of Education and Culture officially recognised three multi-sport training centres and three sport-specific training centres. However, as these institutes are independent and state funding only marginally contributes to elite sport, the centres deliver youth sport and health enhancing activities as well. Almost 30 Finnish NGBs co-operate with sport institutes in varying ways. Over the past years, a local network of 19 sport academies has been developed in the largest cities to deliver athletes' daily training and education needs. This network is co-ordinated by the NOC.

Brazil is the only country where there are no specific national training centres for elite sport. While there are a range of high level multi-functional sport facilities, and despite the availability of some high standard facilities, the existing facilities are a legacy of the Pan American Games held in 2007. However, there remain 18 sports that have specific training centres for elite sport managed by their NGBs and there are also other training centres, usually private or one-off initiatives provided by regional governments. Winning the right to host major sporting events often drives construction and renovation of elite sport facilities, and Brazil is a good example in this regard. As an extension of the 2007 Pan American Games, many of the 34 competition venues that are prepared for the 2016 Olympic Games in Rio de Janeiro have been operational for years prior to the Games, eight underwent some permanent works, seven are temporary facilities and nine have been constructed as permanent legacy venues. As a host nation of the 2014 FIFA World Cup, 12 football venues were either built or renovated in different states across Brazil. Building 'sport for all' facilities and providing opportunities for younger athletes to train in quality facilities, close to their home environment, is a current challenge for Brazilian sport development.

Table 34: Overview of national and regional training centres

	AUS	BRA	CAN	DEN	ESP	FIN	FLA	FRA	JPN	S. KOR	NED	N. IRL	POR	SUI	WAL
Centralised National Training Centres (NTC)															
(a) 1 NTC- all in (centralised)	X							X	X						
(b) ≠ NTCs regionally distributed (multisport, centralised for each sport, elite sport only)			X 7 CSC	X 2	X 3					X 2	X 4	X 1(+1)	1(+3)	X 3	
(c) One NTC per sport, regionally distributed (centralised for each sport; sometimes not only elite sport)				X		X 4+2*	X ±6**			2	5			X	3
Decentralised, Regional Trainings Centres (RTC)															
(d) RTC (decentralised (athletes of the same sport train in different RTCs, that prioritise elite sport–nationally co-ordinated)	X 8			X 21	X 15		NA	X 16		0	0	X 3		X NA	
(e) RTC (athletes train in regular training facilities that are suitable for high-level competition–run by NGBs)		X 18	X			X	X		X 22	X			X		X

** In Finland these four multisport centres and two sport-specific trainings centres are not only for elite sport purposes and are not connected to the NOC** In Flanders there are six elite sport schools, where elite athletes can train during the day; in most sports, the facilities are developed around these schools.*

Support services available at the NTC

> **To what extent are services available at the main facility where athletes train?**

It can be argued that an important reason to centralise training facilities is to make support services available at the main facility where athletes do their training. A question along those lines was asked in the elite sport climate survey, in particular with regard to services provided by sports physicians, medical specialists, physiotherapists, massage therapists, mental coaches/psychologists, nutritionists, sport scientists (e.g., biomechanics support), lifestyle/career advisers and study counselling services. Two key points are presented in Figure 55. First, the greatest availability of centralised services was found in Australia, South Korea and Spain, all countries with multifunctional national trainings centres. It is striking that over 50% of Australian top 16 athletes reported that they can make use of most services on site, including services from psychologists, nutritionists, sport scientists and study counsellors, whereas for most of the other nations ratings against these attributes were very low. Second, performance directors report the availability of services at training venues more extensively than athletes. It could be that, although many services are provided by NGBs, the athletes are not always aware of the opportunity that these services are available.

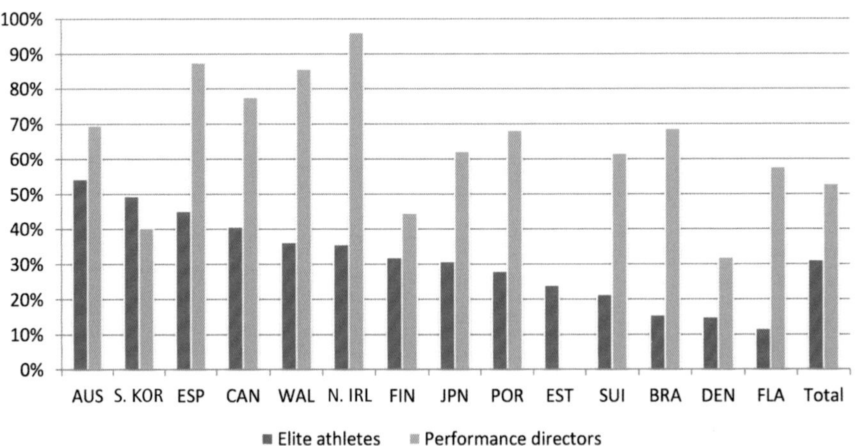

Figure 55: Can athletes make use of various support services (sum of 9 sub-items) at the main facility where they do most of their training? According to top 16 elite athletes (n=1266) and performance directors (n=137)

Regional training facilities

In addition to using centralised facilities, most countries also reported using decentralised facilities, indicating the widespread use of nationally and regionally co-ordinated training facilities. These countries are Australia, Canada, Denmark, France, Northern Ireland, Portugal, Spain, and Switzerland. An overview was provided in Table 35. Other countries have similar regional training centres (RTCs) that are mostly co-ordinated by NGBs. Team sports, for example, often train in facilities run by clubs.

Smaller countries may have a competitive advantage in the development of training facilities

A key question around centralisation and decentralisation of training facilities is concerned with talent development. Should talented athletes train in their home environment, or should they train together with their peers in one location? In this respect, an interesting approach to the development of regional trainings centres is offered by Denmark and the Netherlands. Team Denmark has enlisted 21 local municipal authorities to support and prioritise elite sport (see Pillar 2). These municipalities have a formal agreement with Team Denmark requiring them to support and dedicate resources to sports that are recognised and supported by Team Denmark. Facility access, special training for talented young athletes and educational courses in physical education are among the initiatives offered to athletes as part of the municipal programme. In the Netherlands, since 1992 NOC*NSF has developed 'Regional Olympic Networks' (originally 13, now reduced to 7). A network consists of municipalities, elite sport organisations, sport service offices and facilities providing medical services and education. The network's focus is not solely on elite sport as they also aim to strengthen sport clubs, enhance talent development and support elite athletes. As such the network creates an environment for local elite sport/talent development, as well as engagement with industry and local communities.

A network of regional support services exists in the Netherlands and in Denmark

Only a few countries report a strictly decentralised (Canada, Flanders, Netherlands) or centralised (Northern Ireland, Brazil) system. In most countries the organisation varies by sport, which makes it difficult to cluster the different systems. In Finland, Flanders and Northern Ireland the training centres are not solely for elite sport purposes.

Table 35 provides an overview of the number of athletes training in these centres. Some countries only focus on their senior elite athletes, others also on juniors.

Table 35: Number of athletes that train at the national and regional training centres

	AUS	BRA	CAN	DEN	FIN	FLA	FRA	JPN	S. KOR	NED	N. IRL	POR	ESP	SUI	WAL
National senior athletes	718		1,533 sen+ jun	NA	22		382		1,143	190			485	NA	
National junior athletes					62		197			446			0	NA	
Regional senior athletes	2,542		3,665 sen+ jun	NA	9		970		–				4,728		
Regional junior athletes		660			8		1,286		–				1,676		
Total	3,260	660	5,198	N/A	101	N/A	2,835	N/A		636	N/A	N/A	6,889	791	N/A

Countries organise training facilities according to resources available

In conclusion it appears that countries organise training facilities according to resources available. In larger countries the need for a combined centralised and decentralised network of training facilities may be more prominent than in smaller countries. In this respect, smaller countries may develop a competitive advantage in Pillar 6 because they do not have to combat the 'tyranny of distance' and the consequent increases in the complexity of co-ordination and facility and services replication.

Finally, some countries such as Australia, Canada, Denmark (only for Team Denmark sports), Flanders, Japan, Portugal, Spain and Wallonia provide priority access to training facilities to elite athletes. In Portugal and Spain this is even regulated by law. Six of the 14 countries do not provide such access (Brazil, Finland, France, Nothern Ireland, the Netherlands and Switzerland).

Funding of facilities

In terms of funding, all countries reported that the government plays a role in funding national and elite sport centres. In Australia, France and Spain the funding differs depending on whether the centre is national or regional. In Australia and France the national centres are funded by the (national) government/public services, while the regional centres are funded by collaborations between local (state) government and sponsors. In Spain, the national centre is paid for by the national sports council whereas the regional centre is funded by the government. Many of the institute networks evolved from publicly funded sources and commercial partnerships. As such INSEP and Japanese training institutes are—while government funded—operating as PPPs (public private partnerships), a partnership between government institutions and commercial partners, with the purpose of design, build, finance, and maintenance (DBFM) of infrastructure (De Knop, 2007).

Assessment of facilities by athletes and coaches

The extent to which athletes and coaches are satisfied with the national and regional training facilities is measured in the elite sport climate survey. The results are shown in Figure 56. Japan had the highest number of (top 16) athletes and (international) coaches rating the availability and quality of the training facilities as sufficient. The lowest ratings were from Portugal, Flanders, Brazil and Wallonia.

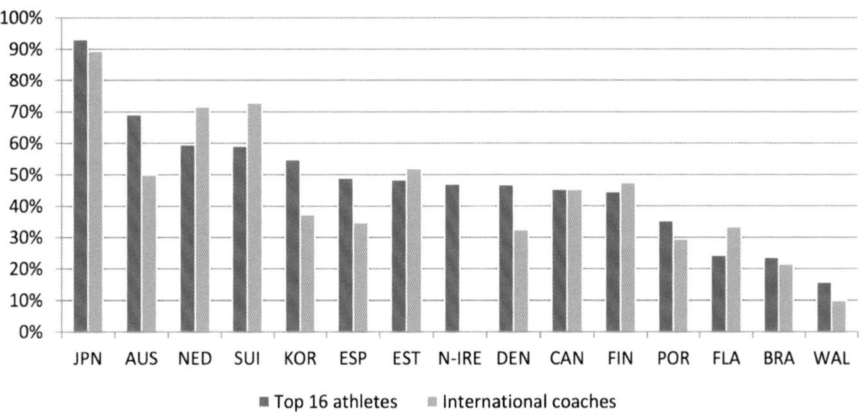

Figure 56: Total percentage of top 16 athletes (n=1,320) and international-level coaches (n=639) rating the quality of training facilities as (very) sufficient (sum of 2 sub factors)

10.4 Summary points in Pillar 6

- Most nations realise the importance of providing elite-level athletes with access to facilities that enable them to train in appropriate conditions at any moment of the day, with appropriate equipment and with access to a variety of support services.
- The models by which facilities are made available varies considerably across nations. There is evidence of a range of models from highly centralised national provision through to highly devolved local provision. For example, while Australia (AIS), France (INSEP) and Japan (JISS) have comprehensive centralised and multisport national training centres (NTCs), other countries take a decentralised view; for example Canada with a network of NTCs and the Netherlands with nine centres (including one national and four multisports centres); in many countries NTCs are organised around single sports, with less sophisticated and cheaper training centres.
- Models of provision have evolved around the context of local circumstances and conditions in various nations. For example in Australia there has been a shift away from state-funded central provision to more commercially operated local provision. By contrast in Denmark the approach appears to be making best strategic use of the facilities and partnerships that already exist, and by formal agreements with 'elite sport municipalities'.
- The quality of existing training facilities is rated highly but there seems to be a dearth of facilities nevertheless.
- Prevalence of high-quality facilities leads to a higher likelihood of winning medals. While it would be tempting to claim that world-class facilities lead to success in international sport, the direction of the relationship is unknown and should be the focus of future research.
- Taking a strategic approach to the provision of elite sport training facilities can be a source of increased success for various reasons. It can help to reduce negative factors such as homesickness and travel times as well as enabling positive benefits such as providing athlete and coaching services cost effectively by achieving economies of scale. There is no generic blueprint, rather local factors based on country size, existing levels of provision and sporting priorities will ultimately determine how many facilities are required and where they will be built.
- Athletes are more critical about the availability of services in their main training facility than coaches and performance directors.

Chapter 10 references

Andersen, S. S. and Ronglan, L. T. (2012). *Nordic Elite Sport: Same Ambitions, Different Tracks.* Copenhagen Business School Press.

Bergsgard, N. A., Houlihan, B., Mangset, P., Nødland, S. I. and Rommetvedt, H. (2007). *Sport Policy: A comparative analysis of stability and change.* London, UK: Elsevier.

De Bosscher, V., Bingham, J., Shibli, S., van Bottenburg, M. and De Knop, P. (2008). *The global Sporting Arms Race. An international comparative study on sports policy factors leading to international sporting success.* Aachen: Meyer & Meyer.

De Knop, P. (2007). *PPS en sportinfrastructuur [PPP and Sports infrastructure].* P. De Knop (Ed.). Brugge: Van den Broele.

Green, M. and Houlihan, B. (2005). *Elite Sport Development. Policy learning and political priorities.* New York: Routledge.

Houlihan, B. and Green, M. (2008). *Comparative Elite Sport Development. Systems, structures and public policy.* London, UK: Elsevier.

Mäkinen, J. (2012). The anatomy of elite sports organization in Finland. In *Nordic elite sport. Same ambitions–different tracks.* Svein Andersen and Lars Tore Ronglan (Eds.). Universitetsforlaget; Oslo. pp. 209-223.

Oakley, B. and Green, M. (2001). The production of Olympic champions: International perspectives on elite sport development system. *European journal for sport management, 8*, 83-105.

LAPUA
KARELIA

11 Pillar 7: Coach provision and coach development

11.1 Concepts and definition

Research into athletes' talent development processes is well established and conceptualised by multiple research approaches such as the LTAD model (e.g., Bayli and Hamilton, 2004), the 10-year rule (e.g., Côte, 1999), deliberate practice (e.g., Ericsson, Krampe and Tesch-romer, 1993) and the developmental model of sport participation (e.g., Ericsson, Côte and Fraser-Thomas, 2007). By contrast, coach development literature is in its relative infancy (Truyens, De Bosscher, Heyndels and De Knop, in press). The complexity of the coaching development and support process is difficult to capture by using a 'one size fits all' approach (Truyens et al., in press). One of the main conclusions of the SPLISS 1.0 study in 2008 was that coach education was well developed in the sample's successful nations (the United Kingdom, Italy and the Netherlands), but there was a general dissatisfaction with the terms and conditions that coaches enjoyed in their sport-related employment. There were also poor mechanisms for the combination of coaching and other paid work (De Bosscher et al., 2008).

The number of good coaches, coach education opportunities, support for living circumstances, and, the status of coaches are the four main areas of Pillar 7

This Pillar investigates four main areas: the number of well-trained and experienced coaches; coach education and opportunities to develop world-class coaches; the personal living circumstances of coaches and their opportunities to become professional; and, the status and recognition of coaches in the sample nations. This is captured in 17 CSFs and 96 subfactors. From the elite sport climate survey three key features should be noted. First, of the total sample of elite coaches (n=1376) more than a quarter are Swiss coaches (27.6%), followed by coaches from Estonia, Australia and Flanders, which collectively represent 62% of the total sample. Overall findings are thus largely influenced by this sample bias and data will be weighted accordingly when overall results are discussed. Second, only 14% of all coaches were females. Third, the performance level at which coaches worked differed by country, and was higher in Spain, Japan and Canada (with over 16% training top 16 world athletes). Flanders, Estonia and Switzerland also included national youth talent coaches in their sample. When significant survey results were found in these sub groups, we focused only on the subset of international level coaches (n=677, or 49%).

11.2 Key findings

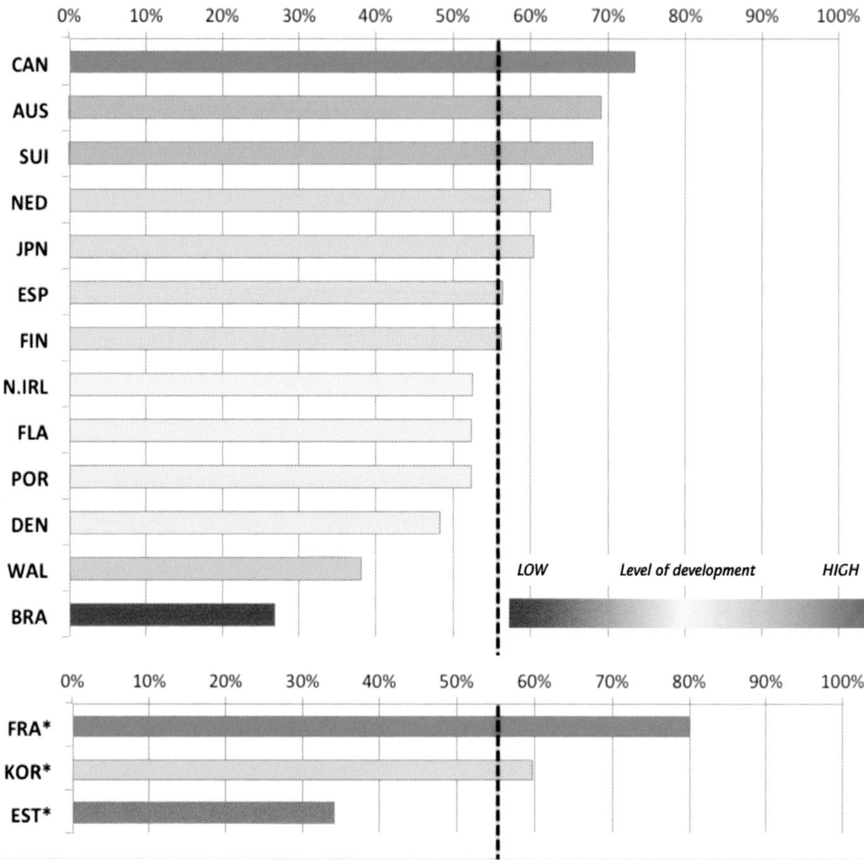

** Note: 13 nations + 3 regions (FLA, WAL, N. IRL). Only partial data available in France (no elite sport climate survey); South Korea and Estonia (no inventory). Caution is therefore needed with the interpretation of scores in these nations.*

Figure 57: Total scores of the SPLISS sample nations against the 7 CSFs of Pillar 7

The relationship with success in Pillar 7 is stronger in winter sports than summer sports

The results of Pillar 7 highlight the importance of coaches as a component of an effective elite sport system. The total scores correlate highly with the success scores of the sample nations both in summer and winter sports.[33] The results from the inventory are very much in line with the survey results.

33 The correlation between Pillar 7 scores for summer sports and success is: $r_s = 0.606^*$ ($p = 0.028$) and winter sports: $r_s = 0.779^{**}$ ($p = 0.002$).

Interestingly, this is one of the few Pillars where the relationship with success is even stronger for winter sports than for summer sports. France, Canada, Australia and Switzerland achieve the highest scores; although caution must be exercised when interpreting the total score values in France, as they do not include coaches' assessments from the surveys. What these countries have in common is a well-structured coach education system that is rated positively by the elite coaches; and provisions to improve coaches' personal circumstances such that they can engage in their sport on a full-time basis. Furthermore, these countries seem to have a longer tradition of recognising coaching as a genuine profession through formal contracts, and in the cases of Canada and Switzerland the presence of a trade union for coaches. Although Brazil underperforms in all of these system attributes, Brazilian athletes assess the level and expertise of their coaches as being reasonably satisfactory. Scores are also low in Wallonia as a result of lower opportunities for coaches to develop skills at a world-class level, and the lower level of income reported by the coaches in the sample.

The results from the inventory are very much in line with the survey results, in which the Netherlands has the highest scores, followed by Canada and Switzerland.

Higher level coaches are not more likely to have completed a coaching qualification. They are more likely to have more international experience as an athlete

When looking at the CSFs that correlate most with success, a few interesting findings emerge. First, there is almost a 'zero' relationship with the number of elite coaches that are qualified in each country and that country's level of success. Similarly, the survey findings revealed that higher level coaches were no more likely to have completed a coaching qualification than national/talent coaches, and there was actually a slightly negative relationship.[34] This finding is consistent with coaching literature that highlights the relatively low impact of traditional coach education on the processes by which coaches gain knowledge. This finding emphasises the importance of learning experience, mentoring from more experienced coaches, and coaches' experience of being an athlete in the sport (Ericsson et al., 2007). Meanwhile, the CSFs do show that the successful nations all provide high-quality services for coaches to support their continuous professional development, as well as having highly developed coach education systems. This finding is stronger in winter sports, which is probably related to the high scores of Switzerland and Canada, two successful winter

Opportunities given to coaches to discuss their experience with other coaches is an important CSF in Pillar 7

34 The correlation between the highest level coaches ever trained and whether they completed a coach education course is: $r_s = -0.134^{**}$ ($p < 000$), $n = 905$.

sport nations, scoring well at Pillar 7. Furthermore, the CSF within Pillar 7 that correlates most with success (CSF 7.10) is concerned with the opportunities given to coaches so that they are able to communicate and discuss their personal development with other elite coaches. These conclusions lend theoretical credence to the examination of a broad range of experiences in the development of high-performance coaches: mentoring, qualifications and personal experience that are increasingly formalised and embedded within coach education systems.

Higher level coaches have more experience as an international level athlete

Second, the surveys with 1,376 coaches revealed that higher level coaches were more likely to have had international experience as an athlete in the same sport in which they were coaching than lower level coaches. This finding provides some support for speculation in previous work (e.g., Ericsson et al., 2007; Lynch and Mallet, 2006) where researchers were unable to confirm this contention due to relatively few respondents.

Coaches in more successful nations have higher living standards.

Third, it is perhaps not surprising that coaches' general monthly income from their elite sport activities and their standard of living is higher in successful countries (CSF 7.11), both in summer sports and winter sports when compared with less successful countries. This finding is also the case for questions about elite sport coaching being a full-time primary activity (CSF 7.12b). These results confirm nations' increased recognition of the elite coach profession and an increasing process of coaching careers being professionalised. The increased ease of worker migration and the increasing acceptance of 'foreign' coaches have created a global market for elite coaches and performance directors. This is yet further evidence of an escalating global sporting arms race.

The status of the elite sport coaching profession is slow in developing.

Finally, the status of coaches and the recognition of the elite sport coaching profession are still seen as underdeveloped attributes in most sample nations' elite sport development system. The only exception is France, which seems to be more advanced at the level of state co-ordination; however as elite sport climate surveys were not conducted in France we cannot confirm this assertion from the coaches themselves. Despite the increased professionalisation of coaching, many coaches do not enjoy the working conditions and benefits found in more conventional professional occupations. Higher quality working conditions seem to be valued higher in those countries that do well in winter sports. This finding could possibly be explained by the fact that winter sports have a longer tradition as a professional occupation such as in ski resorts, ice hockey or commercial skating teams.

11.3 Comparative and descriptive analysis

11.3.1 Sufficient number of well-trained and experienced elite coaches

Critical success factors		INVENTORY	SURVEY			
I. There is a sufficient number of well-trained and experienced elite coaches in the country		O	A	C	PD	
CSF 7.1	There is a database of coaches and elite coaches that is updated yearly and contains details of qualifications and the date qualifications were achieved	X				P2
CSF 7.2	A sufficient number of elite coaches are qualified: They have undertaken governing body training or other refresher training specifically in elite sport; or a training course at international level	X		X	X	
CSF 7.3	Coaches have experience at the elite level in their own career as an athlete			X		
CSF 7.4	The NSA has a strategy for NGBs to attract the world's best coaches and external experts to train elite athletes and to improve the expertise of domestic coaches working at elite level	X				P2
CSF 7.6	Athletes are satisfied with the level and expertise of their coaches during talent development and as an elite athlete		X			

Source of information: O: overall sport inventory; A: athletes' survey; C: coaches' survey; PD: performance directors' survey; right column shows where the CSFs possibly interlink with other Pillars.

Number of coaches

Switzerland and Australia have the highest number of coaches per head of population with a minimum qualification

Not all countries have coaches databases (BRA, DEN, FIN, FRA), and those with databases do not have all the necessary information to quantify the precise number of active coaches. Table 36 displays the number of qualified coaches in each country across two categories: the minimum qualification standard and the highest qualification level that exists in the country. This latter category is not necessarily the elite level, as not all countries organise coach qualifications at this level, a point which will be developed later in this chapter. After standardising by adjusting for population, Switzerland and Australia are top in terms of the number of coaches with the minimum qualification (1%), and Australia performs best at elite level with one such coach per 2,310 head of population.

Table 36: Total number of qualified coaches at designated levels

	Minimum qualification (initiation/instructor)	*Inhabitants per coach*	Highest qualification	*Inhabitants per coach*
AUS	221,888	104	8,400	2,310
CAN	15,204	2,311	152	231,191
DEN*	NA	NA	108	51,852
FIN*	10,000	543	525	10,350
FLA	23,000	276	2,600	2,442
JPN	337,805	377	4,708	27,050
NED	20,000	840	NA	NA
N. IRL*	15,200	119	NA	NA
POR	19,000	556	2,748	3,844
SUI	100,000	81	1,000	8,058
WAL	12,100	293	812	4,367
FRA	NA	NA	3200 (II)	4,367

**Estimation (no database available in these countries).*
Note: The coaches with the highest qualification, concerns the number of coaches who had been enrolled at the highest level of coaches' education that exist in a country; variances can in part be explained by different qualification levels in the countries (e.g., not all countries have an elite coach qualification level). No data available in Brazil, Spain, France.

Looking at the total number of currently active elite coaches, the highest numbers are found in Japan (4,708), Switzerland (1,200) and the Netherlands (239), with Switzerland having the best ratio of active elite coaches per capita, with one elite coach per 6,715 head of population. Denmark has by far the lowest number of coaches per capita, with only one elite coach per 124,444 head of population (Table 37). In this respect, an interesting point of note is that some countries provide incentives to enhance the number of qualified coaches, although this was not a point that was raised in the elite sport climate inventory by the Danish researcher.

Table 37: Total number of active and professional (elite) coaches

	Active elite coaches	*Inhabitants per coach*	Fully professional
AUS	475	48,632	299
CAN	723	48,604	NA
DEN*	45	124,444	42
FIN*	400	13,585	NA
FLA	79	80,380	73
JPN	4,708	27,050	NA
NED	239	70,264	NA
N. IRL*	19	95,263	13
POR	421	25,088	NA
SUI	1,200	6,715	400
WAL	NA	NA	NA
FRA	900	65,684	500

*Note: *In Denmark, this is an estimation based on the number of coaches involved in the SPLISS-study (within an Olympic sport and coaching a senior athlete who is supported by Team Denmark).*

Good athletes... good coaches?

Higher level coaches used to practice sport at a higher level than an athlete

According to some authors, international experience as an athlete is a major advantage for coaches (Ericsson et al. 2007; Truyens et al., in press) (CSF 7.3). Irwin, Hanton and Kerwin (2005) found that 45% of the elite coaches in their study identified prior experience of competing as a gymnast was an important source of coaching knowledge in gymnastics. Some studies concluded differently. For example Lynch and Mallet (2006) reported that although experience as an athlete might be useful in developing coaching expertise, it does not appear that elite-level ability in track and field was a prerequisite for success in coaching international track and field athletes. In the SPLISS elite sport climate survey, it appears that more coaches who had ever coached at a higher level, had participated as an elite athlete in sport themselves than coaches who had worked at a lower level. Table 38 illustrates this point with, approximately 50% of the international-level coaches (world top 16/8/3/continental top 8) having been elite athletes in their sport compared with only 27% of the national-level coaches. Sub analysing the data by nation reveals that the proportion of elite coaches who were former elite athletes increases to a peak score of 83% in South Korea and is remarkably lower in other countries with scores of less than 50% in Estonia, Brazil, Flanders, Finland, Switzerland and Wallonia (Figure 59). This is a particularly interesting finding for sport policymakers with regard to coach education, as it is often a heated topic for debate as to whether good athletes are also good coaches.

Table 38: Cross tabulation of the highest level coaches ever trained and the level they had participated in sport

Highest level trained as a coach (n=1188)	At which level did you participate in sport yourself?		
	International/ elite level	National level	Recreational/other
World top 3/8	56.9%	32.4%	7.6%
World top 16/continental top 8	46.5%	39.4%	8.1%
National level/other	27.3%	53.2%	0%

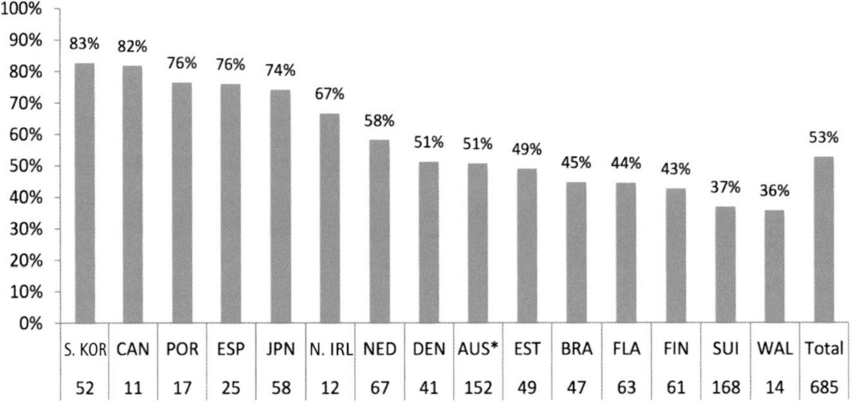

** Australian database includes 'all' coaches respondents; **note small samples (<20) for some countries.*

Figure 59: International-level coaches that participated in sport at an international level as a former elite athlete

Athletes' rating the expertise of their coaches

Higher level athletes rate the expertise of their coaches higher

Finally, athletes' perception of their coaches' expertise was rated fairly high to very high in all countries, with scores ranging from 70% to 83% positive ratings in all countries, except South Korea where only 62% of the athletes rated the expertise of their coach as high or very high. Also, the data revealed that higher level athletes rated the expertise of their coaches higher than the relatively lower level athletes. Moreover most athletes reported that their current coach was the most appropriate coach for them and considered that they still have much to learn from him/her. This latter point was again particularly pronounced for higher level athletes. Figures were slightly lower in South Korea, Brazil and Flanders as shown in Figure 60.

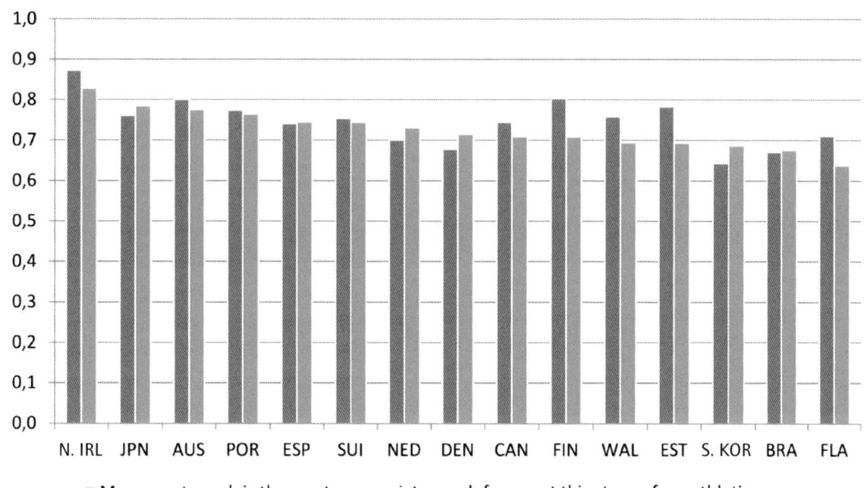

Figure 60: Rating score of top 16 athletes on two statements (mentioned in the graph) (n=1365)

11.3.2 Opportunities to develop an (elite) coaching career

Critical success factors		INVENTORY	SURVEY			
II. Coaches get sufficient opportunities to develop their coaching career to become a world-class elite coach		O	A	C	PD	
CSF 7.6	There is a nationally co-ordinated agency (often within the NSA) responsible for (elite) coaches' education that aligns with the different levels of NGB courses and facilitates NGBs in the organisation of coach development and defines coaching profiles	X				
CSF 7.7	There is a well-developed coach education system from the lowest level (courses for the recreational trainer/coach) to the highest level (education of elite coaches)	X		X	X	
CSF 7.8	There are several services (such as regular refresher courses, information exchange opportunities) and resources supporting the continuous professional development of coaches	X		X	X	
CSF 7.9	Coaches can receive specialist advice from other areas to help them improve the standard of their athletes (psychology, nutrition, physiology, biomechanics, and data analysis)	X			X	
CSF 7.10	Elite coaches are able to communicate and discuss their personal development as elite coaches and the development of elite athletes with other elite coaches (non-sport specific)	X				

Source of information: O: overall sport inventory; A: athletes' survey; C: coaches' survey; PD: performance directors' survey; right column shows where the CSFs are possible on the interface with other Pillars.

Although those who claim coaching to be an art form would have us believe that good coaches are 'born and not made,' such a view is increasingly outmoded, with experts' knowledge in many fields (and how it is acquired) currently being the focus of considerable investigation (Cushion, Armour and Jones, 2003). In a review of the development of coaching as a profession, Woodman (1993) confirmed the assertion that the key to improved coaching lies with coach education and development. This view has resulted in the implementation of coach education programmes worldwide (Cushion et al., 2003). Yet, coaching experience and the observation of other coaches remain primary sources of knowledge for coaches and their coaching practice (Cushion, 2001; Gould, Gianinni, Krane and Hodge, 1990). Furthermore, according to some authors, coaches spent a relatively small amount of time in formal coaching education (Erickson et al., 2007). Coaches, therefore, often serve an informal apprenticeship of prolonged observation, which enables them to develop a familiarity with the task of coaching (Cushion, 2001). Of course there is no 'one size fits all' pedagogy in the day to-day lives of coaches and their practice. From a structural viewpoint the SPLISS 2.0 study reveals that Switzerland and Canada have the best scores on the coach development opportunities, followed by Australia, Finland and Japan, for the way in which their coach education system is developed and in particular the opportunities offered for elite coaches to improve their expertise at the highest levels, as well as the way this assessed by the coaches in the elite sport climate surveys.

National co-ordinated coaches qualification structures

Most countries have developed a nationally co-ordinated coach qualification structure

With regard to coach education, coaching qualifications have changed over time from unco-ordinated systems, in which each NGB developed its own qualification levels and content, to highly nationally co-ordinated structures with guidelines for each NGB and a framework of national qualification levels. The benefits of national co-ordination are that it ensures national standards, guarantees comparability between sports, can facilitate national recognition of the coach (Truyens et al., in press) and can reduce the administrative costs (such as organisation, promotion) because it is all centralised. Consequently, different countries have developed national qualification frameworks, some countries have a strong hands-on approach whereas others allow NGBs to have flexibility within a broad framework (e.g., Australia). Brazil is the only country with no nationally co-ordinated coaching qualification scheme. Here, each NGB is responsible for coach accreditation; however some changes have recently been proposed by the Brazilian Olympic Committee in 2013. Denmark's national agency sets standards for the higher levels of coaching, but the lower levels are left for the NGBs. Since 1999, the European structure for the five levels of coaches' training has facilitated a gradual convergence towards a common European framework for the recognition of coaching qualifications (EENSEE, 2007). The European Qualification Framework (EQF) proposes a five level structure for the recognition of coaches. After changes in line with European treaties, it now distinguishes between participation-oriented and performance-oriented sports coaching and has recently been made more competence based (EENSEE, 2007). Eight (European) SPLISS countries (Denmark, Spain, Finland, Flanders, Northern Ireland, Portugal and Switzerland) evaluate their national qualifications against this EQF.

There is considerable variation in the levels and time spent at each coach education level; entry levels for basic qualification are sometimes too high

There is considerable variation in the levels and number of hours provided at each coach education level in the different countries, which makes them difficult to compare on a like-for-like basis. An interesting element in the Portuguese system, is that the career pathway for coaches is determined not just by the training course and a one season internship, but additionally a specified minimum level of coaching experience is required before coaches can move up to a higher level (between 1-2 years, depending on the level). One lesson to learn is that some countries provide low entry barriers for coaches at the beginners/initiation level (e.g., 16 hours in Flanders, 8-10 hours in Northern Ireland); whereas others require over 100 hours of time investment even for the lowest levels (e.g., Spain, Portugal, the Netherlands, Switzerland, Finland). Further research is needed to analyse the impact this has with regard to the number of coaches in countries, as many nations face an insufficient number of qualified coaches at the grassroots level and some authors indicated that formalised learning is not always valued by coaches as much as their day-to-day learning experience (Bohlke, 2007). In this respect, it may be advisable for countries to lower the entry barriers and increase the number of recognised coaches with a minimum basic qualification level. An interesting initiative to enhance the number of qualified talent coaches was taken by the Finnish Olympic Committee who in partnership with NGBs hired 50 youth coaches to support the coaching of talented young athletes.

Coaches completing a qualification

82% of the international level coaches have completed some level of coach qualification; less than half of the (international level) coaches rate the coach education as sufficient or good

From the survey results, it appears that most international level coaches (on average 82%), have completed some level of coach qualification and scores of 100% were found in Spain, Portugal and Canada. This score is lower in Japan (57%), and lies between 70-80% in the Netherlands, South Korea, Finland, Wallonia and Denmark. Interestingly, coaches that train(ed) athletes at higher levels showed no evidence of having completed coach qualification courses more frequently than other coaches.

Rating qualification levels

The coaches were asked to rate the level of the coaching development certification in their sport. Figure 61 shows generally low ratings among international-level coaches, with on average 45% of the coaches rating the coaching development certification structure in their sport as sufficient or good; these figures were higher than 'all' coaches from the surveys (including national-level coaches). Swiss coaches are remarkably more positive (79% sufficient/good) than the other nations. Spain, Wallonia and Northern Ireland received relatively poor ratings.

Higher level coaches undertake more (refresher) courses to improve their expertise

Furthermore most countries (except Brazil, Portugal and Wallonia) organise regular coaching seminars or clinics at a national level that are designed to increase the expertise of elite coaches. From the data, there appears to be a desire for more opportunities to improve the level of expertise at the highest level. The Netherlands, followed by Switzerland and Finland in particular, stand out as the countries where the highest number of coaches consider that there are enough accredited refresher courses for elite-level coaches organised in their country (Figure 62). The data also revealed that higher level coaches undertake more (refresher) courses to improve their expertise than lower level coaches.

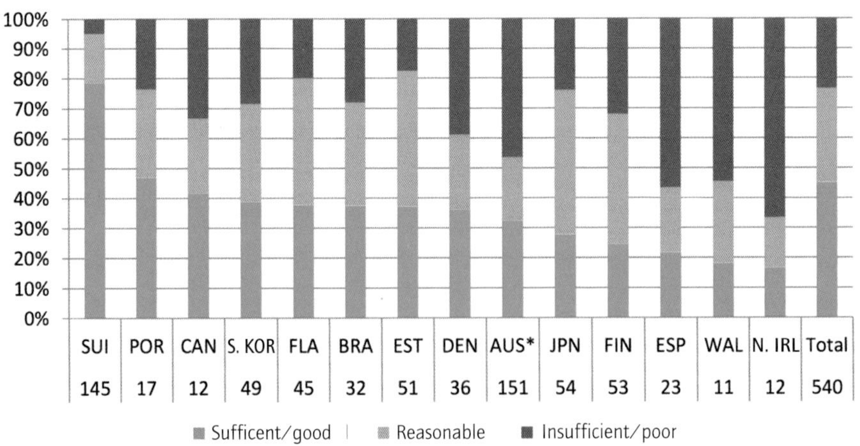

*Figure 61: Rating by international-level coaches of the governing body's (or other recognised organiser) coaching development certification structure in their sport (n=572) (Note: * Australian database includes 'all' coaches)*

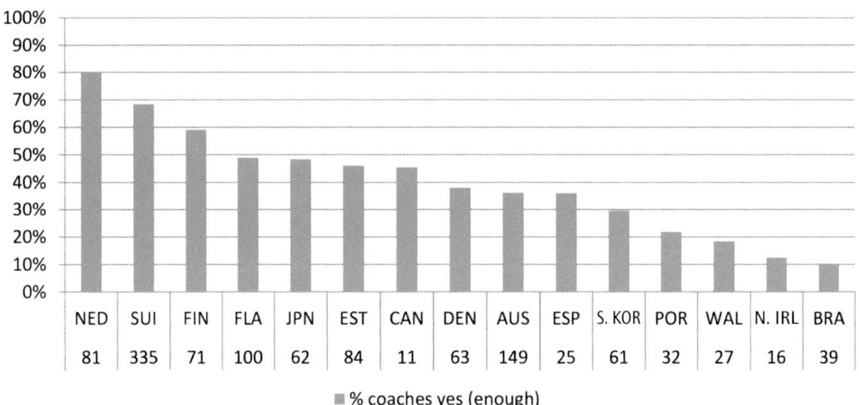

Figure 62: Percentages of (all) coaches that considers that there are enough accredited refresher courses in their country for elite-level coaches (n=1254)

In only five countries are coaches' qualifications required to be regularly updated

Perhaps somewhat surprisingly, only five countries (Australia, Canada, Japan, Portugal, and Switzerland) make it compulsory for coaches at national level to keep their coaching qualifications up to date. For example in Switzerland, coaches need to update their qualifications if they want to get subsidies from the Federal Office of Sport (FOSPO). In Portugal coaches lose their training licence after five years of non-competing. In the other countries the expression 'once a coach, means always a coach' applies. This is interesting, as coaching is such a dynamic profession, that regular qualification updates through continuous professional development would seem a necessity. Flanders and Northern Ireland state that this requirement is sport-specific.

Elite-level qualification

Good coach qualifications at the elite level sometimes take two years; and includes international internships, university involvement and collaboration with (inter)national top coaches

Nine countries have a qualification level specifically for elite coaches: Canada, Denmark, Spain, Finland, the Netherlands, Portugal, Switzerland and France. However, as indicated by the Danish researcher, it is not always a compulsory requirement for elite athlete coaches to obtain this qualification. While general coach development in Switzerland received high ratings by coaches, only 14 out of 36 performance directors indicated that there exists a coach qualification level exclusively for coaches working with elite athletes in their sport. At the elite level, evidence suggests that both the experience of the coach and encounters with experienced coaches are fundamental to the shaping of the coach habitus and coaching practice. Clearly, then, influencing such experiences would affect the acquisition and development of coaches' knowledge (Cushion at al., 2003).

Table 39 displays an overview of some characteristics of elite coach education systems. Finland in particular seems to have a well-developed elite coach development system. In some countries, the total time investment for coaches to be qualified at the elite level, is spread over one to two years (Canada, Denmark, Finland, Portugal) and even three years in Switzerland (for 2 levels). The courses are characterised by the specific training needs of elite athletes, international elite sport requirements, coaching and competing in special circumstances, planning, effectiveness, leadership, management and wider elite sport development issues. An example from Canada is provided in Table 40. One key characteristics of coach education at the elite-level, is that it is tailor-made, adapted to an individual's needs, and organised for only a selected group of (potential) top coaches. Furthermore, mentoring by national top-level coaches or international coaches appears to have become an increasingly more structured and formal part of coach education at the elite level. It is also a key finding in past coaching research that mentoring needs to be in operation in coach education, because experience and collaboration with other coaches are both still highlighted as the most important facets of coach development (Cushion et al., 2003). While it used to be unstructured in the past (Cushion et al., 2003) it has increasingly been embedded in the more progressive elite coach development systems.

The costs of courses of this type (elite level) are not known for each country but are typically higher than for lower levels of coach qualifications, and most of the time they are partly or completely funded by governments or NGBs. (Table 39). In Switzerland, the federal government (FDHA) also compensates coaches for the potential loss of earnings as a result of attending such courses. In Finland, the elite coach qualification is fully in the hands of universities and in Canada the NCI 'Advanced Coaching Diploma' is a highly respected two-year diploma similar to a trade such as being an electrician and is regarded as a form of higher education. In some countries there exists collaboration with universities, or a master's degree, that offers coaching, although a doubt was raised as to whether these are sufficiently adapted to the coaching profession and provide the experience needed to develop as an elite coach.

Table 39: Countries with specific qualifications for the elite level (Y = yes)

		International elite coaches involved in course	International internships	University involved in the course?	University qualification for elite coaches exists?	Price: Funded for coaches?
CANADA	NCI, Advanced Coaching Diploma, 2 years, 45 units the first year and 42 the second year, 261 in total (3 hours/unit)		Possible but not standardised	Yes	Yes	± €2,000 for Canadians and ± €8,500 for internationals; Funding depends on NGB
DENMARK	400 sessions, around 1½-2 years to complete (not full-time)					± €5,400 Funded mostly
FINLAND	Level IV, 1 year (coach's special vocational degree), international level class room courses, observational field experiences, supervised coach experience, distance learning, national and international co-operation with a top coach		Yes	Yes	Yes (fully by universities)	App. €2,000 (2014) half of the expenses paid by NOC and coach associations
FRANCE	There is theoretically one highest level (level II), around 1200h for elite coaches. Presently, many elite coaches have a level III qualification (i.e., for competition coaches). Access to level II is done through recognition of elite sport experience. Level II is compulsory in professional team sports (in football, app. 900 h; 35 days a year) but recognition of elite sport experience is taken into account.	Yes	Possible but not standardised	NO NGBs		Certification is delivered by NGBs

JAPAN	(a) JASA Coach IV, 193h core subjects (62h classrooms, 131h distance learning); > 40h of sport specific (b) JOC National coach Academy (since 2008) is not a qualification, but a coaching programme which JOC coaching directors (a coach who is certified and rewarded by JOC) have to complete; it is a 8-9 week curriculum of instruction (intensive course of 4 days + distance learning and in field of training; international co-operation with a top coach)					JASA Coach IV: about €450 JOC: about €2150 (some NGBs assist in this payment), remark that the 'National coach' (coaching director for selected NGBs by government) receive a salary of around €100,000 a year from government
NETHER-LANDS	Level 4, 300h, spread over 18 months (talent coaches & head coaches) Topcoach 5, 350h (117 theory, 233 practice), spread over 21 months (75 credits in total)			Yes	No	Between €1,250-2,000 per person; The NSA supports NGBs financially. In total €2 mln in 2010*
PORTUGAL	2 levels (grade 3 and 4): theory 182h and 270h, respectively; internships: a sport season (1100h and 1500h) + coach experience before moving to a next level	Yes			Yes	–
SPAIN	(minimum) 3 levels: 520h approximately for the 1st level: 210h specific module, 110h common module, 200h internship; 500h for the 2nd level and 600h for the 3rd level	Yes				Funding depends on sport, NGB and NOC; approximately, between €1,200 and €3,000 for each level
SWITZER-LAND	2 Levels: 450 hours 1st level, elite sport coach (youth) (300h internship) and 900 h 2nd level (certified elite coach), spread over 3 years: class-room courses (120h, 250h); observational field experiences (30h, 50h); supervised coach experience (N/A), distance learning in own environment (50, 100); National and international co-operation with a top coach (N/A)	Yes	Yes two-week intern-ship highest inter-nati-onal level	Yes		The cost is paid, by the federal government (FOSPO-FDHA), which amounts to up to €221,000 for the first level (30 participants/year) and €655,000 for the second level (20 participants/ year)

Note: In Northern Ireland Level 3 is the highest coaching award that is delivered. Coaches wishing to get qualified to Level 4 (elite-level coaching) will generally travel to England where this level of coach education is much more readily available.

Table 40: Content of the two-year elite qualification level, example of Canada

I. Coaching leadership (24 units)
1. Effective leadership behaviour (4 units), creating your coaching philosophy (3 units)
2. Leading change (3 units), living your coaching philosophy (3 units)
3. Building effective teams (5 units)
4. Leading a programme (6 units)
II. Coaching effectiveness (21 units)
1. Analysing coaching and athlete performance (6 units)
2. Skill development and biomechanics (5 units)
3. Innovating practices and coaching intervention (4 credits)
4. Mentoring athletes in training and competition (6 units)
III. Performance planning (24 units)
1. Auditing sport performance (9 credits)
2. Developing integrated training plans (6 units)
3. Detailing the training plan (5 units)
4. Managing the training plan (4 units)
IV. Training and competition readiness (18 units)
1. Health and safety (3 units)
2. Talent identification and selection (3 units)
3. Preparing for competition (7 credits)
4. Strategic planning for training and competition (5 units)
Year 1 (part A) total units= 45 with a midterm presentation; Year 2 (part B) total units= 42 with a final presentation

Source: http://www.coach.ca/information-for-canadian-coaches-p135934

Fast-track coach qualification for former athletes

Keeping athletes in the sport through fast-track qualification courses (in 7 countries)

In the previous section it was shown that higher level coaches have taken part in sports at higher levels themselves. In the world of coaching there is a strange conundrum that great athletes rarely make great coaches. While former athletes may provide very sound advice and guidance it appears that more often than not they fail rather than succeed (McGee, 2014). However, given our data, there is now strong evidence that international experience as an elite athlete is an advantage for coaches to develop at higher levels. In this respect it can be recommended that retired athletes are retained in their sports, and allowed to fast track the qualification course to qualify as an elite coach. This approach is encouraged in seven of the sample countries (Denmark, Spain, Finland, Japan, the Netherlands, Switzerland and France). The Finnish Coaches' Association organises a course for former elite athletes (with a tailored time frame of approximately six months) to enable them to start coaching after retiring from their own elite sport career. In France former athletes have priority access to enter an examination leading to the title of 'professeur de sport' and also receive a free scholarship. In Australia athletes can be fast tracked into an elite coaching role through the National Coaching Scholarship programme, or alternatively receive some recognition of prior learning for certain training modules.. However, some countries have doubts about this strategy. For example the Swiss researcher indicated that the attempt to involve former athletes in the coaching system was seen as something of a weakness.

11.3.3 Sufficient individual living circumstances of coaches

Critical success factors		INVENTORY	SURVEY			
III. Coaches individual living circumstances are sufficient for them to become professional coaches		O	A	C	PD	
CSF 7.11	Coaches' general monthly income (total gross annual income) plus income from their sport activities is sufficiently high to provide a good standard of living.			X		P1
CSF 7.12	Elite sport coaching is—or can be—a full-time primary activity for the best elite coaches. There is a co-ordinated support programme for coaches that allows them to dedicate themselves sufficiently to their sport and to spend sufficient time with their elite athletes and emerging young talents.	X		X		
CSF 7.13	Employers are supportive by taking into account the training needs of elite coaches			X		

Source of information: O: overall sport inventory; A: athletes' survey; C: coaches' survey; PD: performance directors' survey; right column shows where the CSFs are possible on the interface with other Pillars.

Time spent on training activities

Higher level and full-time coaches spend more time on training. Coaches spend on average 31 hours per week on coaching; 31% spend over 40 hours a week

Before elaborating on the living conditions of coaches, we provide some insights into the time coaches spend on their training activities. International-level coaches on average spend 31 hours per week on all their coaching activities (which is higher than national-level coaches), including the preparation and follow-up of training activities and scouting. 31% of these coaches spend over 40 hours a week on coaching duties. Figure 63 displays an overview.

Of course there are differences in weekly hours worked by sport, as shown in Table 41. Coaches in weightlifting, rugby, biathlon, ice hockey and modern pentathlon reported that they spent on average more than 40 hours a week, with scores in sailing and aquatics above 35 hours. Kayak, equestrian, curling and bobsled seem to be less time intensive for coaches. These figures influence the overall averages by country. For example, Flanders, Switzerland and Japan have more aquatics coaches in their samples, whereas Estonia and Switzerland have more gymnastics coaches in their samples. Most ice hockey and ski coaches are from Switzerland and over half of the weightlifting and biathlon coaches are from South Korea. Despite this, coaches in Japan and South Korea on average devote the most time to training. This score appears to be lower in Denmark (n=39, of which 4 are aquatics coaches, 7 athletics, 7 rowing, 4 kayak, and 17 other) and in the Netherlands (n=67, of which 8 coaches are in aquatics, 5 in athletics, and 54 other).

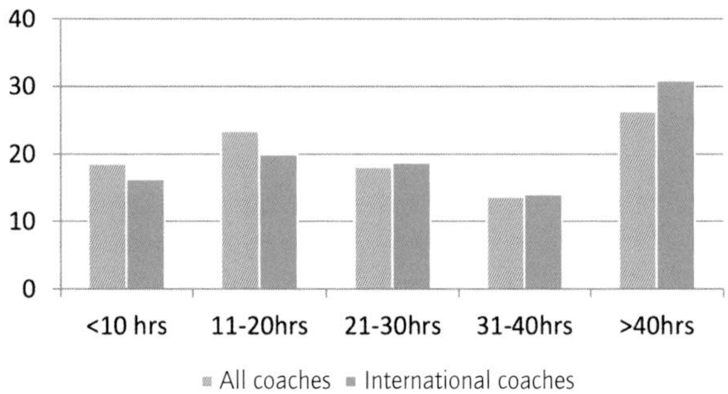

Figure 63: Hours a week that coaches spend on all their coaching activities (including preparation and follow-up of training activities and scouting); comparison by coach level

Table 41: Clustering of sports by four categories of hours that coaches spend on average on training activities (ranked from high to low)

<20 hours	21-30 hours	31-40 hours	41-50 hours
Kayak (n=6), Equestrian (n=20), Curling (n=7) Bobsled (n=1)	Football (n=35), Rowing (n=49), Basketball (n=35), Volleyball (n=53), Cycling (n=32), Judo (n=34), Athletics (n=140), Wrestling (n=29), Badminton (n=26), Shooting (n=22), Hockey (n=11), Boxing (n=9), Archery (n=4), Handball (n=54), Baseball (n=4), Golf (n=1), Luge (n=1)	Sailing (n=25), Aquatics (n=84), Skating (n=31), Skiing (n=122), Tennis (n=32), Triathlon (n=18), Canoe (n=11), Fencing (n=14), Gymnastics (n=58), Table tennis (n=13), Softball (n=3), Taekwondo (n=6)	Weightlifting (n=9), Rugby (n=5), Biathlon (n=9), Ice hockey (n=23), Modern pentathlon (n=5)

It can be assumed that—just as with athletes—over 25 hours a week spent on coaching activities can hardly be combined with a full-time job. A breakdown by country is therefore provided separately for full-time (n=656) and other coaches (n=502) in Figure 64. As can be seen, full-time coaches spend 38 hours per week on coaching, varying from over 50 in Canada and Australia to lesser amounts in the Netherlands and Estonia. The next section investigates this notion in greater depth in relation to the wages of coaches.

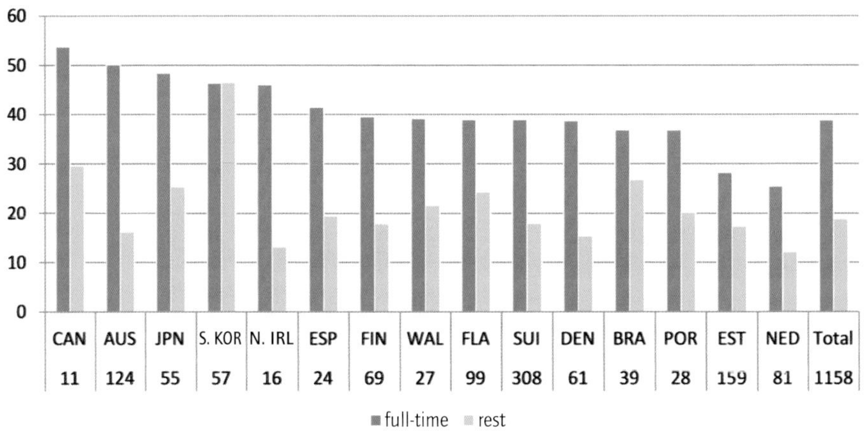

Figure 64: Average hours a week that coaches spend on all their coaching activities; comparison of full-time coaches and others (including preparation and follow-up of training activities and scouting)

Coaching as a full-time activity

> **There is a positive evolution in the working situation of top coaches through funding strategies and employment contracts, but it remains difficult for many coaches to undertake coaching as a full-time profession**

In the SPLISS 1.0 study, it was concluded that financial support for coaches was still in its relative infancy and that it was still difficult for coaches to carry out their roles on a full-time basis (De Bosscher et al., 2008). Potentially high-quality coaches were often lost to coaching because they are forced to seek employment in other areas. This was considered to be an unfortunate finding as there was—at that time—collective realisation in elite sport that athletes need to apply themselves full-time to achieve their potential but coaches were not recognised in the same way. This period (2005 onwards) was actually a turning point in national strategic policies with governments in many countries subsequently setting up employment contracts and different approaches for funding elite-level coaches to address this issue. This point is confirmed in the SPLISS 2.0 study, as all sample countries, except Brazil, offer direct financial support for coaches to become full-time professionals. This provision is offered as a monthly wage, and in addition, most countries provide reimbursement costs, and in some countries coaches can get a car (Australia, France, Spain and Switzerland), depending on the NGB. Additionally, half of the countries provide bonuses for performances (Australia, Canada, Finland, Portugal, Spain, Switzerland and Wallonia). For example, in Canada, the coach of Olympic medallists will receive approximately €6,600 per gold medal, €5,000 per silver medal and €3,300 per bronze medal. This is half the amount that the actual medal-winning athletes receive. It should be noted that while coaches are allowed to earn additional money (e.g., sponsorships) over and above their direct funding, Canada and Japan put limitations on the extra income, so that it does not affect their primary obligations. Furthermore, coaches (except in the Netherlands) are allowed to combine their national coaching position with other coaching activities, such as in sport clubs.

However, despite this positive evolution, the coaches' survey still shows that it remains difficult for some coaches to carry out their coaching job as a full-time activity.

72% of the international coaches receive a monthly salary for their coaching activities; 39% find this insufficient to pay for living costs as a full-time or part-time coach

It was previously reported that 60% of the coaches in the sample described themselves as being a full-time coach. The data show that on average 72% of all coaches operating at an international level receive a monthly salary for their coaching activities. However, 39% of the coaches found this support was insufficient to pay for their living costs either as a full-time or as a part-time coach. Figure 65, which sub-analyses the data by country, reveals that Japan has the highest number of (international) coaches who find the financial support they receive sufficient to operate full-time or part-time, and in the Netherlands there is the highest number of coaches who state that they can operate full-time on the basis of the salary they receive. The financial support is clearly seen as insufficient in Northern Ireland, Brazil, Estonia and South Korea. In Portugal, coaches indicate it is insufficient to operate as a full-time coach, but adequate for part-time coaching. The Portuguese researcher confirmed a significant decrease in the funding available for coaching following the global financial crisis that started in 2008.

Coaches who are sufficiently paid to commit full-time or part-time to their sport report that they can spend enough time with their athletes

These data are related to whether or not coaches considered that they are able to spend enough time with their elite athletes in order to enable them to perform at the highest level. The survey findings reveal that those coaches who stated that they were paid sufficiently, also report that they are more likely to be able to spend enough time with their athletes than those coaches who say they are paid insufficiently. As can be seen in Figure 66 on average 51% of the international-level coaches consider that they can spend enough time with their athletes. Among those coaches who consider themselves to be paid sufficiently the average is 68% whereas for those who say they are paid insufficiently the average decreases to 41%.

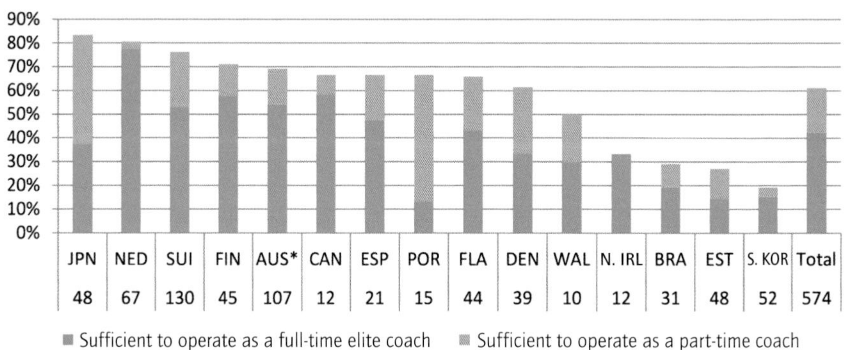

*Figure 65: Percentage of intentional-level coaches assessing the monthly financial support sufficient to pay for their living costs as a full-time or part-time elite coach (Note: * Australian database includes 'all' coaches)*

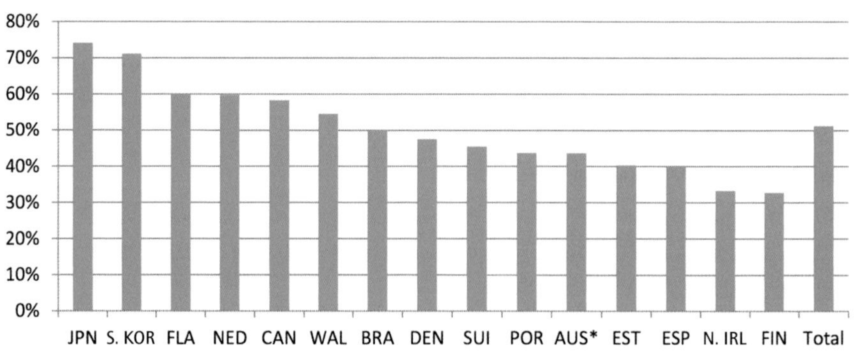

*Figure 66: Percentage of intentional-level coaches assessing that they are able to spend enough time with their elite athletes in order to enable them to perform at the highest level (Note: * Australian database includes 'all' coaches)*

It should also be noted that the coaches who have other paid work alongside their elite sport activities generally gave positive ratings to the support by their employers for their elite coaching career. In particular coaches from, Northern Ireland, Spain and Australia (over 70%) followed by the Netherlands, Switzerland and (>60%) Japan show particularly positive results. Wallonia is the only country where these scores are low with only four coaches (22%) out of the 29 coaches in the sample finding the support of their employers either sufficient or good.

Coaches' income

Coaches were asked how much they earn through their elite sport activities. As there were significant differences between all coaches and 'international-level' coaches, we focussed on the international level only (n=516). Country values are compared in PPP values (international dollars). After excluding outliers of coaches earning more than i$200,000, the average wage of these coaches was around i$36,000, varying from less than i$15,000 in Wallonia and Estonia to over i$60,000 in Canada and South Korea.

Despite high-income categories of some coaches, 13% of full-time international coaches and 34% of coaches coaching top three level athletes, earn below i$12,000

It can be concluded that the income distribution among international-level coaches is quite similar to that of athletes. 36% of the international coaches earn less than i$12,000 per year from their elite sport activities. Of these coaches, 21% reported being full-time coaches. Conversely, of all full-time coaches, 13% reported earning less than i$12,000 a year. While income levels tend to increase with the level of the coaches, among those coaches whose highest level of athletes were world top three athletes; 34% reported to earning less than i$12,000 a year. Overall 35% of the coaches earn more than i$42,000 (88% full-time). There are some differences between men and women, with more men in the higher income categories.

A further breakdown by country in Figure 67 shows that mainly in Wallonia, Estonia and Brazil the income distribution is skewed towards the lower income categories, where more than 50% of the coaches at international level earn less than i$12,000 from their elite sport activities. A higher number of international coaches in South Korea, Canada and the Netherlands earn in the highest income bracket. Despite the guaranteed anonymity of the question, low response rates in some countries have to be reported (Northern Ireland, n=11; Canada, n=8; Japan, n=11 and Portugal, n=11).

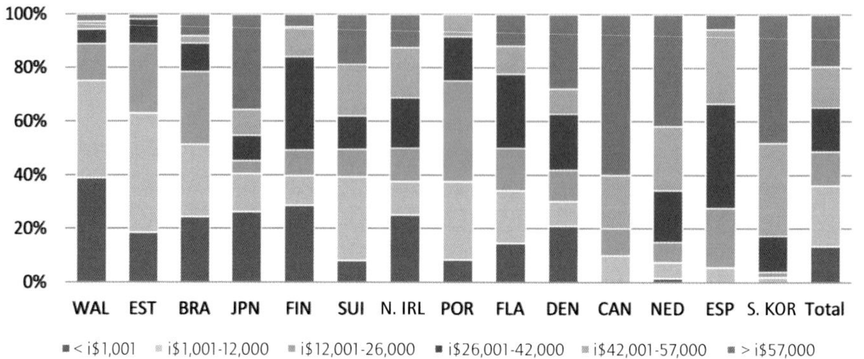

Figure 67: Annual income from elite sport activities (PPP values) of international-level coaches (n=565)

Finally, a further breakdown by sport in Figure 68 (only the sports with a minimum response of 10 coaches) show that in this sample, ice hockey, tennis, table tennis, hockey, and sailing are the sports where these international coaches earn the most. These results need to be interpreted in context of sports that are popular in those countries, and that a sport such as, for example, table tennis, is unlikely to be representative for coaches across all nations.

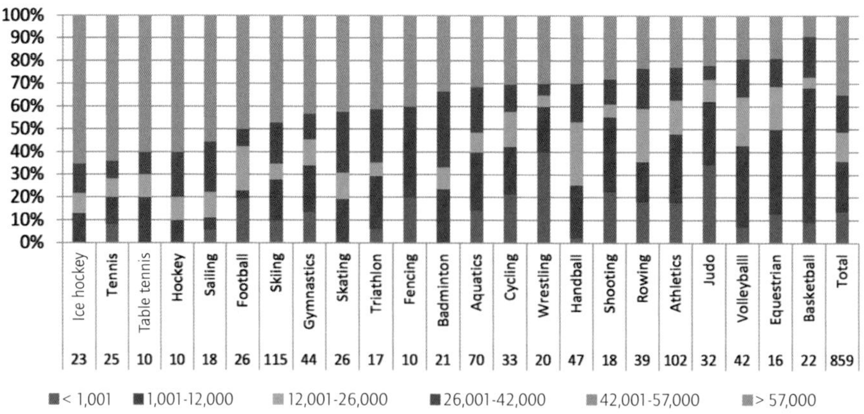

Figure 68: Annual income by sport (by category), from elite sport activities (PPP values) (n=859)

11.3.4 The status and recognition of coaches

Critical success factors		INVENTORY	SURVEY			
IV. The status of coaches: The job of coaches is recognised as valuable throughout the country		O	A	C	PD	
CSF 7.14	The job of a coach is recognised in the country and the career prospects are high			X		
CSF 7.15	Coaches have a written work contract for training activities; the job of a coach is contractually recognised and protected	X		X		
CSF 7.16	There is a trade union for sports coaches and trainers	X				
CSF 7.17	A coaching qualification is mandatory to work in sport clubs and with young talents	X				P3,4

Source of information: O: overall sport inventory; A: athletes' survey; C: coaches' survey; PD: performance directors' survey; right column shows where the CSFs are possible on the interface with other Pillars.

Recognition of the job of coaches

60% of the coaches disagrees that the job of the coach is sufficiently recognised (n=1144)

Despite the improved working conditions for coaches, the literature on policy development and approaches towards the role of coaches is limited. Most policy studies pay attention to the vital importance of the coach in athlete development (e.g., De Bosscher et al., 2006; Green and Houlihan, 2005; Anderson and Ronglan, 2012), but little research exists from the perspective of the coach. According to Duffy, North and Muir (2013), some change is notable and the role of sport coaching in support of policy and legacy objectives is becoming more widely recognised. For example in preparation of the London 2012 Olympic and Paralympic Games, the UK Coaching framework was developed on the assumption that coaching is a mechanism through which sport policy outcomes can be achieved. However, according to Digel (2008) the job of being a coach in sport remains insufficiently recognised. For example in Germany, the employment contracts of top-level coaches were found to be inadequate, their payment was unequal and insufficient, coaching was often not their only job and there was no clear professional profile for coaches. These observations from Germany are highly consistent with the findings in this study. In the elite sport climate survey coaches were asked to give their opinion on different statements. The data revealed for example that less than 40% of coaches agreed or strongly agreed that *'the opportunities coaches get in their country to develop as an expert coach at the highest international level in their sport are well developed'*; 33% disagreed or strongly disagreed. Furthermore, as shown in Figure 69, only 16% found that *'the job of an elite coach is sufficiently recognised in their country'*, with the majority of respondents (60%) disagreeing with the statement. The results were largely negative in all countries, with the highest scores recorded in Denmark (27% agreed) and Australia (24% agreed). There were no differences found between the scores of international- and national-level coaches. The Netherlands posed the question to coaches slightly differently (as yes/no), but it was concluded by van Bottenburg et al. (2012) that despite the fact that 52% of the coaches find the job insufficiently recognised, this score had actually improved significantly in 2011 compared with 2008.

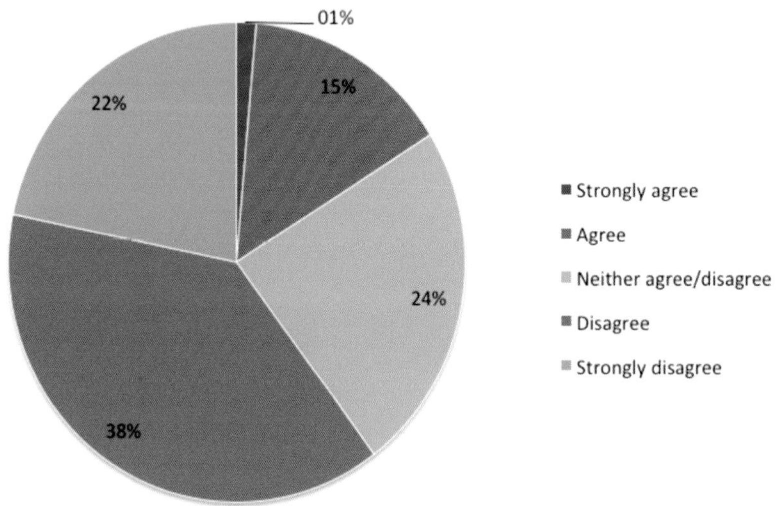

Figure 69: Ratings for the statement, 'the job of elite coach is sufficiently recognised in my country', by all coaches (n=1144)

31% of coaches do not have a written contract of employment

The coaching profession is not entirely comparable to other professions. Coaches do not always have contracts of employment, and if they do, they are mostly short term and do not seem to have the same legal status that is found in more conventional jobs. In the inventory, it was reported that coaches have written contracts in all countries except Brazil and Portugal. These contracts are obligatory in only eight countries (Brazil, Canada, Denmark, Spain, Flanders, Japan, the Netherlands and France) and are seldom agreed on an open-ended basis as is often the case in other professions. Consequently some coaches prefer to combine coaching with another job, which gives them longer term security and certainty of income. Of course, the general position we have described varies by sport. For example in Australia, Canada and Denmark coaches are usually hired on an annual basis, unless they are in a sport or an institution working on a four-year cycle, normally around the Olympic Games.

Recognition of coaches in France: national regulation, national agreement, coaches as civil servants

France can be seen as an example of a nation that recognises the coaching profession more seriously than other nations. First, there is a national regulation which makes it compulsory for coaches to achieve a coaching qualification. Second, there is a national agreement in professional team sports, between employers' unions, employees' unions, sport governing bodies and the state which defines the necessary qualifications, form of contract and wages which coaches should have. Third, there exists a competitive entrance examination to the administrative rank of 'professeur de sport' which recognises coaches as 'civil servants'. These coaches can subsequently be employed as a 'conseiller technique sportif'[35] by the state or be placed in sport federations to help develop and coach elite athletes. This means that even 'poorly developed' sports can have access to full-time professionally qualified coaches. As France did not participate in the surveys of athletes, coaches and performance directors, these findings from the overall elite sport policy inventory cannot be confirmed by the opinions of the coaches themselves. For the other countries, on average 31% of the coaches in the sample did not have a written contract of employment, and this statistic varied from a low score of 8-10% in the Netherlands, South Korea and Canada to a high score of 50% in Switzerland and Brazil.

Finally, in only four countries (Canada, Spain, Portugal, and France) is it a mandatory requirement for coaches to be qualified to work with sport clubs and talented young athletes. However, Canada does not have control systems for these qualifications. Coaching policies still have a long way to go in order to be delivered on a more formal basis, particularly in the case of less commercial sports.

35 There are 1674 'Conseillers techniques sportifs' in France: 64 are performance directors, 340 are entraîneurs nationaux (national coaches), 1,270 are 'conseillers techniques régionaux'. These coaches mainly work for talent development and coaching of future elite athletes (who train in regional institutes). Furthermore there are 500 coaches in professional sports; there is an estimate of 900 coaches working for elite sport in the NGB.

11.4 Key points in Pillar 7

- There are strong and significant correlations between the overall quality of coaching provision in the sample nations and medal-winning success in Olympic sports.
- Coaching is increasingly recognised as a profession in its own right and is becoming a less weak link in an elite sport development system. However, the athletes remain rewarded/supported better and a majority of coaches continue to find that their coaching work is insufficiently recognised. There is evidence of considerable variations in practice where less qualified and experienced coaches operate in developing nations and smaller nations. There are also considerable variations in the qualifications and experience of coaches between different sports.
- There seems to be a move towards nationally co-ordinated coaching qualification structures as well as requirements for continuous professional development.
- It appears that being a former international athlete is a source of competitive advantage for elite level coaches. Some 57% of international-level coaches in the sample were former international-level athletes compared with 27% amongst national-level coaches. Some nations are responding to this situation by fast tracking selected athletes into coaching.
- Coaching is a full-time occupation with the typical commitment around 31 hours per week and a minority (31%) working over 40 hours per week. For many coaches it is necessary to supplement their income with employment elsewhere. Coaches who are sufficiently remunerated are more likely to spend the required time with their athletes compared to those who are insufficiently remunerated.
- Coaches earn money for their efforts and can supplement their basic income from coaching with other work, sponsorship and prize money. There is a global market for coaching talent and in extreme cases we have seen coaches earning over €200,000 per annum. For the most part, coaches receive salaries that are broadly in line with average salaries in their home country.
- While there are examples of the role of the coach being recognised nationally as a worthwhile occupation, some 31% of sample reported that they did not have a written contract of employment. Addressing the employment and security needs of coaches in the future will be a means towards sustainable success for nations that wish to develop leading edge elite sport development systems. Job security and commitment, in that regard, enable good people to stay.

Chapter 11 references

Andersen, S. and Tore Ronglan, L. (2012). *Nordic Elite Sport. Same ambitions, different tracks.* Norway: AIT Otta AS.

Bölhke, N. (2007). New Insights in the nature of best practice in elite sport system management – exemplified with the organisation of coach education. New Studies in Athletics. *The IAAF Quarterly Magazine for Coaches Education, 22* (1), 49-59.

Côte, J. (1999). The influence of the family in the development of talent in sport. *The Sport Psychologist, 13,* 395-417.

Cushion, C. J. (2001). *Coaching research and coach education: Do the sum of the parts equal the whole?* SportaPolis Retrieved from http://www.sportsmedia. org/Sportapolisnewsletter4.htm.

Cushion, C. J., Armour, K. M. and Robyn L. Jones (2003). Coach Education and Continuing Professional Development: Experience and Learning to Coach, Quest, 55:3, 215-230

De Bosscher, V., Bingham, J., Shibli, S., van Bottenburg, M. and De Knop, P. (2008). *The global Sporting Arms Race. An international comparative study on sports policy factors leading to international sporting success.* Aachen: Meyer & Meyer.

De Bosscher, V., De Knop, P., van Bottenburg, M. and Shibli, S. (2006). A Conceptual Framework for Analysing Sports Policy Factors Leading to International Sporting Success. *European Sport Management Quarterly, 6* (2), 185-215.

Digel, H. (2008). Coach Profession Profile. Report from the University of Tübingen, retrieved 15/05/2009 from http://www.bisp.de/SharedDocs/Downloads/Praesentationen_Referate_Veranstaltungen/PK_Trainerprojekte_Berufsfeld_Englisch.pdf?__blob=publicationFil

Duffy, P., North J. and Muir, B. (2013) Understanding the impact of sport coaching on legacy. *International Journal of Sport Policy and Politics, 5:2,* 165-182, DOI: 10.1080/19406940.2012.665380

EENSSEE. (2007). Review of the eu 5-level structure for the recognition of coaching qualifications. Report Complied by the European Coaching Council, a subcommittee of the European Network of Sports Science, Education and Employment: European Network of Sport Science, Education & Employment. Retrieved 1/04/2014 from http://www.icce.ws/_assets/files/documents/ECC_5_level_review.pdf

Erickson, K., Côte, J. and Fraser-Thomas, J. (2007). Sport Experience, Milestones, and Educational Activities Associated with High-Performance Coaches' Development. *The Sport Psychologist, 21,* 302-316.

Ericsson, K. A., Krampe, T. and Tesch-romer, C. (1993). The role of Deliberate Practice in the Acquisition of Expert Performance. *Psychological Review, 100* (3), 363-406.

Green, M. and Houlihan, B. (2005). *Elite sport development. Policy learning and political priorities.* London and New York: Routledge.

Gould, D., Gianinni, J., Krane, V. and Hodge, K. (1990). Educational needs of elite U.S. national Pan American and Olympic coaches. *Journal of Teaching in Physical Education, 9,* 322-344.

Irwin, G., Hanton, S. and Kerwin, D. G. (2005). The conceptual process of skill progression development in artistic gymnastics. *Journal of Sports Sciences, 23* (10), 1089-1099.

Lynch, M. and Mallet, C. (2006). Becoming a successful high performance track and field coach. *Modern Athlete & Coach, 4* (1), 15-20.

Mc Gee, B. (2014). Do great athletes make great coaches? Internet source, retrieved 2/04/2014, http://d3multisport.com/general/do-great-athletes-make-great-coaches/

Truyens, J., De Bosscher, V., Heyndels, B. and De Knop, P. (in press). The coach development and support structures for elite athletics; the development of an international benchmark instrument. *International Journal of Sport Science and Coaching.*

Van Bottenburg, M., Dijk, B., Elling, A. and Reijgersberg, N. (2012). *Bloed, Zweet en tranen. En een moment van glorie. 3-meting topsportklimaat in Nederland. [Blood, sweat and tears. And a moment of glory. 3-measurement elite sport climate in the Netherlands].* Nieuwegein: Arko Sports Media.

Woodman, L. (1993). Coaching: A Science, an art, an emerging profession. *Sport Science Review, 2* (2), 1-13.

バスクリン
MIZUNO

12 Pillar 8: National and international competition/events

12.1 Concepts and definition

Competition, both at national and international level, is an important factor in the development of athletes (Crespo, Miley and Couraud, 2001; Green and Houlihan, 2005; Oakley and Green, 2001). It allows athletes and teams to measure themselves against rivals and to make progression towards taking part in events that are perceived to be the pinnacle of achievement such as the Olympic Games. International competition opportunities can be enhanced for athletes when major sports events are organised in their own nation, as has been shown in many studies on the Olympic Games (e.g., Bernard and Busse, 2004; Johnson and Ali, 2002; Kuper and Sterken, 2003). For example, opportunities for tennis players to participate in professional tournaments staged in their own country has been shown to be a factor which influences sporting success (Crespo, Reid, Miley and Atienza 2003; Reid, Crespo, Atienza and Dimmock 2007). Crespo et al. (2003) point out that in tennis European players appear to have a substantial advantage as 53% of the current ATP calendar is hosted in Europe, and the evidence suggests that there are positive performance effects for countries that organise professional tournaments. Beyond tennis there seems to be a dearth of research regarding the effects of national and international competition structures and sporting success.

Pillar 8 is concerned with the number of international events organised, the strategic planning behind it, the opportunities for athletes to participate in international competition and national competition level

Our analysis of Pillar 8 is limited to three key areas: First, the number of international evens organised and the extent to which there is a national policy and support system for the organisation of major international sports events in each nation. The analysis reviews the role of events in elite sports development, and the extent to which countries make strategic investments in planning and delivering events. Second, the opportunities for athletes to participate in international competitions; and third, the extent to which there is an appropriate level of national competitions in which athletes can participate.

Policy responses were received from 14 countries and sub-national regions. In this Pillar we looked at seven CSFs and 51 sub-factors.

12.2 Key findings

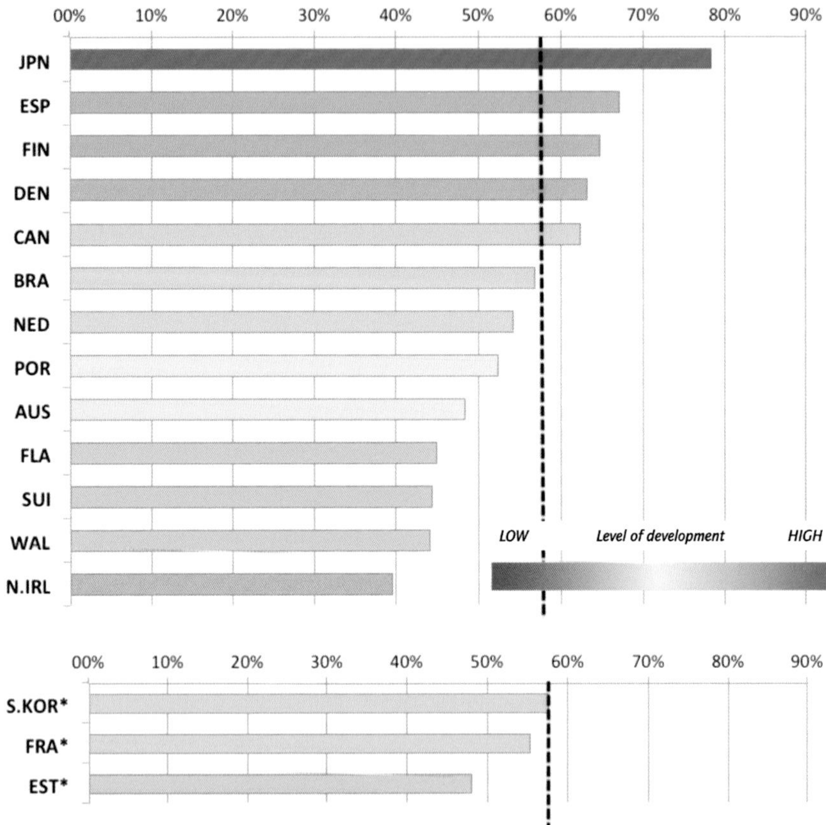

** Note: 13 nations + 3 regions (FLA, WAL, N. IRL). Only partial data available in France (no elite sport climate survey); South Korea and Estonia (no inventory). Caution is therefore needed with the interpretation of scores.*

Figure 70: Total scores of the SPLISS sample nations against the 7 CSFs of Pillar 8

Japan scored highest on this Pillar as shown in Figure 70, which can be explained by two main elements in this Pillar: first, the high degree of national co-ordination; and second, the relatively high number of events organised in the country. The survey responses also confirm Japan's position of pre-eminence in event organisation, with a clear focus on identification of opportunities for athletes to participate in national competition as well as in international competition. Despite the relatively low number of events organised in Finland compared with the average across the sample nations, Finland's high score is explained by good support services and high satisfaction scores from athletes concerning their opportunities to participate in international competition. National co-ordination is high in Denmark, but this comes with fewer international events staged in the country. Despite a high level of co-ordination and the high number of events organised in Canada, athletes, coaches and performance directors do not rate this provision highly. Canada received the lowest scores on the elite sport climate surveys for Pillar 8. With a score of 48%, Australia also underperforms compared with its scores on other Pillars. This is likely to be related to the geographic remoteness of the country, where long-distance traveling to and from Australia may be seen as a barrier to taking part in international sport. As noted by Crespo et al. (2003) being relatively close to many high-performance events is one of the reasons why European countries may have a competitive advantage over others in Pillar 8.

Pillar 8 (national and international competition) correlates well with summer sports but not with winter sports

Overall scores on this Pillar correlate well with success in summer sports but not with winter sports.[36] A possible explanation for this may well be the fact that the majority of nations in the sample are summer sport nations. This means that they can have high scores on Pillar 8, but not be successful in winter sports. Winter sports are mostly dependent on weather and natural sportscape conditions. This means that winter sportscape countries are most likely to host winter sport events. This in turn leads to an overrepresentation of locally born and bred athletes—athletes with an 'unfair' advantage when it comes to accessing international events (that are local to them). In this sample there are only a few mainly smaller winter sport nations that can 'drive' the correlation between a high score on the Pillar and success in winter sports. One of the most successful winter sport nations—Switzerland—scores low on this Pillar which might be the explanation why we did not find a significant correlation between success and a high score on Pillar 8.

Two critical success factors appear to be most prominent in relation to success of the SPLISS countries: first, the number of international events that have been organised in the country; and second for summer sports only, national co-ordination and long-term planning regarding the organisation of major international sports events.[37]

---

36 The correlation of the Pillar 8 scores with success is: $r_{s(summer)} = .577^*$ ($p = 0.039$) and $r_{s(winter)} = -0.271$ ($p = 0.370$).

37 The correlation of the CSF on (1) the number of international events organised in the country is: $r_{s(summer)} = .609$ ($p = 0.035$); $r_{s(winter)} = .075$ ($p = 0.817$); the correlation on national co-ordination and long-term planning with success is $r_{s(winter)} = .556^*$ ($p = 0.039$); $r_{s(summer)} = .522$ ($p = 0.056$) ($n = 14$).

Figure 71 shows the overall scores (positive evaluation of access to (inter)national competition) for the elite sport climate survey plotted against each nation's overall score for Pillar 8. It should be noted that South Korea and Estonia did not return an inventory for this Pillar, and France did not conduct the surveys. From the results of those countries that completed both documents, two key observations can be made.

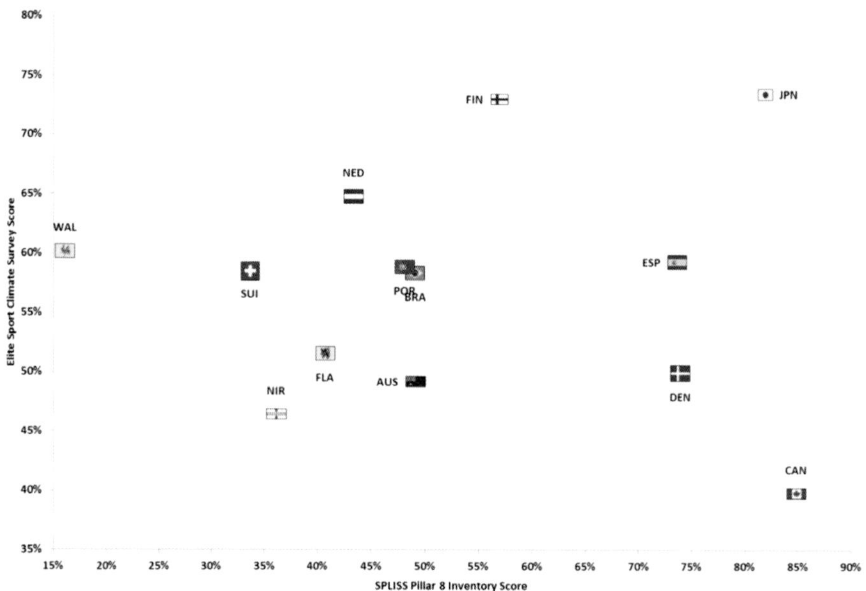

Figure 71: Comparison between Pillar 8 inventory score and elite sport climate survey score

Planning and hosting events does not necessarily translate into opportunities for athletes and coaches to compete and succeed internationally

First, inventories and surveys are not clearly related,[38] as those nations with the highest degree of co-ordination and integration do not necessarily score well on the surveys. Canada and Denmark, despite their event-specific agencies, are among the lowest scoring countries on the surveys. Planning and hosting events does not necessarily translate into opportunities for athletes and coaches to compete and succeed internationally.

Second, it is interesting to note that the three countries with the lowest inventory scores have some form of devolved government, either through sub-national entities in the case of Northern Ireland and

38 The correlation of the surveys and the inventory scores is only: r_s = .0.044 (p = 0.887).

the two Belgian regions, or through a federal/canton structure in Switzerland. The tensions between national and local objectives are perhaps best illustrated by Switzerland's bid to host the 2022 Winter Olympic Games. The Swiss Olympic Committee chose St. Moritz as its preferred location in 2011, but voters rejected the proposal on grounds of cost in a referendum in 2013, forcing organisers to abandon the bid. In the case of Northern Ireland world-class events are the responsibility of UK Sport which operates across the four home nations, England, Scotland, Wales and Northern Ireland.

Northern Ireland's inventory score was among the lowest of all the SPLISS countries, ahead of only Switzerland and Wallonia. The low score is indicative of the complex nature of sports governance in Northern Ireland, with athletes able to compete for Northern Ireland, Great Britain, and Ireland internationally, depending on the sport, the event and their own cultural and political allegiances.

We conclude from our data that the organisation of events (the number of events and the level of competition of events) may need to be considered separately from the views of athletes, coaches and performance directors, when it comes to assessing its value and usefulness for performance enhancement. In other words, for athletes to truly capitalise on the opportunity to improve their performance, it seems insufficient merely to have access to (more) events. How preparation for and access to events is facilitated and planned for by policymakers remains an important component of athlete satisfaction, and the ultimate achievement of sporting success.

Canada has the highest inventory score of all the SPLISS countries, at 84.6%, but the lowest survey score (39.8%). Thus, while an objective analysis suggests that considerable infrastructure is in place to plan and deliver the staging of international events in Canada, the athletes who take part in them, along with the coaches and performance directors who guide them, evidently do not feel well supported by their national governing bodies and other high level sporting organisations.

This may be to some extent a function of the funding of events in Canada, which is directed through a specific agency (The Hosting Programme) that has economic, and political objectives as well as sporting objectives. By giving control of event planning and delivery to such an organisation, NGBs may be excluded from the planning process, with the result that domestic athletes may feel they do not have sufficient home advantage opportunities. The single most important issue for Canada is the national competition structure, as athletes coaches and performance directors feel that it does not prepare athletes well for international competition. Additionally, the Canadian participants report that their country does not bring enough international events to Canada, and that athletes therefore do not have enough opportunities to compete on the international stage as a result.

Co-ordination and organisation of international events

It is possible to present this Pillar on elite event planning and delivery across two axes–degree of national co-ordination against the number of events (Figure 72). The degree of co-ordination ranges from complete autonomy to complete integration of co-operation and planning at national level as part of a national strategic policy.

There is no direct relationship with the number of events staged and the level of co-ordination and planning

Canada, Denmark and Japan exhibit a high degree of long-term centralised co-ordination and planning. This underpins the ability of NSAs and NGBs to bid for, fund, plan and deliver events. While Spain and also Portugal stage a significant number of events, organisers have more autonomy. Switzerland and Flanders have relative autonomy and stage an average number of events. The Netherlands exhibits a long-term event planning approach, but only limited co-ordination is provided. Some co-ordination takes place through government providing assistance to national governing bodies and cities in the bidding and organising process of events. At the other end of the scale, Northern Ireland and Wallonia stage only a small number of international events and are characterised by a low level of co-ordination, while Finland delivered few events in spite of its reasonable co-ordination score. South Korea did not participate in the Pillar 8 inventory, but it stages many international events, as expressed by the substantial amounts of money provided by government (53% of total elite sport funding), and explained earlier in the commentary to Pillar 1.

Figure 72: The planning, co-ordination and delivery of elite sport events

NUMBER OF EVENTS				
	High Frequent	ESP	POR	JPN CAN
	↑	SUI	NED* FRA BRA	DEN
	Low occasional	N. IRL FLA WAL*	AUS FIN	–
		'Autonomy' Low	→	'Integration' High
		DEGREE OF NATIONAL CO-ORDINATION/PLANNING		

*Note: *In the Netherlands and Wallonia only (perceived) survey data on the number of events are available.*

In theory, best practice within the continuum might reasonably be considered as being high and to the right, such that countries aim in principle to *increase* the level of co-ordination and planning, with a resultant *increase* in the number of events staged. The exception to this rule is Spain, which staged fewer events in 2010 (240) than in 2009 (302).[39] Meanwhile Australia, France and Switzerland have a stated aim of increasing the level of co-ordination and planning of events by developing a long-term event planning structure. At this stage of interpretation it is also important to note the fact that some or even most nations, and their national policy development agencies may have nationally co-ordinated event bidding and hosting strategies for quite different reasons than the development of talented athletes. Politicians and in turn their policy advisors and bureaucrats will more often be interested in the wider impacts of hosting events, and these impacts are increasingly used to justify planning and bidding for events. These impacts include sporting benefits, such as increased participation through 'inspiration' or 'demonstration effects', as well as social, economic and political benefits. Global financial pressures may possibly explain why the number of events in Spain has fallen, and why funding has declined in Portugal and Wallonia.

Some caution is necessary in analysing the data, due to the data gaps in the inventories and the non-completion of the surveys in some nations. Spain and the Netherlands did not supply financial data; Wallonia and the Netherlands did not submit a total for the number of events staged. The positioning of the Netherlands in Figure 72 was derived from the survey results and an estimate based on known world and European championship events staged in Olympic sports (e.g., 2010 World Artistic Gymnastics Championships, Rotterdam; 2011 UCI World Track Cycling Championships, Apeldoorn; 2011 World Table Tennis Championships, Rotterdam). The Australian and French data suffer from the fact that centralised data is not held by the Australian Sports Commission, or INSEP, but sits with the NGBs. This highlights the issue of potential under-reporting of events staged, which may give a misleading impression of a country's position on the continuum.

---

39 Over the past three years, Spain has staged 60 international events at world level (world championships, world cups (tests)) and 34 continental events (e.g., European championships, Pacific Rim, European Cup). When including all other international evens (e.g., European and world championship tests), the number is 45.

12.3 Comparative and descriptive analysis

12.3.1 Co-ordination and long-term planning of international elite sport events

Critical success factors		INVENTORY	SURVEY			
I. There is nationally co-ordinated planning to increase the number of international elite sport events that are organised in the country in a wide range of sports		O	A	C	PD	
CSF 8.1	There is a national co-ordination and long-term planning of (elite sport) event organisation and funding (including NGB co-ordination and planning)	X			X	P2
CSF 8.2	NGBs and cities/municipalities or others are provided with assistance and advice on the organisation of major international elite sports events	X				
CSF 8.3	NGBs and cities/municipalities or others receive funding for the bidding for, and the staging of, major international elite sports events	X				P1
CSF 8.4	There is a high number of international events that have been organised in the country over the past five years in a (wide) range of sports for junior and senior athletes	X	X	X	X	

Source of information: O: overall sport inventory; A: athletes' survey; C: coaches' survey; PD: performance directors' survey; right column shows where the CSFs are possible on the interface with other Pillars.

Co-ordination and long-term planning

It can be argued that countries engage in hosting events for economic, social/cultural/political and different sporting reasons (e.g., stimulating grassroots and elite sport development). Australia, Canada, Denmark, Finland, the Netherlands and Wallonia aim to achieve benefits in all three categories, with in particular Australia, Canada and Denmark having well developed plans in that regard.

Only five countries engage in nationally co-ordinating the planning and organisation of international events

National co-ordination is organised in two different ways. All countries, except Northern Ireland, Switzerland and Spain have a nationally co-ordinated major event funding plan. However, only five countries (Australia, Denmark, Finland, Japan and the Netherlands) engage in nationally co-ordinating the planning and organisation of events. Despite this, the overall management and organisation of major sporting events is the responsibility of the relevant NGBs (or local organising committees) in most nations. As such the level of support varies from event to event depending on the individual requirements of the event and the level of commitment made by government. NGBs reporting the highest level of planning were in Brazil, Spain, Japan, Korea, Portugal and Wallonia.

Only five countries (Canada, Denmark, Japan, the Netherlands and Switzerland) report having a long-term event planning strategy in place. Canada (The Hosting Programme) and Denmark (Sport Event Denmark), each have a single agency specifically created to fulfil this role. Northern Ireland's event programme ended in 2009-2010. Finland, France and Japan are developing long-term plans, but these are not yet in place. The planning cycle is typically four years (i.e., one Olympic cycle), although in the Netherlands, the planning calendar stretches as far ahead as 2024. Australia and France reported that the organisation of international events depends on the national governing bodies as well as individual cities and states. Consequently this activity is not planned at national level.

Some countries also provide a certain level of assistance for the process of bidding for and hosting events, although often staff are seconded to the NGB in such roles. There are a few examples of permanently employed staff (nationally) whose specific role focusses solely on bidding for and organising events: Finland (three people), France (two) and Canada (number unknown).

Most countries provide financial support for event organisers, but there is some variation in the way that this is provided and co-ordinated. Flanders, Canada, Finland and Wallonia provide financial support to event organisers, while in Japan and the Netherlands, the NSA takes a more central role as a co-organiser involving local government and national governing bodies. Canada and Denmark's event agencies (The Hosting Programme and Sport Event Denmark, respectively) are funded directly by central government, the latter in conjunction with Denmark's NOC. Switzerland describes itself as a country with inadequate levels of co-ordination, though the federal government has recently introduced legislation to strengthen its involvement. They created a multi-year plan, co-ordinated in consultation with the Swiss Olympic Committee, with the aim of developing an event calendar for international sports events eight to ten years ahead and which is integrated with government's medium- to long-term financial planning.

12.3.2 Commercial and broadcast co-operation

A minority of countries (Denmark, Japan, Northern Ireland, the Netherlands and Switzerland) have entered directly into negotiations with commercial partners for the organisation of events. In the case of Northern Ireland and the Netherlands, this happens on an event-by-event basis but is a matter of routine in Denmark, Japan and Switzerland. Denmark and Japan (along with Canada, which has an historical agreement with CNBC), also negotiate agreements with national broadcasters. In the remaining countries, government departments and National Sport Organisations tend to stay out of negotiations, leaving this to NGBs. The main reason for this is that the commercial rights to these events are most often held by the international governing bodies, which subsequently award them to a host city or nation (e.g., IOC, FIFA).

12.3.3 Funding for bidding and hosting events

Awarding of funding for international events is nationally co-ordinated in most nations

The majority of countries report that the awarding of funding is nationally co-ordinated, with the exceptions being Northern Ireland, Spain and Switzerland. This reflects the administrative and political structure in Northern Ireland and more particularly in Switzerland, where regional governments have significant influence. Northern Ireland's situation is further complicated by a two-tier political administration, which has the potential to create conflict between local and national objectives. In addition, some sports' governing bodies operate with cross-border jurisdiction. Hockey, boxing and rugby for example are governed on an All-Ireland rather than on a UK basis.

NGBs in all countries can receive funding for hosting events, although the amount of funding varies considerably from country to country, and according to the level of competition involved. Funding tends to be provided by means of seeding grants, with specific rates of investment for different levels of competition. For example, in Flanders organisers may claim up to €30,000 for a world championship and €15,000 for a continental championship. In France the amount of funding available is higher for world-level events (about a third of the overall staging cost on average), than for continental or other international events (18% and 13% of staging costs, respectively). Elsewhere, funding is distributed on a more ad hoc basis.

It is interesting to consider the total amount of funding provided for international events especially in light of the total elite sport funding, as presented in Pillar 1. South Korea spent 53% of the total elite sport funding in 2010 on the organisation of international events, such as the Asian Games, IAAF World Championships, and the Universiade. Exact information could not be provided by the Australian researcher because event data is not collected by the Australian Sports Commission, rather, this is often held by individual NSOs, 20% of the funding (derived from Pillar 1) appears to be devoted to international events. Portugal (14%) and Flanders (10.5%) are the only other nations that spend more than 10% of their elite sport budget on events..

Table 42: Yearly funding provided for the staging/organisation of major international high performance sports events in 2010

	AUS	BRA	CAN	DEN	FIN	FLA	S. KOR	JPN	POR	SUI	WAL
Funding 2010, m€	–	1.86	8.02	0.49	0.50	1.19	–	0.51	1.31	0.41	0.24
% of total elite sport funding	20%	–	–	2.1%	2.5%	10.5%	53.3%	2.8%	14.0%	–	–

Note with table: these figures are only a snapshot of 2010 and differ from year to year.

12.3.4 Hosting events

The country hosting the most senior international events (in Olympic sports) over the period 2009-2010 was Spain, with a total of 546 (of which 94 were at world or European level), followed by Japan (319) and Canada (127). Denmark staged 83 events in total, but did not record any breakdown by competitive level or distinction between senior and junior competition.

In countries where event data is collected by individual NGBs (e.g., Australia and France) it was nearly impossible for us to compile a reliable total number. The figures reported next are therefore likely to under-represent the number of international sports events staged in each country, since events may be staged independently without NSA involvement. As such, when conducting a sport-by-sport analysis of the world championships and continental championships organised over the past three years, Australia reported an approximate number of 18 events held over the past three years (including annual Australian Open championships for golf and tennis), the French researcher reported 25, including only those events where the national governing bodies applied for funding to the CNDS (Centre National pour le Développement du Sport).

Athletes, coaches and performance directors were asked to assess if sufficient numbers of international events were organised in their country and in their sport. It can be argued that views of athletes, coaches and performance directors might reasonably differ in regard to what is an 'appropriate' level of competition (Figure 73).

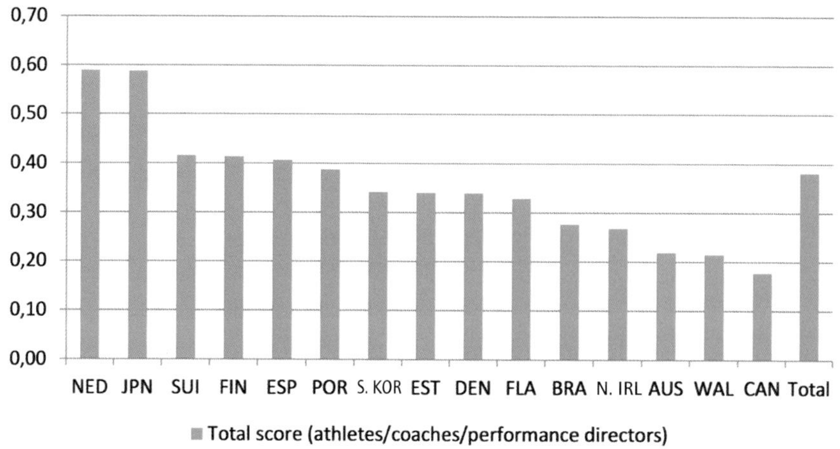

Figure 73: Total scores for the perceptions of athletes, coaches and performance directors on whether there are sufficient events in their country in their sport

12.3.5 Opportunities to participate in international competitions

Critical success factors		INVENTORY	SURVEY			
II. Athletes can participate sufficiently in international (high-level) competitions		O	A	C	PD	
CSF 8.5	There are sufficient opportunities for young talents and elite athletes to participate in international competitions, at the right age		X	X	X	P5
CSF 8.6	Young talents, athletes and coaches can receive reimbursement of their costs for participating in international competitions	X	X	X	X	P1

Source of information: O: overall sport inventory; A: athletes' survey: C: coaches' survey; PD: performance directors' survey; right column shows where the CSFs are possible on the interface with other Pillars.

Opportunities to participate

The second part of the analysis of this Pillar concerns the opportunities provided to elite athletes and young talents to participate in international competition.

Athletes are more satisfied than coaches with the number of international competitions they can take part in. Higher level athletes and coaches are more satisfied

Approximately 75% of the athletes who responded are happy with the number of opportunities they have to participate in international competition. Only in South Korea do athletes suggest that they would like to compete in more international events hosted in other countries. Coaches appear to be slightly less satisfied with the number of competitive opportunities, but overall the majority (67%) agrees that athletes are offered sufficient opportunities to compete. In Australia, Canada, South Korea, Northern Ireland and Estonia, less than half of all coaches are happy with the number of competitive opportunities (see Figure 74). Not surprisingly, top 16 level athletes and international level coaches are more satisfied than their counterparts at lower levels.

The views of performance directors confirm that there are at least a 'reasonable' number of competitive opportunities, with Canadian and South Korean performance directors the only dissenting voices. Flanders and Wallonia in particular had a very high proportion of performance directors who were happy with the number of competitions for senior athletes. For young talents, the scores were generally lower, with Canada and South Korea again scoring towards the bottom end of the distribution.

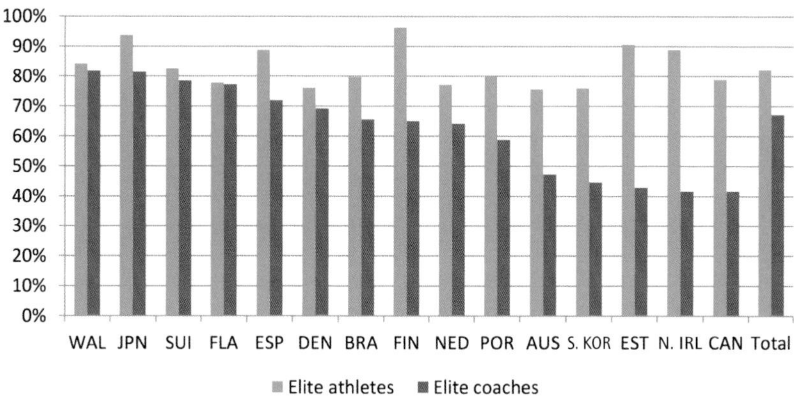

Note: Australian data contain 'all' athletes and coaches as the data did not allow to distinct by level.

Figure 74: Can you, given your level, take part in enough international competitions? According to top 16 athletes and international level coaches.

Reimbursement of international competition costs

Generally senior level athletes and their coaches receive national funding to compete in international competition. The exceptions are Brazil and France, where funding is provided mainly by municipalities. In all but four countries (Brazil, Canada, France and the Netherlands), national funding is also provided to young athletes and talented coaches to facilitate participation in international competition.

Our results show that there is considerable consistency across the nations in terms of the financial support that athletes and coaches receive for participation in international competition. Around two-thirds of all elite athletes state that they receive support to compete. This is higher among top 16 athletes (75%). Only Brazilian athletes bucked this trend, with 48% of them (top 16) stating that they do not receive support. A similar proportion of athletes agree that the support they receive is sufficient to compete, ranging from 52% in Brazil to over 85% in Finland, the Netherlands and Japan.

As reported previously, the views of elite coaches are different to those of the athletes, in that fewer of them receive direct financial support (58%), and fewer still (45%) consider their funding sufficient. There is significant variation between countries, with fewer than 10% of coaches in Northern Ireland receiving funding, compared with 90% in South Korea and 100% in Canada. Interestingly, Switzerland has the highest proportion of coaches who say their funding is sufficient, but only 27% actually receive funding. Funding for coaches is concentrated in a small number of sports—and those that are funded, are funded well.

12.3.6 National competition level

Critical success factors		INVENTORY	SURVEY			
III. The national competition has relatively high standard compared with the international standards		O	A	C	PD	
CSF 8.7	The national competition structure in each sport provides a competitive environment at an international top level at each age*	X	X	X	X	

Source of information: O: overall sport inventory; A: athletes' survey; C: coaches' survey; PD: performance directors' survey; right column shows where the CSFs are possible on the interface with other Pillars.

Numerous competitive opportunities are a key ingredient of successful athlete development programmes. For example in tennis, Crespo et al. (2003) observed a strong relationship (r=0.82) between the number of professional tournaments played and the ATP ranking (i.e., Association of Tennis Professionals, men) list in 2002. Interestingly, the authors also found that this relationship had reduced over the last 10 years.

In the last section of this Pillar, stakeholders were asked to rate the level and frequency of national-level competitions in their sport that translates to the opportunities they have as young and senior athletes to participate in national-level competition. On average one-third of the athletes and coaches report that the level of the national competition for juniors (young talents) is (very) low. For senior athletes this is a little higher. From Figure 75 we can see that coaches and athletes rate the national competition level differently. For young talents, the lowest ratings among coaches are found in Canada and Northern Ireland and among athletes in Flanders, Wallonia, Brazil and Canada, all with more than 40% of the respondents reporting a (very) low level of competition. For senior athletes the level is rated lower (Figure 76), mainly among coaches in Northern Ireland, Wallonia, Australia, Finland and Canada and among athletes in Flanders, Wallonia, Finland, Canada and Brazil.

Canada as one of the nations with arguably the most integrated and co-ordinated approach to staging international events, is evaluated by athletes, coaches and performance directors as having the least developed national competition structure. It might be argued that in such circumstances, the international competitive environment takes on additional importance, filling a void for athletes in those nations that lack sufficient opportunities at home. It has to be noted that the Canadian coaches' sample was the smallest of all responding nations (n=12) and therefore not representative.

In Northern Ireland the lower level of satisfaction with the level of national competition, may be related to the country's sub-national status. 'National' competition in Northern Ireland is one level below competition at the level of Great Britain or All-Ireland, which athletes would need to compete at in order to achieve world championship or Olympic qualification in most sports.

Conversely, the existence of any gap, whether actual or perceived, between performing at the national and international level, could put athletes at a disadvantage in comparison with their counterparts in other nations. It should also be noted that if athletes are competing internationally, competitive opportunities at national level might be less of a priority for athletes and their coaches, but an important opportunity for those nations where the national competition level is high.

The (low) level of national competition can lead to an experience gap compared to what athletes competing at an international level expect

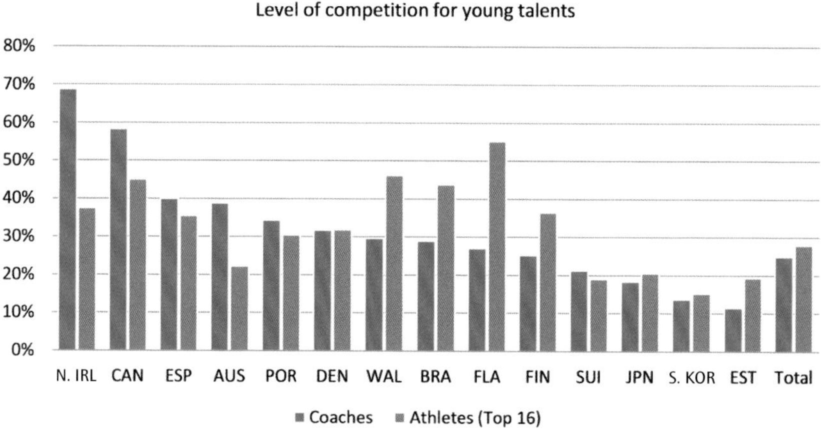

Figure 75: Percentage of coaches and athletes (top 16) rating the level of national competitions in their sport for young talents as (very) low

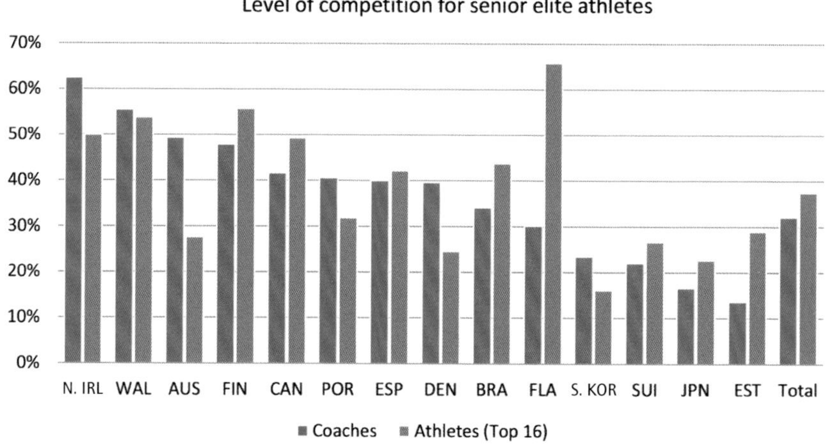

Figure 76: Percentage of coaches and athletes (top 16) rating the level and frequency of national competitions in their sport for senior athletes as (very) low

12.4 Summary points in Pillar 8

- Nations have different reasons for hosting international sports events. These include achieving economic impact; place marketing impacts; cultural impacts; the pursuit of political ambitions; and a variety of sporting impacts. It is clear that elite sport development goals are not the only objectives for hosting such events and are possibly of an even lower priority than other objectives.
- While hosting major sports events can be seen as a source of competitive advantage it is not necessarily a feature of an elite sport development system that is controllable. Events are often in short supply and have high demand to stage them (bidding wars); there is an element of political decision-making as to where events are hosted as well as a tendency for the location of events to be rotated.
- Funding for athletes, coaches and performance directors to take part in international competition varies considerably by nation. The more enlightened nations in terms of their elite sport development systems accept that taking part in international competition is a cost of doing business and funding it accordingly.
- National level competition is more controllable and predictable than international competition. With the exception of two of the larger nations (AUS and CAN) and the devolved nation (NIR) satisfaction levels for domestic competition are generally high.

Chapter 12 references

Bernard, A. B. and Busse, M. R. (2004). Who wins the Olympic Games? Economic resources and medal totals. *Review of Economics & Statistics, 86* (1), 413-417.

Crespo, M., Miley, D. and Couraud, F. (2001). An overall vision of player development. In *Tennis Player Development* (pp. 13-18). M. Crespo, M. Reid, and D. Miley (Eds.). London: ITF LTd.

Crespo, M., Reid, M., Miley, D. and Atienza, F. (2003) The relationship between professional tournament structure on the national level and success in men's professional tennis. *Journal of Science and Medicine in Sport, 6*, 3-13.

Green, M. and Houlihan, B. (2005). *Elite Sport Development. Policy learning and political priorities.* New York: Routledge.

Johnson, K. N. and Ali, A. (2002). *A tale of two seasons: participation and medal counts at the summer and winter Olympic Games.* Retrieved February 15, 2003, from Wellesley college, Massachusetts http://www.wellesley.edu/economics/wkpapers/wellwp_0010.pdf

Kuper, G. and Sterken, E. (2003). Olympic participation and performance since 1896: University of Groningen, Research Institute SOM (Systems, Organisations and Management).

Oakley, B. and Green, M. (2001). The production of Olympic champions: International perspectives on elite sport development system. *European Journal for Sport Management, 8*, 83-105.

Reid, M., Crespo, M., Atienza, F. and Dimmock, J. (2007a) Tournament structure and nations' success in women's professional tennis. *Journal of Sport Sciences, 25*, 1221-1228.

BEL
VAN ACKER
BEL

13 Pillar 9: Sport science support, scientific research and innovation in elite sport

13.1 Concepts and definition

Innovative scientific research is one of the fastest growing fields of interest in elite sport over the past decade and is proving to be an increasingly important factor in the battle for sporting success. In the SPLISS 1.0 study it was still an underdeveloped area in five of the six nations (except Norway). and it was stated that 'in terms of indicating where nations might be able to derive a source of differentiation and competitive advantage, scientific support and innovation as an integrated part of elite sport is still an area for improvement' (De Bosscher et al., 2008, p. 133). Sports science and sports medicine support was one of the key characteristics of the German Democratic Republic (GDR), where approximately 600 staff worked on top secret sports science research projects (Houlihan and Green, 2008, p. 23) and in the Soviet sport system fundamental research was embedded in all elements of an athletic career by a network of research institutes (Smolianov and Zakus, 2008). Australia was one of the early adopters of elite squad development through a highly scientific approach and Australia remains a leading country in regard to the application of science to sport (Green and Houlihan, 2005). While the Australian Sports Medicine Federation was formed as early as 1963, the early engagement of science with sport has been in regard to equipment and apparel rather than focusing on the preparation and training of competitors. Part of the explanation for this is, according to Houlihan and Green (2008), *'that there is profit to be made from boat design in sailing and the sale of sports clothing, but little profit to be made from scientific research into training, nutrition and psychological preparation for competition. The use of athlete-centred sports science and medicine became more prevalent when governments decided to invest public money in its development'* (p. 177). The Belgian high jump athlete Tia Hellebaut, who won gold in Beijing 2008, is a good example of how sport science support in biomechanics is likely to have made the difference between being on the podium rather than just being an Olympian. Detailed 3-D kinematic video footage was recorded with high-speed cameras in six international level competitions in the two years prior to the Beijing Olympics (Malcolm and De Clercq, 2013). This project was funded by government. After the event, Belgian newspapers wrote that only two female high jumpers received such scientific support, namely Hellebaut and the Croatian Blanka Vlasic, who won the silver medal.

In addition to sports medicine and sports science support, innovation and sports engineering play important roles as well. Innovation concerns the development (and implementation) of a new idea, a new product or a new service, in order to create competitive advantage in an increasingly competitive environment (Winand, 2013). In high-performance management, continued organisational success depends on the ability of organisations to learn and to innovate (Kloot and Martin, 2000). Sharkskin swimming suits or aerodynamic skeleton bobs in winter sports are good examples of how innovative engineering can make a difference and where countries that structurally invest in these activities derive an advantage over others.

In this study, Pillar 9 is concerned with the support provided for sport science, scientific research and innovation and as a result of this support, with an integrated approach to the collection, co-ordination and dissemination of scientific research. The Pillar consists of nine CSFs and 65 sub-factors.

13.2 Key findings

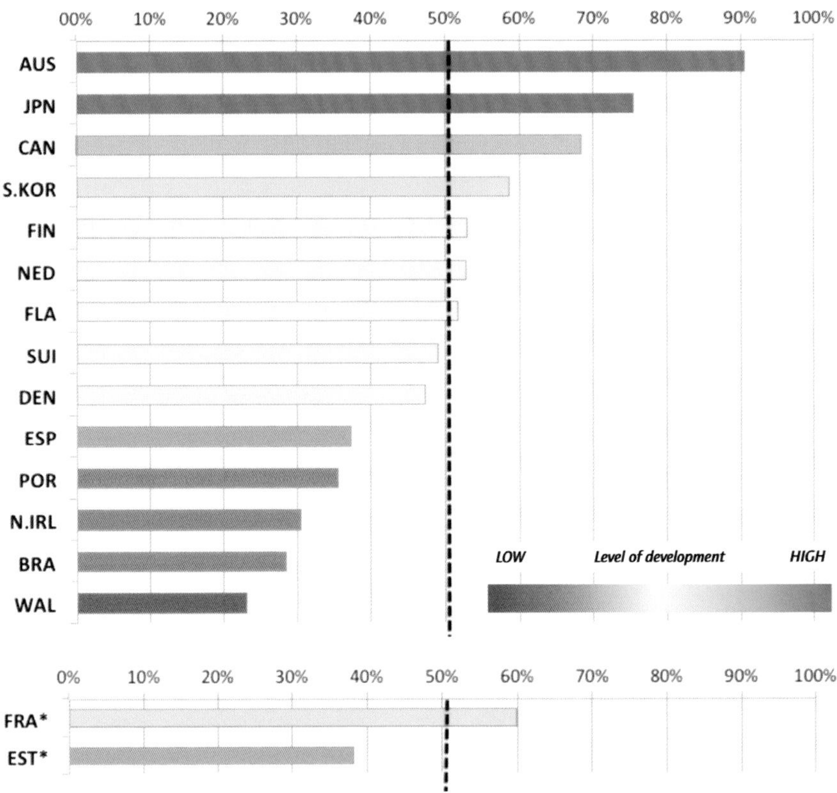

** Note: 13 nations + 3 regions (FLA, WAL, N. IRL). Only partial data are available in France (no elite sport climate survey); Estonia (no inventory). Caution is therefore needed with the interpretation of scores.*

*Figure 77: Total scores of the SPLISS sample nations against the 9 CSFs of Pillar 9**

The best performing nations in summer sports and winter sports generally score well in scientific research and innovation. They have a national sport research centre, and co-ordinate, disseminate and communicate scientific information well

The scores on Pillar 9 enable us to conclude that the best performing nations in summer sports and in winter sports, also have the highest scores for scientific research amongst our sample nations.[40] The average score is 50.2%, with Australia the highest scoring nation, followed by Japan and Canada. These countries stand out as a result of the important role of the national training centres in research, respectively the Australian Institute of Sport and the Japanese Institute of Sport Science,

40 The total scores are significantly correlated with success: Spearman's rank correlation with success in summer sports delivering a $r_s = .710$, and in winter sports $r_s = .784$ ($p < 0.01$).

and the network of seven Canadian Sport Centres that collaborate with the NGBs. Compared with France (note: incomplete data, only information from the inventory), the best performing country in the sample in summer sports, sport science development at INSEP is less explicit. Switzerland's (FOSPO in Magglingen) and Finland's (KIHU) sport research institutes are also notable for their research, with Magglingen having a stronger focus on elite sport. Australia is also well developed with regard to all critical success factors including the co-ordination, dissemination and communication of scientific information. Every element in the process is implemented with so much care, that the country outperforms all others on this Pillar. This finding also provides further evidence of a long-term strategic approach that Australia initiated earlier than many other countries. Interestingly, while over 80% of the Australian coaches stated that they used scientific information frequently, the coaches' satisfaction with the applicability of research and the wider dissemination of results is only moderate. Satisfaction with this factor was higher in Japan, Canada, Switzerland and Flanders.

Pillar 9 is still relatively under developed (in descending order) in Denmark, Spain, Portugal, Northern Ireland, Brazil and Wallonia, which all score below the average. In these countries the national co-ordination and dissemination of scientific research as well as the financial support provided for research are not yet seen as key elements for elite sport success.

The countries with the highest budget for elite sport in Pillar 1 also spend most on sport science research

It is perhaps not surprising that the countries with the highest budget for elite sport in Pillar 1 also spend most on sport science research. The total amount spent on Pillar 9 comprises around 16% of the total elite sport expenditures in Australia and 13% in Japan, while this is less than 3% in the worst performing countries. The relatively high importance awarded to the factors in this Pillar is also shown in Switzerland (8.5% of total elite sport expenditures) and Flanders (11%), although caution must be exercised when interpreting financial data due to comparability issues. It is noteworthy that the development of sport science does not seem to depend on the wealth of the sample countries[41] as best demonstrated by Brazil. Our assessment is that this is an area in which Brazil could gain competitive advantage for its host Olympic Games in 2016 or more realistically Tokyo 2020 because of the lead in time required to deliver positive results.

41 Correlation between GDP/CAP and the scores on Pillar 9: $r_s = 0.102$ (summer sports; $p = 0.708$) and 0.411 (winter sports; $p = 0.114$).

Evaluations by stakeholders are generally not very high in Pillar 9

Remarkably, from a stakeholders' viewpoint (mainly the coaches), it is perceived that there is generally room for improvement on this Pillar in all countries, as the average score of all aggregated CSFs obtained from the elite sport climate survey (by athletes, coaches and performing directors) is just 35%. Looking at the views of coaches we found almost universal dissatisfaction with the applicability and the dissemination of research data for their particular sport. It can be argued that coaches always want applied findings that will assist them in improving training and competition practice immediately. In that regard there may well be a clear difference (in perception and in application) between fundamental research (long term, and not linked to a direct coaching or competition research question) and applied research (where researchers solve questions that coaches, athletes or administrators pose). It is clear that a perceived gap exists between what universities deliver and what 'sport' is demanding. However, this does not necessarily mean that scientists are not delivering new knowledge, rather they are not delivering on the immediate needs of coaches and athletes. For the development of true competitive advantage, our view is that fundamental research remains critical, but should be translated more for the practitioners in the field.

The CSF that can be identified as the most important element of Pillar 9, in terms of its relationship with success, is concerned with the existence of a national research centre that conducts applied elite sport research and co-ordinates research activities on elite sport nationally. Also the most successful nations tend to collaborate strongly with universities and (sport) research centres with which they have formal agreements. As expected, CSFs are partially correlated to the financial support received for research and innovation. The next section shows the more detailed descriptive results.

13.3 Comparative and descriptive analysis

13.3.1 Support for scientific research

Critical success factors P9		INVENTORY	SURVEY			
I. There is sufficient support for scientific research and innovation and sport science is provided at each level of elite sport development		O	A	C	PD	
CSF 9.1	There is (sufficient) financial support with specific subsidies for scientific research and innovation in elite sport	X		X		P1
CSF 9.2	Different areas of elite athlete development (all Pillars) are supported by applied scientific research and innovation projects and there are 'field laboratories' and/or embedded scientists that in situ develop, test and/or apply new technologies in co-operation with coaches and athletes at elite sport training centres	X				All

Source of information: O: overall sport inventory; A: athletes' survey, C: coaches' survey; PD: performance directors' survey. Right column shows if the CSFs are possibly interlinked with other Pillars.

It is difficult to make like for like comparisons when it comes to the funding of scientific research and innovation. There remains confusion over what exactly scientific research and innovation entails as well as the data available about distinct research project funding from sport science and sport medicine support services. The purpose of Pillar 9 is to capture the broad conception of scientific research supporting elite sport performance.

Coaches can be competitive in Pillar 9; only 28% of all coaches find the research in their sport sufficient

The data available show that research and innovation is highly embedded in elite sport development in Australia, Canada, Japan and Switzerland in particular. In Australia 16% of the total elite sport funding (€22.6m) is spent on this Pillar, of which €1.4 million is specifically spent on research projects, and the rest on tailor-made sport science support services. The AIS (Australian Institute of Sport) has a Performance Research Section that is charged with the distribution of research funds, monitoring of research project progress, dissemination of research outputs and the implementation of research outcomes into elite training environments. They also initiate and run research and development activities in elite sport. These include a Technical Research Laboratory, an Applied Sensors Unit and a Data Analytics Unit. The AIS has established a number of high-performance research funds which target the short-, medium- and long-term strategy of the organisation, from targeted sports research funding, to NGBs or national institute network scientists, the AIS PhD Scheme and the 'Big Idea' fund aimed at one or two ideas that might offer significant competitive advantage to Australian sport. Longer term outcomes are also achieved through the AIS' strategic partnerships with the Commonwealth Scientific and Industrial Research Organisation (CSIRO), National ICT Australia (NICTA) and the partnership with Victoria University's Institute for Sport, Exercise and Active Living (ISEAL). Each of these are genuine partnerships with roughly 50/50 inputs of both cash and in-kind, with the outcomes targeted at the strategic aims of the AIS. Finally, field laboratories are set up that develop, test and/or apply research and new technologies *in situ* for 26 sports. Despite these seemingly high support services, only 29% of the 148 Australian coaches who took part in the research consider that there is sufficient scientific research related to their area of elite sport (Figure 78). These figures are higher in Japan and Switzerland with 41% assessing this to be sufficient. Figure 78 also shows that according to the coaches there is room for improvement, as only one quarter feel that they are sufficiently supported, with scores being the lowest in Brazil, Northern Ireland and Portugal.

In Canada, Own the Podium (OTP) is the hub of Canada's scientific research and innovation initiatives, with nine full-time staff employed for the national co-ordination of research. OTP is funded by a series of partners (including the federal government). OTP focuses both at establishing and servicing Integrated Support Teams (IST) through the NGBs and the network of seven Canadian Sport Centres. The Canadian Sport Centres collaborate with NGBs to provide integrated support team programmes for training groups through a network of in-house and contracted experts. This programme will work with 'field laboratories' and scientific experts. As another example OTP's Top Secret Programme, is a research and development project designed to provide Canada's winter athletes with the best equipment, technology, and knowledge which provided them with a unique competitive edge when Canada hosted the Winter Olympics in 2010. The programme includes over 150 researchers from 17 universities and institutions across the country who have been working to improve equipment, technology, information and training for Canadian athletes through the federally-financed Own the Podium programme's five-year, $8-million Top Secret Project. Finally the National Research Council (NRC) provides services to Own The Podium and works collaboratively with them on their Sport Research Initiative. For example the NRC's most relevant sport research project in winter sports is focused on testing and improving aerodynamics in sport-specific equipment and clothing, by utilising the services within the NRC-IAR (Institute for Aerospace Research) and with 'field laboratories' (NRC 2x3-m wind tunnel) expert scientists. The federal government has three primarily research councils. They include NSERC (National Science and Engineering Research Council of Canada), SSHRC (Social Sciences and Humanities Research Council) and CIHR (Canadian Institutes of Health Research). Each of these will support elite sport projects submitted by research groups within universities but these are not co-ordinated by Sport Canada.

In Japan 56 people (22 of whom are full-time permanent staff) work in three departments of the national research institute JISS (Japanese Institute of Sport Science). JISS has a sports sciences department (e.g., physiology, psychology and biomechanics; measurement and analysis); a sports medicine department (e.g., rehabilitation, physiotherapy, injuries); and a sports information department that gathers and disseminates information, maintains databases (e.g., game analysis, sports medicine and science research, strategy and tactics, sporting records, and sports policy), and builds domestic and international networks aimed at facilitating exchange of information.

More than 10% of the total funding on elite sport is therefore spent on research in Japan but also in Flanders. With the exception of Wallonia, all countries provide specific financial support for scientific research and innovation in elite sport. **Appendix 1** provides an overview of the research funding (research projects and sport science support) and the delivery structures in each country. The figures do not include university investments (or academic research funds) on elite sport and private sector investments that are not nationally co-ordinated. We acknowledge that private research investments in commercial sports are substantial in some countries, where top teams and clubs carry out their own research and companies invest in sports technology and equipment.

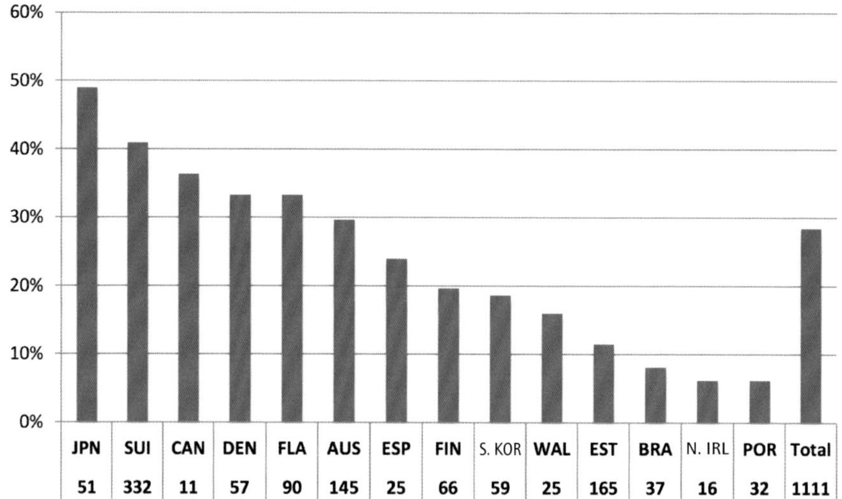

Note: The Netherlands did not ask this question in their surveys.

Figure 78: Do coaches consider that there is sufficient scientific research in their country related to their area in elite sport (all coaches, no significant differences between subgroups)

13.3.2 Co-ordination and dissemination of scientific research

Critical success factors P9		INVENTORY	SURVEY			
II. Co-ordination and dissemination of scientific information and innovative research		O	A	C	PD	
CSF 9.3	There is a national research centre that conducts applied elite sport research, co-ordinates research activities on elite sport nationally and has (or NSA has) a specific responsibility for developing and co-ordinating innovation projects in elite sport	X		X	X	
CSF 9.4	There is a specific responsibility within the NGB for developing and co-ordinating innovative research projects in elite sport				X	P2
CSF 9.5	Scientific support/innovation in elite sport is provided in strong co-operation with universities /and (sport) research centres	X				
CSF9.6	There is a regularly updated database of scientific research that can be consulted by coaches and NGBs	X				P2
CSF 9.7	There is a network to communicate and disseminate scientific information to the NGBs, clubs, elite athletes and coaches. Coaches receive scientific information from NGBs and other organisations	X	X	X		P2
CSF 9.8	Coaches make use of sport scientific information on elite sport in their training activities			X	X	P7
CSF 9.9	Scientific research is embedded in coaches' education and coaches are taught how to search for scientific information and how to use research outcomes as part of their coaching	X				P7

Source of information: O: overall sport inventory; A: athletes' survey; C: coaches' survey; PD: performance directors' survey. Right column shows if the CSFs are possibly interlinked with other Pillars.

National research report

How strongly each nation scores on Pillar 9 is determined by the attention paid by each nation to the quality and existence of scientific research and innovation, the national co-ordination of research activities (CSF 9.2-9.5), the translation of research knowledge into practical use for coaches, the dissemination of information (CSF 9.6) and the way scientific knowledge is applied in training activities (CSF 9.7 and 9.8). There is often a divide between the research theorists and the practical users–the coaches and athletes. There is a perception among coaches that much of the research conducted in the area of sports science has limited practical value and application in regard to preparing their athletes and that the outcomes of research are presented in a form that may be too technical and formal for coaches to be able to translate into action (Williams, 2005). In spite of this, literature shows that elite coaches value sport science knowledge. Both sports science researchers and elite coaches in an Australian study agreed that sport science research influences what elite coaches do with their athletes, and that technical aspects of coaching need to be based on sports science/sports medicine research (Williams, 2005). We have presented the process of production and distribution of scientific information applied to sport in Figure 79.

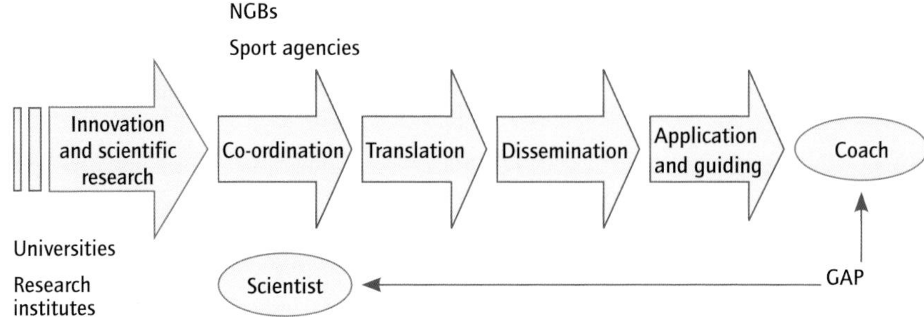

Figure 79: From research to practice: processes of scientific research and innovation applied to elite sport

Use of scientific research by coaches

78% the international elite coaches make use of scientific research in relation to their training activities.

Most elite coaches indicate that they make use of scientific research in relation to their training activities. This is shown in Figure 80. Scores are significantly higher for coaches of athletes competing at international level. Only in Brazil, Wallonia and Estonia do less than 70% of the coaches use scientifically based information to support their training programmes.

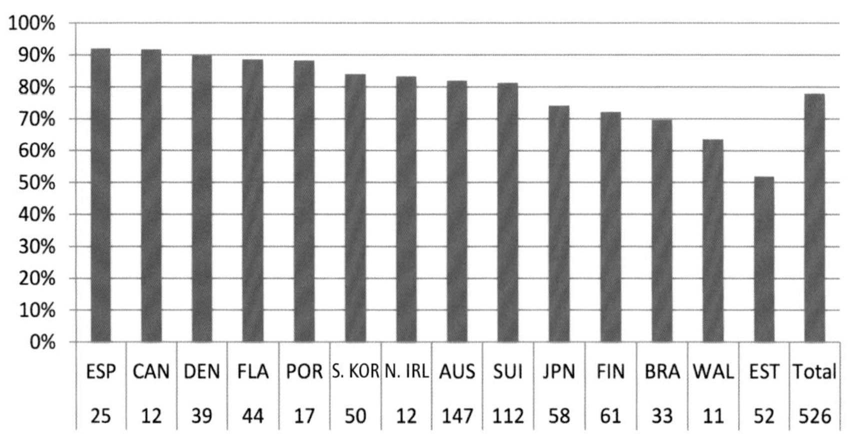

Note: The Netherlands did not ask this question in their surveys.

Figure 80: Percentage of coaches that used scientific information over the past 12 months actively for their training activities (only international level coaches)

Many NGBs appoint staff specifically for the collection and dissemination of scientific information

As revealed by the overall inventory of the SPLISS countries, elite sport research is conducted mainly in two environments: first, by (often government-funded) research institutes (typically as part of the national training centre), and second, in universities. Ten countries (AUS, BRA, CAN, ESP, FIN, FRA, JPN, S. KOR, NED, SUI) have a national sport research centre, of which the Australian, Canadian, Japanese and French are the most comprehensively developed. Only in Finland, Brazil and Korea are those centres not integrated with the national training centre. Due to increased professionalisation of elite sport globally, some NGBs have also appointed staff members with specialist sport science expertise (CSF 9.3). In Japan 79% of the performance directors (11 out of 14 NGBs) indicate that they have appointed a person responsible for the collection and dissemination of scientific information specifically in their sport and 64% (n=9) have appointed a sport scientist who collaborates closely with elite coaches. This score is remarkably higher than all other countries in the sample.

Countries try to close a gap between universities and practitioners/coaches

In many countries the NSA also collaborates with universities in regard to elite sport research. It seems that in this space the gap between theory and practice is perceived to be substantial. The pressure for academics to publish in peer-reviewed journals often leads to a failure to translate the research into practice that can be used in the high-performance environment of coaches and athletes. Williams (2005) argued in Australia that important qualities of elite coaches were related to *'keeping up to date with the latest developments in coaching'* and *'using the latest methods/technology'*; important qualities of a sports science researcher were *'knowledge of the sport(s) with which they work'*, *'practicality of research conducted'* and *'experience of working with coaches/athletes'*. These findings indicate the importance of collaboration between academics and practitioners. In four countries (AUS, FRA, JPN, NED) there are national agreements in place between the NSA and universities concerned with co-operation around elite sport research. Once again, Japan and Australia seem to be more advanced than other countries. In Japan this is part of the Basic Act on Sports (MEXT, 2011) that defines the responsibility of the national government with regard to research and organising a system that promotes co-operation within the nation, and between quasi-governmental agencies, universities, sport organisations and the private sector. At the local level JISS (Japanese Institute of Sport Science) has completed partnership deals with three domestic universities. The Australian Sport Research Network's (ASRN) purpose is to develop collaborations with key stakeholders to identify, prioritise and enable industry relevant evidence-based research that will lead to, among other things, greater sporting excellence. The purpose is to develop and maintain active links between universities and the sport industry, to facilitate the conduct of research and scholarship in sport, to facilitate the scholarly debate and knowledge exchange and to foster and facilitate liaison, communication and co-operation between members and other interested parties. Eight countries (CAN, DEN, FLA, S. KOR POR, SPA, SUI, N. IRL, WAL) reported that they had research collaborations in place but without a national agreement.

Dissemination of scientific information is strongly developed in Japan and Canada.

As can be seen in Figure 79 the next critical step relates to the dissemination of scientific knowledge among the main users: the coaches. Williams (2005) identified that Australian coaches mainly seek information from other coaches, or through conferences, workshops and coaching journals, and that coaches prefer audiovisual modes of communication to written communication. Accordingly the elite sport climate survey questioned coaches whether they received regular correspondence from their national governing body or club that contained scientific knowledge related to high performance in their sport and whether their national governing body, club or national sport agency during the past 12 months had organised relevant update seminars. Coaches in Canada generally score the highest, although we need to note this is based on a very small sample. Most Canadian and Japanese coaches also agree that scientific knowledge is sufficiently disseminated (Figure 81). The Canadian researcher reported that most scientific work is closely related to the sports and coaching processes, which supports this result. It is worth noting that Canada hosts a SIRC (Sport Information Research Centre) which has a high profile and which may in turn explain why coaches think they have relatively easy access to scientific literature.

In the other strong sport research nation, Australia, respondents are less satisfied with the quality and amount of information they receive, despite a number of supportive policies in that regard. The results are more positive in Switzerland, Japan and Korea. The weakest scores can be found in Brazil, Wallonia and Portugal. It needs to be noted that sample sizes differ between countries, however, no significant differences were identified between subgroups such as the level of the coaches.

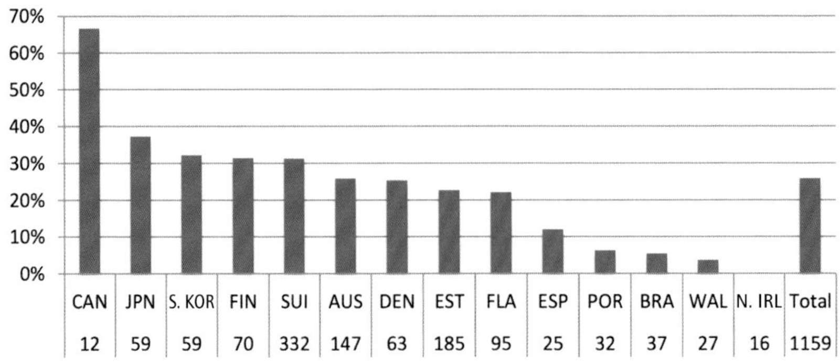

Note: The Netherlands did not ask this question in their surveys.

Figure 81: Coaches' opinion on the sufficiency of dissemination of scientific knowledge (all coaches, no differences between subgroups)

Scientific knowledge and development needs to be part of coach development.

Finally athletes and coaches were asked to rate the practical applicability of scientific research (biomechanics, physiology), new technology developments and innovation in their sport, and how they rate the opportunities to make use of it. The results are shown in Figure 82. Scores were significantly higher for top 16 elite athletes and international-level coaches. In Switzerland, Finland, Denmark, South Korea, Australia, Northern Ireland and Flanders the practical value of scientific research was rated higher than the sample average.

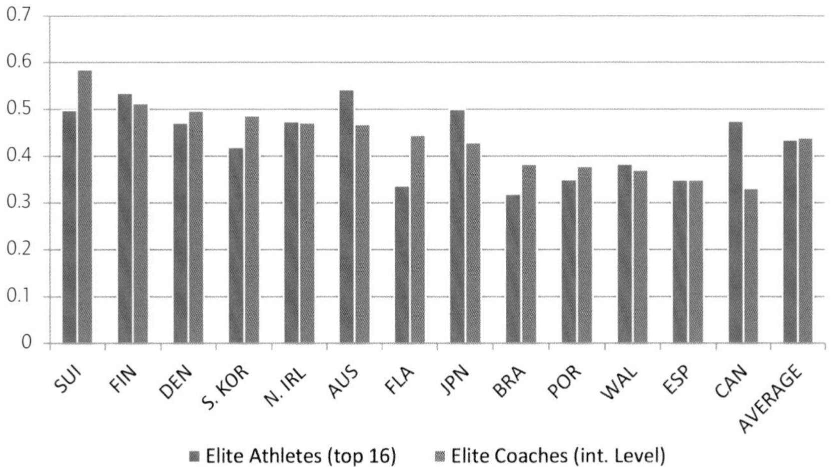

Note: The Netherlands did not ask this question in their surveys.

Figure 82: Total sum of scores (n=13 items) on rating the applicability of scientific research, new technology developments and innovation in their sport and the opportunities to make use of it. Evaluation by top 16 athletes and international-level coaches

If scientific knowledge and information are important, it needs to be part of coaches' education. This is the case in most countries (except Northern Ireland and the Netherlands). Australia, South Korea, Canada and Finland seem to be the most advanced in this regard. In Australia, there are specific modules within the NGB coaching accreditation that cover research and the use of technology and a selection of coaches receive scholarships, where embedded research and technology development is part of the programme, and they have the opportunity to liaise directly with scientists. Furthermore they learn skills to search for scientific information, and they receive information from the National Sport Information Centre (NSIC). In Canada the Coaching Association of Canada (CAC) fosters the Coaching Research programme as an essential component for athlete and coach development, and in Finland Level II and III coaches are taught how to search for scientific information. In South Korea the 1st and 2nd degree coach education programme run by Korea Institute of Sport Science (KISS), includes the writing of a dissertation, supervised by researchers at KISS.

13.4 Summary points in Pillar 9

- Over the past decades, scientific research has grown as an important source of competitive advantage for elite sport development systems. The presence of a highly developed approach to Pillar 9 is evidence of nations taking a long-term strategic approach to achieving elite sporting success.
- Investment in scientific research is positively correlated with the financial resources made available to elite sport within nations (Pillar 1). However, investment in Pillar 9 is not necessarily a function of a nation's wealth, rather a policy decision as to how resources are allocated and used. Nations making conscious decisions about the value of scientific research and supporting these decisions with the requisite amount of funding over time are likely to have a competitive advantage over nations that rely on passive macroeconomic variables such as population and national wealth.
- The most important critical success factor of Pillar 9 in terms of success is the existence of a national research centre which carries out research itself as well as taking a co-ordination role directing research activity in elite sport nationally.
- Stakeholders in the system, coaches, performance directors and athletes, generally do not rate their nations highly on Pillar 9. This may in part be due to tensions between pure research and applied research. It is clear that what coaches require needs to be practical and actionable interpretation of research.
- The higher the level of coaches and athletes, the more scientific research appears to be used and valued. It seems that at the top of the elite performance is where scientific support can make its most valuable (winning margins) contributions.

Chapter 13 references

De Bosscher, V., Bingham, J., Shibli, S., van Bottenburg, M. and De Knop, P. (2008). *The global Sporting Arms Race. An international comparative study on sports policy factors leading to international sporting success.* Aachen: Meyer & Meyer.

Green, M. and Houlihan, B. (2005). *Elite Sport Development. Policy learning and political priorities.* New York: Routledge.

Houlihan, B. and Green, M. (2008). *Comparative Elite Sport Development. Systems, structures and public policy.* London, UK: Elsevier.

Kloot, L. and Martin, J. (2000). Strategic performance management: A balanced approach to performance management issues in local government. *Management Accounting Research, 11* (2), 231-251. doi: http://dx.doi.org/10.1006/mare.2000.0130

Malcolm, P. and De Clercq, D. (2013). Best Practice in biomechanics and how it can be used in hig-performance sport: the longitudinal follow-up during competition of an elite high-jump athlete. In *Managing high performance sport* (pp. 199-205). I. P. S. and V. D. Bosscher (Ed.). London and New York: Routledge.

Smolianov, P. and Zakus, D. H. (2008). Exploring high performance management in Olympic sport with reference to practices in the former USSR and Russia. *International Journal of Sport Management, 9*, 206-232.

Williams, S. J. (2005). *A Case Study of the Relationship between Sports Science Research Practice and Elite Coaches' Perceived Needs.* (PhD), University of Canberra, Canberra.

Winand, M. (2013). *Innovative sport federations: Attitude, perceptions and innovation champion.* Paper presented at the EURAM 13th conference Democratising Management, Istanbul, Turkey.

Appendix I: Overview of the research funding (research projects and sport science support) and the delivery structures and processes

COUNTRY	Notes
AUSTRALIA 16% €22.58m	Includes sport science/ medicine support services NB: €1.4m research projects only
BRAZIL 2.44% €1.60m	An average of the years 2003-2009 was taken (incl. sport science)
CANADA 5.71% €6.68m	This amount includes sport science, sport medicine and integrated support team.
DENMARK 1.3% €0.20m	Including only TD funded research projects
FINLAND 6.0% €1.72m	This includes the state support to KIHU (€1.170m), NOC projects, ministry projects (€0.55m) and administration
FLANDERS 11.1% €2.03m	Includes sport science support

Structures and processes
• The majority of elite sport research funding comes from ASC/AIS (Commonwealth state funding), although state-level institutes and academies (state government funding) is also available, as is stated by the National Institute System Intergovernmental Agreement (NISIA) (signed 2011). • AIS has short-, medium- and long-term research funds. All research at the AIS can be categorised into the AIS' five research themes: (1) Athlete preparation, (2) athlete resilience (3) podium preparedness (4) skill, techniques and tactics (5) athlete/coach pathways.
• 2 programmes: (1) CENESP (Center of Excellence in Sport) network composed by scientific centres of institutions of higher education, the National Olympic Committee, the National Paralympic Committee, the sports administration entities at the local, state and national levels, and the private sector; however this network in sport science ended in 2007 (since 1995); (2) the programme 'Brazil in Elite Sports–Champion Brazil', is managed by the Ministry of Sports with financial resources from Federal General.
• Own The Podium (OTP) is the foundation of Canada's scientific research and innovation initiatives. Each NGB receives funding to support athletes with highest medal potential (SSSM= support sport science and sport medicine) • Canada has 7 sport centres (4) and institutes (3) delivering services to athletes, training group and coaches. Most of the institutes are doing research directly related to the needs of their training groups. • OTP, in collaboration with SIRC (www.sirc.ca), is publishing two or three times per year an electronic magazine for coaches and high performance directors cal 'SIRCuit' that present the most recent researches relevant to the work of technical leaders. SIRC has one of the larger collection of sport related publication, not limited to HP Sport, and offer litterature review services and access to their publication database and Sport Discus. Coaching Association and Coaches of Canada are publishing 'Coach Plan' that present best practices and other information for coaches. • Note: OTP is one of the only collaborative initiatives in Canada, combining the Canadian Sport Policy set by the GOC through Sport Canada (a branch of the Heritage department), the COC/CPC, the NSOs and the network of Canadian Sport Centers. Funding is provided by Sport Canada, yet is operated as a separate initiative from Sport Canada.
• Two funding levels 1) Team Denmark (elite sport research funding), 2) Ministry of Culture–Committee for Scientific Research and other institutions (foundations, NSA.) Overall research funding. The figures only include TD. • Team Denmark's (TD) Research Committee has over the period 2006-2010 focused on two strategic areas: (1) sport psychology and (2) talent development. • TD's research strategy is based on co-operation with the three research institutions: the Department of Exercise and Sport Sciences (Copenhagen University), the Section of Sport Science (Aarhus University) and the Institute of Sports Science and Clinical Biomechanics (University of Southern Denmark) and other researchers involved in elite sport and performance optimisation.
• Elite sport research and development projects are funded by the NOC and Paralympic Committee. The state sport council (scientific committee) funds sport science projects. • The Research Institute for Olympic Sports (KIHU) is the main organisation providing research related to elite sport development (in Olympic sports) and applying the research results to practical coaching and coaches' education.
Federal Government and NSA provide support for research projects; the priority is: 1) optimising the performance of elite athletes and teams, 2) talent detection, 3) material development and technology, 4) policy.

COUNTRY	Notes
FRANCE NA €2.67m	Includes research projects (0.378), 20 INSEP personnel (0.629) + shift (0.263) + 4 FTE natonal institutes winter and sailing (0.407) Excludes funding from NGBs to universities Sport science support mainly comes through NGB funding
JAPAN 12.9% €5.74m	Data include the multi support programme (athlete support, research and development) and sport medical and science research from JISS
PORTUGAL 0.5% €0.90m	Not available
SPAIN 0.4% €0.27m	0.4% includes research projects only; excludes sport science support
NETHERLANDS 4.55% (est.) €2.50m	Note: excludes some money from NOC*NSF for NGBs or trainings centres that is sometimes included sport science support
N-IRELAND 16.8% €0.24m	Includes sport science support

Structures and processes

• National sport government (sport ministry) and INSEP organise a grant programme in two domains:
  • Science and elite sport with the aim to help elite athletes to improve their performance in int. event and Olympic games
  • Science and medicine in elite sport in the aim to improve knowledge in elite sport diseases and to have medical support for elite athletes.
• Note: there is no national planning of elite sport research funding; this is mainly co-ordinated by the NGBs themselves.

• There are two types of research budgets: the government programme called multisupport programme and the JISS.
• Japan Institute of Sport Sciences (JISS) receives funding from state organisations (MEXT; Sport and Youth bureau) via National Agency for the Advancement of Sports and Health (NAASH).
• JISS provides scientific support for athletes and coaches to resolve problems in Olympic Sports. JISS provides testing, measurements, and seminars utilising scientific methods and findings and gives individual consultations and guidance for each athlete. 66 people are working on sport science, in (formerly) 3 departments:
  • Sports Sciences (e.g., physiology, psychology and biomechanics; measurement and analysis)
  • Sports Medicine: treatment and services (incl. rehabilitation, physiotherapy) and applied research (injuries)
  • Sports Information: gathers and disseminates information; maintains databases (e.g., game analysis, sports medicine and science research, strategy and tactics, sporting records, and sports policy); builds domestic and international networks aimed at facilitating the exchange of information.
  • Note: after reformations, the structure has changed, for example the information department is now part of JSC, as the Department of Information and International Relations.
• However, apart from newsletters, the information dissemination is limited and coaches and NGBs get scientific information from their own network, universities, and academic societies.

• The NSA has made a contract with three universities in order to guarantee scientific and technical support to the assessment, counselling and training control of elite athletes.
• The National sport Agency (CDS) is responsible for the research funding. • This happens through the announcement of subsidies for universities and public agencies for research projects on elite sport (CSD Announcement, section 1. Scientific support, technological development and generation of knowledge applied to high-performance level).
• The purpose is to develop innovative applications for the elite sport. Subsidies are given to InnoSportNL , from NOC*NSF and the ministry of welfare, health and sports (VWS). • Note: this does not include sport by sport investments to NGBs, of which it is unknown how much is directed to sport science support. This also excludes money from the ambition funds (€5.5m) that also partly go to scientific research or technological developments.
• This is mainly sport science support; for scientific research, there is one person's PhD related to elite sport (recovery and the timing of training sessions). Funded by Sport Northern Ireland. • Scientific research and innovation is taking a course of natural evolution in Northern Ireland. During the early days, SINI was about establishing services, delivering them and showing that they made an impact. As well as maintaining its current workload, SINI is looking at the next stage which includes the ingenuity to apply research to new sporting situations, in particular over the next five years. If SINI had some way of driving the work and innovation between sport and the capacity within universities, positive outcomes could be achieved.

COUNTRY	Notes
SWITZERLAND 8.5% €4.9m	Excludes anti-doping funding Includes Magglingen (€3,42m), NGBs (€0.2m), SLF (€0.8), commission technology and innovation (€0.5m), federal sport commission ESK (€1.0m)
WALLONIA	

Notes: Data from South Korea are not available.

Structures and processes
• Research projects: three national research funds through which Swiss sport can apply research funding: the Swiss Federal Sports Commission (ESK). The Commission for Technology and Innovation (CTI) and the Swiss National Science Foundation (SNSF) are mainly concerned with general sport research. • SFISM Magglingen on behalf of FOSPO is also entitled to co-ordinate the re-search money provided by the national research funds for sport and elite sport. SFISM employs app. 110 people, 20% of the activities is research (in addition to teaching and service provision). • Institute for Snow and Avalanche Research (SLF) is an interdisciplinary research and service centre for winter sports (e.g., snow analyses and weather forecasts), with app. 130 employees. • Note: big NGBs such as the SFA, the SIHA, Swiss Ski and Swiss Tennis have their own, albeit mostly modest research budgets (app. €200,000).
• The researcher reported that there is no national funding for research projects and that elite sport research is mainly executed through the national (academic) scientific research foundation.

14 Conclusions: Successful elite sport policies

14.1 Introduction

In this chapter we review the results of the SPLISS 2.0 project from two different perspectives. First, we provide an analysis of the sample nations' performance against the nine Pillars. We present this as a topline report so that readers can derive the strategic points that emerge. Second, we analyse the performance of some sample nations in isolation in order to provide a more detailed look at how individual nations perform against the various benchmarks for each Pillar. In the concluding section of the chapter we take a helicopter view to address some of the wider issues in theory and elite sport development literature.

14.2 Overview per Pillar

Figure 83 presents the Pillar scores for all of the nations. The countries are ranked according to success in summer sports, measured as market share of medals during Olympic Games and world championships over a four-year time period (2009-2012). We need to take note of the fact that some countries focus heavily on winter sports, notably Canada, Switzerland and Finland. The colour-coded scoring system (traffic lights) is a helpful tool primarily to facilitate interpretation and comparison; to simplify the visualisation of results; and to identify any specific characteristics in the overall results for the nine Pillars and their relationship with success. Figure 83 is a one-page summary of more than 3,000 pages of inventory data and survey results of 3,142 elite athletes, 1,376 elite coaches and 241 performance directors who completed the elite sport climate survey.

As a reminder, the percentage scores are the aggregated scores within each Pillar of data collected through the inventories (by the researchers) and the elite sport climate surveys (by the athletes, coaches and performance directors). A total of 750 sub factors have been aggregated over the nine Pillars. Countries with incomplete datasets are indicated with an asterisk. France did not conduct the elite sport climate surveys with athletes, coaches or performance directors, Estonia only submitted inventory data for Pillar 1 but did conduct athlete and coaches surveys; and Korea did not provide inventories for Pillars 4, 7 and 8.

In Figure 83 nations are ranked from most to least successful in regard to their performance in the 1,065 Summer Olympic Games and world championship events contested between 2009 and 2012. France (dark green cell) achieves the highest score on this output indicator and is listed first in the table, whereas Wallonia with the lowest score is at the bottom of the table.

As a general overview of Figure 83, it can be seen that higher performing countries in summer sports, also tend to have higher scores on the nine Pillars.[42] There are some exceptions such as Brazil, scoring low on most Pillars (except Pillars 1 and 8); and across all countries, low scores on Pillar 3 (sports participation) and Pillar 4 (talent); and, in the case of France a low score on Pillar 2 (governance, organisation and structure). In the case of talent identification and development it was shown earlier that smaller countries perform better and with regard to sport participation we indicated that comparing the sport participation level in different nations is highly problematic for methodological reasons.

At the bottom half of Figure 83, less successful countries still display yellow or green traffic lights in Pillar 4 (talent ID and development), Pillar 5 (athletic career and post-career support) and 6 (training facilities). In SPLISS 1.0 we argued that the absence of the discrimination in the scores on Pillars 5 and 6 lends weight to the fact that elite sport systems have become more homogeneous and, on a short-term basis, these Pillars are possible drivers of an effective system. This is confirmed by the SPLISS 2.0 results.

For winter sports, the relationship between success and the nine Pillars is less pronounced. This may be attributable to winter sports being more specialised than summer sports and that fewer nations prioritise winter sports. This result needs to be considered in light of the fact that we did not separate winter and summer sport funding and as such allocate separate funding (inputs) streams to sporting success (outputs). A further external factor that cannot be influenced by policymakers is the dependency of winter sports on the natural (landscape and climate) environment, such as mountains and snow. As a result, the ability to 'manage' elite sport success in winter sports decreases for countries in which the natural conditions do not favor winter sports, while nations with favorable winter sport conditions have an advantage over other nations to turn their investments into elite sporting success. This is strengthened by the fact that the Winter Olympic Games is much smaller than the Summer Olympic Games with around one-third of the number of events but also less competition as fewer nations take part.

---

42 The average scores of nations on the Pillars is associated with success in summer sports: $rs = 0.776^{**}$, $p<0.01$, $n=16$.

LOW — Level of development — HIGH

Summer	Winter		P1 Financial support	P2 Governance, structure & organisation	P3 Sports participation	P4 TalentidID & development	P5 Athletic career & post career	P6 Training facilities	P7 Coach education & provision	P8 (inter) national competition	P9 Scientific research & innovation	Average
4,29%	4,38%	**FRA***	69%	37%	52%	45%	66%	72%	80%	55%	60%	60%
4,08%	1,21%	**AUS**	60%	64%	54%	49%	76%	66%	69%	48%	90%	64%
3,91%	1,96%	**JAP**	61%	58%	33%	45%	67%	74%	60%	78%	75%	62%
2,39%	6,59%	S. KOR*	70%	47%	38%	54%	54%	55%	59%	57%	59%	55%
1,78%	4,83%	**NED**	45%	69%	62%	68%	77%	65%	62%	54%	53%	62%
1,69%	0,00%	**ESP**	56%	50%	33%	55%	76%	74%	56%	67%	37%	56%
1,53%	12,27%	**CAN**	55%	58%	43%	23%	65%	63%	73%	62%	68%	57%
1,44%	0,00%	**BRA**	66%	38%	35%	18%	38%	33%	27%	57%	28%	38%
0,73%	0,09%	**DEN**	28%	53%	71%	61%	63%	49%	48%	63%	47%	54%
0,56%	3,22%	**SUI**	45%	58%	62%	70%	58%	61%	68%	44%	49%	58%
0,26%	2,52%	**FIN**	36%	47%	50%	49%	70%	43%	56%	65%	53%	52%
0,15%	0,00%	N. IRL	30%	42%	42%	41%	63%	60%	52%	40%	31%	45%
0,15%	0,10%	**EST***	26%	34%	NA	64%	34%	56%	34%	48%	38%	42%
0,18%	0,19%	**FLA**	41%	48%	48%	71%	66%	47%	52%	45%	52%	53%
0,15%	0,00%	**POR**	25%	34%	41%	44%	49%	48%	52%	52%	35%	43%
0,09%	0,00%	**WAL**	33%	36%	46,2%	59%	54%	37%	38%	44%	23%	39%
		Average	47%	48%	47%	50%	61%	56%	56%	55%	50%	

Figure 83: Success of countries and their scores on the nine elite sport policy Pillars

14.2.1 Topline findings

One of the overriding questions driving this book is 'which policy factors lead to elite sporting success?' Table 43 in that regard presents a ranking (success) correlation with total scores on the Pillars. In other words, is the success ranking of nations reflected in a similar ranking within the Pillars?

Table 43: Spearman's rank correlations (r^2) for 9 Pillars with success (market share summer and winter sports, 2009-2012)

	r_s summer	Sig	r_s winter	Sig	N
Pillar 1 (financial support)	**0.909****	0.000	**0.588***	0.039	16
Pillar 2 (organisation and structure)	**0.720****	0.004	**0.685****	0.007	14
Pillar 3 (sport participation)	0.049	0.873	0.267	0.377	13
Pillar 4 (talent ID/TD)	- 0.148	0.707	0.237	0.435	13
Pillar 5 (post) athletic career support	0.483	0.080	0.322	0.261	14
Pillar 6 (facilities)	**0.704****	0.005	0.354	0.214	14
Pillar 7 (coaches)	**0.606***	0.028	**0.779****	0.002	13
Pillar 8 (inter)national competition	**0.577***	0.039	**0.271**	0.370	13
Pillar 9 (scientific research)	**0.71****	0.004	**0.784****	0.001	14

*Note: ** P<0.01; * p<0.05; the correlations are taken only for the countries where data are complete, which explains the different N-values.*

Most Pillars relate well with international success. Pillar 3 (participation), Pillar 4 (talent), Pillar 5 (athlete support)

Overall most Pillars correlate positively and significantly with success, either in summer or winter sports: Pillar 1 (financial support), Pillar 2 (structure and organisation), Pillar 7 (coaches) and Pillar 9 (scientific research) are the four Pillars that correlate significantly with sporting success for both summer and winter sports. Pillar 6 (facilities) and Pillar 8 (international competition) correlate significantly with summer sports only.

Pillar 5 (athlete support) needs a strong development, but nations will not gain a competitive advantage

An interesting finding was that Pillar 5 does not correlate significantly with success, which may be explained by the relatively high level of development that was found in all nations (including low performing nations). This point is best appreciated by noting that the average score for Pillar 5 was 61%, which in turn is five percentage points higher than the next highest scoring Pillar. Our interpretation of this is that globally the average athletic career support is exceptionally high (compared to other Pillars), possibly because this was the first Pillar that countries thought of and invested in after they started professionalising their elite sport policy. Today, countries need to reach a high level of support for their elite athletes. If they fail to do so, their athletes will lag behind. But if they do, they will not gain competitive advantage because all other nations bring this Pillar to roughly the same level.

14.2.2 Pillar 1—Money in—medals out!?

It can be argued that money spent on elite sport is the best possible explanation for success in summer sports. This is consistent with the SPLISS 1.0 study in which it was found that those nations that spent the most money in absolute terms on elite sport tended to be the most successful in terms of medal-winning success. Wealthy nations and developing nations that decide to allocate significant funding towards elite sporting success will be more successful.

Diminishing returns to scale: money is important, but 'more' money in does not equal 'more' medals out

While 'money in equals medals out' it does not follow that 'MORE money in equals more medals out'. As a matter of fact in the case of most nations, more money was required to invest in the system, just to maintain a consistent level of success. In reality the nature of the global sporting arms race is such that there are diminishing returns to scale in terms of additional resources and the extra output achieved from them. In SPLISS 2.0 we requested historical elite sport investment information which paints a picture of a continued global sporting arms race. This is illustrated in Figure 84: Relative increase/decrease of financial support (government and lotteries) (inputs) and market shares (outputs) since 2001 (or the most relevant year according to the dataset)—Summer sports84 (summer sports) and Figure 85 (winter sports). For example, France invested 101% more in 2011 than 2002 (€187m against €93m). Meanwhile its market share of Olympic Games and world championships in summer sports decreased by 30% in London compared with Sydney and in winter sports declined by 21% in Vancouver compared with Salt Lake City.

Nations suffering from diminishing returns on investment were Australia, France, Finland and Belgium whose expenditures increased over a 10-year period (between 2001 and 2011) but market share decreased (in relative terms), both in summer and winter sports. As the home nation of the Sydney Olympic Games, Australia improved its success from Atlanta 1996 with the nation's highest ever market share in Sydney (6.3%). While Australia has been a recent best practice example of elite sport development and has inspired many other countries to emulate them in the process, it is clear that the competition is increasing. Countries such as Japan (summer sports), South Korea (winter sports) and Brazil (summer sports) are investing heavily and they are becoming more successful, taking market share from the established nations. Because the supply of success, that is, medal winning opportunities, is essentially fixed in the Summer Olympic Games, there is a zero sum game being played out. For every gain of a medal there has to be the loss of a medal. It is for this reason that nations seem prepared to invest heavily in simply maintaining their market share.

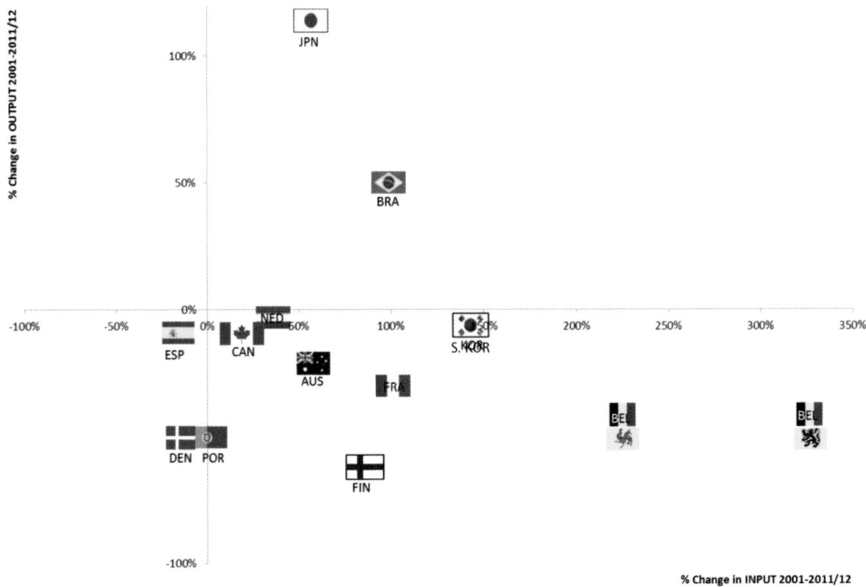

Figure 84: Relative increase/decrease of financial support (government and lotteries) (inputs) and market shares (outputs) since 2001 (or the most relevant year according to the dataset)–Summer sports

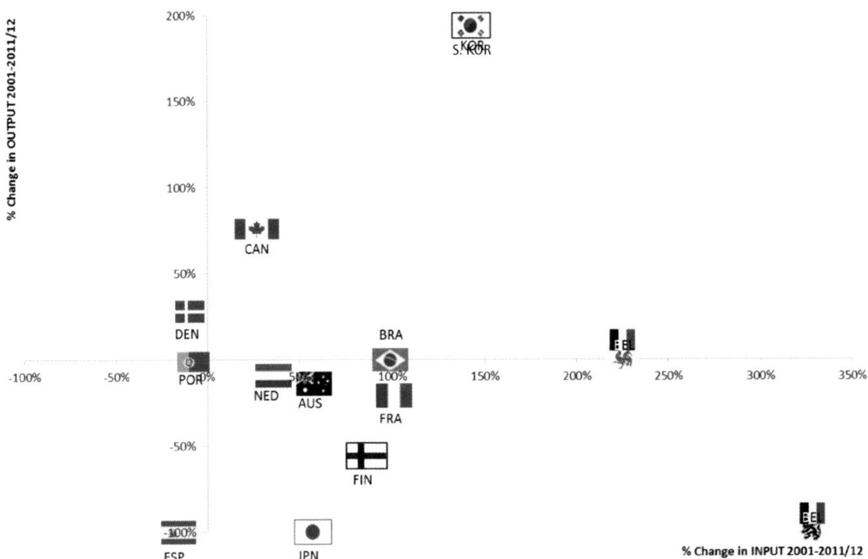

Figure 85: Relative increase/decrease of financial support (government and lotteries) (inputs) and market shares (outputs) since 2001 (or the most relevant year according to the dataset)—Winter sports

After identifying the absolute amount of financial resources that are invested, it is also important to consider the efficiency of nations, or the relative performance of nations. Efficient nations achieve 'more' success with 'less' investment. Ultimately, efficient nations need to be analysed in further detail when it comes to which Pillars they invest in most, and how integration between Pillars is achieved. Figure 86 and Figure 87 present this 'money in–medals out' (efficiency) relationship for the sample nations with expenditures shown in PPP values.[43] As a reminder, elite sport expenditures in our measurement include (a) government funding, (b) national lotteries, (c) NOCs and (d) nationally co-ordinated sponsorship (excluding possible overlaps between each funding source). Nation-by-nation diagnostics of the 16 nations show that Australia, France, Japan and the Netherlands can be identified as the most efficient nations in summer sports given their investment in elite sport because they are located above the line of best fit. Denmark and Spain perform more or less in line with the expectations. Switzerland and Canada also do well in summer sports given that both nations spend over 30% of their elite sport funding on winter sports (much

43 A linear regression analysis with case-wise diagnostics was conducted to support this graph. The dotted line in the graphs is an estimation based on residuals. Noting the limitation of a small sample, analysis of residuals helps to, under ceteris paribus conditions, compare the predicted success, based on the independent variable (here elite sport expenditures), with actual success. The higher the residual, the better it performs given its elite sport expenditure, and the more efficient the country can be assumed to be (see De Bosscher, 2007).

higher than all other nations). The countries that underperform in summer sports are Brazil and South Korea which can be identified as the most inefficient. However, when the funding spent on international events in South Korea (€134m or i$224, 53%) is excluded, South Korea would return to the average. Furthermore, for smaller nations with limited funding in absolute terms, it appears to be difficult to achieve some level of success that is in line with their relative level of investment (Belgium, Finland, Portugal, Estonia and Northern Ireland).

Australia, France, Japan and the Netherlands are the most efficient nations in summer sports

It seems that there might be a minimum level of absolute funding required for an elite sporting system to start delivering results and the key question therefore is: what is the minimum amount of absolute funding a nation would have to invest in order to start delivering elite sport success? In searching for an answer to this question, a minimum threshold starting point might be the €34m spent by Denmark as it is a tipping point for achieving a market share of more than 0.5% and the delivery of performance as expected (on the regression line).

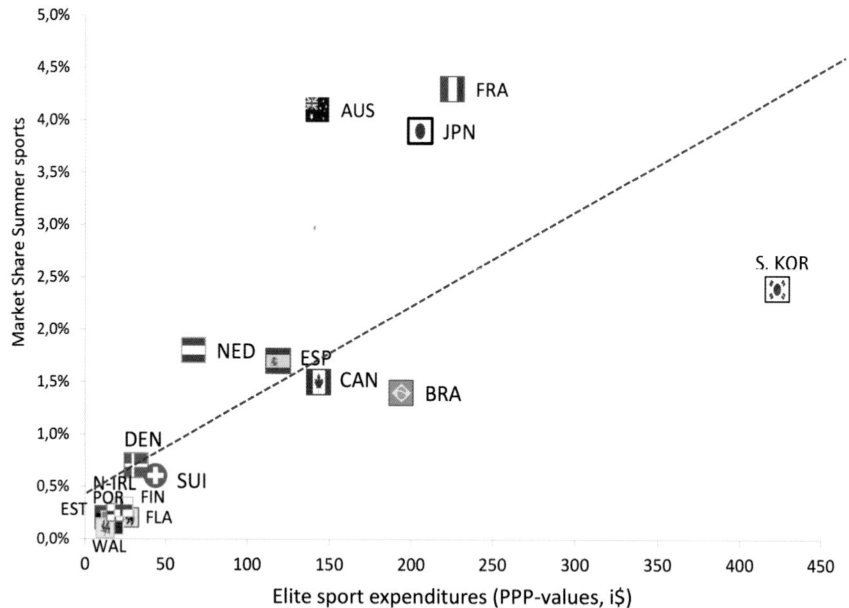

Figure 86: Elite sport expenditures per year (PPP) and the market share of the SPLISS nations in summer sports at world championships and Olympic Games (2009-2012)

For winter sports, the correlation between investment and success is lower. This is in part because elite sport expenditures in this figure, were not specified for winter sports only, as not all countries invest in winter sports, and only some achieved any of success.[44] Despite these limitations, as shown in Figure 87, Canada, the Netherlands, France, Switzerland and to a lesser extent Finland can be seen to perform above expectations in winter sports, given their elite sport expenditures. This supports our earlier statement that nations with favorable winter sport conditions have an advantage over other nations to turn their investments into elite sporting success.

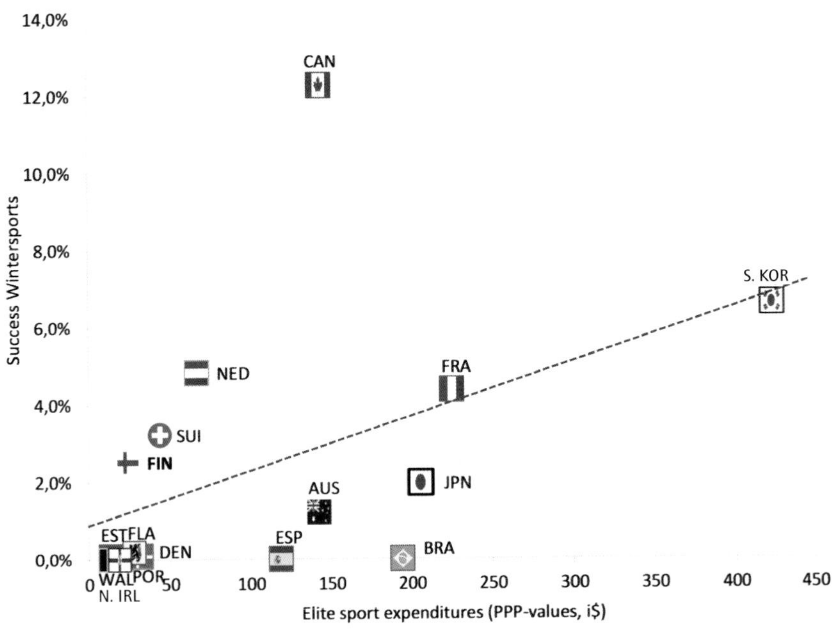

Figure 87: Elite sport expenditures per year (PPP values) and the market share of the SPLISS nations in winter sports at world championships and Olympic Games (2009-2012)

In summary, there are three key messages arising from the analysis of Pillar 1 against success. First, there is a strong positive relationship between the absolute amount of elite sport funding invested by nations and their success. Second, there are diminishing returns on investment where merely investing more money does not automatically lead to more success. This point confirms the nature and continuation of the global sporting arms race. Third, within the sample there is considerable variation in the efficiency ratios of investment to success. There are clear indications that some nations use the resources that are invested more efficiently than others. This finding

44 Data allocated to NGBs and sport programmes for winter sports only are available, but in some countries they do not represent total elite sport expenditures because of the small share of funding that is divided on a sport by sport basis; for example in South Korea and Japan funding is mostly used for elite athletes' training at the national training centres (for which sport by sport figures are not available).

in itself confirms the importance of investigating the other Pillars that represent the throughput policy factors in more depth. There is much to be learned from which factors are invested in; how they relate to each other; and how they are managed in an integrated approach by policymakers.

14.2.3 Pillar 2—Efficient nations are organised and structured better

The most efficient nations (input-output) also perform best on Pillar 2 (organisation and structure)

An interesting point of note is that precisely those countries that we have identified as being the most efficient (Australia, Japan, France and the Netherlands for summer sports; Canada, the Netherlands, and Switzerland for winter sports), are also the countries that perform best on Pillar 2: 'organisation, governance and structure of elite sport', all with green traffic lights and scores far above the average. It can be argued that these countries have the most integrated approach to elite sport development and the characteristics they tend to have in common are:

- Full-time management staff in the NSA
- Strong national co-ordination of activities and financial inputs which is evidence of a clear decision making structure
- Autonomy is given to NGBs, but with a certain degree of government control, such as formal objectives and transparent measurement instruments to evaluate NGB funding criteria
- NSA policy that is regularly evaluated by athletes, coaches, and performance directors, who are represented in the decision-making process of the NSA
- Long-term planning of elite sport policies
- Communication with athletes, coaches and performance directors

France is an exception to this finding with low scores on Pillar 2 (37%, the third lowest score). Caution is needed, however, as France did not complete the surveys, and thus scores are only based on inventory information. France seems to be currently in the process of changing policies from a very state-centred approach in the 1980s (Oakley and Green, 2001) to a current approach that involves more private engagement and involvement. This is true at both the national training centre (INSEP) and at the level of NGBs, via a 'sport runs sport' approach where funded organisations are held more accountable for delivering on agreed objectives. Only limited co-ordination exists between regional trainings centres (CREPS, Centres de Resource, d'Expertise et de Performance Sportive), and stakeholders are involved in policy decisions to a limited extent. For the first time the sport budget of the French state was below the budget of the National Centre for the Development of Sport (CNDS). The Pillar 2 score also reflects the rivalry between the French Olympic Committee and the state. However, one of the strengths of the French elite sport system remains that state technical staff working for the sport federations are trained and funded by the ministry. As such there is still a strong 'hands on' approach from the government when it comes to administrative issues, such as the decision that surveys of athletes and coaches from France could not be included in the SPLISS project.

Finland also presents a mild outlier if we consider its winter sport efficiency. With an average score for Pillar 2 (ranked 9th) it has a fragmented elite sport policy. In Finland the organisations responsible for elite sport are disparate. Despite the fact that the NOC and the Ministry of Education and Culture participate in elite sport strategy processes, there is no clear co-ordination for elite sport.

While this section has identified that there is a strong positive relationship between Pillar 1 (financial inputs) and Pillar 2 (governance, organisation and structure of elite sport policies), it is also clear that how Pillar scores were compiled varies greatly between nations. Similar summary scores may be the result of (the combination of) quite different subfactor scores. There is therefore no generic blueprint that can be transferred into any national context with the guarantee of delivering success. None of these approaches are necessarily right or wrong, and it is simply a case of finding a set of ingredients that work effectively in a given context. Consequently, the most appropriate role for governments is one of enabling rather than delivering. High-performance sport is a highly specialised and dynamic environment that does not lend itself well to bureaucracy that can be copied and pasted across national governmental systems, or across different sports. A compromise approach is for governments to provide funding but with strings attached in the form of agreed objectives and outputs that must be achieved to maintain the relationship. Governments as facilitators (providing funding) of system effectiveness (setting results targets and enabling sport organisations to achieve them) seems to be the approach that leads to countries being most likely to be successful.

Pillar 2 (organisation and structure) does not cause success directly, is less expensive, but takes time to develop and may be a pre-condition without which success is unlikely

Pillar 2 is a complex Pillar as it is likely to be the case that effective organisation of elite sport systems does not cause success directly but it is probably a pre-condition without which success is unlikely. Robinson and Minikin (2012) have observed that systems in small or less-developed countries with a limited tradition of elite sport development lack central co-ordination and governance. Setting up elaborate, complex and integrated systems for co-ordination, organisation and governance (Pillar 2) takes time and experience and cannot be considered a quick fix for achieving sporting success. In the longer term it can be argued that nations with a well-developed Pillar 2 may be able to achieve sustainable competitive advantage because this Pillar is less about money in and more about doing things right and doing the right things. The Netherlands scores highest on Pillar 2 (69%) and for a nation of some 17 million people, it also consistently 'punches above its weight' in summer and winter sports (see Figure 86 and Figure 87).

As a final observation in regard to Pillar 2 it is worth noting that although national co-ordination can be seen as a strength of the system, it does not imply centralised governance. Confident national co-ordination allows for local differentiation and the ability to take a contingency approach to the particular circumstances, and a realisation that unique characteristics and circumstances, such as a nation's geography or culture, require a sport-specific and local approach.

14.2.4 Pillars 3 and 4—The non-significant Pillars: Does sport participation, talent identification and development really not matter?

It might come as a surprise to many that sport participation levels of the population as a whole and talent identification/development do not directly influence nations' sporting success. Relatively low scores on talent identification and development systems were found in successful countries and higher scores were notable in smaller countries. In regard to sport participation (Pillar 3) some high performing countries such as Australia and France, only have average sports participation scores. The key question for policymakers is whether sport participation and related talent selection and development are irrelevant to the medal-winning capacity of countries?

We can look at this in two ways. On the one hand, it still holds true that countries first need sport participants before they can create elite athletes. Each elite athlete was once just a beginner in his or her sport and dependent on teachers and coaches at schools and clubs to develop his or her talent. On the other hand, while it seems obvious that nations need a talent pool in order to have the chance to be successful in elite sport, there is no strong argument that countries need a broad participation base in sport in order to excel in elite sport. Investing in sport participation and physical education might be valuable from a social and public health perspective and may also contribute to future success by delivering more athletes in the talent pool. However, understandably, this kind of investment is not directly related to elite sporting success, especially in the short term. The activities that need to take place between the numbers associated with participation and talent, and the success outcomes such as medals seem to mediate to such an extent that the relationship between participating and winning is too hard to prove with the data that we have available.

First, the reality is that in most nations elite sport development is a separate system, with independent system drivers, compared with grassroots sport. Analysing the relationship by linking sports participation to success is therefore not the right way to discover if and how this relationship works. Our data show that nations which spend most on grassroots sport are not the most successful nations. Second, all of the nations in this project have a base participation system in place (except Brazil), with varying (sometimes hard to measure) levels of participation. But in countries where organised sport is in its infancy, such as developing countries, sports participation may need to be a first priority to attract young people to sport, before bringing them into elite development pathways. As such, success could possibly decrease for countries without a sports participation basis. Third, beyond the (non)existence of a grassroots sporting system, we need to consider the specificity of sports. Sports where specialisation occurs early (e.g., soccer) or those where peak performance occurs at a young age (e.g., gymnastics) require a different approach to those sports that emphasise later specialisation (e.g., rowing) or when peak performance is achieved at a later age (e.g., triathlon) (Vaeyens et al., 2008). Fourth, predictability of talent differs per sport and varies with age. For example, sport disciplines where one or two variables have a high predictive value (e.g., track and field, sprint) will be more suitable for effective talent identification compared to multi-skilled disciplines (e.g., tennis, volleyball). Furthermore, the prediction of success is likely to be easier in more 'closed' (e.g., run 100 metres) rather than 'open' sports (e.g., score a goal) because movements in closed sports are less affected by the environment and fewer variables are likely to impact on performance (Vaeyens et al., 2008). This is why national governing bodies have invested more resources in talent identification models within more closed sports (e.g., rowing, cycling, athletics, canoeing and weightlifting) and are now recruiting potential medal winners at later ages, for example through talent transfer or by identifying 'sporting giants', such as in the UK. Talent development research shows the downside of a too narrow approach to elite sport development, and the pitfalls of identifying talent too early. Several researchers have emphasised the need for deliberate play (maximising fun, intrinsic motivation and enjoyment) with adapted sport rules, in order to decrease drop-out rates (from sport in general and from young talents in particular), to reduce injuries and to improve sustainable sport participation, personal development and the achievement of expertise (e.g., Côté, 1999; Wiersma, 2008; Vaeyens et al., 2008). Discussions in regard to early specialisation (e.g., Côté, Fraser and Thomas, 2007, identifying talent at an early age and subjecting young people to intensive performance programmes in a single sport) and diversification (also known as late specialisation) (Wiersma, 2000), participation in a variety of sports and activities through which an athlete develops multilateral physical, social and psychological skills are inherent to talent development and need to be carefully considered in elite sport policy planning.

Our research design delivers no evidence of a direct link between policy actions that are intended to drive sports participation or talent development and the level of success in elite sport that countries achieve. It seems that Pillars 3 and 4 are not priority Pillars for short-term (quick fix) success in sport, but in the longer term may provide a foundation for temporary competitive advantage by delivering more talented athletes for selection into elite sport. As smaller (less populated) nations have higher scores on Pillars 3 and 4, it seems that higher populated countries have relied more on the vast size of their participation and talent pool.

If larger countries start to invest more in these Pillars it may well deliver scope for performance improvement at the expense of smaller nations. Some evidence was shown in the results from the surveys completed by elite athletes (n=2423), revealing that the age at which they first received extra attention as an emerging talent from their NGB was 17 years old (SD ±3.6 years). As many skills are 'best trainable' before the age of 12, there seems to be scope to intervene positively in athlete (development) careers at an early age, and as such to invest in high quality delivered in sport clubs to learn basic competencies. If we look at the issue of grassroots participation from a different perspective, we find that predominantly Muslim countries systematically underperform in summer sports particularly (De Bosscher, 2007). In these nations, women who make up around 50% of the population, are often discouraged from taking part in sport generally and elite sport specifically. From this extreme perspective, we can see that in instances where there is no tradition of sports participation for half of the population, success in elite sport nationally is at best modest.

Overall it is important to acknowledge that the quality and reliability of sport participation data available from most of the countries is at best acceptable and at worst questionable. Different methodologies and means of data collection make it hard to compare participation rates between countries. There is also limited data on the frequency and intensity of sport participation, which is critical information in order to conduct a meaningful Pillar 3 analysis. Except for Brazil all nations in the sample have reasonable levels of sport participation and as such our data lacks discriminatory depth. As such we cannot use the outcomes of our study to answer the question if sport participation levels have a direct effect on elite sport success of nations. At best we can hypothesise that the effect of sport participation levels is mediated by other factors, which need to be explored in future research.

14.2.5 Pillar 5 (athletic career support)–Non-significant but essential

Pillar 5 deals with athletic career and post-career support. This Pillar did not correlate significantly with success. We contend that this can be largely explained by the fact that most nations are doing essentially the same things in regard to athletic career support. The most important of these appear to be providing athletes with the money and time to train and compete as if they were full-time professional athletes. Apart from low scoring nations such as Brazil and Estonia, the nations in our sample shared similar scores. Lack of discrimination between nations confirms that it is the Pillar in which we see the most homogenised approach to elite sport development.

Within this Pillar, the most important CSF (significantly correlating with success) concerns athletes' monthly income: average income, the amount of money they invest from their own income in their elite sport activities, and whether the income is sufficient to train on a full-time basis. NSAs want to treat athletes as employees, providing a secured wage that allows for full-time dedication to elite sport. However, the data showed that there is still a significant cohort of top 16 athletes (48%) who do not earn enough on a monthly basis to consider elite sport as their full-time profession. For female athletes this is even harder as they earn less than their male colleagues.

From our results we derive the assertion that also post-career support for athletes is still not fully recognised by administrators as a policy area worthy of significant attention. During the athletes' career, preparation for the post- athletic career increasingly is considered, but after retirement, the support is limited.

14.2.6 Pillars 6, 7, 8 and 9—The significant Pillars: Facilities, coaching, competition, and scientific research have a direct influence on sporting performance

A common characteristic of facilities (Pillar 6), coaching (Pillar 7) and access to competition (Pillar 8) is that they directly 'touch' athletes who operate in an elite sport development system. These Pillars are the drivers of an effective elite sport system. We need to exercise a degree of caution here in the sense that correlations indicate a relationship but not the direction or cause of a relationship. It would be convenient to assume that Pillars 6, 7 and 8 cause elite sporting success, but this is not proven. What we can say is that these Pillars are linked to success, but it is also possible that elite sport success causes Pillars 6, 7 and 8. In other words, success may be rewarded with further investment. As such, it seems likely that causality may work in both directions. For example, in the UK systematic investment in elite sport was first made in 1997 and proved to be successful, as evidenced by the results in Beijing 2008 and London 2012 when the UK was the host nation. Success breeds success and, in the case of the UK, has led to further investment such as the extra £20 million awarded to UK Sport to prepare for the Rio 2016 Olympic Games. A goal has been set to win one more medal than the number achieved in London 2012 (66 v 65).

Quite obviously Pillars 6, 7 and 8 are closely linked. Elite level athletes require access to specialised and state of the art facilities in which they can train, have priority access, and which are equipped to the appropriate standards for elite sport; where the best expert coaches can optimise the talent that they are working with. This also includes access to on-site scientific support (Pillar 9). There is a global market for best coaching talent, and it is common to see foreign coaches working in nations where there is a systematic approach to elite sport development. Ultimately, elite athletes need to be tested in international competition and either at home or abroad, governments may decide that funding athletes to take part in such competitions is a legitimate 'cost of doing business'.

Of the four Pillars discussed in this section, Pillar 9 (scientific research and innovation) is more likely to deliver a long-term source of competitive advantage rather than contribute to immediate medal-winning results. It requires time and experience to develop a comprehensive national research centre that carries out research as well as co-ordinating research activity in elite sport nationally, which was the most important critical success factor on Pillar 9. Sport science support is all about making the difference to the narrow margins that are the difference between winning and losing. Any innovation or new insight that helps athletes to improve performance, whether it be techniques to improve human performance or equipment performance, will always be highly sought after in the pursuit of competitive advantage. It is noteworthy that Australia scores the highest (90%) on Pillar 9, and it is also the nation that has actively been developing an elite sport development system for the longest of all nations in our sample. Japan is the second highest scoring nation (75%) and has made huge investments in research and innovation, such as the US$250 million in the Japan Institute of Sport Sciences. Furthermore, the results of Pillar 9 indicated that sport science research still fails to deliver applied (real-life applications) value for those who work closest to the elite performance–the athletes and their coaches.

14.2.7 The characteristics of efficient nations

In summer sports, the most efficient nations that we identified were Australia, Japan, the Netherlands and France as these were the nations that achieved comparatively higher levels of output than their investment would otherwise predict (Figure 86). These countries have the highest average scores on all Pillars, and they all do particularly well in Pillars 5 (athletic career support), 6 (training facilities) and 7 (coaches). Apart from the Netherlands, these nations also spent the most money on elite sport, and they all score reasonably well on Pillar 9 (scientific research). As discussed Pillars 5, 6, and 7 can be seen as making immediate (short-term) contributions to sporting success. New nations entering the market of international sport competitions, setting up a strategic approach to elite sport, may need to prioritise investing in these Pillars first.

In Figure 88 it can be seen that although the four most successful nations have above average output scores and similar overall average scores (60% to 64%) the way in which scores are composed varies considerably. France's relative strengths lie in Pillar 7 (80%), Pillar 6 (72%) and Pillar 1 (69%) whereas it has a clear weakness in Pillar 2 (37%). The Netherlands by contrast has the highest score of all nations on Pillar 2 (69%) and nearly in Pillar 3 (62%) and Pillar 4 (68%), whilst having the lowest score on Pillar 1 (45%). This implies that it is not necessarily money that is most important in achieving success, and that an appropriate structure, organisation and integrated co-ordination can also have a positive impact on success. It also shows that an efficient model can be achieved in different ways: not only based on overperforming in coaching, competition and/or scientific support (e.g., France, Australia and Japan), but also on a strong organisational model that is built on, and profits from, a high level of sport participation and a powerful sport club system fostering talent development.

	P1	P2	P3	P4	P5	P6	P7	P8	P9	Average
FRA*	69%	37%	52%	45%	67%	72%	80%	55%	60%	60%
AUS	60%	64%	54%	49%	76%	66%	69%	48%	90%	64%
JAP	61%	59%	33%	45%	67%	74%	60%	78%	75%	62%
NED	45%	69%	62%	68%	77%	65%	62%	54%	53%	62%

Figure 88: The top four SPLISS 2.0 nations in financial efficiency in summer sports (referring to Figure 86)

Whereas the low investments (P1) in the Netherlands are compensated for by a strong organisational model (P2) and participation base (P3, P4), Japan's poor participation base (Pillar 3) is compensated for by high scores on facilities (Pillar 6), access to international competition (Pillar 8) and research and innovation (Pillar 9). Australia suffers from the 'tyranny of distance' for access to international competition (Pillar 8) but compensates for this with high scores on research and innovation (Pillar 9), athletic career support (Pillar 5) and coaching (Pillar 7). Arguably a mature system such as that of Australia could focus further on investing in research and innovation as competitive advantage is derived from innovation rather than imitation. System leaders need to innovate in order to stay ahead of the competition.

The four countries performing above average (and expectations) in winter sports given the resources at their disposal were the Netherlands, Canada, Switzerland and Finland (Figure 89).

	P1	P2	P3	P4	P5	P6	P7	P8	P9	Average
NED	45%	69%	62%	68%	77%	65%	62%	54%	53%	62%
CAN	55%	58%	43%	23%	65%	63%	73%	62%	68%	57%
SUI	45%	58%	62%	70%	58%	61%	68%	44%	49%	58%
FIN	36%	47%	50%	49%	70%	43%	56%	65%	53%	52%

Figure 89: The top four SPLISS 2.0 nations in financial efficiency in winter sports (referring to Figure 86)

As indicated in Figure 89, the successful winter sports nations have average to high scores across Pillar 5 (athletic career support) and Pillar 7 (coaches). None of these countries has green traffic light scores on Pillar 1 (financial support), but all four countries clearly prioritise winter sports in their funding criteria. In addition, as winter sports are organised on a more autonomous basis, for example, in ski resorts or on a more commercial basis (e.g., commercial ice skating, ice hockey teams), these are factors that are likely to be less influenced by national investments. Winter sports are also more likely to be funded by private organisations.

Figures 88 and 89 show that different combinations of factors can lead to international sporting success. In recent years many nations have sought to increase their success by adopting a more strategic approach to elite athlete development and by copying best practice from early mover nations (imitation rather than innovation). Australia and Canada were among the early adopters of strategic elite sport policy approaches, and they built their systems partly modeled on the high performance structures of former communist nations. As a consequence, Australia and its Australian Institute of Sport have been powerful examples for many other nations to emulate. As a result, the current elite sport literature reports that elite sport development is characterised by increasing institutionalisation, government involvement and homogenisation (Oakley and Green, 2001; Green and Houlihan, 2005). However, the SPLISS 2.0 results also show that although overall Pillar scores may be similar, nations have different scores on CSFs. A contingency approach–the design of a model which fits best with the unique situation that a country finds itself in–may well be the best solution for individual nations developing or advancing their elite performance systems. These findings are consistent with the notion of *'glocalisations'* which reflect a homogenized (global) response to generic (macro) factors impacting on success but with heterogeneous applications (local adaptations) when it comes to the unique national situation and competitive environment. Geography and the cultural context, plus path dependency as identified by Houlihan and Green (2008) all seem to play an important role in how countries make these design and policy decisions. This will be illustrated in the nation-by-nation analysis in the next section. Accordingly, countries have particular strengths (and weaknesses) in different Pillars. Countries also combine CSFs in different ways. This finding is in line with Anderson and Ronglan's (2012) work that illustrated how different sports had similar ambitions but different tracks to achieve this as exemplified by Swedish golf and tennis, Norwegian handball, Finnish ice hockey and Danish track cycling.

There is no structural or managerial blueprint that can be simply lifted from one context and placed in another that will guarantee success. The reality is that there are a set of broad principles around a common framework that can be adapted to local circumstances in a culturally appropriate manner. Accordingly, the key challenge for nations remains to find the right blend of system ingredients and processes that work best in their own context and culture, encouraging them to 'benchlearn', from rivals rather than merely benchmarking against them.

14.2.8 Pillar-by-Pillar analysis: Key points

In summary our Pillar-by-Pillar analysis delivers eight key points.

- Pillar 1—financial support—correlates strongest with elite sport success. As per the SPLISS 1.0 results we find that the absolute amount of funding invested in elite sport is the factor most strongly related to success.
- While 'money in correlates with medals out' it does not follow that 'MORE money in leads to more medals out'—there are diminishing returns to scale of investment where merely investing more money does not automatically lead to more success. This confirms the assumption that there exists a situation in elite sport policy that can be likened to a global sporting arms race.
- Pillar 2—A strategic and co-ordinated approach to sport system management is likely to impact positively on sporting success and is seen as a characteristic of efficient nations. We consider Pillar 2 to be the building block of an elite sport system in the sense that it does not lead to success on its own but is an important component to have in order to enable success. Setting up elaborate, complex and integrated systems for co-ordination, organisation and governance takes time and experience and cannot be considered a quick fix for achieving sporting success. Nations with a well-developed Pillar 2 may be able to achieve sustainable competitive advantage because this is less about money in and more about doing things right and doing the right things.
- The most appropriate role for governments is one of enabling rather than delivering. High-performance sport does not lend itself well to bureaucracy that can be copied and pasted across national governmental systems, or across different sports. Governments as facilitators and enablers seems to be the approach that leads to countries being most likely to be successful.
- We found no significant direct relationship between grassroots participation (Pillar 3), talent identification and development (Pillar 4) and elite sport success. As noted there are measurement issues with Pillars, but irrespective of those it is our view that the impact on elite sport success of Pillars 3 and 4 is mediated more by other factors than it is in Pillars 5 to 9. There is a considerable time between the podium and participation and a high drop-out rate between those identified as talented and those who reach the top. We argue that participation indirectly influences success (in the long-term) because of it positively delivering a continuous supply of young talents. This intuitive importance of the influence of participation numbers and talent identification processes on elite sporting success justifies further research into these relationships.

- We also did not find a significant correlation between athletic career and post-career support (Pillar 5) and sporting success, which we attribute to nations taking a broadly similar approach to this Pillar which is creating an environment that enables athletes to train and compete as full-time professional athletes. Future research with a bigger sample of diverse nations might be required to further advance our understanding of this Pillar.
- There is a significant relationship between facilities, top-level coaching and access to international competition (Pillars 6, 7 and 8) and success. These are drivers of an effective elite sport system. Our basic argument in regard to the direct impact that these factors have on sporting success, is that all three literally 'touch' the athlete and his/her performance. Poor facilities, poor coaching and limited access to international competition are all likely to have an immediate negative impact on athletic performance.
- Scientific research and innovation (Pillar 9) is positively linked to success, and more strongly than was found in SPLISS 1.0. High scores on this Pillar are indicative of nations taking a mid- to longer-term view towards achieving or sustaining elite sport success. Superior scientific support in elite sport development typifies nations that want to be leaders, not followers. Sport science is about staying ahead of other competitors, coming up with new methods, approaches and equipment that enable athletes to achieve a competitive advantage over international competitors. If science allows the elite sport system to continuously offer short-term advantage to athletes, the sport science support itself becomes a source of sustainable competitive advantage.
- There is no evidence of an elite sport development system blueprint that can be generically applied to every nation. Although broad consensus exists on the basic ingredients of a system, the mix of how those ingredients are combined varies considerably between nations. The key challenge for nations is to benchlearn, instead of benchmark, and to use the best principles (not best practice) of efficient and effective elite sport policies that can be applied to their own context.

Having taken a Pillar-by-Pillar view we now proceed to look at performance in the nine Pillars on a nation-by-nation approach.

14.3 Pillar performance per nation

In this section we consider the performance of the sample nations against all of the Pillars. Using radar graphs to visualise nations' performance, we plot the nations' scores against the sample average and against the maximum scores on each Pillar. This approach enables us to derive the relative strengths and weaknesses of each nation quickly and also get an indication about the most obvious areas for improvement.

The SPLISS 2.0 nations as a cohort are an interesting sample. In terms of their macro-economic characteristics they account for about 8% of the world's population and 10% of global wealth. However, during the four years 2009-2012 they accounted for 23% of the success achieved in summer sports and 37% of the success achieved in winter sports. In addition they also produced 26% of the Olympians who took part in London 2012. In global sporting terms, therefore, the SPLISS 2.0 nations should be viewed as being more successful than average and any weaknesses identified should be considered as being relative to each other rather than absolute in a global sense. Radar graphs for all 16 sport systems (from 15 nations) in the sample are shown in Figure 90.

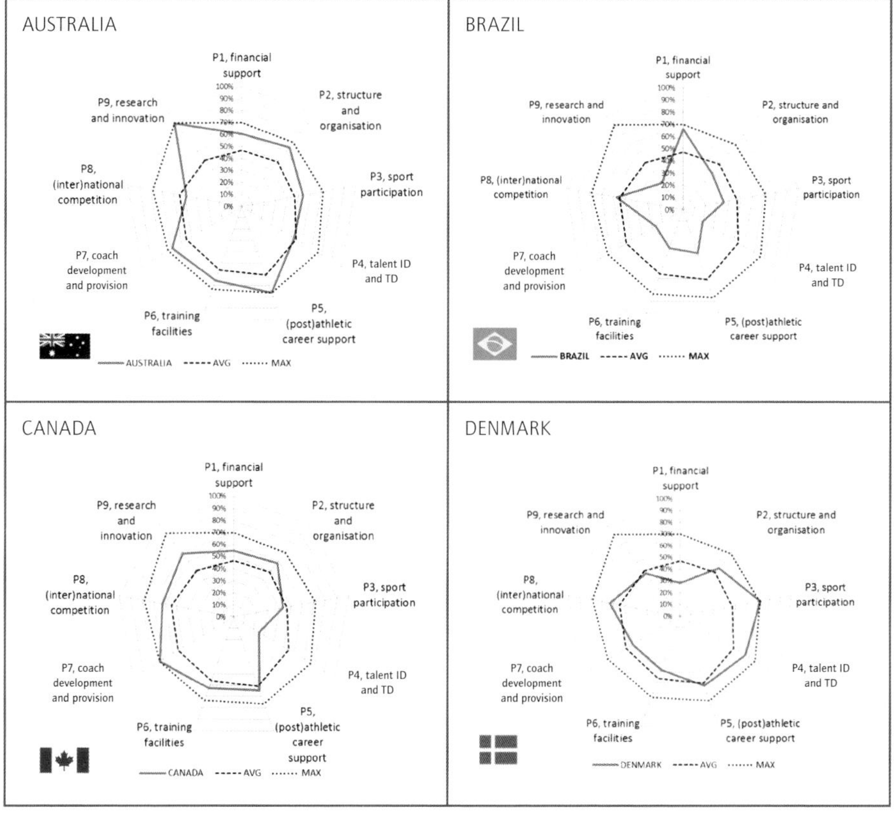

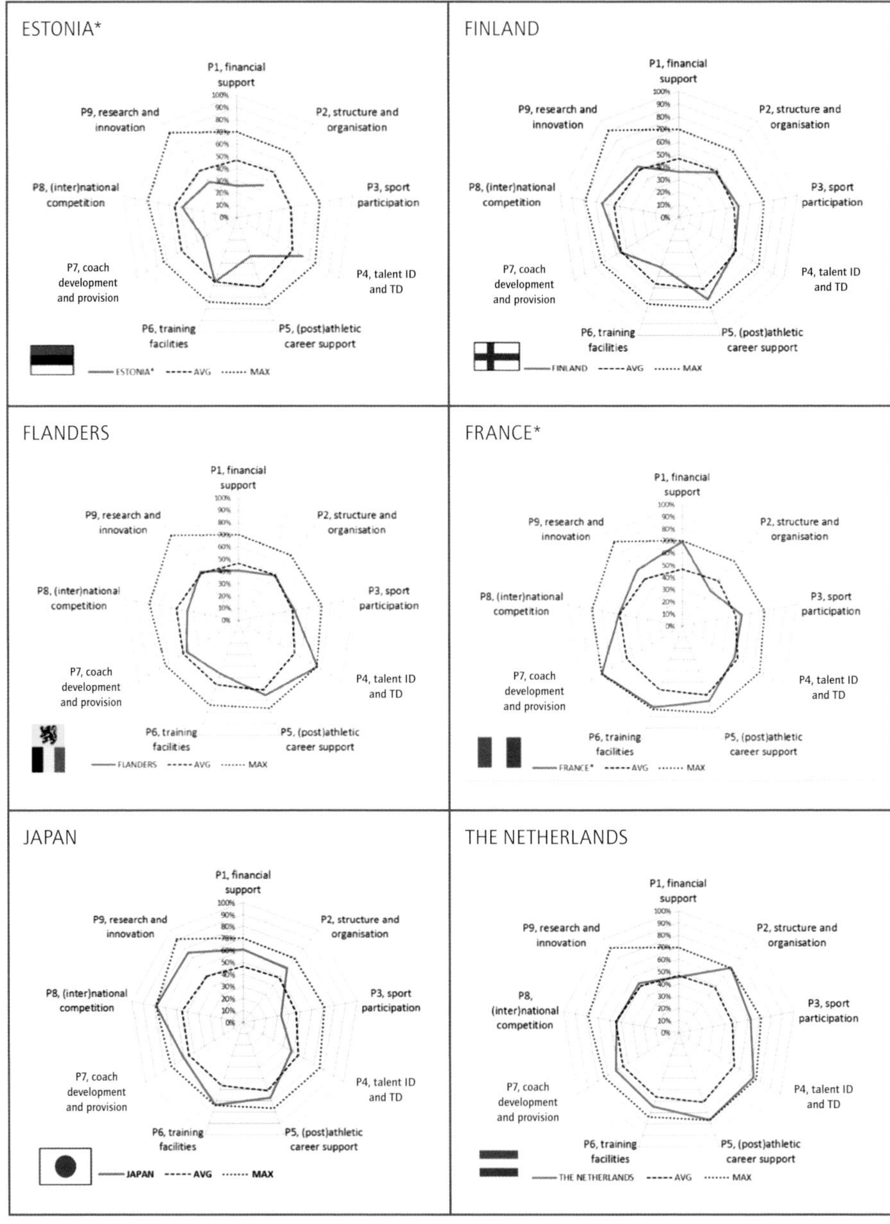

ESTONIA*
P1, financial support
P2, structure and organisation
P3, sport participation
P4, talent ID and TD
P5, (post)athletic career support
P6, training facilities
P7, coach development and provision
P8, (inter)national competition
P9, research and innovation
ESTONIA* AVG MAX
FINLAND
FINLAND AVG MAX
FLANDERS
FLANDERS AVG MAX
FRANCE*
FRANCE* AVG MAX
JAPAN
JAPAN AVG MAX
THE NETHERLANDS
THE NETHERLANDS AVG MAX

** Note of caution: incomplete dataset in France (no elite sport climate survey); Estonia (no inventory); and South Korea (no inventory in Pillars 4, 7 and 8).*

Figure 90: Radar graphs for the SPLISS 2.0 nations compared to the sample average and maximum scores in 15 nations

Rather than going into detail for each of the 16 nations we focus instead on some thematic issues that arise from a high-level examination of the data.

14.3.1 Successful nations in summer sports

Australia achieved the highest combined Pillar score

Our first key theme is concerned with success in the broad portfolio of summer sports nations (Figure 91). Australia has improved its success rate over more than 20 years since the establishment of the AIS in 1981. Chapter 4 also revealed that Australia was the most successful nation given its population and wealth (relative success) and was most successful at achieving top eight places in the SPLISS 2.0 sample. To that end the Australian system has become a benchmark for many other nations that have decided to increase their elite sport investment. Australia is a mature well-developed system which scores well in terms of efficiency and it is also innovation driven in the pursuit of sustained competitive advantage. Australia achieved the highest combined Pillar score of all countries. Its greatest strengths are in Pillar 9 (research and innovation) and Pillar 5 (athletic career support). Australia scores above the average on seven of the nine Pillars and is below average on Pillar 4 (talent) and Pillar 8 (national and international competition). Japan is a nation that can be seen as a late developer in adopting best practices from, among others, Australia. Since the National Training Centre was established in 2008, Japan has gained a competitive strength in Pillar 6 (facilities). Japan's scores exceed all countries on Pillars 6 (training facilities) and 8 (national and international competition). Only on Pillars 3 (participation) and 4 (talent) are Japan's scores below average.

Even successful countries do things differently

France has quite a different configuration of factors compared to Australia and Japan. It has some of the highest scores on Pillar 7 (coaches), Pillar 1 (financial support) and Pillar 6 (training facilities) and on Pillar 2 (organisation) it scores surprisingly low. As noted earlier findings for France need to be considered in light of two possible explanations. First operationally there is tension between the French Olympic Committee and the state which may lead to a sub-optimal organisational framework. Second, methodologically the missing elite sport climate survey data may also have an impact in this regard. Overall we can conclude that even successful countries do things differently and as such can continue to learn from each other. This realisation also offers considerable scope to carve out strategies that focus on Pillars where countries feel that they may have a comparative advantage and enable them to outperform other nations.

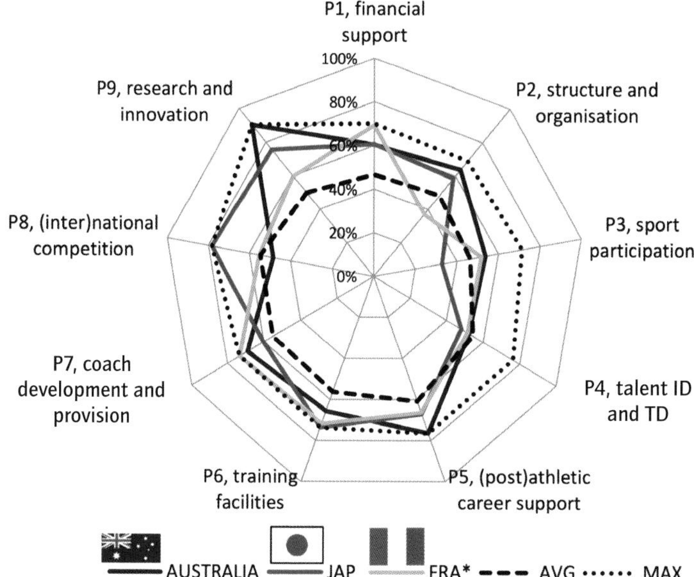

**Note of caution: incomplete dataset in France (no elite sport climate survey)*

Figure 91: Radar graph of Australia, France and Japan compared to the average and maximum scores of 15 nations*

14.3.2 Successful nations in winter sports

For winter sport sports we examine the top three performing countries Canada, the Netherlands and South Korea (Figure 92).

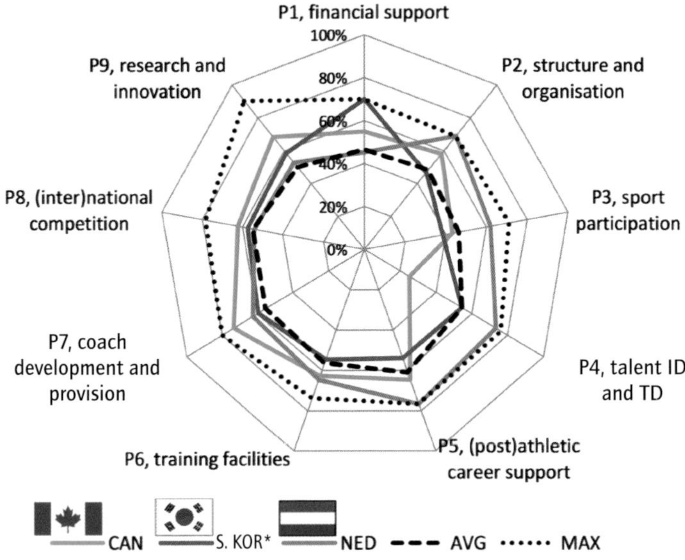

Figure 92: Radar graph of Canada, South Korea, and the Netherlands compared to the average and maximum scores of 15 nations*

Figure 92 shows the strengths of Canada in Pillars 7 (coaches), 8 ((inter)national competition) and 9 (research innovation), whereas the strengths of the Netherlands are on the right side of the graph (in Pillars 2, 3, 4, 6), showing the importance of its organisational model that not only enhances sport participation and talent development (mainly in speed skating) but also proves to be effective and efficient in turning this broad base into later elite sporting success (at least in this sport). Canada has (along with France[45]) the best score of all nations on coaching provision and development (Pillar 7). Furthermore Canada scores well on international competition (Pillar 8) which was confirmed by Green and Houlihan (2005) as 'the enthusiasm of Canadian cities to host major international sports events and the willingness of the federal government to provide some

45 France has the highest Pillar 7 scores on the inventory only; as it did not complete the surveys, these scores are not wholly reliable.

support for facility development which may be traced back to the motive of enhancing national identity through a high international profile' (p.168). Canada also has a developing academic sport science culture that is increasingly making direct contributions to elite sport. While Canada probably suffers most from the national measurement in this project (and Canada's responsibilities are divided over the states for education and sports participation, which impacts on Pillars 3-4), it is likely that in the long run Canada can increase its competitive position by developing a more co-ordinated approach to the development of talented young athletes.

Almost diametrically opposed to the Canada scores, are the scores for the Netherlands showing relative strengths in Pillars 2 (organisation), 3 (participation), 4 (talent ID and development) and 5 (athletic career support). The Netherlands is ranked third in winter sport success and fifth in summer sports in spite of being ranked 8th with a score below average on P1 (financial support). However, in winter sports, 42 of the 46 (91%) medals won from 2009-2012, were in speed skating; two in snowboard and two in short track. Still, this country can serve as a good example of a nation that uses its resources wisely to 'punch above its weight', not just in winter sports but in summer sports, too.

As a general view, the radar graphs confirm previous findings in relation to the efficiency or the input–output relationship, where South Korea was not identified as being particularly successful given the fact that it spends the most on elite sport (and where purchasing power parity is low). South Korea achieves only around the average on most Pillars. Digging deeper into South Korea's investment in elite sport one may conclude that an important objective is international exposure, through the organisation of international events (53% of elite sport expenditures). Furthermore the results in Pillar 5 showed that South Korea also had the highest average funding for athletes (in PPP values) and the highest number of athletes in the higher income categories. Funding is clearly an important tool for South Korea to facilitate its elite sport ambitions.

Comparing Figure 91 and Figure 92, it is interesting to compare the Netherlands with Australia as their population and economic productivity is similar. Australia has a longer tradition of facilitating elite success and to this day the Netherlands has only modest elite sport investments from national collective sources. Both have different relative strengths with the Netherlands scoring high on on Pillars 2, 3 and 4 (organisation, participation and talent) and Australia standing out for its approach to research and innovation (Pillar 9). Australia performs relatively better in Summer Olympic sports but the Netherlands is more successful in Winter Olympic sports, notably speed skating in which it has recently developed very strong competitive advantage. As such, both countries represent different pathways to success, as the product of several decades of elite sport policies and sport for all policies. Furthermore, taking both figures together, there are sizeable differences in the populations of these six countries, varying from relatively small nations (Australia, 23 million and the Netherlands, 17 million), to bigger (Canada, 35 million), big (South Korea, 49 million: France, 66 million) and the biggest (Japan, 127 million). In relative terms, the residual analysis in chapter 4 clustered all these nations as positive performers given their population and wealth, with Australia being the most successful country, ranked 6th worldwide (in top three places), followed by France (10th), the Netherlands (15th), South Korea (16th) and Japan (18th). It is notable that these nations produced different levels of efficiency in converting their populations into Olympians, top eight places and medallists. While Australia and France were highly successful at producing finalists, they were relatively less successful at converting these into medallists (36% of their top eight places converted to medallists). By contrast, South Korea (48%) and Japan (49%) enjoyed much higher success rates in converting their finalists into medal winners. The issues of efficiency of production and conversion of raw material into medal-winning success is a whole new direction for future research to investigate.

We speculate that, similar to the Global Competitiveness Report, produced by the World Economic Forum (WEF, 2012), in which countries are mapped according to their 'competitiveness readiness', similar principles may apply to the competitiveness of elite sport systems. Without delving too deep into the intricacies of the global competitiveness index of the WEF, countries are separated into factor driven, efficiency driven and innovation driven economies. Low levels of labour specialisation typify factor driven economies whereas innovation driven economies are extremely specialised. Efficiency driven economies are developing towards levels of sophistication that make them use available resources more economically. In regard to global competitiveness in elite sport systems, we argue in this book that similar principles apply. Some systems are highly developed and integrated and capitalise on the wide availability of well-educated and highly skilled elite sport labour. In addition, they have access to a range of services and skills that make the system increasingly efficient and innovative, leading to larger numbers of athletes achieving top eight places. Other systems 'spill' a lot of resources, are relatively under developed, and still require the implementation of more efficient elite sport production processes, complemented by local elite sport professionals who are available on the ground, rather than imported from more developed nations. In short, long-term sustainable competitiveness of nations in elite sport is likely to be a function of structures and systems rather than luck.

14.3.3 Small nations

Switzerland, Finland and Denmark can be identified as small nations (with a population < 10 million) that have average success rates in summer sports (Denmark and Switzerland) or winter sports (Finland and Switzerland) in absolute terms, and do well in relative terms (given their population and wealth). Figure 93 shows the comparative radar graph. These nations also show different strengths in different Pillars. For Switzerland and Denmark, the general pattern is quite similar to the Netherlands, with higher scores on Pillars 2 (structure), Pillar 3 (participation) and Pillar 4 (talent). In addition, Switzerland has well-developed coaches (Pillar 7) and good facilities (Pillar 6), whereas in Denmark, scores are higher on (inter)national competition (Pillar 8) and (post) athletic career support (Pillar 5). It can be argued that these smaller nations can differentiate themselves from bigger nations in their ability to utilise the potential of their athletes to create elite sport achievements and to co-ordinate elite sport, with relatively high autonomy given to the sports. Referring to Ronglan (2014), 'the competitive advantage of these nations has not been a comprehensive elite sport system but an ability to utilise the potential embedded in the popular movement to 'also' create some elite sport achievements' (p. 16). This is also further evidence that there is no 'one size fits all' approach that is applicable to all nations. What Ronglan (2014) details about certain Nordic countries are examples of culturally specific adaptations of basic principles that have evolved in a context sensitive manner.

Finland's scores are quite different, with high levels of development in Pillars 8 (international competition) and Pillar 5 (athletic career support). The country has a low level of co-ordination, which is expressed by average scores in Pillars 2 (structure) and Pillar 4 (talent).

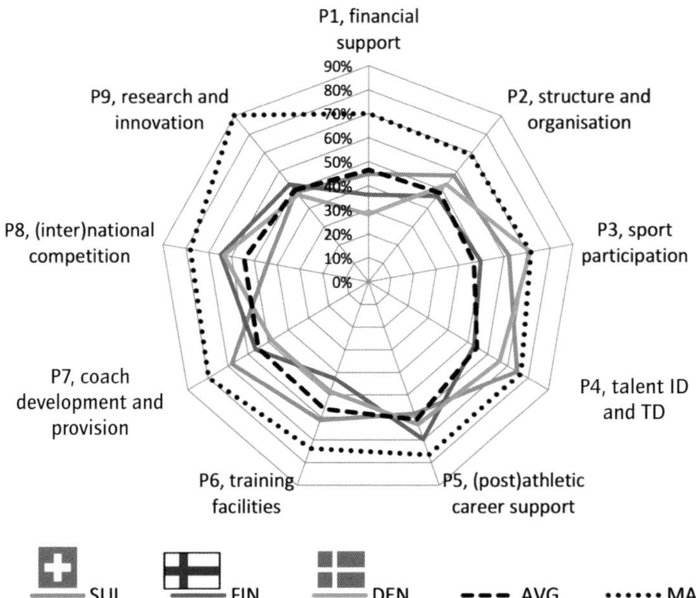

Figure 93: Radar graph of Denmark, Finland and Switzerland compared to the average and maximum scores of 15 nations

14.3.4 Small and unsuccessful nations

Belgium (Flanders/Wallonia) and Portugal (Figure 94) are comparable countries in terms of their population, and are among the least successful nations of the sample. Given their population and GDP/Cap (chapter 4, relative success), they perform below expectations. The score differences between Flanders (the northern, Dutch-speaking part of Belgium) and Wallonia (southern, French- and German-speaking) confirm that there are policy differences in both regions. Similarly Northern Ireland is comparable to Belgium in terms of the specific state structure, although there is no national policy organisation in Belgium, except for the National Olympic Committee, while in Northern Ireland some sports are co-ordinated nationally, by UK Sport.

The rules of the game are dictated by what rival nations are doing and not by what an individual nation is doing compared to the past

Over the past decade, Flanders has invested strategically in elite sport by, for example, tripling elite sport funding, although it is still low in relative terms compared to other nations. Examples of specific strategic initiatives include the establishment of elite sport schools (1998); setting up a department with sole responsibility for elite sport within the national sport administration Bloso (2003); full-time athletes (1995) and coaches (2007) paid by Bloso; athletic career coaches (2007); and, specific elite sport science support (2007). While in the SPLISS 1.0 project Flanders scored below the average on all Pillars, except Pillar 4 (talent), it now comes close to the average in Pillars 2 (organisation), 3 (sport participation), 5 (athletic career support) and 9 (scientific research and innovation). Despite these policy improvements, Flemish success remains limited. The rules of the game are dictated by what rival nations are doing and not on what an individual nation is doing now compared to what it did in the past (De Bosscher et al., 2008). The absolute (minimum) amount of funding put into the system, as speculated on earlier, is an important target to achieve. Wallonia has not shown a similar evolution in strategic planning as evidenced by lower scores than Flanders on all Pillars. Portugal also scores lower on all Pillars except for the access to international competition (Pillar 8) and coaches (Pillar 7).

In the case of Northern Ireland, SPLISS 2.0 included an audit of the nation's 'high performance' system rather than elite sport system, the latter being co-ordinated by UK Sport. Northern Ireland scores slightly above average on Pillars 5, 6 and 7.

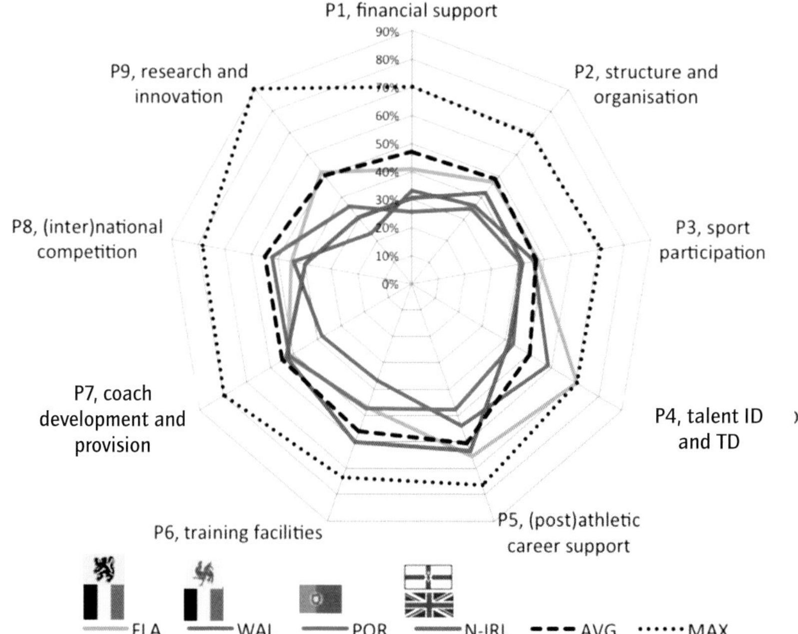

Figure 94: Radar graph of Flanders/Wallonia and Portugal compared to the average and maximum scores of 15 nations

For all of these nations, sporting success is also below what would be expected given the level of investment (see Figure 86 and Figure 87) which causes us to revisit the question, is there a minimum threshold of investment that nations need to make in order to have a globally competitive elite sport development system?

14.3.5 Future hosts of the Olympic Games

At the time of writing this book, Rio 2016 and Tokyo 2020 were future events, and it is therefore useful to look at the profiles of future hosts of the Summer Olympic Games. It is well-documented that countries hosting the Olympic Games have a home advantage and tend to win more medals. Nations like Australia (Sydney, 2000), Greece (Athens, 2004), China (Beijing, 2008) and the United Kingdom (London, 2012) all performed better during their home Olympics and also in the Games prior to being the host nation. They also received more investment and benefited from a more strategic national approach to elite sport development. Japan and Brazil were the only countries in the sample that increased their market share of success following increased investments made over the period 2001 to 2012.

Looking at the nine Pillars for Brazil, and how elite athletes, coaches and performance directors have evaluated them, there is a strong belief that with an increasing national strategic approach to elite sport policy development, Brazil may improve its future medal tally. National government, lotteries and the Olympic Committee collectively invested around €147 million on a yearly basis in elite sport. It is estimated that another €65 million by the state companies (€222m in total in 2011-2012) is invested, although it is less clear if and how this funding is genuinely nationally co-ordinated and allocated. Brazil is a typical example showing that it takes time to turn investments in elite sport into success. Money alone cannot guarantee success; the crucial question is how the money is spent. The main weakness in Brazil, covering all Pillars, is that there is no clear overall plan, leadership and co-ordination to be successful in elite sport in the short term. As outlined in Figure 95, the only Pillar where Brazil scores around the average of the other 15 nations (except for Pillar 1) is Pillar 8 (access to international competition). There is significant funding available in Brazil (Pillar 1) but the allocation of funding remains quite undirected. The magnitude of the gaps between the scores for Brazil and the sample average are the greatest in Pillars 7 (coaches), 4 (talent) and 6 (facilities). Sport participation is a long-term development that also has a low score. Brazil exhibited only a small pre-hosting effect in London 2012, winning just two more medals than in Beijing 2008. Despite the potential that the country has, it seems that 2016 may be too early for Brazil to perform well and in line with previous host nations. The 2016 Olympic Games may provide the country with a platform from which it can build towards achieving longer term success.

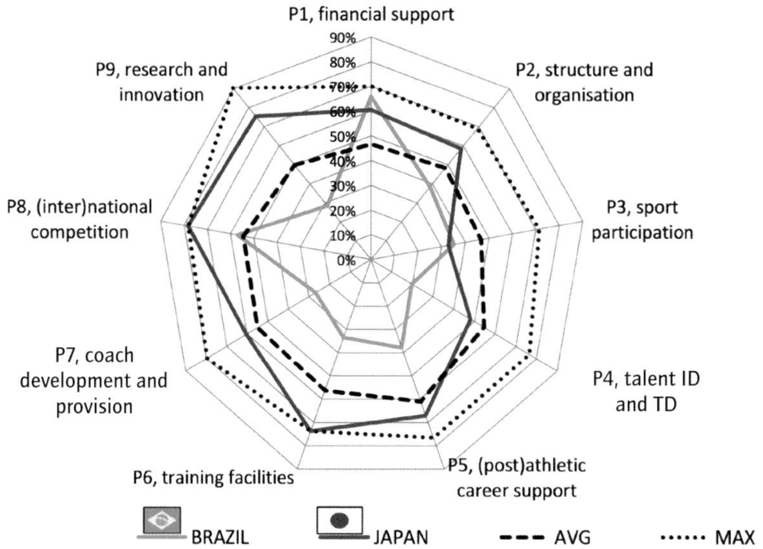

Figure 95: Radar graph of Brazil compared to Japan compared to the average and maximum scores of 15 nations

Japan performs far better than Brazil on all of the nine Pillars, except for sports participation (Pillar 3), where both countries perform below average. The total elite sport budget (€208 million) is the second highest after South Korea. It has a relative strength in research and innovation, training facilities (the national training centre in Tokyo and the 22 sport-specific training centres), and (international) competition. Japan has a long high-performance history and is probably well set up to work towards a very successful home Olympic Games.

14.3.6 Nation-by-nation analysis: Key points

The nation-by-nation analysis delivers four key points.

- The findings confirm that there is no generic blueprint for success. It is clear that success can be achieved by various configurations of the nine Pillars. Elite sport pathways require a contingency approach, with a model that fits best with the unique situation that a country is placed in.
- The case of the Netherlands shows that it is possible for a nation to perform well in elite sport with a relatively modest financial investment. The Netherlands' key strength is its approach to structure, governance and co-ordination in a country characterised by a high level of sport participation and a powerful sport club system fostering talent development.

- There is no blueprint for correcting the performance of nations that are less successful in elite sport. Weaker nations do not share distinct areas of weakness although a surprising number of them perform well on Pillar 4 (talent). This may have to do with the realisation that there is not large population to deliver a steady stream of talent.
- The future hosts of the Olympic Games, Brazil in 2016, and Japan in 2020, appear to be in different states of readiness to achieve success. Brazil is likely to struggle to achieve the uplift normally achieved by hosts, but Japan appears to be on a successful trajectory.
- We reiterate our reference to the Global Competitiveness Report, produced by the World Economic Forum, where more 'efficient' or even 'innovative' nations achieve better (economic) results with similar latent capacity. We believe that an important part of unexplained medal-winning variance is explained by system efficiencies. The nine Pillar SPLISS model allows zooming in on what the constituents are, which in turn may lead to more efficient production of elite success.

14.4 Key issues in elite sport policy development

In this concluding section we look at some key issues that arise from our analysis. First, we examine the keys to achieving sporting success. Thus far we have looked at the aggregate scores for the nine Pillars as a simple way of assessing nations' performance. In reality each Pillar is composed of numerous sub factors and as such we can also conduct an analysis of sub factors that can facilitate success. Second we look at elite sport policy theory development and how the SPLISS 2.0 project has contributed. We also reflect on directions for future research. Third we look at two strategic issues—centralised versus decentralised approaches to national co-ordination, and whether prioritisation of specific sports can be an effective strategy in the long term. We conclude the book with some reflections on the development of elite sport development systems.

14.4.1 The keys to success

When we delve deeper into the 96 critical success factors that are the building blocks of the nine Pillars we find that 22 factors significantly correlate with success either in summer or in winter sports (at the 0.05 level).[46] This subset of 22 significant CSFs is shown in Table 44.

---

46 50 CSFs have a positive correlation with success that is higher than 0.3.

Table 44: Key success drivers per Pillar, based on significant correlations with success (in either summer or winter sports, ordered from highest to lowest correlation)

PILLAR 1 (Financial support)	Summer	Winter
Total national expenditure on elite sport (CSF 1.4)	**	*
Total national (elite) sport funding for NGBs, and/or sport clubs (CSF 1.7 and 1.8)	**	X
Increase/decrease in national expenditure on sport–4 years (CSF 1.3)	**	X
Expenditure on elite sport as a proportion of expenditure on sport (CSF 1.5)	**	
Total national expenditure on elite sport (CSF 1.4)	**	X
PILLAR 2 (Governance, organisation and structure)		
Full-time management staff in the NSA (CSF 2.12)	**	**
National co-ordination; decision-making structure (CSF 2.1)	*	*
Objective and transparent measurement instrument to evaluate NGBs (CSF 2.11)	X	*
NSA policy regularly evaluated by athletes, coaches, and PD (CSF 2.7b, ESC)	X	*
Athletes and coaches represented in NSA decision-making process (CSF 2.9)		*
PILLAR 5 (Athletic career support)		
Athletes' have a sufficient monthly income (CSF 5.1)	*	
PILLAR 6 (Training facilities)		
High-quality national elite sport centre(s) (CSF 6.5)	**	X
PILLAR 7 (Coach support and provisions)		
(Non-sport specific) Communication platform for elite coaches (CSF 7.10)	X	**
Sufficient general monthly income of coaches (CSF 7.11)	**	*
A trade union for coaches (CSF 7.16)		**
Services/resources for continuous elite coach development (CSF 7.8b, ESC)		*
Elite sport coaching as a full-time activity/coaches spend sufficient time with elite athletes/talents (CSF 7.12 and 7.12b, ESC)	*	X
PILLAR 8 (National and international competition/events)		
A high number of international events organised in the country (CSF 8.4)	*	
National co-ordination and long-term planning of events (CSF 8.1)	X	*
PILLAR 9 (Scientific research and innovation)		
National research centre (CSF 9.3)	**	**
(Sufficient) Financial support for research and innovation (CSF 9.1)	**	**
A communication and dissemination network (CSF 9.7 and 9.7b, ESC)		*
Strong co-operation with universities and (sport) research centres (CSF 9.5)	*	x

*Note: **when P<0.01; * when p<0.05; X when the correlation is above 0.3 and is significant in either summer or winter sports.*

Elite sport expenditure is the best predictor of outputs, with the highest correlation to success. This is further corroborated by the fact that three out of the five CSFs that have a correlation higher than 0.7, are in some way related to the financial resources of nations as listed here:

- Full-time management staff in the NSA for support of elite coaches, elite athletes and others (Pillar 2)
- There is a high-quality national elite sport centre(s) including: an administrative headquarters; hotel facilities/overnight accommodation; available sports medics, sports scientists; a close link with universities and the education of younger athletes (Pillar 6)
- There is (sufficient) financial support with specific subsidies for scientific research and innovation in elite sport (Pillar 9)
- Elite coaches are able to communicate and discuss their personal development as elite coaches and the development of elite athletes with other elite coaches (non-sport specific) (Pillar 7)
- There is a trade union for sports coaches (Pillar 7)

All of these CSFs are critically enhanced by sufficient financial resources (Pillar 1) and effective structure, governance and co-ordination. This finding lends further weight to the hypothesis that there may well be a minimum 'entry level' of investment required for a nation of any size to have an effective system and that money alone does not guarantee success because of the need for some level of proficiency in Pillar 2. The influence of Pillar 2 is the additional importance of knowledge and experience–two attributes that can only be bought to a limited extent. The development of a comprehensive, well-structured and smooth-running (culture) system cannot be fast tracked.

14.4.2 Theory development

The original SPLISS 1.0 study was a considerable advancement of knowledge concerning elite sport development systems at the national level.[47] One of the main characteristics of the SPLISS model, is that in addition to the nine Pillars, each of these Pillars is operationalised by critical success factors (CSFs) and sub factors that are measured as composite indicators (OECD, 2008), echoing

47 At time of writing this book, the original paper 'A Conceptual Framework for Analysing Sports Policy Factors Leading to International Sporting Success', De Bosscher, et al. (2006), published in European Sport Management Quarterly was the second most cited and fifth most read paper in the journal's history, which illustrates the need for a comprehensive theoretical framework at that time. Taylor and Francis (Routledge), 2.07. 2014, Scopus http://www.tandfonline.com/action/showMostReadArticles?journalCode=resm20#.Uygld02PKDY). Another theoretical paper, 'Explaining international sporting success. An International comparison of elite sport systems and policies in six nations' published in 2009 in Sport Management Review won the Best paper award and was the 4th most cited (9.07.2014), Elsevier, http://www.journals.elsevier.com/sport-management-review/most-cited-articles, Scopus).

methodologies from economies, competitiveness and strategic management literature. One of the key findings from this project is that high performing countries show strengths in different sets of Pillars and each Pillar score is composed of different configurations of CSFs. The past research has found an emerging consensus regarding convergence in relation to sport policy, but with room for diversity. Houlihan (2012) points to the problematic use of convergence and the lack of clarity 'under what conditions we can expect convergence in sport policy' (p. 112). The SPLISS results cannot illuminate the full complexity and richness of sport policy change but can provide a deeper understanding into some substantive resources that are mostly similar and key CSFs that are present among high performing countries and are possibly evidence of convergence. Similarly, some nations show large variations in a range of CSFs. These CSFs can be seen as combinations of resources and capabilities useful as guidelines to researchers and policymakers, which need to be adapted to local circumstances in a culturally relevant manner. Similarly, a competitiveness study aiming to validate SPLISS at the sport-specific level in athletics by Truyens et al. (2014) concluded:

'A competitive advantage can be achieved by countries that develop specific resource configurations and dynamic capabilities that take advantage of the opportunities within its external environment. These configurations do not need to be identical among different competitors. As a matter of fact, in order to achieve a competitive advantage one would look for the 'best' resource configurations... From a resource-based perspective, a CSF represents a specific resource configuration which is assumed to be developed in the same manner by all competitors. However, in terms of capabilities, it can be assumed that these capabilities differentiate between countries according to their external environment and the resource allocation provided in their country (cf. educational opportunities, scientific co-operation with universities or research centres, etc.).' (p. 484)

Reflections on the structure and process of elite sport policy are of interest to many, and we are the first to acknowledge that we have only been looking at the tip of the iceberg. There is still much work to do to develop and validate a coherent theory that better describes causal relationships between CSFs and success and also further advances construct validity. According to Gliner and Morgan (2000), construct validity 'is a continuing process of experimentation and modification leading to the refinement of the instrument that measures the construct' (p. 80). The major challenge for the SPLISS project is the many extraneous factors influencing success (we refer to the SWOT analysis in chapter 3). Ongoing research is required to further validate the conceptual model and the related CSFs.

One concern in that regard is related to the context in which sport systems are embedded. As stated in the theory chapter of this book (chapter 2), while the SPLISS model and its constituent CSFs are comprehensive, it is not an all-embracing model that can be applied to any situation, any country or any context. This was well illustrated by Andersen and Ronglan (2012) who used three different success stories from Swedish golf, Norwegian handball and Danish track cycling. They indicated that not only did the paths to success differ, but also the context in which these developments took place. Sport operates in an open system as it is influenced by the social, cultural and economic conditions of the community (Chelladurai, 2009).

Furthermore, the SPLISS framework focuses on the input-throughput-output factors that are predominantly driven by national governments and national sporting organisations. The framework does not take into account environmental factors such as inputs and throughputs from private organisations. Therefore, it takes a rather closed systems, perspective on elite sport policy. Brouwers, Sotiriadou, and De Bosscher (2015) argue the use of an open systems perspective when examining factors that influence elite sport success which allows the role of the private sector (e.g., sport academies, third party organisations and other private initiatives) to be taken into account. While chapter 2 described the interdependency of factors influencing success at the meso- and macro-levels and the environment of elite sport as a source of world-class performance (Digel et al., 2000), the focus is on those factors that can be controlled, or are 'developable'—and within these finding the best 'fruitology' (Hofstede, 1998)[48] of factors that can be compared.

Because of its government-driven policy-oriented focus, the SPLISS project also excludes the more commercial or 'market models' of elite athlete development. It is likely that a 'commercial' approach to elite sport development differs from a government-led approach, as can be observed in sports such as football, tennis or cycling. As truly mass spectator and mass participation sports, the media value and in its wake the commercial (sponsorship) value of these sports have delivered unprecedented resources to fuel the further development of elite sport systems. This 'co-financing' of elite sport by the private sector is currently not captured in the SPLISS model. Again this is illustrative of the different approaches to success and the absence of a 'one size fits all' model.

14.4.3 Methodology development

The use of mixed methodology research methods and quantitative measurement as a technique to compare the management of elite sport policies of nations moved SPLISS beyond the dominant body of elite sport system research which is characterised by using descriptive comparative research models only. By transforming qualitative and quantitative data (the critical success factors of a conceptual model) into a scoring system comparable to economic competitiveness studies, SPLISS

48 This refers to the metaphor made by Hofstede in chapter 3, saying that every comparison between nations is like a comparison between aples and oranges and it is important to find a common language.

has taken the next step in understanding more clearly how elite sport success is, or can be, created. The mixed methods methodology was seen as a useful tool for several reasons. It assists in the pursuit of data completeness and provides a more holistic understanding of research problems than either approach alone (Creswell and Plano Clark, 2007), and it enabled fuller and more reflective analysis of the data. The scoring system, in particular, making use of composite indicators, is shown to be a useful tool: (a) to move beyond the descriptive level of comparison and to extract meaning from qualitative data and to verify interpretations; (b) to facilitate pattern recognition that relates inputs and throughputs to outputs (Sandelowski et al., 2009); and (c) to improve criterion validation of the conceptual model, that contributes to identifying possible relationships between policies and success. Furthermore a key characteristic of the scoring system methodology used in this project is that data from a variety of perspectives (inventories and surveys) are included from people with different responsibilities such as policymakers, athletes and coaches. This approach enables the quality of elite sport development systems within a nation to be triangulated on the basis of the perceptions of the primary users. As reported in the economics' literature, the final composite scores help to summarise complex, multi-dimensional realities with a view to supporting decision makers (OECD, 2008). The traffic lights presented in Figure 83 show how 750 sub-factors divided over nine Pillars including the responses of 3,142 elite athletes, 1,376 elite coaches and 241 performance directors can be distilled down to one page.

However, the SPLISS project is not a quantitative study and qualitative information for the CSFs in the nine Pillars is of major importance for enhancing our understanding of elite sport systems and explaining the subsequently derived scores. The danger of the scoring system is that, while it is easy to interpret and to facilitate communication with a general public and policymakers, it may also send misleading policy messages if misinterpreted. Misinterpretation is likely, if dimensions that are difficult to measure are ignored (OECD, 2008), such as the socio-cultural context of nations, or the specificity of sports. At best, the SPLISS methodology is a proxy for a set of indicators that should be interpreted without dropping the underlying information base. The key point of note is that the radar graphs and traffic lights are not a stand-alone evaluation of elite sport policies, they cannot be isolated from the general descriptive information on elite sport policies written in this book. Essentially, qualitative and quantitative data remain complementary. The main purpose of the SPLISS project was to investigate the 'black box' of 'policy throughput', not only in regard to what happens between input and outputs, but also get a sense of the usefulness and quality of those actions by having them rated by stakeholders. In this respect, another danger of this methodology is that the methods that are used in SPLISS are time consuming and this, in combination with the fact that the use of surveys in an international context is expensive, makes comparative mixed research methods studies very labour intensive. As a consequence practice sometimes develops faster than theory.

We refer to the SWOT analysis of the SPLISS 2.0 project as it was presented in chapter 3 for a detailed overview.

14.4.4 Implementation: Lesson drawing and policy transfer

The 'global sporting arms race' and the subsequent pressures to be seen to succeed on the world stage has led to a drive towards the exchange and transfer of sporting practices between nations (Bloyce and Smith, 2010). Some national-level elite sport development systems seem to have the characteristics of role models in which certain nations that are judged to be successful are selected as the target for an often uncritical reproduction in an admirer's domestic context (Collins and Bailey, 2012). Typical examples are the former communist countries and Australia, which have all been benchmarks for many other countries. While the SPLISS 2.0 project attempts to provide a model that can be used as a guiding tool for nations to evaluate their effectiveness, it can become problematic when nations use this information to benchmark themselves and simply transfer best practices, Pillars and critical success to their context. It is unclear under what conditions we can expect best practices to work in other contexts or structures or indeed which factors or their characteristics are reciprocal. The discussion of this phenomenon in sport was raised by Houlihan and Green (2008), who borrowed the concepts of 'policy learning', 'lesson drawing' and 'policy transfer' from the social policy literature. They state that one of the most significant obstacles in the implementation of policies, is the inherent difficulty of translating ideas and strategies from one context into another. Furthermore, Collins and Bailey (2012) raise the issue of 'scienciness', by which they mean the illusion of scientific credibility and validity of the principles behind a sport system which are highly technical and specialist, but which usually lack underpinning evidence. Effective transfer of practices from one setting to another assumes that the drivers of such change really understand these nuances. Despite the search for a common (or similar) path towards elite sport development, the reality seems to be that this is not always the case. Furthermore, the results have shown that there is no generic blueprint–no sets of Pillars, critical success factors or recognised best practices that can be copied and pasted between different contexts. There is broad consensus on the ingredients that go into the elite success recipe but countries combine ingredients in their own unique ways. Accordingly, the key challenges for nations remain to 'benchlearn' instead of 'benchmark': apply best principles of efficient elite sport policies to their own context; and to seek best broad brush principles of efficient and effective elite sport policies rather than looking for simplistic transfer of best practice. The challenge remains to find the right blend of system ingredients and processes that will work best for given nations in their own context and culture.

14.4.5 Centralised versus decentralised approaches to national co-ordination: Who takes control over elite sport?

A central theme running through the evolution of successful elite sport development is the notion of a strategic, planned and co-ordinated approach (Houlihan and Green, 2008). In that regard governments drive and fund elite sport systems and make NGBs increasingly dependent on government strategies, funding streams and politics. Over time, this has led to increasing government involvement and institutionalisation of elite sport (e.g., Bergsgard et al., 2008; Houlihan and Green, 2008). All countries in the SPLISS sample provide evidence of central governments shaping policy to suit their own agendas. However, as was notable in Pillar 2, sport policy development has not been immune to the various influences of New Public Management (NPM) and the related requirement for a far greater emphasis on evidence-based policy making (Green, 2009).

NPM seeks to reorganise public sector organisations, to introduce elements of competition into public service provision as well as to 'borrow' private sector management techniques (Eliassen and Sitter, 2008 cited by Green, 2009, p. 125). Despite national co-ordination and increased government funding, elite sport development remains dependent on NGBs as the organisations that are ultimately responsible for the advancement of the sport. Typical examples of NPM application to elite sport policies are the integration of core business principles, external accountability of national governing bodies, the widespread use of performance indicators, target-setting, benchmarking, performance management and the explicit attempts to alter the cultures of organisations and staff, so that they more closely resemble those found in the private, or for-profit sector (Grix, 2009).

All of these elements of NPM were found to a greater or lesser extent in the SPLISS sample nations, and some of them related positively and significantly with success (e.g., having a formal objective and transparent measurement instrument to evaluate the NGB funding criteria). An example of this is provided by the performance contract in Denmark between the Ministry of Culture and Team Denmark. The contract comes with increasing prioritisation and reduced funding for the majority of NGBs—in part related to more liberal politics during that period (Storm, 2012). Further evidence can be found in Australia, France and other countries that have had 25-30+ years of government running elite sport development, where a shift has taken place from a highly centralised approach towards the principles of 'sport runs sport' and increasing the accountability of NGBs. These NGBs now have the freedom to determine the ways in which funding is spent, and to make use of the support services offered by the Australian Sports Commission. However, one point of note applicable to the SPLISS project is, as some scholars have argued, that all of these movements are evidence of a trend towards increasing government control rather than increasing sport's autonomy (Goodwin and Grix, 2011). Although governance in elite sport has moved towards the principles of decentralisation, collaboration and partnerships, all such relationships remain co-ordinated by a state that is more concerned with 'steering' (guiding, shaping, leading) than 'rowing' (intervening at the operational level of policy delivery) (Green, 2009). The reason for this evolution, as explained by Green (2009), could be that the need for control and co-ordination is more pronounced in elite sport than in other sport settings, which is in line with Mintzberg (1994) who outlines the preference for centralisation when a high degree of specialisation is required such as in elite sport.

In conclusion, in search of policy solutions governments are continuously balancing the need for co-ordination, control and coherence (a top down approach) with the need for empowerment, responsiveness, and market confidence through a bottom up approach (Mäkinen, 2013). It seems to us that during an escalating global sporting arms race—an era that we are in now—where nations feel increasing pressure to perform, to position, to achieve global recognition, there must also be a sense of control and prioritisation, but best results are achieved from nationally driven policies (NSA and NGBs), those that focus on the aspirational target, but minimise control and standardisation so to allow for sport-specific implementation.

14.4.6 Is prioritisation an effective long-term strategy?

Our analysis did not confirm effectiveness of prioritisation over diversification approaches

It seems to be increasingly assumed by policymakers that more money needs to be invested in fewer sports to ensure success (particularly at elite levels) and that this focus helps to drive government decision making. The Pillar 1 results showed that all countries, intentionally or otherwise, prioritise the use of funding, either by focusing only on Olympic sports, or by providing a disproportionately high share of the funding to a minority of sports. Our analysis did not show any evidence of countries that prioritise their funding to win more medals being more successful and in some cases the relationship even seemed to be negative (see CSF 2.18). Furthermore the results could not confirm, nor reject, the notion that nations that invest across many sports are successful in more sports. France (diverse approach) and Australia (prioritised approach, since the 1980s) were illustrated as the most extreme examples. Australia has seen its success decreasing over the past decade. France on the other hand has remained successful by investing in a wider range of sports. What these findings may be showing is some anecdotal evidence to state that the strategic choice for a priority funding approach does not show a strong relationship with increased success especially not in the longer term. A priority funding approach will also lead to those sports not receiving funding falling further behind from a global perspective and it might be harder for them to catch up when funding fortunes change. In the UK, UK Sport's no-compromise approach has been highly successful in enabling established medal-winning sports to achieve spectacularly successful results (for example track cycling). However there has also been widespread criticism about funding cuts to other sports (e.g., women's water polo) as any future medal success now seems impossible. The Swiss researchers argued that such a 'no-compromise' approach would not work in the Swiss system. Next to elite success, the Swiss system aims to produce socially desirable results, by investing in sports that are highly valued by Swiss citizens.

In the long run, the question remains what is the more strategic way forward, diversification or specialisation? Both strategies have delivered results for different countries. Shilbury (2006) argued that some sports may be fortunate to attract the funding they require consistently and are therefore able to reduce their dependence on government funding. Governments and other funders of elite sport need to recognise that their funding will not continue to support the range of programmes and activities that sports will be required to run in order to grow and develop in an increasingly competitive environment. Future research could be conducted into the best fit strategies for smaller versus bigger countries, and for developed versus developing countries (in terms of their elite sport system). For example it makes intuitive sense to keep investing in many medal-yielding sports in which a country already has reputation, expertise and experience. It also makes sense to invest in culturally and geographically (e.g., snow sports) relevant sports for a country. Culture, geography, demography and economy can all be potential sources of short- or long-term competitive advantage.

The SPLISS 2.0 data suggest that countries with an average elite sport budget seem to spread funding across more sports and countries with either a bigger or smaller budget take a more targeted approach. Our results also indicate that nations that prioritise elite sport funding over grassroots funding, are (slightly) more successful. This is also a finding that requires further investigation in future studies that include nations that take either a grassroots or elite sport perspective.

14.5 Reflections: What next for elite sport?

Elite sport policy finds itself at an interesting crossroads as we move into the Rio 2016, PyeongChang 2018 and Tokyo 2020 Olympic cycles. The evidence indicates that more nations are taking part in these events, more nations are winning medals and more nations are achieving top eight places. Nonetheless in London 2012, 89 out of 204 nations went home without even a top eight place and 119 did not win a medal as shown in Figure 96.

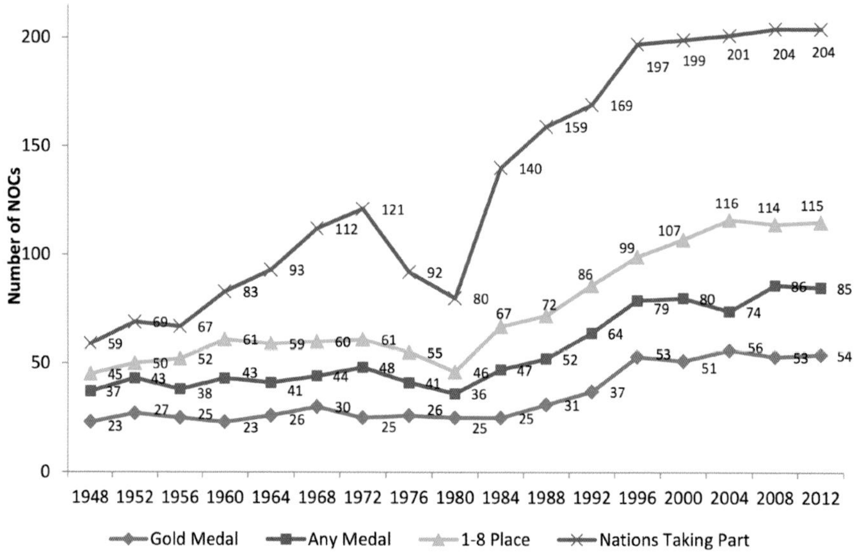

Figure 96: Number of NOCs taking part in the Olympic Summer games, the number winning top eight places and medals

> **Of the 962 medal-winning events in London, only 52% are contestable by any nation. The IOC has been winning the battle to share success more widely**

The IOC wishes to pursue a policy of universality whereby the entire Olympic family is represented at the Games. It would also like to see a greater spread of medals away from the traditionally dominant countries to a much more diverse portfolio of medal-winning nations. To this end there have been steps to limit how many medals nations can contest, such that in London 2012 of the 962 medal-winning opportunities the maximum contestable by any nation was 497 (52%). By contrast, there are nations that have invested heavily in developing competitive advantage and who are unwilling to see their established strengths diminished. What has played out in practice is an interesting scenario as shown in Figure 97 which demonstrates trends in the proportion of nations winning a gold medal, any medal or a top eight place since 1948.

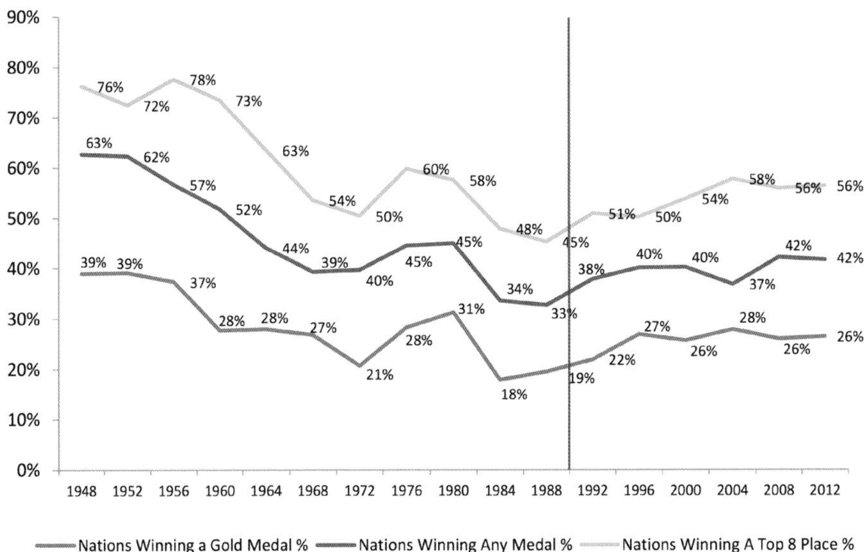

Figure 98: Trends in the proportion of nations winning a gold medal, any medal or a top eight place since 1948

In 1948 75% of nations won a top eight place, 63% won a medal of some sort and 30% won a gold medal. These proportions fell steadily in the intervening years and reached their lowest levels in the boycotted Games of 1984. In what we consider to be the modern era, that is, from 1988 onwards, the pattern has reversed, and there are upward trend lines demonstrating that at London 2012 56% of nations won a top eight place, 47% won a medal and 26% won a gold medal. It would appear that since 1988 the IOC has been winning the battle to share success in all of its forms more widely. For nations that do not win medals or indeed top eight places, there must come at some point a realisation that the market for Olympic medal success is difficult if not impossible to break into. At the end of the SPLISS 1.0 book we posed the question to governments, to what extent do you wish to be a part of this game? In a world in which resources are scarce and there are many competing interests for them, it would be tempting, and indeed rational, for nations which are not successful to stop their investment in elite sport and to spend the money on something else instead. Should this happen, the product that is the Olympic Games would be devalued, and it is quite likely that the value of commercial property rights would be reduced.

There needs to be a wider debate about the role of elite sport for society

There are two potential solutions to this problem. First, given that medal-based measures of success are relevant only to a minority of nations (the last time the majority of nations won a medal was in 1960, 52%), it may be useful to manage nations' expectations using non-medal-based measures which could include: top eight places; top 16 places; number of Olympians qualified to take part in the event; number of events contested; and number of medals contested. In this regard further development and dissemination of the 'relative success' model as described in chapter 4, may be useful in helping nations to get a more realistic sense of what positive achievement might look like. Second, there needs to be wider debate about the role that elite sport plays in society. Is there any evidence that elite sport success creates role models who inspire the next generation of athletes and stimulates grassroots participation? Is there any evidence that the public in most countries accept the notion that 'it's not the winning that matters but the taking part'? Is there any evidence that the Olympic Games creates a national 'feel good factor' once every four years that justifies the investment in elite sport development systems? If there is evidence that elite sport is somehow good for society, then nations may continue to invest in it and be prepared to accept the expense without expectation of medal-winning success. What appears to be happening currently in the world of elite sport is similar to a game of Poker, in which all of the players are waiting to see who blinks first.

Chapter 14 references

Andersen, S. S. & Ronglan, L. T. (2012). *Nordic Elite Sport: Same Ambitions, Different Tracks.* Copenhagen Business School Press.

Bergsgard, N. A., Houlihan, B., Mangset, P., Nødland, S. I. and Rommetvedt, H. (2007). *Sport Policy: A comparative analysis of stability and change.* London, UK: Elsevier.

Bloyce, D. and Smith, A. (2010). *Sport policy and development.* New York: Routledge.

Brouwers, J., Sotiriadou, P. and De Bosscher, V. (2015). Sport-specific policies and factors that influence international success: The case of tennis. *Sport Management Review* (0). doi: http://dx.doi.org/10.1016/j.smr.2014.10.003

Chelladurai, P. (2009). *Managing organisations for sport and physical activity: A systems perspective.* Arizona: Holcomb Hathaway Publishers.

Collins, D. and Bailey, R. (2013). 'Scienciness' and the allure of second-hand strategy in talent identification and development. *International Journal of Sport Policy and Politics, 5* (2), 183-191. doi: 10.1080/19406940.2012.656682

Côté, J. and Fraser-Thomas, J. (2007). Play, practice, and athlete development. In *Developing sport exercise: Researchers and coaches put theory into practice.* D. Farrow, J. Baker and C. Macmahon (Eds.). New York: Routledge.

Côté, J. (1999). The influence of the family in the development of talent in sport. *Sport Psychologist, 13* (4), 395.

De Bosscher, V. (2007). *Sports policy factors leading to international sporting success.* Published doctoral thesis. Brussels: VUBPRESS.

De Bosscher, V., Bingham, J., Shibli, S., Van Bottenburg, M. and De Knop, P. (2008). *The global sporting arms race. An international comparative study on sports policy factors leading to international sporting success.* Aachen: Meyer & Meyer.

De Bosscher, V., De Knop, P., van Bottenburg, M. and Shibli, S. (2006). A Conceptual Framework for Analysing Sports Policy Factors Leading to International Sporting Success. *European Sport Management Quarterly, 6* (2), 185-215.

Digel, H. (2000). *Resources for world class performances in sport – a comparison of competitive sport systems.*

Eliassen, K. A. and Sitter, N. (2008). *Understanding public management.* London: SAGE.

Gliner, J. A. and Morgan, G. A. (2000). *Research methods in applied settings: an integrated approach to design and analysis.* Mahwah, NJ: Lawrence Erlbaum Associates.

Goodwin, M. and Grix, J. (2011). Bringing structures back in: The 'governance narrative', the 'decentred approach' and 'asymmetrical network governance' in the education and sport policy communities. *Public Administration, 89* (2), 537-556. doi: 10.1111/j.1467-9299.2011.01921.x

Green, M. (2009). Podium or participation? Analysing policy priorities under changing modes of sport governance in the United Kingdom. *International Journal of Sport Policy and Politics, 1* (2), 121-144. doi: 10.1080/19406940902950697

Green, M. and Houlihan, B. (2005). *Elite Sport Development. Policy learning and political priorities.* New York: Routledge.

Grix, J. (2009). The impact of UK sport policy on the governance of athletics. *International Journal of Sport Policy, 1* (1), 31-49.

Hofstede, G. (1998). A case for comparing apples with oranges: International differences in values. *International Journal of Comparative Sociology, 39*, 16-31.

Houlihan, B. (2012). Sport policy convergence: a framework for analysis. *European Sport Management Quarterly, 2*, 111-135

Houlihan, B. and Green, M. (2008). *Comparative Elite Sport Development. Systems, structures and public policy.* London, UK: Elsevier.

Mäkinen, J. (2012). The elite sport reforms in New Zealand: the comparative view. In EASM (2013). *Proceedings of the 21th conference of the European Association of Sport Management.* Istanbul (Turkey), September 11-15.

Mintzberg, H. (1994). *Organisatiestructuren [Organisational structures].* Schoonhoven: Academic Service.

Oakley, B. and Green, M. (2001). The production of Olympic champions: International perspectives on elite sport development system. *European Journal for Sport Management, 8*, 83-105.

OECD (Producer). (2008). *Handbook on Constructing Composite Indicators: Methodology and User Guide.* Retrieved from www.oecd.org/std/42495745.pdf

Robinson, L. and Minikin, B. (2012). Understanding the competitive advantage of National Olympic Committees. *Managing Leisure, 17* (2/3), 139-154.

Ronglan, L. T. (2014). Elite sport in Scandinavian welfare states: legitimacy under pressure? *International Journal of Sport Policy and Politics*, 1-19. doi: 10.1080/19406940.2014.987309

Sandelowski, M., Voils, C. I. and Knafl, G. (2009). On quantitizing. *Journal of Mixed Methods Research, 3* (3), 208-222. doi: 10.1177/1558689809334210

Shilbury, D. (2000). Considering future sport delivery systems. *Sport Management Review, 3*, 199-221.

Storm, R. K. (2012) Danish elite sport and Team Denmark: new trends? In *Nordic Elite Sport. Same ambitions, different tracks*. S. Andersen and L. Tore Ronglan (Eds). Norway: AIT Otta AS.

Storm, R. K. (2012). *The discourse of the trickle-down fffect: An assessment of the consequences of Hegemonic closure in sport.* Paper presented at the 20th Conference of the European Association of Sport Management, Aalborg, Denmark.

Truyens, J., De Bosscher, V., Heyndels, B. and Westerbeek, H. (2014). A resource-based perspective on countries' competitive advantage in elite athletics. *International Journal of Sport Policy and Politics,* 1-31. doi: 10.1080/19406940.2013.839954

Vaeyens, R., Lenoir, M., Williams, A. M. and Philippaerts, R. (2008). Talent identification and development programmes in sport: Current models and future directions. *Sports Medicine, 38* (9), 703-714.

Wiersma, L. D. (2000). Risks and benefits of youth sport specialization: perspectives and recommendations. *Pediatric exercise science, 12* (1), 13-22.

WEF (2012). *The Global Competitiveness Report 2011-2012. World Economic Forum.* Geneva: World Economic Forum.

Credits

Cover design:	Andreas Reuel
Cover photos:	©imago/sportfotodienst: top left & right:
	©picture alliance/dpa: bottom left & right:
Jacket design:	Andreas Reuel
Layout:	Cornelia Knorr
Typesetting:	www.satzstudio-hilger.de
Inside photos:	©picture alliance/dpa: p. 11, 36, 86, 108, 132, 180, 196, 232, 260, 278, 350
	©imago/sportfotodienst: p. 14, 328
	©Ulrich Känzig/BASPO: p. 58
Graphics:	©Simon Shibli: Chapter 4
	All other graphics: ©Veerle De Bosscher
Copyediting:	Elizabeth Evans